A STUDY OF CONTEMPORARY GHANA

VOLUME TWO - SOME ASPECTS OF SOCIAL STRUCTURE

VOLUME II:

SOME ASPECTS OF SOCIAL STRUCTURE

Contributors

C. G. BAETA

Professor of Indigenous and Comparative Religions,
University of Ghana

J. C. CALDWELL

Fellow in Demography,
The Australian National University,
formerly Senior Research Fellow in Demography
and Associate Professor of Sociology,
University of Ghana

G. E. HURD

Lecturer in Sociology,
University of Leicester,
formerly Lecturer in Sociology,
University of Ghana

N. A. OLLENNU

Judge of the Supreme Court
of Ghana

P. A. TETTEH

Senior Lecturer in Planning,
Kumasi University of Science and Technology

VOLUME I:

THE ECONOMY OF GHANA
already published

A STUDY OF CONTEMPORARY GHANA

VOLUME TWO

SOME ASPECTS OF SOCIAL STRUCTURE

DIRECTED AND EDITED

BY

WALTER BIRMINGHAM

I. NEUSTADT

E. N. OMABOE

London
Published for the Ghana Academy of Sciences by
GEORGE ALLEN & UNWIN LTD
RUSKIN HOUSE · MUSEUM STREET

PRINTED IN GREAT BRITIAN
in 10 *on* 11 *point Times Roman type*
BY SIMSON SHAND LTD
LONDON, HERTFORD AND HARLOW

CONTENTS

PREFACE

In the preface to the first volume of this study we described its origins and its general objectives. We acknowledged there our indebtedness for the co-operation and assistance we received from many organizations and individuals. We wish to say once more how much we valued the support given us from the very early stages of the project by the Ghana Academy of Sciences, and the generous assistance which the Ford Foundation gave towards the cost of the research. It is a pleasure to acknowledge here the tireless assistance of Mrs R. Bridger, of the Faculty of the Social Sciences, University of Leicester. With unfailing patience and imaginative understanding she saw to the considerable and essential technical minutiae involved in preparing the manuscript for the press. We are also grateful for her judicious prodding, gentle yet firm, which has effectively hastened the appearance of this volume.

This volume could not have been produced in the absence of the comprehensive 1960 Population Census of Ghana. The successful completion of this Census was in many respects a remarkable feat, and our thanks and admiration must be given once more and unstintingly to the officers of the Central Bureau of Statistics and the Census Office. The assistance given by the Population Council in establishing demographic studies at the University of Ghana allowed full use to be made of the Census data as they came to be available. It has financed the demographic research programme which has been drawn on so extensively in this volume. Dr J. C. Caldwell, who has now returned to the Department of Demography of the Australian National University, was in charge of this programme at the time we undertook the planning and the general direction of the project and was able to receive valuable help from his colleagues and not least from the students and research assistants associated with the programme. We would like to express our appreciation to the Department of Demography of the Australian National University which has provided help with processing facilities.

We must emphasize the part played by Dr J. C. Caldwell in the direction and execution of what represents the major part of this volume, i.e. an analysis of the structure and movements of population in Ghana. We were glad to be able to call on his expert services in analysing and ordering the wealth of data provided by the 1960 Population Census and other studies carried out by the Central Bureau of Statistics. Dr Caldwell agreed not only to analyse the major demographic sources available at the Census Office, but, at the suggestion of the Ghana Academy of Sciences, to incorporate in this study some of the work he was already undertaking, and, in addition, to organize some essential supplementary survey work. This survey work was carried out from the University of Ghana, though it could only achieve its maximum value because of the availability of the vast framework of the Census findings into which it could meaningfully fit its own results.

Full descriptions of the surveys carried out by Dr Caldwell are in the process of being published in the appropriate learned journals. But, as he was in full agreement with the Directors of the project and the officers of the Ghana Academy of Sciences that the findings should be made available in Ghana as soon as possible, much of this work is being described in this volume for the first time. Some of Dr Caldwell's surveys have been re-coded and re-processed for other publications for which time was not so limited as in the case of this work. Thus there may be small numerical differences between some of the figures published here and those found in the separate publications. It is not anticipated that any of these minor discrepancies will be of any great significance.

The analysis of Ghana's demographic data gives rise to complex problems. The fundamental problem is that much of the census material is not yet buttressed by other comparable data. A single comprehensive census cannot by its nature be as valuable as a series of two or more of such censuses. Without such a series the demographer must make various assumptions, of the kind which are explained in this volume, before estimating rates of change or correcting distorted data. Similarly, one census can be used in conjunction with an effective nation-wide system of birth and death registration to estimate the level of vital rates, but, where such systems are lacking, as they are as yet throughout tropical Africa, indirect methods must be used. In much the same way, census data may be difficult to interpret in an immigrant land like Ghana, in the absence of a complete check on all movements in and out of the country. Such data will in time be available.

Some problems in the analysis continue to be a cause of concern. In a society such as Ghana at the present stage of its development, it is impossible to achieve complete accuracy in age statement. This weakness, together with inadequate data on the distribution of either mortality or fertility by age, underlies much of the hesitancy displayed in this study by statements with qualifications such as 'probably . . .' or even 'possibly. . . '. For the study of mortality and for the construction of stable population models, mortality schedules from elsewhere (the United Nations Model Life Tables and the Princeton Office of Population Research sets of tables) have been borrowed. This is not a wholly satisfactory procedure, but it has been found that most of the major conclusions reached in the population chapters are not fundamentally affected by different, but soundly based, mortality assumptions. Definitions of marriage and estimates of the periods during which females were married or were at some risk of conception also provided difficulties.

Perhaps the hardest decision made in the present work was when to call a halt to the collection of data so that the analysis could be rounded off with a view to hastening publication. Dr Caldwell's main period of research extended from early 1962 until early 1964. By this time, *Volumes I* and *II* and the *Advance Report of Volumes III* and *IV* of the 1960 Population Census were available. As the *Advance Report* was based on a careful 10 *per cent* sample of the census punch cards, it was thought that it would give as accurate a picture of national data as would be warranted for a large-scale study of this type. This has proved to be the case. As this volume is going to press, *Volumes III* and *IV*, as well as *Special Reports* on towns and tribes, have become available. Checking has shown that this extra material does not in any way modify the conclusions drawn from the tables in the *Advance Report*. In fact, they provide a very good illustration of the accuracy of such samples. Nevertheless, it should be remembered that the figures quoted are those from the *Advance Report*, which differ sometimes noticeably, but never significantly, from the exact figures now available in *Volumes III* and *IV*. A few additional footnotes have been added to draw attention to extra information, now available, and casting further light on some of the statements made.

It remains true, nevertheless, that the material to be made available by *The Post-Enumeration Survey* should yield further valuable information, not only on the accuracy of the original census, but also on a range of matters relating to fertility and migration. In the event, it was thought right that the material in this volume should be made available as soon as practicable. But, another valuable study or an extension of this study should be undertaken from the full census data in due course.

We referred in the preface to the first volume to the initial difficulties and delays which we encountered in the execution of the project as a whole. The study had been planned as a single work which would describe a series of aspects of contemporary Ghanaian society and, above all, bring together in a handy and systematic form some of the scattered and unanalysed but available material on Ghana as a whole. In the event, the section on the economy of Ghana became a substantial volume in itself whose contributors were able to incorporate a good deal of original research material in the analysis of available sources. The necessity of reducing the scope of the remaining part of the work, the large part assigned, for good reasons, to the demographic section, and some considerable fresh problems, including availability of data, encountered in carrying out the suitable completion of a number of planned chapters on certain other aspects of the Ghanaian social scene have given this volume a somewhat different scope and character from those originally envisaged. Some may regret, in particular, the absence of suitable essays on the changes in the political system of the country, and on the complex relationships between the traditional and the newly emerging systems of social stratification—to name only two of the more obvious omissions. Other serious lacunae could be readily indicated—not the least, an account of the remarkable social welfare institutions which have come to be developed in Ghana; or, for that matter, an analysis of the social aspects of the Volta River Project, an enterprise which is in many ways uniquely interesting as an example of planned social change.[1] Similarly we would have wished to accord much more space and a more thoroughgoing treatment to the presentation of some of those aspects of Ghanaian society which are treated only briefly in this volume (Mr Hurd who is responsible for the section on Education has in effect continued with his original work into aspects of the relationship

[1] A volume of papers read at the Volta Resettlement Symposium, held in Kumasi, March 23–7, 1965, under the auspices of the Volta River Authority, Accra, and the Faculty of Architecture, University of Science and Technology, Kumasi, Ghana (mimeographed, now being prepared for publication) gives some fascinating glimpses of this: in particular the paper by Mr G. W. Amarteifio, who was more directly concerned with the complex human problems involved in the resettlement of large numbers of people. (The economic aspects of the Project have been dealt with in Vol. I of our study.)

between education and social mobility in Ghana, and his results are to appear elsewhere). Some may even question the legitimacy of the reference to 'social structure' in the title of this volume.

This volume has not been produced as a specialist monograph, and most technical terms are explained. We hope that it, too, will serve as a work of reference for public servants, university staff and students, teachers in training colleges, and in the senior years of secondary schools.

As in the first volume the work of contributors has been here ascribed to them individually. Similarly full credit and responsibility for the content of each contribution are with the individual authors. We are particularly pleased to have been able to include contributions from Ghanaian scholars. It is indeed our hope that the enterprise which we have initiated in these two volumes may be taken over, before long, by the rising generation of Ghanaian social scientists. As we said in the preface to the first volume, they may be able to use this work as 'a benchmark for future studies of social and economic changes in Ghana'.

As general directors and editors of the work as a whole we must assume the responsibility for the final form of this volume. We know full well the limitations and the deficiencies from which it too suffers; and in this case, too, we would welcome constructive comment.

W.B.B.
I.N.
E.N.O.

LIST OF TABLES

LIST OF FIGURES

LIST OF MAPS

CHAPTER I

POPULATION: GENERAL CHARACTERISTICS

1. INTRODUCTION

Man has long been a feature of the African continent. In their turn important characteristics of the continent, such as the boundaries of the regions exhibiting different types of natural vegetation, and even the natural vegetation itself, have been profoundly affected by his presence. Excavations during the past decade in East Africa suggest that parts of Africa were probably the original home of mankind, and more recent diggings near Lake Chad indicate that West Africa too may have housed human beings or their closely-related ancestors for tens of thousands of generations. Such a long period of occupancy, however, has not solved all the problems of human settlement, and some more recently occupied parts of the earth have been more generous in the returns they have offered for man's labour.

Africa contains not much less than a quarter of the world's land area[1] but only about $8\frac{1}{2}$ per cent of its inhabitants. Thus, while the world as a whole supports an average population density of sixty persons per square mile, Africa averages only twenty-two or little more than a third as much.

Admittedly, global population figures always indicate the extent to which most of the world is dwarfed by the staggering numbers found in Asia, and especially in China and the Indian sub-continent. This one continent contains almost four-sevenths of the people of the world. In 1961[2] Africa's population was estimated to be 261 million. This may be put into perspective by the realization that it was 28 per cent greater than North America's 204 million and 20 per cent more than USSR's 218 million. It amounted to about three-fifths of the population of Europe outside the USSR.

In natural terms, and to a large extent human and cultural ones, Africa has two subdivisions. The dividing line is the Sahara Desert. South of it lie two-thirds of the continent's area and two-thirds of its people. Here, 171 million people now occupy $7\frac{3}{4}$ million square miles of land. Considering its great extent, this is one of the most homogeneous areas of the earth's surface. The vast majority of it lies within the tropics, the greatest single area of the world's land surface to do so. The landscape and climate vary only a moderate amount over thousands of miles. Its history, unlike that of North Africa, has not been intimately bound up with the rise and fall of Mediterranean civilizations.

But the real homogeneity of sub-Saharan Africa lies in its people. Both its indigenous people and visitors from outside have long tended to think of

[1] $22 \cdot 4$ per cent according to the United Nations *Demographic Year Books* which ignore some of the polar lands.

[2] United Nations *1962 Demographic Year Book*, which at the time of writing was the most recent published estimate.

B

it as Black Africa or *Afrique noire*, and the theme of blackness is quite a common one in the signs and symbols of independence in many of the new countries of the region. In spite of differences of language and of standard of living, the great majority of the 97 per cent of the population, which in ancestral terms may be regarded as indigenous, share basic similarities in culture and social organization. Now they are also aware of common problems of economic development.

Whilst one of the earth's inhabitants in every twelve lives in Africa, one in every eighteen is found in sub-Saharan Africa. The negro peoples, using the term in its widest sense, make up a little over one-twentieth of mankind, all of whom originated in sub-Saharan Africa, where the vast majority are still to be found.

One of the most distinctive divisions of tropical Africa is West Africa. This is the region hedged in by the Sahara Desert to the north and by the Atlantic Ocean to the south and west. The eastern boundary is usually taken to be the Cameroon Mountains. Its area is anything from 1 million to 2 million square miles depending on the amount of the Sahara which is included. Its population, unlike that of any other major segment of Africa, has never contained an appreciable fraction of non-Africans. It holds somewhat less than half the population of sub-Saharan Africa. Its 80 million people live in almost a score of countries and territories. But over half of these are to be found in Nigeria and almost a fifth of the remainder in Ghana.

The area of modern Ghana is 92,100 square miles. This is approximately the size of the United Kingdom. Unlike Africa as a whole, Ghana contains neither desert, nor rugged ranges, nor particularly uninhabitable arid savannah. Thus with seventy-three persons per square mile in 1960, it exhibits a population density above the world average, although, if the parallel above is continued, amounting to less than a seventh of that of the United Kingdom. The 1960 Census enumerated 6,726,820 people or $0 \cdot 22$ per cent of the world's population living on what represents $0 \cdot 20$ per cent of the world's land area.

In terms of Africa, Ghana's position is more striking. It accounts for $2 \cdot 6$ per cent of its population on only $0 \cdot 8$ per cent of its surface. Over 4 per cent of all the inhabitants and almost $4\frac{1}{2}$ per cent of the African population of sub-Saharan Africa is to be found there.

Many of the geographical and historical generalizations which may be made about Africa have at least some application to Ghana and its inhabitants. Four points are frequently made by geographers when describing the continent. It lies astride the equator, so that, unlike any other continent, nearly four-fifths of it is found within the tropics. It consists of a series of tablelands of varying heights and lacks lowland plains. Because of excessive evaporation as much as because of limited precipitation, insufficiency of water is a widespread problem. A monotonously regular coastline is nowhere studded with gulfs and bights leading far inland.

Tropical location is certainly of importance in any attempt to explain the pattern of economic development. Industrialization has so far been a phenomenon almost exclusively confined to temperate lands. Even if this does not mean that its adaptation to tropical conditions is inherently more difficult, it does mean that much of the stock of existing knowledge relating to the industries and agriculture of affluent societies is not directly applicable to tropical Africa. The so-called 'north-south' problem of economic development is really a 'temperate-tropical' problem.

The hinterland of Ghana is not very hilly, and, even north of the forest, aridity is a seasonal rather than a general problem. The north is, however, too dry to support forest, and so cannot share in the cash incomes derived from forest tree crops. The position is aggravated by the high cost of moving produce from the north to the southern markets or ports. Water transport has been of no great importance within Ghana, although the position may alter when the lake behind the Volta River Dam is full. The tsetse fly has seen to it that horses and cattle have played no significant role in transportation. Until quite recent times human beings provided almost the sole means of moving goods. In the long run forms of transport produced by the Industrial Revolution portend more for the future of Africa than for any other continent. But as yet economic change in northern Ghana is impeded by difficulties of transport and above all by problems of cheap transportation. The north is still the area where subsistence agriculture predominates, and where the cash economy is of minor importance.

Historians have drawn attention to the long period during which the Sahara provided West Africa with its chief link with the outside world, during which time cultural and economic change tended to be greatest amongst the people of the savannah. During the last 500 years the position has changed dramatically. The ships which have come down the west coast of Africa to the Gulf of Guinea have been able to carry hundreds of times as much cargo as could the ships of the desert. Not all was gain, for it was soon discovered that they could also be used for removing people as slaves. Nevertheless, from that time, the direction of external cultural influences upon West Africa was reversed, and the coast and forest people have experienced more rapid economic advance than have their fellows inland. In Ghana this has been accentuated by the fact that modern technology has bent the West African forest to its service more readily than the wooded grasslands of the savannah. The former can grow a range of tree crops, of which, in Ghana, cocoa is by far the most important, while the latter is bedevilled by problems of tsetse fly, distance from the coast and seasonal water problems.

In the last century the European presence moved inland from the coast. Cultural diffusion northwards from the sea-shore points of contact had long been taking place. But the period of European administration in most of tropical Africa has been, however marked its effect, surprisingly short. There are men still alive who can remember the partition of Africa. Only fifty-five years separated the Orders in Council which defined the Gold Coast Colony and established British authority over Ashanti and the Northern Territory, and the attainment by Ghana of Independence.

The division of Africa is of continuing significance, for it created new borders and new institutions. In the mid-twentieth century most of the countries so created are probably too small and the borders of many pass clumsily through distinct ethnic groups. Of much more doubtful validity, however, is the critical note which is sometimes heard in the statement that the new territories of West Africa cut across the natural divisions of the country. It is, in fact, precisely because of these divisions that it was important that the new nations of West Africa should have axes perpendicular to the coast. This was the way that most migration streams flowed. This allowed the inland areas access to the coast. And in the fullness of time, with the growth of a desire for national development, this was to permit some of the revenue from the coast and forest to be spent in the drier lands of the north.

The last decade has seen Independence come to Ghana, and subsequently to most of tropical Africa. It has witnessed a quickening interest in economic development and an increase in governmental expenditure. Throughout much of tropical Africa the growth of towns has accelerated and the rural-urban migration stream has thickened. At the same time a more critical eye has been fastened upon the movements of peoples across national borders. The partition of Africa tended to halt the age-old mass movements of African peoples. The rise of national States may eventually reduce even the numbers of individual migrants crossing borders.

This, then, provides a very sketchy background for a study of the population of Ghana. Any understanding of the characteristics of the population requires some appreciation of the dichotomy which has existed between the richer south and the poorer north, for the division is apparent in the data of mortality, population growth, education, occupation, urbanization and other characteristics of the people.

2. POPULATION ESTIMATES

Population trends in either Africa or Ghana prior to this century are really unknown. Two eminent demographers[1] have suggested that the whole continent may have had a population of around 100 million in 1650 and that this may have amounted to about a fifth of the world's total. There is no satisfactory evidence at all for this figure. It is arrived at partly by agreement with a guess Riccioli made in 1661 and partly by retrospective estimation from the somewhat firmer figures of the early twentieth century, buttressed by beliefs about the effects of slave trading and other aspects of contact between Africans and Europeans.

It is probably true that the combined effect of high mortality rates and relatively slow economic development resulted in Africa exhibiting the lowest continental rate of population growth in the two or three centuries preceding the present one. It is by no means so certain that population actually declined. Nor is it altogether credible that in the 270 years separating the mid-seventeenth-century estimates and the firmer United Nations' figure of 136 million people for 1920, Africa's population increased by only a third compared with a threefold multiplication by the next slowest growing population, that of Asia. By comparison it might be noted that the subsequent forty years apparently witnessed almost a doubling in the numbers of the people of Africa.

[1] See A. M. Carr-Saunders, *World Population: Past Growth and Present Trends*, Oxford, 1936, pp. 29–45; W. F. Willcox, 'Increase in the population of the earth and of the continents since 1650', in W. F. Willcox (ed.), *International Migrations*, National Bureau of Economic Research, New York, 1931, vol. II, pp. 33–82; United Nations, Population Division, *The Determinants and Consequences of Population Trends*, New York, 1953, pp. 10–11.

In Ghana, too, even the vaguest outline of the magnitude of the population can be drawn only for the last three-quarters of a century. Previously, chiefs in many areas had from time to time counted their people by requiring each to deposit some object such as a grain or a shell in a receptacle. The national census, however, arose from the needs of the British Colonial Government or the present Government of Ghana when administering much more extensive domains.

The present borders of Ghana have only been established since the First World War. However, in 1891, a census was made of the Colony of the Gold Coast and in 1901 the enumeration area was extended to include Ashanti and parts of the Northern Territories. Altogether seven censuses have been taken, those of 1891, 1901, 1911, 1921, 1931, 1948 and 1960, and of these the last four have covered the area of modern Ghana.

It is difficult to compare the populations counted by the various censuses, not only because of changes in the area covered, but mainly because the earlier censuses were undoubtedly incomplete in their enumeration. Indeed, by modern standards only the 1960 Census might be strictly classed as a proper census at all, and even it has not found all its problems easy to solve. The early censuses were carried out at very little cost and in the first two the traditional method of counting described above was still retained. Not until 1931 was the population enumerated individually, and not until 1960 was all the collected information recorded separately for each individual.

Thus, some of the rapid population growth which is apparently attested by Table 1.1 is the result of increasingly more complete enumeration of the population. Somewhat off-setting this was the tendency in 1891 and 1901 to add liberal estimates for population not counted in certain difficult areas.

Nevertheless, the censuses constitute a record of continuing population growth. Even around the turn of the century population growth in the area enumerated bore no witness to support theories of population stagnation or limited growth. However, such evidence can hardly be used as a test case for the whole continent, for Ghana has long attracted substantial immigration. The earlier censuses provide insufficient evidence to allow an adequate distinction to be made between natural increase and gain from immigration.

For the area constituting the pre-War I Gold Coast Colony, the census record now covers sixty-nine years. It purports to show a quadrupling of population from about three-quarters of a million people to well over 3 million. The apparent rate of population growth for the period averages 2·1 per cent per annum, being the product of an average rate of growth of 1·4 per cent for the years before 1921 and 2·7 per cent after it. Fifty-nine years of records exist for what is now Ashanti and Brong-Ahafo. They indicate a multiplication of population between 1901 and 1960 by almost fivefold at an average annual rate of 2·8 per cent. The slower growth of the Northern and Upper Regions is evident, for, even if the relatively very incomplete 1901 return for the area is accepted, growth between then and 1960 has been only three-and-a-half times at an average rate of 2·2 per cent per year.

Table 1.1 is confined to the period since 1921, when the area of modern Ghana was attained by the attachment of mandated territory from the old German Togoland. If the figures are taken as they stand, the population has approximately trebled in four decades. The acceptance of the estimate

of probable error, namely 5 per cent underenumeration in 1921, incorpor-
ated in the 1931 Census Report would not lower this figure below 2·8
times, but the real error of 40 years ago could have been considerably
greater than the one suggested.

TABLE 1.1

POPULATION SIZE AND DENSITY, 1921–60

Census	1921	1931	1948	1960
Population (thousands)	2,298	3,164	4,118	6,727
Population density (persons per square mile)	25	34	45	73

Sources: Ghana Population Censuses.

Accepting the census figures as published would imply an average
annual rate of population growth between 1921 and 1960 of 2·8 per cent
per annum. Table 1·2 analyses the period in terms of growth during the
three component intercensal periods. The picture presented is one of rapid
population increase in the first and last periods separated by an interval of
relatively slow growth.

One obvious reaction to these figures is to conclude that the three
censuses are mutually irreconcilable, and to argue further that the 1948
Census probably failed to enumerate quite large numbers of people. As will
be seen later, there is some support for the idea arising from a detailed
study of the 1948 and 1960 Censuses. If the 1948 results are disregarded, the
1931–60 rate of growth becomes 2·7 per cent per annum. Such an average
growth rate would not have been impossible in an immigrant country, and
would imply that the 1948 Census should have enumerated about 4,925,000
persons. Further, it would have meant that the underenumeration in that
year had amounted to over 800,000 persons or about one-sixth of the
population.

This is probably not the case, although some undercount almost
certainly did occur in 1948. It has become commonplace to point to the
dichotomy between economically developed countries, where population
growth rates react to economic conditions because of the widespread
practice of family planning, and developing countries, where such a
relationship between demographic and economic trends does not yet exist.
There are, however, developing countries which do show a relationship
between economic growth and population. The relation is achieved not
through the level of births but through that of net immigration. In some
developing countries the employment market, especially for immigrants
who tend to enter the more modernized sector, is markedly affected by
overseas economic conditions. These are countries which produce raw
materials, such as tropical tree crops, for overseas industries. The economic
depression of the 1930s affected employment in two ways. Firstly, the sale of
crops became more difficult and the returns dwindled. Secondly, government spending dropped with revenues, for the administration's income
depended to a considerable extent either directly on the value of exports or
indirectly on them through duties on imports bought with the resulting
foreign exchange. In such circumstances an immigrant stream can easily

shrink or even reverse its direction, especially in areas where immigrants had rarely intended to migrate for a lifetime and had long assumed that they would attempt to return home if unemployed. Thus Malaya exhibited average annual rates of population growth between the censuses of 1921, 1931, 1947 and 1957 of 2·7 per cent, 1·9 per cent and 2·8 per cent respectively. There are obvious parallels between this pattern and that of Ghana; parallels which would be closer still if Malaya had allowed immigration to continue after the Second World War as freely as did Ghana. Economic depression, and even war, can have marked effects on the demographic structure of such countries.

TABLE 1.2

POPULATION INCREASE, 1921–60

Intercensal period	Population increase (thousands)	Percentage increase	Average annual percentage increase
1921–60	4,429	193	2·8
1921–31	865	38	3·2
1931–48	955	30	1·6
1948–60	2,608	63	4·2
1931–60	3,563	113	2·7

3. POPULATION PROFILE

The United Nations declared 1960–1 to be the World Census Year and encouraged countries to hold censuses around that time. The previous decade had witnessed the achievement of independence by many countries which had previously been colonies and the decision by a big proportion of them to undertake economic development plans. Equally, there were good reasons for holding censuses in many colonies which were soon to become self-governing.

Ghana carried out by far its most ambitious census to date in March 1960. This was followed up by a Post Enumeration Sample Survey of about 5 per cent of the population in June and July of the same year. The purpose of the Survey was to provide a check on the accuracy of the Census and to undertake a more extensive investigation of certain aspects of Ghanaian society than was possible in the full Census. Publication of the detailed findings of the Census began to appear from 1963.[1]

Thus, in view of the data available at the time of writing and of the adoption of the *Seven-Year Development Plan*,[2] the present time is a good one to provide a stock-taking of the human resources of Ghana. Such stock-takings are an essential feature of social and economic planning. Findings are now available both from the 1960 Census and from other governmental and private investigations.[3]

---

[1] *1960 Population Census of Ghana*, Vols. I and II and *Advance Report* of Vols. III and IV.

[2] *Seven-Year Plan for National Reconstruction and Development: Financial Years, 1963/4–1969/70*, Accra, 1964.

[3] i.e. the investigations financed by the Population Council as part of the demography teaching and research programme it supported in the University of Ghana.

(i) *Aspects of Ethnic Composition*[1]

The population of Ghana is almost entirely African. People of African origin made up 99·77 per cent of the country's population in 1960. Earlier the proportion had been even higher, 99·84 per cent in 1948 and 99·91 per cent in 1921. The non-African section of the population continued to increase disproportionately rapidly between censuses, but it is still insignificant numerically. There has never been in West Africa the equivalent of the large numbers of people of non-African ancestry found in parts of eastern, southern and northern Africa.

In 1921 non-Africans were found in Ghana in the proportion of one person per 1,131 inhabitants. By 1948 this had risen to about one in 600, and by 1960 to one in 430. In 1960 people of European origin, which includes Americans and Australians, made up about four-fifths of the 15,680 non-Africans. It must come as some surprise to people living in the wealthier suburbs of Accra or shopping in the largest department stores of that city to learn that only one person in every 563 in Ghana is European and only one in every 907 is British.

For these reasons, this and the subsequent chapters will concentrate almost entirely on the African population. However, before passing on from the non-African population, some observations might be made on some of the interesting changes which have been occurring in the structure of this group.

The approach of Ghana to independence and its final attainment in 1957 did not mean a diminution in the number of Europeans living in the country. In fact the twelve years between 1948 and 1960 witnessed well over a doubling in the European community from 5,157 to 11,950 persons[2] while the number of Africans increased by only two-thirds.

Within the European community two significant changes did occur. The first change was the fall in the British[3] proportion of this community from 82 per cent to 62 per cent. The explanation lies in the Ghanaianization of many administrative posts in the public service, commerce and army previously held by the British, and in the tendency of the new Government of Ghana to seek more widely for its foreign employees. In actuality the numbers of the British in Ghana have not fallen. They rose between 1948 and 1960 from 4,211 to 7,420. But at the same time the non-British European population increased in size spectacularly. In the former year they numbered less than a thousand. In the ensuing twelve years they increased almost five-fold to 4,530. By 1964 they may have made up the majority of the European population.

The other change within the European population was a further increase in the tendency to bring wives to Ghana and to undertake a normal family life within the country. In twelve years the sex ratio fell from 317 males per hundred females to 141. Nor was this change a result of the fall in the British proportion of the community, for the sex ratios of British and non-

---

[1] At the time of writing only limited data were available on these aspects. The position has subsequently been improved by the publication of further information from which the following summary has been constructed. Table 1.33.

[2] The 1948 figures include 281 persons in ships. In 1960, too, such persons were apparently enumerated.

[3] British is defined as persons from the United Kingdom or Ireland.

British European communities remained very similar. Back in 1921 the sex ratio had been 747, a figure which was so much lower than in earlier times that it prompted the Chief Census Officer to observe that it proved that 'Europeans are now usually accompanied by their wives'. There are still comparatively few children or second generation Europeans in Ghana. In 1960 only 7 per cent had been born in Ghana, compared with figures of 26 per cent for the Asian community and 36 per cent for African immigrant communities.

The number of Asians increased between 1948 and 1960 by 133 per cent, a rate of growth approximating that of the European population. By the latter year, however, there were only 3,730 of them. Between 1948 and 1960 the proportion of Lebanese and Syrians had fallen from 85 per cent to 59 per cent while that of Indians and Pakistanis had climbed from 12 per cent to 25 per cent. It is possible that the Asian communities have doubts about their continued residence, for, unlike the experience of the European community, there is apparently a declining tendency to bring women-folk to Ghana or to keep them there. Between the two most recent censuses their sex ratio climbed from 165 to 180 males per hundred females, the change being even more pronounced in the Lebanese and Syrian community.

Table 1.3 shows that Ghana is one of Africa's immigrant lands. Admittedly, almost 92 per cent of the population had been born in the country, but this included children of immigrants who did not regard Ghana as the ancestral home of their people. Of less than $6\frac{3}{4}$ million people enumerated in the country in 1960, over 800,000 were classified as of foreign origin and of these over half a million were born elsewhere. The term 'foreign origin' is used to describe persons whose fathers or grandfathers, or in matrilineal societies their mothers or grandmothers, came from a foreign country. The use of this definition is justifiable in West Africa, where migrants to foreign lands usually regard their migration as temporary and intend to return some day to their native land. In a survey of adult Nigerian and Togolese immigrants in Ghana,[1] less than 6 per cent stated that they did not intend to return ultimately to their homelands, although the majority had lived in Ghana for more than ten years. The figure would almost certainly be much higher for those of foreign origin who identified themselves more with Ghana because they had arrived as young children or who were born there.

Thus, at the time of the 1960 Census, one in twelve of the population was of foreign birth and more than an eighth were of foreign origin. The true figures may be somewhat higher, because of the feeling of insecurity that so easily arises amongst migrants and which makes some reluctant to admit birth in other countries. More significantly still, those of foreign birth had more than trebled in number since 1948 and had doubled in the proportion they made up of the whole population.

In some sectors of the society the impact of foreigners has been greater than these figures might indicate. Almost two-thirds of the persons of foreign birth are males. They are heavily concentrated in the main working age groups. Thus, while only 10·4 per cent of all males were born outside Ghana, 19·4 per cent of those in the 25–54 years of age range were. They

[1] See Appendix. Population Council programme carried out in 1963 from the University of Ghana, *International Migration Survey.*

are not drawn evenly to all parts of Ghana, but mostly proceed to the more economically developed areas of southern Ghana. The proportion of foreign born in the whole country is 8·3 per cent, but in Accra it is 15·4 per cent. Thus, almost a third of the males, 25–54 years of age, in Accra are of foreign birth, and, if the national ratio of those of foreign origin to those of foreign birth holds almost half may be of foreign origin. Throughout the southern and more modernized sector of the Ghanaian economy, immigrant workers are to be found in great numbers. The society and economy of southern Ghana is in many ways an African counterpart to the countries of overseas European settlement. To each, people came from other areas of similar culture for their personal economic betterment.

TABLE 1.3

POPULATION OF NATIVE BIRTH, FOREIGN BIRTH, NATIVE ORIGIN AND FOREIGN ORIGIN*
(Numbers in thousands, percentages of all males
or females or total population in Ghana)

	Males	Females	Both sexes
Born in Ghana:			
Numbers	3,047	3,120	6,167
Percentages	89·6	93·8	91·7
Born elsewhere:			
Numbers	353	207	560
Percentages	10·4	6·2	8·3
Ghanaian origin:			
Numbers	2,908	2,991	5,899
Percentages	85·5	89·9	86·6
Foreign origin:			
Numbers	492	336	828
Percentages	14·5	10·1	13·4

* Most persons of foreign birth are also of foreign origin, but the foreign-origin category does include some persons of Ghanaian descent who were born abroad but who have subsequently come to the country.
Source: 1960 Census.

The detailed mechanics of international migration will be left to a later chapter. However, this sketch of the chief features of Ghana's population would be incomplete without a brief analysis of the migrants' origins, for they do not merge imperceptibly into traditional Ghanaian society and do not usually expect to do so.

Over four-fifths of the population of foreign origin in Ghana is derived from three countries, Togo, Upper Volta and Nigeria. Over a third have been contributed by the first, and almost a quarter each by the other two. Most other immigration has been on a relatively small scale with the possible exception of that from the Ivory Coast, the majority of which has been localized movement into the Northern Region. Most of the immigration has been, by African standards at least, over relatively short distances. Only about one African in a thousand has come from outside West Africa, while almost two-thirds have originated from adjoining countries. In some ways the most anomalous movement has been that from Nigeria, which lies beyond two intervening countries. The explanation probably lies in the relatively short distance from south-west Nigeria to south-east Ghana, the common use of English as the national language and a history of administration by the same colonial power.

TABLE 1.4

POPULATION OF FOREIGN ORIGIN, 1960

Country of origin	Number (thousands)	Percentage of all persons of foreign origin
Togo	281	34·0
Upper Volta	195	23·5
Nigeria	191	23·1
Ivory Coast	54	6·6
Dahomey	32	3·8
Niger	25	3·0
Mali	19	2·3
Liberia	9	1·0
Other parts of Africa	7	0·8
AFRICAN total	812	98·1
Countries outside Africa	16	1·9
TOTAL for all countries	827	100·0

Source: 1960 Census.

(ii) *Age and Sex*

Probably the single most important type of data collected by censuses or surveys is that on age and sex. The age and sex composition of a population can be analysed to reveal much of the demographic change occurring in the society and to indicate the problems to be faced by social and economic planners. Certain planning decisions will in fact be radically different in societies of different age structures.

In most of the developing world severe difficulties arise when attempts are made to collect adequate age data. The problem is not merely one of organizing a major census and assembling and training an adequate number of skilful and conscientious enumerators. The real difficulty is that a large proportion of the population do not know their own ages accurately and that the age of a human being cannot be told by inspection. Such societies have hitherto not experienced the pressure imposed in the more developed societies in fields like education, employment and insurance to treat age as of special importance. In many cultures the European system of reckoning age has never been fully accepted.

Until 1960, census-takers in Ghana had attempted to secure age data only in four large age groups. By 1960 something more precise was needed for the purposes of administration, and the spread of education and of quantitative concepts in the society made such precision more possible. Hence age data are now available by single years.

These data are shown in Figures 1.1 and 1.2 and in Table 1.5. Some of the problems met with are presented in striking form in Figure 1.1. It is obvious that it is most improbable that eight times as many people are aged 60 as 61, or that far more had ages in 1960 ending in even numbers or five than in odd numbers.

Such discrepancies are not as serious as they first look. Figure 1.2 demonstrates that, when the age data are assembled into five-year age groups, they assume a rather more probable configuration. Indeed the data in this form are on the whole internally consistent and conform broadly with what is known about fertility, mortality and growth rates in the

Figure 1.1

GHANA: POPULATION PYRAMID BY SINGLE YEAR AGE GROUPS,

1960

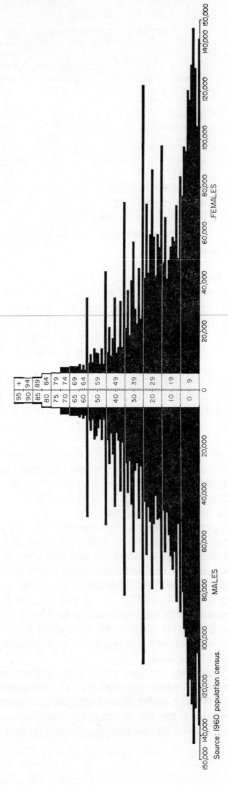

Source: 1960 population census.

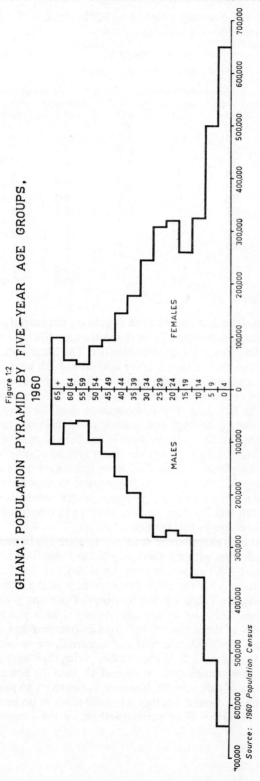

Figure 1:2
GHANA: POPULATION PYRAMID BY FIVE—YEAR AGE GROUPS, 1960

Source: 1960 Population Census

country. From the planning point of view, the data, with certain adjustments, are certainly usable and are indeed very valuable.

TABLE 1.5

POPULATION BY FIVE-YEAR AGE GROUPS, 1960

| Age | Numbers (thousands) | | | Percentage distribution | | |
	both sexes	male	female	both sexes	male	female
0–4	1,294	639	655	19·2	18·8	19·6
5–9	1,020	514	506	15·2	15·1	15·2
10–14	683	358	325	10·1	10·5	9·8
15–19	541	277	264	8·0	8·1	7·9
20–4	587	268	319	8·7	7·9	9·6
25–9	589	281	308	8·8	8·3	9·2
30–4	489	242	247	7·3	7·1	7·4
35–9	373	196	177	5·5	5·8	5·3
40–4	312	167	145	4·6	4·9	4·4
45–9	219	124	95	3·3	3·6	2·9
50–4	180	97	83	2·7	2·9	2·5
55–9	109	60	49	1·6	1·8	1·5
60–4	119	64	55	1·8	1·9	1·7
65+	212	113	99	3·2	3·3	3·0
All ages	6,727	3,400	3,327	100·0	100·0	100·0

Source: 1960 Census.

Most age misstatement occurs when people are not sure of their ages and choose an approximate figure. In so doing they are likely to round off the age to one ending in 0, 5 or an even number. The latter is more markedly the case in Ghana than in some other societies which have been studied. Much of this inexactitude is not serious when ages are aggregated into five-year groups or when various techniques are used for smoothing out the rises and falls in the data. The misstatement does, however, indicate an uncertainty about the real age and in some cases this uncertainty may not be over a matter of only a year or two. It has been found everywhere that preference for certain digits in age statement instead of others can be used as some measure of the likelihood of more serious errors in the age data. Certainly those groups in the society more prone to error are more likely to contain individuals who, through ignorance, may misstate their true age by many years. With this in mind, we shall attempt to pinpoint those Ghanaians most likely to err in this fashion.

A simple test is to examine the tendency to state age in numbers ending in zero. When dealing with numbers as great as those found in the census, one would expect, if all ages were correctly stated, the number of 10-year-olds to be approximately the same as the average of the numbers of nine- and 11-year-olds. In Table 1.6 the numbers of persons giving their ages as 10, 20, 40 and 60 years of age are expressed as a percentage of the average numbers of those giving their ages as one year less and one year more than that. If no misstatement had occurred, we would expect that percentage to be around 100. If the number giving their ages as 40 is twice the average of those enumerated as 39 and 41, then the percentage will be 200. The purpose of this exercise, however, is not to try to gauge the order of inaccuracy but to discern whether it is more likely to occur among males than females, or urban than rural dwellers, or the educated than the uneducated.

TABLE 1.6

COMPARISON OF THOSE ENUMERATED AT CERTAIN AGES COMPARED WITH THE AVERAGES OF
THE AGES IMMEDIATELY PRECEDING AND FOLLOWING THEM, BY SEX, URBAN-RURAL RESIDENCE
AND SCHOOLING, 1960 (EXPRESSED AS PERCENTAGES)

Age	Tota popula- tion	Males	Females	Urban popula- tion	Rural popula- tion	Now at school	Has had some schooling	Never attended school
10	134	135	133	129	136	120	138	155
20	175	165	183	164	179	Not available		
40	392	371	418	362	401	Not available		
60	583	557	616	601	579	Not available		

Source: 1960 Census.

It is immediately clear that age statement becomes increasingly unreliable with age. Older people have a greater span of time on which to keep track; they have lived for a longer time in a less quantitative culture than that which prevails in modern Ghana; and they include a bigger proportion of uneducated persons.

A glance at some of the other data can serve as a check on some of these hypotheses.

From 20 years of age males score consistently better than females. But the margin is less than one would expect from the greater involvement of males in the more modernized economy, the larger proportion of them educated, especially amongst the older age groups, and from the result of using similar tests in other countries. Notice, for instance, the scores at 10 years of age, where females held a slight margin in spite of the fact that the proportion of them at school in 1960 was only about three-fifths as great as was that of males. Similarly, urban scores are better than rural ones, but again not by the margin that might be expected if the sole factors involved were education and involvement in modern, quantitative society. In 1960 the proportion of the population over 6 years of age who had been to school or were still there was almost twice as high in urban as in rural areas.

The effect of schooling on accuracy in age statement is clear enough, even though the statistics are available for only one of the ages under examination. That any education is important is suggested by the difference between the figures for those who have had some schooling and those who have had none. It might be argued that the impact of school lay not only in the education given but also in the emphasis placed on age when children are put in a certain grade.

Finally, the question might be asked whether the respective figures for those with schooling and those without are affected from one area of the country to another by the general level of education and literacy in the area. The analysis in Table 1.7 has been confined to those who either are still at school or have never been there, as the intermediate group is too small in some regions to benefit by analysis. The Regions have been graded from those with the greatest proportion of residents who have attended school to those with the least. The answer to the question posed above is that, at least in the case of children, who admittedly are normally more likely to be assisted by others in stating their age, it is not merely personal education that counts but that of the society in general. This is especially clear when comparing the Northern Region with the rest of the country. The percentages for those still at school in the Western and Northern Regions were almost as high as for those in the Volta Region who had never been to school.

TABLE 1.7

COMPARISON OF THOSE ENUMERATED AS TEN YEARS OF AGE WITH THE AVERAGES OF THOSE ENUMERATED AS NINE AND ELEVEN YEARS OF AGE, BY REGION, 1960 (EXPRESSED AS PERCENTAGES)

Region	Now at school	Never at school
Accra Capital District	116	139
Eastern	114	144
Volta	119	128
Ashanti	121	144
Western	127	137
Brong-Ahafo	119	146
Northern and Upper	125	168

Source: 1960 Census

A further look at Figure 1.2 shows that, even by 5-year age groups, the population pyramid is not the simple one exhibited by countries of fairly stable population growth. The pyramid is restricted in the age groups immediately following 10 years of age and bulges in the 20s.

Such a pattern has been common recently in European age pyramids where the gap resulted from the very low birth rates of the depression and war years. There is, however, no real question of a similar phenomenon having taken place in Ghana.

Another possibility would seem to be that the bulges above 20 years of age are caused by the addition to the population of immigrants who arrive as young adults. A further examination of Figure 1.2 will show that this explanation is sufficient to account for much of the distortion on the male side of the pyramid but for very little on the female side.

The sole satisfactory solution to the problem is the explanation that in the age statistics large numbers of females between 10 and 20 years of age and somewhat smaller numbers of males between 10 and 25 years of age have had their ages advanced in the Census age tables. The probability of this occurrence receives support from an examination of the age structure recorded for the individual Regions, and indeed by the inspection of data from other African countries.

The basic form of the age pyramid described for the whole of Ghana is found in each Region. But the distortions are only just perceptible in such areas as the Eastern and Volta Regions, where educational levels are high. In contrast, they completely dominate the pyramid for the Upper and Northern Regions. In this case twice as many women were enumerated in the 25–29 years of age range as in the 15–19 years one. On the other hand, in the Volta Region only 1·6 per cent more were enumerated. One would expect, of course, to find fewer women in the older age group, as indeed can be seen in the stable population pyramid of Figure 1.3, where the size of the 25–29 age group amounts to little more than two-thirds of that of the 15–19 age one.

A similar pattern seems to occur throughout West Africa. In the Congo, for instance, the most swollen female age group, the 30–34 years of age one, is 47 per cent bigger than the denuded 15–19 years of age group. This may be compared with the maximum equivalent contrast in Ghana where the 25–29 years of age group exceeds the 15–19 years of age group by only 17 per cent.

Various reasons can be advanced for the occurrence of these patterns. Some are connected with the problems faced by enumerators when estimating age in areas where few people have any exact idea of their own age. The assumption that all females who had reached puberty were over 15 years of age could lead to some loss from the 10–14 years of age group. Similarly, the assumption that all females who had married and had borne one or two children were over 20 years old could remove substantial numbers from the 15–19 years of age group, especially in the remote areas. There is some tendency to regard those who are supported as 'children' and those who support themselves or are married as 'adults'. As more boys stay on at school, and as females marry appreciably earlier, relatives could easily describe as adult a larger proportion of adolescent females than males. This would noticeably affect age tables if some enumerators were forced to translate such descriptive terms into age categories.

A further examination of this phenomenon is warranted because some of the age groups most affected are those important in the study of fertility. In Figure 1.3 an attempt has been made to compare the enumerated population with the age distribution of the hypothetical *stable population* which seems to come closest to fitting the known facts of fertility, mortality and rate of population increase. The attempt cannot be wholly satisfactory because some distortion of the age structure has been brought about by the presence of large numbers of immigrants. There is no simple solution because a subtraction of the foreign-born would leave in the statistics large numbers of native-born children whose existence is to be attributed solely to the arrival in Ghana of their immigrant parents. Correction could be attempted only if statistics were published showing the age of population of *foreign origin*.[1]

It can be seen that the discrepancies between the two pyramids imply a deficiency in the census enumeration of females, 10–19 years of age, of about 23 per cent below what might have been expected. In contrast the 30–34 years of age range was about 19 per cent greater than stable population analysis would indicate. In numbers this means that the former age range was found to be about 175,000 below expectation and the latter 140,000 above. Taking immigration into account, the losses and gains were probably not quite as great as cited here. But that there was a very considerable advancement of female ages from the age ranges immediately younger than 20 years cannot be doubted.

Age advancement has also taken place amongst males. Here, however, the magnitude of immigration has so distorted the age data as to make the

---

[1] With the publication of the full Volume III of the 1960 Census these figures are now available. An examination of Tables 1 and 14 of that volume demonstrates that the anomalies in age distribution which have been discussed are also present in only a very slightly modified form in the population of Ghanaian origin. They arise largely from a differential pattern of age misstatement and not from the age pattern of immigrants.

C

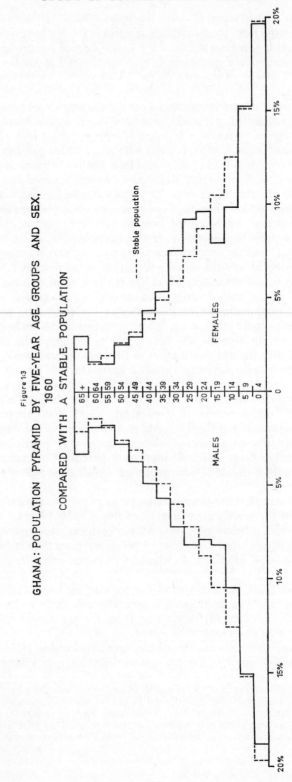

Figure 1:3

GHANA: POPULATION PYRAMID BY FIVE-YEAR AGE GROUPS AND SEX, 1960

COMPARED WITH A STABLE POPULATION

extent of the advancement less in all probability than Figure 1.3 would suggest and hence less than the female advancement. It would also appear that the advancement of male ages has resulted in a more uniform enlargement of the older male age groups, and not in the pronounced swelling of the 20–34 years of age range found amongst the females. These suggestions receive support from an examination of the age pyramid for the Northern and Upper Regions, Figure 1.4, where immigration is less than in the case of any other Region and where the tendency towards age misstatement is most pronounced. On the other hand, emigration from the Region has undoubtedly contributed to the rather unusual shape of the pyramid.

Two other features of the pyramids might be noted. There is some tendency, as in most countries, for some of the aged to succumb to the temptation to exaggerate their ages. The 65 years of age and over group is over a third greater than might be expected from stable population analysis. At the other end of the scale, the youngest age group is somewhat smaller.

It is worth while pursuing further the study of the age data of young children, for the size of this group is of critical importance when attempting to estimate the level of fertility. In a country like Ghana, exhibiting a fairly substantial rate of natural growth, one would expect that the births each year would exceed those of the previous year. Furthermore, the older age groups of children will be relatively more reduced in numbers by the cumulative effect of deaths. Thus, the graphing of those enumerated by the census in single years of age groups should produce a portion of an age pyramid with sides sloping inwards as age advances. Figure 1.5 shows that the published data of the 1960 Census produce no such effect for at least the first four years of age.

Census age data for young children are notorious for exhibiting peculiarities. There are two common causes, and both result in a relative denuding of this age group. One is that young children, especially the newly born who are not yet named, are often ignored by relatives and missed out by enumerators. The other is that various ways of counting age, whether specifically enshrined in the culture or not, can result in many children being regarded as either under one or one year old for shorter periods than is actually the case. Indeed, if there is age misstatement, and if the tendency to advance age exceeds that to reduce it, which is usually the case, then the youngest age group will be reduced in size. Children can leave the 0–4 years of age group in this way, for instance, but no child can be advanced to it from an age younger than that of birth.

In the 1960 Census of Ghana, age misstatement is probably the main culprit. If we were to take the contrary view and to assert that nearly complete enumeration is first found only at 3 years of age and that the pyramiding first observable between 3 and 4 years of age should be projected backwards to base level, then we would in effect be maintaining that a quarter of all children in their first three years of life had been omitted. This would mean that in the country in 1960 there were, not three-quarters of a million children of this age but a third as many more again or a full million. This is incompatible, as will be seen later, with what is known of the fertility level and rate of increase of the population. Indeed, it would imply a level of fertility in Ghana well above that ever found anywhere in the world.

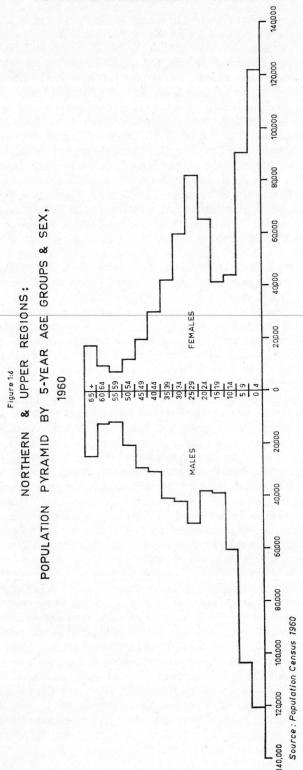

Figure 1:4

NORTHERN & UPPER REGIONS:

POPULATION PYRAMID BY 5-YEAR AGE GROUPS & SEX,
1960

Source: Population Census 1960

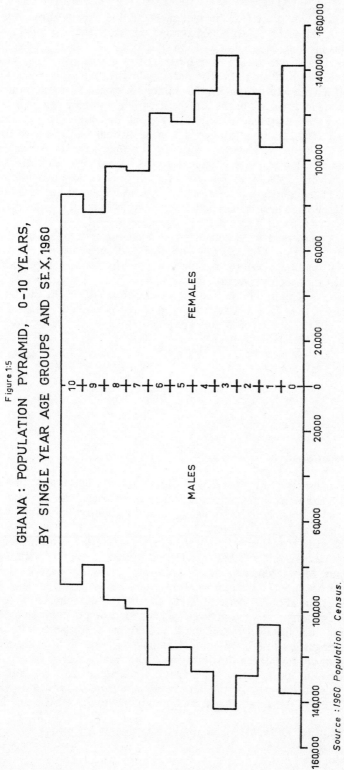

Figure 1:5

GHANA : POPULATION PYRAMID, 0-10 YEARS,
BY SINGLE YEAR AGE GROUPS AND SEX, 1960

Source : 1960 Population Census.

The truth would seem to be that most of this phenomenon, but not necessarily all, is to be explained by age misstatement. An independent check has been made in Ghana of the stated ages of a sample of children whose real ages were known from birth registration records.[1] The sample was necessarily confined to the compulsory Registration areas which are all urban. It may have also omitted the children of some of the least educated in these areas, for such births are the least likely to be registered. If the pattern of age misstatement within this group had prevailed throughout Ghana in 1960, the 0–4 years of age group would have been relatively reduced in size by $4\frac{1}{2}$ per cent. Allowing for some underenumeration of children under 1 year, the true figure was possibly over 5 per cent. However, in the following analysis caution has prevailed and a conservative minimum figure has been used as a correction factor. Correction has been made as if the 0–4 group had been underenumerated relative to adult females by 3 per cent.

However, errors in age statement or even in enumeration do not obscure the main features of Ghana's population and its age structure.

The outstanding fact of the population is that its rate of natural increase is so great that each generation is much larger than its predecessor. Thus the number of children in the country is very great indeed. As can be seen in Table 1.8, over four-ninths of the population is under 15 years of age. Indeed, half the people of Ghana are under 18.

TABLE 1.8

POPULATION IN MAJOR AGE GROUPS, BY SEX, 1960 (PERCENTAGES)

Age	Males	Females	Both sexes
Under 15	44·4	44·6	44·5
15–44	42·1	43·9	43·0
45–64	10·2	8·5	9·3
Over 65	3·3	3·0	3·2

Source: 1960 Census.

Such an age structure must have profound social and economic implications. For example, the expenditure pattern of a society with a median age of 18 years is unlikely to be similar to that of a country like Britain where the median age is twice as great.

Ghana's age structure is by no means unique. Rather is it an example, although perhaps a somewhat extreme example, of a country with a high birth rate. Most tropical African countries apparently have a slightly smaller proportion of their population under 15 years of age, the range extending from about 35 per cent to 45 per cent. It is of interest to note that Togo, which apparently has an even higher proportion of children, adjoins Ghana and belongs to the same major cultural area. In the world outside Africa, the proportion of the population under 15 years is little more than 20 per cent in some of the slow-growing economically developed countries of Western Europe, just over 30 per cent in some of the temperate countries of overseas European settlement and Japan, and from 40 per cent to 45 per cent in many of the developing areas found in the tropics of Asia and Latin America.

[1] See Appendix. Population Council Programme, *Registration Survey*.

Much has been written elsewhere about the significance of child-dependency of the type found in Ghana and of the strain thrown upon the economy by the existence of disproportionately large numbers of children. The direct economic strain is of two main types, that of providing education and that of meeting such needs as food, clothing and shelter. Both are a burden because of the relatively small size of the work force from which the national wealth originates.

The country as a whole finds the provision of education difficult only if it aims at providing schooling facilities for a substantial fraction of its children. Such an aim has been a very recent development in tropical Africa and has been associated to a very considerable extent with the hopes raised by the achievement of independence. By 1960 the number of persons in Ghanaian schools amounted to 36 per cent of those 5–19 years old.[1] Britain's proportion of 81 per cent was two-and-a-half times as large. But Ghana's problems in providing schools, equipment and teachers were relatively greater than this comparison might suggest for a much higher proportion of her population than that of Great Britain was of school age. Thus the proportions of the total populations of Britain and Ghana at school were 17 per cent and 11 per cent respectively. The difference this time is not two-and-a-half times but only one-and-two-thirds times.

Other economic strains imposed by a high child dependency ratio are more debatable. In a non-subsistence economy, where all children are at school and play no part in production, it is demonstrable that children are economically totally dependent. In a fully subsistence economy, where children can do much to provide their own food and other needs from a very young age, especially if the possibility of schooling does not exist, it is doubtful whether their presence imposes any extra burden. An intermediate situation exists in a country, where not all children are at school, and, where most of those who are, go to day school only. In rural Ghana, almost one-third of families claim that children of 10–14 years of age earn their keep even when they do go to school. Nevertheless, it would be true to say that, as countries become more economically developed, and as the population becomes more urbanized, the economic strain of supporting a relatively large number of children becomes proportionately greater.

The real strain imposed by a high child-dependency ratio is not adequately revealed by static analysis. The high ratio is proof that the next adult generation will be much larger than the present one. This means that all facilities in the country must continue to be multiplied. The implications of this will be considered later when the problem of continued high rates of population growth is examined.

On the other hand, as Table 1.9 shows, the dependency problem of fast growing populations is usually mitigated by the fact that their proportion of dependent aged population is normally very small. This is only to a small extent the effect of relatively high mortality levels; it is largely a consequence of the greater size of each successive generation in a rapidly growing population. If it is true that persons in the age groups under 15 and over 65 years are usually supported by those of working age, then 48 per cent of Ghana's population is dependent compared with 41 per cent in the United States and 34 per cent in Britain. This can be put in clearer form in terms of

[1] Not quite all persons in Ghanaian schools were in fact 5–19 years of age.

production and consumption, if we assume that each member of the population consumes the same amount. This is, of course, not true in the case of young children, so the comparisons about to be drawn are not quite as marked as shown. Taking Sweden, which has one of the world's lowest total dependency ratios, as standard, it can be seen that the same labour in Ghana will result in only 79 per cent as much consumption because of the extra dependent population to support. Most developing countries have to support such demographic loads in addition to the problems created by scarce capital and insufficiently skilled labour forces.

TABLE 1.9

DEPENDENCY, 1960: GHANA AND SELECTED OTHER COUNTRIES (PERCENTAGES)

Country	Population under 15	Population 15–64	Population over 65	Demographic efficiency* (Sweden=100)
Ghana	44·5	52·3	3·2	79
Malaya	45·1	52·2	2·7	79
Thailand	42·3	55·3	2·4	83
Ceylon	40·7	57·4	1·9	87
India	39·6	56·8	3·6	86
Venezuela	42·1	55·2	2·7	83
Brazil	41·9	55·7	2·4	84
Argentina	30·9	63·9	5·2	96
USSR	34·3	55·2	10·5	83
Japan	30·0	64·2	5·8	97
Australia	30·1	61·5	8·4	93
Canada	33·8	58·6	7·6	88
USA	31·2	59·5	9·3	90
United Kingdom	22·2	65·9	11·9	99
France	25·6	62·4	12·0	94
Sweden	21·8	66·2	12·0	100

* i.e. ratio of total population to population 15–64 years of age, in Sweden, divided by the same measure for the country concerned.
Source: United Nations *Demographic Year Books.*

It is often assumed, frequently correctly, that high population growth rates in many developing countries have been brought about by steeply declining infant mortality rates and that this has boosted the child dependency level. Changes in age structure, however, are often not great, especially in high fertility populations, unless the fertility level itself has changed. There is little evidence of such a change in Ghana. The age structure of the population has apparently remained surprisingly stable for at least 40 years. Table 1.10 shows this for the 1921, 1948 and 1960 Censuses. The age groups are the only ones that can be used to give comparability between the censuses. The fact that the 1921 figures were for the Colony and Ashanti only makes surprisingly little difference. The proportions of both sexes found in the same area in 1960 were 46·7 per cent, 42·1 per cent and 11·2 per cent for each of the three age groups.

While the age structure of Ghana as a whole has remained remarkably steady over the years, the same cannot be said from area to area. The proportion of the population under 15 years of age ranged in 1960 from 46·5 per cent in Ashanti to 42·8 per cent in the combined Northern and

TABLE 1.10

AGE STRUCTURE, BY SEX, 1921, 1948 and 1960 (PERCENTAGES)

Age	Sex	Censuses		
		1921*	1948	1960
Under 16 years:	males	43·4	43·6	46·5
	females	44·8	42·5	46·1
	both sexes	44·1	43·0	46·3
16–45 years:	males	43·0	42·5	41·3
	females	41·5	43·9	43·2
	both sexes	42·3	43·2	42·1
over 46 years:	males	13·6	13·9	12·2
	females	13·7	13·6	10·5
	both sexes	13·6	13·8	11·8

* Colony and Ashanti only.

Upper Regions. The contrast, arising from different levels of fertility and natural growth, was greater than this because migration, most pronounced amongst males, worked towards lessening the differences. Thus the proportion of females under 15 years of age was 47·7 per cent in the former area and only 40·1 per cent in the latter. The differences were more pronounced still in the Local Authority areas. In parts of Ashanti and the Central Region half the population was found to be under 15 years of age, while in the majority of the Upper Region less than 40 per cent of the population was in this group.

Finally, it should be remarked that not only is the population of Ghana youthful, but so is every subsection. Thus, most women of childbearing age are in their younger and more prolific years. Similarly, taking the labour force to be synonymous with the 15–64 years of age range, half the labour force is to be found in the youngest third of this range. The median-aged worker is only 30 years old. The work force may be more vital but it can hardly contain the same proportion of men with long experience as is the case in more slowly growing populations. Of course, this may be of no concern where the most valuable type of experience is that of the new imported economy. Thus in Ghana one member in nine of the labour force is over 50 years of age, while in Britain almost 30 per cent are.

Related to the question of the age structure of the community is that of the sex structure, for although sex is objectively distinguishable in a sense that age is not, a differential in age misstatement by sex complicates the assessment of the sex balance within any individual age group. That such differentials do occur in Ghana we have already seen.

Considerable interest centres on the question of the sex balance and the sex ratio at birth of the peoples of tropical Africa. Evidence has been adduced to show that the sex ratio at birth is probably lower than that found in any other large area of the world. Certainly, the negro community of the United States exhibits sex ratios in every age group well below those of the white community. One calculation showed that the sex ratio of the population of tropical Africa as a whole was 95·6 males per hundred females compared with 107·2 in the rest of Africa.[1] The only continent

[1] George H. T. Kimble, *Tropical Africa*, New York, 1960, Vol. I, p. 108.

with a sex ratio below that of tropical Africa was Europe, where the cause was not the low sex ratio at birth but the erosion of male population by war and emigration.

As Table 1.11 shows, Ghana does in fact have a slight excess of males. However, this can be explained wholly in terms of immigration, for there are 70 per cent more foreign-born males than females in the country. The sex ratio of the native-born is a little higher than the average for tropical Africa quoted above but still shows a deficit of males.

The sex ratio of native-born Ghanaians is, at 97·7 males per hundred females, well within the experience of those European countries which have not recently been affected by war or massive emigration. For instance, in 1960 the ratios in Sweden and Finland were 99·5 and 93·0 respectively. But these ratios were achieved by an excess of male births, which were subsequently eroded away by higher male mortality at every age until a majority of females remained. This has been the typical European experience. The sex ratios of the under 1 year of age group were, in 1960, 104·8 and 104·0 in the two countries, while the ratios of the whole 0–4 years of age group were 106·0 and 104·3.

This experience is very different from the Ghanaian one. In 1960 the sex ratios for these two age groups was 95·6 and 97·7 in the case of the whole population and 95·7 and 97·6 in the case of the native-born. The 0–4 years of age figures probably give the best picture, for the single years of age figures suggest some sex differential in age misstatement. This picture is in general in line with enumerations of the youngest age groups in earlier censuses.

Even if non-African mortality experience is relevant to Ghana, and if accordingly considerably more male than female infants and small children die, the sex ratio of 97·6 in the 0–4 years of age native-born group is not likely to have resulted from a sex ratio at birth of much over 100. It seems likely, then, that the marked excess of male over female births, which is a feature of much of the world, is not found in Ghana nor perhaps in tropical Africa as a whole.

Another conclusion is also implicit in the Table showing the sex ratios of the native born. The sex ratio for the whole population is 97·7 males per hundred females. Now, Ghana is essentially an immigrant rather than an emigrant country. However, there has undoubtedly been some emigration, especially of the native-born children of foreign immigrants, and probably males have, as in the case of other African migration, proved somewhat more mobile. Therefore, the sex ratio of surviving native-born Ghanaians, found anywhere in the world, is probably a little above 97·7. Perhaps a reasonably good guess would be about 99 males per hundred females or even 100.

Thus the sex ratio for the whole native-born population is apparently very similar to that found at birth. This implies that throughout life the level of male mortality approximates to that of females. This is not the recent Western experience, but it is now known to be the case in India as it may be in some other parts of Asia and Africa. Perhaps in Ghana, as in India, female mortality exceeds that of males during the main child-bearing years but is less in childhood and old age.

The analysis of the sex ratios by age group confirms that there has been

TABLE 1.11

SEX RATIOS, 1960 (MALES PER HUNDRED FEMALES)

(a) all ages

Total population	102·2
Foreign-born	170·6
Native born	97·7

(b) by single-years of age

Age	Total population	Native-born
0	95·6	95·7
1	100·0	–
2	99·0	–
3	97·7	–
4	96·8	–

(c) by five-year age groups

Age	Total population	Native-born
0–4	97·7	97·6
5–9	101·5	102·0
10–14	110·1	110·0
15–19	105·0	103·0
20–4	84·2	79·9
25–9	91·0	83·3
30–4	98·3	88·2
35–9	110·6	98·2
40–4	114·9	100·2
45–9	129·7	115·7
50–4	118·0	105·2
55–9	122·7	109·3
60–4	115·1	104·2
65+	114·0	102·6

age misstatement to a degree which cannot be explained merely in terms of preference for an age ending in one digit rather than another, and that there is a differential by sex in such misstatement. The analysis shows that the tendency during the years of adolescence for the advancement of stated age clearly affects more females than males. One result is an apparent massing of females in the young adult age groups. Thus an examination of the whole 15–44 years of age range gives the impression that males make up only 98·1 per cent of the number of females in spite of the large number of male immigrants, while, amongst the native born, where our studies have indicated that there is probably approximate parity between the sexes in each age group, the deficiency of males appears to be about 9·5 per cent.

That this pattern in the sex ratios is not peculiar to the 1960 Census can be seen in Table 1.12, where the 1948 and 1960 ratios are compared. The very high ratio in the oldest age group in 1960 is largely a product of relatively greater immigration. The higher ratio in the 1948 1–15 years of age group may be explained by a change in the system of taxation. The 1948 Census Report argued that, 'Persons are normally put on the tax roll at age 16 years and fear that the census might be used for this purpose may have resulted in deliberate understatement of age. The error is somewhat more for males than for females but may be in the neighbourhood of 100,000 of each sex.'[1]

[1] 1948 Census Report, p. 13.

TABLE 1.12

SEX RATIOS BY AGE, 1948 AND 1960
(MALES PER HUNDRED FEMALES)

Age group	1948	1960
Under 1	97·4	95·6
1–15	106·8	102·7
16–44	98·9	97·3
45+	104·6	120·0
All ages	102·3	102·2

The sex ratios shown in Table 1.11(c) demonstrate the effect of immigration in heightening adult sex ratios. The decline of the ratios of the total population from 130 in the 45–49 years of age group to 114 in the over 65 years of age group indicates that the older age groups are not as much affected by the presence of migrants, possibly because of re-emigration and perhaps because the great wave of immigration has been a comparatively recent phenomenon. There may also have been lower mortality amongst older aged females than amongst older males. Such a view receives some support from the fall of the sex ratio amongst the native born from 116 to 103 in the same age groups. Both findings may, of course, be largely a product of age misstatement. It is quite possible that the decline in the native-born ratio has also arisen from the return home of immigrants, in that some immigrants have been enumerated as native born. The fact that sex ratios were relatively higher in 1948 in the younger age groups and much lower in the older age groups than was the case in 1960 suggests that the first great wave of post-war immigration was beginning then and has not been sustained in recent years.

In terms of the geographical distribution of sex ratios, the pattern is deeply influenced by migration. There are fewer males than females in areas where economic prospects are either limited or are not increasing as rapidly as in other areas within reach. Sex ratios are below the national average of 102 and in general females outnumber males in the Upper Region, all the Volta Region except the far north, the south-eastern half of the Eastern Region, and the coastal areas except Accra-Tema and Takoradi.[1] Males predominate in most of Ashanti, all of Brong-Ahafo and much of the Western Region, especially in those areas where cocoa-planting is still pressing on into country previously occupied by forest. This also applies to parts of the Central and Eastern Region where planting is either most recent or is still continuing. Of considerable interest is the fact that males predominate in nearly all the country lying north of the thick forest except for the Upper Region in the far north. These are now areas where immigration is at least as important as emigration. The increase of population in this relatively thinly settled area is related to the extension of small-scale agriculture. One factor of importance, especially in Brong-Ahafo East and Buem-Krachi, is increased yam growing for cash sale in the urban markets to the south.

The pattern of sex ratios can, therefore, be used as a tool in the analysis of migration. If, however, the analysis is confined to particular age groups, great care must be exercised to distinguish between the effect of a sex

[1] See map in next chapter.

differentiation in migrational movement and that of a sex differentiation in age misstatement.

(iii) *Population Distribution*
Not only does the composition of the population vary according to age and sex, but also according to place of residence, ethnic group and urban or rural location.

That the population is not evenly distributed is clear from Table 1.13, which is based upon the Regions of the country, and from the map showing population density by Local Authority Area.[1] Ghana's major administrative Regions may be compared with advantage. On the whole they do approximate to the real divisions of the country in cultural, historical, economic and agricultural terms.

Excluding the Accra Capital District, Regional population density can be seen to vary from almost 200 persons per square mile in the Central Region to less than a tenth as many in the Northern Region. The latter indeed makes up more than a quarter of the area of the country but contains only about one-sixteenth of its people. Most Ghanaians live in those parts of the forest which have been longest commercially developed and in the ports to the south. Almost two-thirds of the population live in the part of the country formed by the Eastern, Central, Ashanti and Volta Regions and Accra, although these Regions make up only about one-third of the country's area. Fewer people live in the more recently developed forest lands of the Western and Brong-Ahafo Regions and fewer still are to be found in the country immediately to the north of the forest. However, such a pattern is not sustained indefinitely to the northward. In the far north more populous areas are again encountered. With a population density of 64 persons per square mile, the Upper Region exhibits an intensity of settlement which is three-and-a-half times that of the Northern Region, not far short of twice that of Brong-Ahafo, and much the same as the Western Region. Furthermore, this population is maintained almost entirely by subsistence farming. There is little in the way of the tree cash crops, the commerce and the industry of southern Ghana.

TABLE 1.13

POPULATION DISTRIBUTION BY REGION, 1960

Region	Population (thousands)	Percentage of population of Ghana	Area (sq. miles)	Percentage of area of Ghana	Average population density (persons per sq. mile)
Accra C.D.	492	7·3	995	1·1	494
Eastern	1,094	16·3	7,698	8·4	142
Central	751	11·2	3,815	4·1	197
Western	626	9·3	9,236	10·0	68
Ashanti	1,109	16·5	9,417	10·2	118
Brong-Ahafo	588	8·7	15,273	16·6	38
Volta	777	11·6	7,943	8·6	98
Northern	427	6·3	24,179	26·3	18
Upper	862	12·8	13,544	14·7	64
Ghana	6,727	100·0	92,100	100·0	73

Source: 1960 Census.

[1] See map in next chapter.

The settlement pattern can perhaps best be understood by examining the position in terms of the smaller divisions of the country formed by the Local Authority areas. In south-eastern Ghana a rectangular block of country is found in which every Local Authority area exhibits population densities above the national average. It extends for 175 miles westward from the Togo border and inland for about 75 miles. Densely settled areas extend beyond this rectangle, as if radially from Accra, along the coast westward to Axim, north-west through Kumasi to Sunyani and beyond, and north-east to Kpandu and Hohoe. In southern Ghana sparsely settled areas extend over almost the whole south-west with the exception of a narrow coastal strip from Axim eastward and scattered mining areas. These forests, stretching northward 150 miles to Dormaa Ahenkro and eastward almost as far as to the Upper Pra River, provide the last great frontier area of the once far more extensive forest land.

In population terms, northern Ghana is reached almost immediately after crossing the ridge of hills, which extends from Wenchi through Mampong and Mpraeso, and entering the Volta Basin. In some places, population drops on crossing this ridge from above 200 persons per square mile to a little more than a tenth as much. Except in the far north-east, the most marked dichotomy in Ghana's population distribution is that between the sparsely settled lands which drain into the Volta and the predominantly thickly settled area which drains straight into the sea. This division does not correlate to any marked degree with climate, but is apparently associated to some extent with the quality of the soil.

The anomalous area is found in north-eastern Ghana. Here is an area of savannah-woodland country, receiving only about 40 inches of rain a year, which is uniquely densely settled for this part of Africa. For about 90 miles from west of Navrongo to the border of Togo, and stretching southward for 30 or 40 miles from the Upper Volta border, is an area of 2,500 square miles containing more than 400,000 people at an average of more than 160 persons per square mile. In the Frafra area the density of settlement exceeds 200 persons per square mile. A somewhat similar, but smaller area, in the far north-west exhibits a density of population of more than 100 persons per square mile. It is these areas of dense subsistence farming which provide the Upper Region with its most distinctive quality. They also provide Ghana with its greatest problem area, for, in terms of the present economic structure of the region, these population densities are excessive. In many areas each successive dry season raises questions of food supply. Real food shortages are a typical feature of the annual cycle of events.

At the time of writing, the 1960 Census has provided nothing on the ethnic distribution, or the closely related linguistic distribution, of the native-born population. In 1948 the Census of that year had listed sixty tribes. But well over a third of the population were enumerated as Asante, Ewe or Fanti. In these three groups were found one-seventh, one-eighth and one-ninth of the population respectively. These major groups were geographically strongly localized, 87 per cent of Asantes being found in Ashanti, 85 per cent of Ewes in what is now the Volta Region, and 80 per cent of the Fantis in the Cape Coast District alone of the Central Region. The largest tribes of the north contained only about a third as many people as the major tribal groups of the south. Nevertheless, about one-seventh of the population originating there was attributed to the Frafra and another seventh to the Dagomba. Twenty tribes in the country as a whole were credited with more than 50,000 members each.

In modern Ghana, however, the contrast between ways of life is often most marked, not in terms of the different regions or ethnic groups, but in terms of whether one lives in a large town or in a village. Table 1.14 shows that about half the population of Ghana live either in small villages or in some cases in scattered rural housing (under 1,000 inhabitants), over a quarter live in large villages (between 1,000–5,000 inhabitants), and just under a quarter live in towns (5,000 inhabitants and over).[1] Large towns (50,000 inhabitants or over) house 7·7 per cent of the population, i.e. 5 per cent in Accra and 2·7 per cent in Kumasi.

TABLE 1.14

POPULATION BY SIZE OF LOCALITY, 1960 (PERCENTAGE DISTRIBUTION)

Under 1,000	1,000–5,000	5,000–20,000	20,000–50,000	50,000–250,000	Over 250,000
48·2	28·8	11·4	3·9	2·7	5·0

Source: 1960 Census.

The town population is not evenly distributed. In southern Ghana, west of the Volta River, almost a third of the population lives in towns. In the Brong-Ahafo and Volta Regions less than one-sixth does so, while in northern Ghana less than a twelfth does.

TABLE 1.15

URBAN AND RURAL POPULATION, BY REGION, 1960 (PERCENTAGE DISTRIBUTION)

Region	Urban (localities with more than 5,000 inhabitants)	Rural	Urban (with more than 100,000 inhabitants)
Accra C.D.	80	20	69
Eastern	20	80	—
Central and Western*	26	74	—
Ashanti	25	75	16
Brong-Ahafo	16	84	—
Volta	13	87	—
Northern and Upper*	8	92	—
Ghana	23	77	8

* i.e. using 1960 Regions.
Source: 1960 Census.

The towns attract considerably greater numbers of males than females. Thus 23·5 per cent of Ghana's males are to be found in towns, compared with 22·6 per cent of the females. These differences give rise to a much more marked discrepancy in the balance of the sexes within the towns. In rural Ghana the sex ratio is 101 males per hundred females, but it rises to 106 in the towns and 114 in Accra. This imbalance can lead to social problems, especially in the immigrant quarters of the towns.

The more detailed treatment of urbanization will be left to a later chapter.

[1] Using the definition of the 1960 Census, which defined an urban centre as one with over 5,000 inhabitants.

(iv) *The Educational Pattern*

Mass education in Ghana has been regarded as a possibility only since the Second World War. In the last two decades all developing countries have been faced with the dilemma of whether they can afford to have universal education or whether they can afford not to have it, for its achievement might well decisively hasten economic development. Ghana has decided that it is essential and has in recent years been committing an exceptionally large share of its national income to education.

At the time of the 1948 Census only 4 per cent of the population had received any schooling. By 1960 21 per cent had. In the latter year 27 per cent of the population over 6 years of age had attended school at some time. Of children in the 10–14 years of age range, 42·7 per cent were attending school and a further 6·3 per cent had at some stage attended it. Indeed, amongst 10–14-year-old males, 60·3 per cent had been to school and 54 per cent were still there. The high point was reached in the Accra Capital District, where 78·8 per cent of 10–14-year-old males had been in school at some time and 74·9 per cent were currently there.

TABLE 1.16

POPULATION EVER AT SCHOOL, 1948 AND 1960

	1948	*1960*
(a) Total population (thousands)	4,118	6,727
(b) Number who have attended or are attending school (thousands)	164*	1,405
(c) Percentage (b) forms of (a)	4·0	20·9

* African population only.

The fundamental facts then, of the Ghanaian educational picture are first that there must be a tremendous effort to increase the availability of education and second that the country has to continue to bear the growing economic burden which this must impose. By 1960 three-quarters of a million Ghanaians, of whom two-thirds were males and one-third females, were receiving full-time education. This represented 11 per cent of the population of the whole country and in size was over two-fifths as large as the male labour force, measured in terms of the number of males, 15–64 years of age. In terms of the comparison with the size of the labour force, which is the source of wealth upon which the educational system rests, the United Kingdom, with its much higher level of incomes, supports little more than one-and-a-half times as many people enjoying full-time education.

A vital consideration when assessing the future strain of providing education is the estimate of the demand for education, especially above that age which is likely to mark the upper limit of universal schooling. Below that age, an estimate is relatively easy. At the time of the 1960 Census, 644,000 children between 6 and 11 years of age were not at school. If they had all been provided with schooling and compelled to attend, the numbers at school in this age range would have been multiplied by $2\frac{1}{2}$ and the total population receiving full-time education would have increased by 87 per cent.

The extent to which the demand for the provision of schooling might increase in the adolescent years is a more difficult question. Table 1.17 and

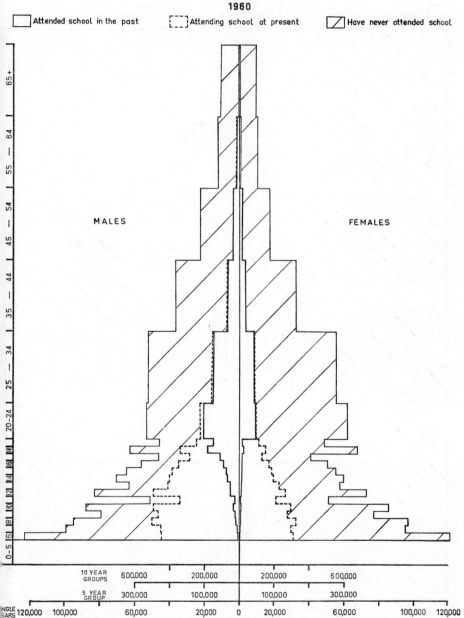

Figure 1·6a
GHANA: EDUCATIONAL AGE PYRAMID,
POPULATION OVER 6 YEARS OF AGE,
1960

☐ Attended school in the past   ⌐ ⌐ Attending school at present   ⟋ Have never attended school

MALES   FEMALES

Source: 1960 Population Census

D

Figure 1:6b.

GHANA: POPULATION RECTANGLE,
SHOWING PROPORTIONS EDUCATED, BY AGE,
1960

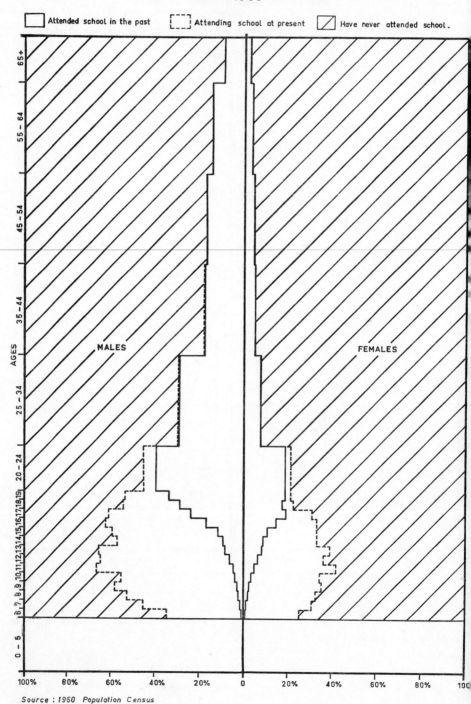

Source : 1960 Population Census

Figures 1.6(a) and 1.6(b) show the usual decline in the numbers attending school during these years. But this in Ghana is a compound of two quite separate factors. One is the tendency of many children to leave school with advancing years. The other is that the rate of educational change has been so great that children in a group ten years younger than another group are educationally in a different generation which has been provided with more educational facilities.

TABLE 1.17

SCHOOL ATTENDANCE BY SEX AND AGE, 1960* (IN THOUSANDS)

	Males			*Females*			*Males with some*
		At school	*Never*		*At school*	*Never*	*schooling per*
	Now at	*in the*	*at*	*Now at*	*in the*	*at*	*hundred females*
	school	*past*	*school*	*school*	*past*	*school*	*with some schooling*
Age	*(per cent of whole age group)*			*(per cent of whole age group)*			
6–9	46	1	53	30	1	69	155
10–14	54	6	40	30	6	64	181
15–19	36	22	42	12	16	72	219
20–4	6	39	55	3	19	78	250
25–34	0	29	71	0	8	92	359
35–44	0	18	82	0	5	95	394
45–54	0	17	83	0	5	95	445
55–64	0	15	85	0	4	96 ⎱	470
65+	0	9	91	0	3	97 ⎰	

* includes attendance at universities, etc.
Source: 1960 Census.

There are some interesting aspects of the educational statistics. Perhaps the most conspicuous is the fact that, although the proportion educated decreases with age, this phenomenon occurs only from the 10–14 years of age group onwards. While only 31 per cent of 6-year-olds have ever been in school, the number thereafter increases until it reaches a maximum of 53–54 per cent in the 11- and 13-year-old groups. Some of the explanation may lie in over-statement of age. Some may lie in cultural resistance to very young children leaving the household for formal tuition. However, it is probable that the main reason is merely the practical difficulties associated with small children walking or securing transport for long distances to school. This suggestion receives support from the fact that the ratio of the percentage of 11-year-olds to that of 6-year-olds at school is about 2.1 in the small rural localities with less than 200 inhabitants which are often a considerable distance from a school, only 1.6 in bigger villages, and 1.4 in centres with more than 5,000 inhabitants.

The high average age of students in the various types of educational institution results both from the belated commencement of school, the fact that economic considerations often force children to discontinue school for a year or two in order to work until such time as they or their relatives can meet the cost of more schooling, and the recent availability of educational facilities in many areas. Thus the six years in which primary school children of each age group form the greatest proportion of all children of that age is from 7 to 12 years, an advance of about one year on the position in Britain. Similarly the most typical four-year span for middle schools is 13 to 16 years, the most typical six-year span for secondary schools is 15 to 20 years, and the most typical three-year span for university students is 23 to 25 years.

There is an even stronger tapering tendency with movement up the educational structure than is evidenced by the proportion educated in each age group. Thus while 512,000 students were to be found in 1960 in primary schools and 183,000 were in middle schools, only 20,000 and 1,000 were in secondary schools and universities respectively. In 1960, the greatest hurdle in the educational system was still the achievement of a standard high enough to secure a place in a secondary school. A few students managed to do this straight from primary school but most had to undertake one or more years in the middle school first. There was no block of similar magnitude in gaining entrance to a university. In 1960 there were 880 students in the sixth forms of the secondary schools and 760 in the first years of universities. Such figures must be treated cautiously. The secondary school leavers were probably greater in number than they had been the previous year. Nor do all pass the final examinations at matriculation level. Furthermore, some of those who do then proceed to overseas universities. On the other hand, a survey[1] indicated that in the early 1960s only about three-fifths of the university intake would have come directly from schools. Therefore, not many more than 450 of the first-year university students probably belonged to this category in 1960. Thus, while reaching the final year of secondary school does not guarantee university entrance, the great majority of such students, and perhaps nearly all the matriculants, do in fact proceed to university studies.

Education has not yet spread evenly throughout the society, for there have been differential financial and cultural pressures. An example of the latter is found in the education of the sexes. Throughout the population well over twice as many males as females have ever been to school. But, as can be seen from Table 1.17, this state of affairs is passing. Amongst the oldest people almost five times as many males as females have been to school, but in the younger years of the primary school at the present time

TABLE 1.18

SCHOOL ATTENDANCE BY REGION, 1960

	(1)	(2)		
Region	Percentage of population 6+ years of age, ever at school	Percentage of population 6–9 years of age, ever at school	Ratio of (2) to (1)	Males per hundred females ever at school
Accra C.D.	47	60	1·3	202
Eastern	35	49	1·4	188
Western and Central	28	40	1·4	263
Ashanti	33	50	1·5	227
Brong-Ahafo	20	33	1·7	276
Volta	34	44	1·3	196
Northern and Upper	6	12	2·2	358
Ghana	27	39	1·4	223

Source: 1960 Census.

[1] See Appendix. Population Council Programme, *University Survey.*

males outnumber females by only one-and-a-half times. All parts of Ghana are not as yet equally affected by this change. In the north there are still three-and-a-half times as many males as females with schooling.

In other ways, too, there is still quite a strong regional differential in Ghana's educational pattern. It has always been easier for a cocoa farmer to send his son to school than it has for a subsistence farmer. Table 1.18 illustrates this, but it also shows that these conditions are passing. A comparison of the numbers of the younger children now at school with the educated members of the adult community reveals that the gains have been greatest where the previous levels were lowest.

The distribution and development of education in Ghana can perhaps be best understood from the census data on the Local Authority areas. In every area of the Northern and Upper Regions, with the single exception of Tamale with its imported administrative officials, less than one person in every twenty-five over 15 years of age has ever had any schooling. While this is true nowhere further south, nevertheless, nowhere in Ghana has a majority of the adult population been to school, although this is almost the case in the Accra and Kpandu areas.

The general pattern of education is fairly clear. Schooling has taken place when it was available and where the population could afford it. Amongst the population over 15 years of age the greatest numbers of educated are found in the older tree crop areas and in the ports. More than a quarter of the adult population has had some schooling in the Akwapim-Akim District, the Kpandu-Ho District, and in such ports, mining towns and administrative centres as Accra, Tema, Keta, Cape Coast, Takoradi-Sekondi, Tarkwa, Oda, Obuasi, Kumasi and Sunyani. An examination of the proportion of 6–14-year-olds who have received some schooling shows how the pattern is being modified. The chief changes are the intensification of education in the districts where it had been available together with an advance of the borders of the rural area containing an abnormally high proportion of population with schooling far into Ashanti. There is now a solid block of territory where over half the population between 6 and 14 years has had some schooling. It extends west to east from Bekwai to Ho and north to south from Ejura to Cape Coast. This is an area of over 10,000 square miles of land where cocoa, coffee and food crops have largely replaced the forest and where in parts gold and diamonds are to be found. Educational advance still lags behind on the coast, except for half a dozen major towns, in the forests of the south-west and far west, and especially in the north. Government assistance has been able to do much, but the ability of the regional economy to sustain high family incomes is still of very great importance.

Interrelated with the regional educational differential is the rural-urban one. Table 1.19 demonstrates clearly that the proportion of persons with schooling climbs steeply as the size of the locality of residence increases. This does have something to do with the tendency of the educated to seek urban jobs. But it is also related to the greater opportunities for education which have persisted in the towns. It might be remarked that until education for all can be arranged there is something to be said, in terms of the strategy of planning for rapid economic modernization, for concentrating a larger than average share of education upon those whose backgrounds have already helped to shape them for adaptation to a modernized society. Even if this has not been the result of planning in modern Ghana, the fact remains that nearly as many children are at school in towns of more than 5,000 inhabitants as in villages with less than 1,000 inhabitants, in spite of the fact that the latter contain more than three times as many people.

TABLE 1.19

SCHOOL ATTENDANCE BY SIZE OF LOCALITY, 1960

Size of locality (No. of inhabitants)	Percentage of population over 6 years of age who have ever attended school	Percentage of population, 6–14 years of age, at present at school
Under 200	14	21
200–499	19	32
500–999	22	38
1,000–1,999	26	41
2,000–4,999	31	47
5,000 and over	43	56

Source: 1960 Census.

(v) The Occupational Pattern

Ghana is a country which is in transition from a state where the vast majority of its people lived in villages to one where a significant fraction of its population live and work in towns. The occupational pattern is therefore undergoing change. For the first time statistics of unemployment are becoming important, for unemployment, as distinct from underemployment, is in West Africa largely a town phenomenon and is one that must necessarily concern governments. Farming is, of course, still of very great importance. In 1960 three-fifths of the working population were farmers compared with about four-fifths twelve years earlier.

In 1960 nearly three-quarters of the adult population regarded themselves as members of the labour force, and of these 94 per cent were in employment. Thus, over $2\frac{1}{2}$ million persons described themselves as employed. The number of employed males was equal to 46 per cent of all males or 89 per cent of the number of males between 15 and 64 years of age. The two main groups withdrawn from active labour were the unemployed and the students, each amounting to about 6 per cent of those over 15 years of age. The balance of those adults outside the labour force could be regarded as the retired and amounted only to about two-thirds of the number of males over 65 years of age. The number of employed females was equal to 30 per cent of all females or 57 per cent of the number of females between 15 and 64 years of age. Over a third of all adult females were listed as outside the labour force by virtue of being home-makers, although it is a reasonable assumption that a substantial proportion of them did in fact undertake some farm work or petty trading. Unemployment and student status accounted for only 3 and 2 per cent respectively of female withdrawals from the labour force, or in total about half that prevailing amongst males. It should be noted, however, that an unemployed female might well list herself as a home-maker. As in the case of males, almost 5 per cent of females over 15 years of age could be regarded as retired, a figure which amounted to little over half the number over 65 years of age.

TABLE 1.20

ECONOMIC ACTIVITY OF POPULATION OVER FIFTEEN YEARS OF AGE, BY SEX, 1960
(PERCENTAGES)

	Employed	Un-employed	Home-makers	Students	Aged or disabled	Other
Males	83·2	5·8	0·6	6·0	3·3	1·1
Females	53·6	3·0	36·7	1·8	4·6	0·3
Both sexes	68·6	4·4	18·4	3·9	4·0	0·7

Source: 1960 Census.

The unemployed thus make up 6·5 and 5·2 per cent respectively of the males and females who regard themselves as potential members of the labour force. It is of importance to try to isolate the incidence of unemployment in the community. In spite of the fact that only 23 per cent of the population is classified as urban, 44 per cent of the unemployed are found in the towns. Thus the incidence of unemployment is twice as high in the towns as in rural Ghana. Nor is it evenly spread in the towns, but tends to be more marked in the larger centres. Thus Accra accounts for a quarter of the urban population of the country but contains a third of the urban unemployed.

The incidence of unemployment is even more localized in terms of age. As shown in Table 1.21, over 60 per cent of male unemployment and over 70 per cent of female unemployment is concentrated in the 15–24 years of age range. Indeed, more than half of all female unemployed are between 15 and 19 years old.

That the two phenomena described above are not unrelated is also suggested by Table 1.21. Adolescents and young adults tend to drift to the towns in large numbers. The proportion of the urban female population found in the 15–19 years of age range is a quarter as high again as the proportion of rural females found at this age. The proportion of males found in the 20–24 years of age range is over one-and-a-half times as great. Part of this phenomenon may be explained by a more marked tendency to overstate age in rural Ghana, but much of it is evidence of a very pronounced movement to the towns by people of this age. The age groups in which these young adults migrate to the towns are the very ones in which the incidence of unemployment is highest. This could suggest two things. Firstly, that rural unemployment in these ages is a cause of such migration, and secondly, that a considerable fraction of the country's unemployed is constituted by young migrants who have reached the towns and cannot, for a period at least, find employment.[1]

[1] New data have lately become available in *Special Report A: Statistics of Towns with 10,000 population or more* from the 1960 Census. These towns contain 18·6 per cent of the total population. Assuming, as does the Census, that an examination of unemployment should be confined to persons over 15 years of age, it might be noted that 30·3 per cent of those of 15 years or more in the whole country are 15–24 years of age. Thus, if the age structure of towns were similar to that of the rest of the country, which would be very roughly the case only for rural-urban migration, and if unemployment were distributed evenly by age, one might expect to find that 5½ per cent of the unemployed were found amongst 15–24 year-olds of these towns. But in 1960 such persons contributed 23 per cent of all unemployment. Thus the move to the towns, and the greater difficulties experienced there by young adults in securing employment, result in an incidence of unemployment over four times greater than might otherwise have been expected.

TABLE 1.21

URBAN AND RURAL POPULATION AND UNEMPLOYED POPULATION BY SEX AND AGE, 1960

Age Group	Percentage of males in each age group		Ratio of urban male percentage to rural male percentage	Percentage of females in each age group		Ratio of urban female percentage to rural female percentage	Percentage of all unemployed in Ghana over 15 years of age in each age group	
	urban	rural		urban	rural		males	females
10–14	9·4	10·9	0·9	11·2	9·4	1·2	—	53
15–19	9·7	7·7	1·3	9·5	7·5	1·3	34	18
20–4	11·0	6·9	1·6	10·9	9·2	1·2	27	8
25–9	11·0	7·4	1·5	9·1	9·3	1·0	15	5
30–4	8·2	6·8	1·2	7·1	7·5	0·9	9	100
All ages	100·0	100·0	1·0	100·0	100·0	1·0	100	

Source: 1960 Census.

Ghana's economy is still primarily agricultural, three-fifths of the labour force being employed in agriculture, forestry, hunting and fishing. Most are farmers, for even fishing and forestry employ only $2 \cdot 2$ per cent and $0 \cdot 5$ per cent of those employed in spite of the prominence of these occupations on the south coast and in the forests of the south-west respectively. Of even less importance, in spite of the grasslands of northern Ghana, is the live-stock industry which employs less than 7,000 people, making up only $0 \cdot 3$ per cent of the labour force. The tsetse fly is mostly to blame, although there is also the fact that the density of human population in the Upper Region demands either a fully crop-growing economy or a mixed farming one in which crop-growing is predominant.

Mining, in spite of its importance as an export industry, employs fewer than 50,000 people, or less than 2 per cent of the labour force. Nevertheless, in recent years it has accounted for about a fifth of Ghana's overseas earnings. Most of these employees work in the gold and diamond mining industries, about 52 per cent in the former and 42 per cent in the latter.

One person in eleven in Ghana is listed as being employed in the manufacturing industry. This does not mean, however, that by 1960 Ghana's plans for industrialization had achieved such startling success. It does mean that, in terms of statistical classification, manufacturing includes many activities which do not take place in vast modern factories. Nearly a quarter of a million people are employed in manufacturing in Ghana. But a third of them are dress-makers or tailors, an eighth make furniture, mostly on a small scale, and a twentieth are motor mechanics. It is, in fact, very difficult to estimate the true number employed in the modern industrial sector. This is demonstrated by the fact that about half of all manufacturing takes place in centres with less than 2,000 people. Thus, although the Accra Capital District is the chief location of modern manufacturing industry in Ghana, it accounts for only one-tenth of those employed in manufacturing. This, for instance, is less than two-thirds the number found in the Volta Region.

Commerce accounts for one-seventh of the employed population. In the non-agricultural sector it accounts for two-fifths. This figure is thrown into better perspective if one realizes that 87 per cent of those employed in commerce are petty traders, and indeed that almost three-quarters of them are female petty traders. Petty trading provides employment for more than a quarter of a million women, or over a quarter of the whole female labour force. It employs almost half as many women as does agriculture.

One person in every fifteen is employed in construction, transport or the provision of such services as electricity, water and sanitary services. The importance of the transportation system provided by the *mammy lorries* and other trucks is underlined by the fact that well over half of the workers in the transport industry are connected with them.

Services include a wide range of employment such as the central government, local administration, education, health and also domestic service. Over two-thirds of all these persons are employed by the Government.

Agriculture is by no means a homogeneous category. Nor, in Ghana, can one in any way draw a meaningful division between a modern non-agricultural sector and a traditional agricultural one. As yet, by far the most important section of the country's modern, cash-earning, market-

TABLE 1.22

PERSONS EMPLOYED IN INDUSTRIES BY SEX, 1960
(NUMBERS OF EMPLOYEES ARE IN THOUSANDS)

	Males		Females		Both sexes	
	No.	%	No.	%	No.	%
Agriculture, forestry, hunting and fishing	1,003	64	576	58	1,579	62
Mining	46	3	2	0	48	2
Manufacturing	136	9	99	10	235	9
Commerce	96	6	276	28	372	15
Construction	87	5	3	0	90	3
Electricity, water and sanitary services	14	1	0	0	14	1
Transport	67	4	1	0	68	3
Services	124	8	31	3	155	6
All industries	1,573	100	988	100	2,561	100

Source: 1960 Census.

orientated economy is found in agriculture. The planting of tree crops, especially cocoa, has already replaced subsistence farming as the dominant form of agriculture in much of the forest area, and has very substantially raised living standards in the process. Average income per head per annum in the Regions of southern Ghana west of the Volta River is everywhere above £50. In the two northern Regions it is £30.[1] Eventually, practically the whole area once covered by forest will produce tree-crop products for sale on the world market. This does not mean that the subsistence growing of food crops for home consumption has not continued and will not continue. It does mean, however, that there is a major source of cash income. The position is very different in the savannah-woodland country which forms the Northern and Upper Regions. On the whole, problems of agriculture and of the economics of transportation have to date prevented the disappearance of the subsistence farming economy. Except in those areas where yams can be grown, not even the most common foodstuffs are saleable in the markets of the large towns of the south where a different dietary régime prevails.

The census does not allow a clear-cut division to be made between subsistence and commercial farming. However, some indication of the importance of subsistence farming is given by noting the fraction formed of all employed in 'agriculture, forestry, hunting and fishing' by those finding employment in 'Field crops and foodstuff production, including vegetables and flowers and mixed farming'. The balance of the employees in this sector of the economy is attributed to 'Oil palm plantation, tea and coffee plantation, cocoa growing, rubber plantation, tobacco growing, agricultural services, forestry, logging, fishing' and in very small numbers to 'hunting' and 'livestock production'. Table 1.23 shows that the proportion made up by the former is 58 per cent for Ghana as a whole. But this is not the typical position throughout the country. The proportion ranges from 37 and 41 per cent in the relatively new cocoa regions of Ashanti and Brong-Ahafo to around 50 per cent in the older regions, to 64 per cent in

[1] R. Szereszewski, Economic Volume of the *Social and Economic Survey of Ghana*, 'Gross Value Added per Capita by Region, 1960'.

the Volta Region, and to 98 per cent in the north. Thus, in much of the south, between a quarter and a third of the labour force is employed in food production, while in the north five-sixths is.

This contrast between the Regions is a feature not merely of food production but of all agriculture. Thus in the Eastern Region, the historic heart of tree-crop agriculture in Ghana, less than three-fifths of the labour force is employed in agriculture. An examination of the distribution of employment by Local Authority areas shows that, apart from the coastal ports, the areas where fewest of the work force are employed in agriculture are precisely those districts where economically advanced agriculture, in the form of the growing of commercial tree crops, has longest been practised. There is nothing very unusual or deplorable in this state of affairs. It is in countries of advanced and efficient agriculture where relatively few are employed in this activity. The most efficient agriculture can not only bring the greatest returns: it can also release the greatest proportion of the labour force for other productive purposes, which in turn raises living standards. Thus, New Zealand and Denmark, two countries highly specialized in agricultural production, employ only 16 and 25 per cent respectively of their work forces in this sphere. Concern is often felt in developing countries for the future of agricultural production in those regions from which many people are migrating to the towns or in which many people are turning to other forms of employment. Admittedly, such migration may raise very considerable problems of urban employment. On the other hand, it may well be a sign of the development of economically efficient agriculture. The true area for concern is in most cases that which maintains a very high level of agricultural employment.

TABLE 1.23

EMPLOYMENT IN AGRICULTURE BY REGION, 1960

Region	(1) Percentage of labour force employed in Agriculture, Forestry, Hunting and Fishing	(2) Percentage of labour force employed in Field crops and Foodstuffs production	Percentage (2) forms of (1)
Accra C.D.	13	6	48
Eastern	59	28	47
Western and Central	58	29	50
Ashanti	62	23	37
Brong-Ahafo	80	33	41
Volta	62	40	64
Northern and Upper	86	84	98
Ghana	62	36	58

Source: 1960 Census.

Some of the patterns of employment serve as indicators of the way Ghana has developed and may continue to develop. The line between urban and rural is by no means distinct in terms of urban-rural division, or at least as those terms are defined in the census. Three-quarters of the rural work force is employed in agriculture, but so is a fifth of the urban work force. The rural proportion employed in manufacturing is about half of that found in the urban areas. A clearer cut division between urban and rural employment is in fact found in commerce rather than in agriculture.

A very interesting rural-urban employment differential is found in terms of age. A far higher proportion of the older population is engaged in agriculture than is the case amongst young adults. Some of the explanation may lie in the tendency of the young to migrate to the town only to return to the village when satiated with town life. However, there is little doubt that it is largely a sign of social and economic change. The young, as in other countries, have adapted themselves more easily to the changes. Furthermore, it is generally the young who have the education needed to secure the town jobs. It may also be noted from Table 1.24 that rural-urban migration is probably strongest in the late adolescent and early adult years. Apparently it is not normally a phenomenon of 14- or 15-year-olds so much as of 18-, 19- or 20-year-olds.

TABLE 1.24

PERCENTAGE OF ALL EMPLOYED MALES
WORKING IN AGRICULTURE BY AGE, 1960

Age group	Employed in agriculture
15–19	65
20–4	52
25–9	53
30–4	59
35–9	63
40–4	69
45–9	70
50–4	75
55–9	78
60–4	84
65+	86
All ages	64

The question of type of employment is intimately bound up with residence and with migration. In much of West Africa farming can only be easily done on the land of one's native district. This, of course, does not apply to those employed in agriculture by the owners of tree plantations, and it is not wholly correct in any case of areas where land is now sold. Nevertheless, the statement is still sufficiently true to mean that migration does much to cut one off from the land. Thus a much higher proportion of the migrant community is employed in non-agricultural activities than is the case within the native-born group. Admittedly, one of the reasons for migration is often to secure a non-agricultural job. This is by no means true of all migration in Ghana, for one of the attractions to migrants seeking to earn money is cash employment in the cocoa lands of the forest in southern Ghana.

Table 1.25 demonstrates all the points just mentioned. It does more than that. It also reveals that inter-regional migration in Ghana produces a work force with a composition surprisingly similar to that resulting from international African migration, especially in terms of the division between agriculture and other employment. Thus, if it should become government policy to speed up urbanization and the growth of non-agricultural employment, this end could probably be achieved by encouraging migration. There

TABLE 1.25

TYPE OF EMPLOYMENT BY AREA OF ORIGIN, MALES, 1960 (PERCENTAGES OF ALL EMPLOYED MALES FROM SAME BIRTH PLACE)

Birthplace	Agriculture, fishing, etc.	Manufacturing	Construction mining, provision of electricity, water, etc.	Commerce	Services	Transport, communications	Total
Same Region	73	9	6	3	5	4	100
Other Region in Ghana	47	10	16	7	15	6	100
Other West African country	49	8	15	15	10	3	100

Source: 1960 Census.

is no evidence, however, that such migration would necessarily have to be international migration. Such ends, if desired, could probably be attained by promoting the movement of people from those areas of Ghana with a predominantly agricultural economy to the areas with a more varied economy. It should be noted that in the field of commerce, which is in Ghana a predominantly female occupation, the percentage of all female employment found within it is 25, 38 and 53 per cent of females from the same Region, another Region and another West African country respectively. Thus, over half the employment secured by immigrant females from other countries is in commerce, and the overwhelming majority takes the form of petty trading. Even amongst males, foreign immigrants are conspicuous in this field, doubtless largely due to the Nigerian penchant for trade.

A few further comments might be made on the occupational statistics produced by the 1960 Census. Employees, as distinct from employers, the self-employed or family workers, form less than one-fifth of the labour force. Less than 4 per cent of occupied females are classified in this way. This is a question which undoubtedly gave trouble to the census-takers, and there is almost certainly considerable doubt about the way casual agricultural employees were classified. The proportion claimed for Ghana is similar to that found elsewhere in predominantly agricultural countries which have begun to develop economically in other ways as well. It is much lower than the five-sixths found in such an industrialized country as the United Kingdom.

Government employment in Ghana is certainly on the increase. In 1960, employees in the public sector amounted to almost two-fifths of all employees. The proportion is now probably higher still. This is especially likely in agriculture. In 1960, government employment in that field amounted to a little over 30,000 persons or to about 2 per cent of the entire agricultural labour force. However, governmental participation in agriculture has increased very greatly since then.

4. HOUSEHOLD, MARRIAGE AND THE FAMILY

Supplementing this brief overall view of the population of Ghana, a few generalizations may be made about the family, as a prelude to later discussion on the likely trends of demographic change. This is not the right point in this study for a sociological consideration of such subjects as family structure or type of marriage. Nor will an accurate estimate of average family size be attempted, for that is the task of the next chapter. Nevertheless, the following observations may do something to put more specific studies into perspective.

Comparatively little information can at the time of writing be gleaned from the Census. The majority of the findings that follow are derived from three sample surveys carried out in the 1962–4 period. One was nation-wide, one dealt only with rural areas and the other was confined to socio-economically superior areas of the four largest towns.[1]

The most valuable information to be derived from the censuses is that on housing. Fortunately similar definitions were employed in 1948 and 1960. In a Report of the latter Census the following was written:

[1] i.e. The surveys listed as (5), (4) and (3) respectively in the Appendix, 'Notes on 1962–4 Population Survey Programme'.

In the Enumerator's Manual, a house or a compound is defined as a self-contained building unit. It is a structurally separate and independent place of abode. The essential features are separateness and independence. An enclosure may be considered as separate if it is surrounded by walls, fences, etc., so that a person or a group of persons can isolate themselves from other persons in the community for the purpose of sleeping, preparing and taking their meals or protecting themselves from hazards of climate such as storms and the sun. . . .

It appears from the Field Reconciliation of the PES (Post-enumeration Survey) House Coverage Check (one of the PES operations aimed at measuring part of the coverage area of the 1960 Census) that the above definition of house/compound was easy to apply in localities with named streets and numbered houses (e.g. urban areas) where one house number generally identified a separate house or compound. But in others, mainly rural localities and, especially, where houses are clustered around in a haphazard fashion, it appeared that the concept of what constituted a house or compound varied sometimes from enumerator to enumerator. In some rural areas, particularly in southern and central Ghana, the structures belonging to or constituting one compound are not always connected or surrounded by a fence or wall. A comparison between the main census enumerator's definition of house/compound and that of the Post Enumeration Survey interviewer would appear to indicate that the former adopted a rather broader concept by grouping as one house/compound two or even three structures which could be regarded as separate houses. On the other hand, there were also (although fewer) cases where the census enumerator treated one house/compound as two separate house/compounds. However, apart from these odd cases of clustered houses, the definition appeared to have been satisfactorily applied.

Subsequently, the Report also points out that in some villages people crowded into the house of a chief or the customary head of the family for enumeration.

On the night of the 1960 Census, 98·6 per cent of the population was found sleeping in houses. Of the remaining 94,000 persons, three types of residence, schools and colleges, army barracks, and lorry parks and markets, each accounted for about a quarter. In Accra 1·3 per cent of the male and 0·2 per cent of the female population were found in lorry parks, markets or elsewhere out-of-doors.

Throughout the country an average of 10·6 persons per house was discovered. This apparently represented an increase of about a quarter since 1948. In that year the average number of persons enumerated had been 8·5 per house and 2·2 per room. In the subsequent intercensal period there was a marked increase in the number of persons per house in southern Ghana but very little change at all in the north. The greatest change of all apparently occurred in the largest towns, for in Accra and Kumasi the number of persons per house nearly doubled.

The average number of persons per house has increased markedly since 1948. Changes in methods of enumeration are unlikely to explain more than a small part of the total increase. It is most improbable, however, that the

TABLE 1.26

PERSONS PER HOUSE AND PER ROOM, 1948 AND 1960 (AVERAGES)

Area (as in 1948)	1948 Persons per house	1948 Persons per room	Rooms per house	1960 Persons per house	1948–60 percentage increase in persons per house
Gold Coast (Ghana)	8·5	2·2	3·8	10·6	25
Colony	7·6	2·2	3·5	9·9	30
Ashanti	9·7	2·3	4·2	11·9	23
Northern Territories	10·0	2·4	4·2	10·3	3
Accra	10·5	2·4	4·4	18·5	76
Kumasi	10·4	2·2	4·5	21·3	105

Source: 1948 and 1960 Censuses.

explanation lies in the failure of house building in Ghana to cope with a population explosion and the consequent increase in overcrowding and discomfort.

The real explanation almost certainly lies in rising standards of living and accelerating urbanization. There are two basic types of house in Ghana. One is the simple village house, usually made of earth or swish. This contains a few rooms. There is no need to add more, for relatives can easily build similar houses nearby. Towns also contain such houses as well as makeshift shanties. But for decades now they have also contained an increasing number of much larger houses specifically built to meet what are felt to be the needs of the town dweller. These are usually large, often consisting of two storeys. They frequently form up to three sides of a courtyard. In this they duplicate to some extent the features of a village compound, and, in fact, many of the rooms open, not to other rooms, but directly into the compound. Thus they are often almost as detached as separate village houses. These large houses usually have walls consisting wholly or partly of cement, which is often painted yellow or white, and are roofed with iron. In addition to this type of house, towns, especially Accra, are beginning to contain many more government built modern houses, which can usually be made to house more persons than the smaller village houses.

Thus, urbanization is likely to result in an increase in the number of big houses and a rise in the average number of persons found per house. It might be noted that in 1948 the variation in the average number of persons per house between different regions was to be explained largely in terms of variation in house size. The number of persons found per room remained surprisingly constant.

Much more confirmation for the hypothesis is provided by Table 1.27, where the number of persons per household has been worked out for the house of median size on the assumption of a linear distribution of households by number of occupants within the published class intervals. It can be seen that the average number of persons found per house increases with the size of the village or towns so as to be, for the country as a whole, almost twice as great for towns with more than 50,000 inhabitants as for villages with less than 100 inhabitants. It is suggested that the difference is achieved not by a general increase in house size with the size of locality but by an increase in the proportion of the type of town house already described.

TABLE 1.27

NUMBER OF PERSONS FOUND IN HOUSES OF MEDIAN SIZE BY LOCALITY SIZE AND REGION, 1960

Region	Size of locality (number of inhabitants)									
	Under 100	100–199	200–499	500–999	1,000–1,999	2,000–4,999	5,000–9,999	10,000–19,999	20,000–49,999	50,000 & over
Accra C.D.	5·4	5·6	5·9	6·2	6·8	7·9	10·0	6·6	—	13·7
Eastern	7·4	7·5	7·8	7·9	7·8	8·3	8·2	12·4	14·3	—
Western and Central	6·5	6·4	6·9	7·2	7·5	8·6	10·5	8·0	13·1	—
Ashanti	7·5	7·2	8·3	9·4	10·7	12·2	14·1	16·8	*	15·9
Brong-Ahafo	7·9	8·7	9·3	9·1	12·0	12·5	16·1	17·8	—	—
Volta	7·1	7·3	7·1	7·2	7·3	8·0	7·8	8·0	—	—
Northern and Upper	7·9	7·6	8·2	8·1	7·5	7·7	8·9	9·2	—	—
Ghana	7·2	7·4	7·7	7·7	8·1	8·8	9·6	9·3	*	14·1

* There appears to be an error in the Census tabulation for this cell.
Source: 1960 Census.

E

Although Table 1.27 shows that the increase in the number of persons per house with increasing locality size is a feature of all Regions of Ghana, it also reveals that locality size alone does not determine that number. It is noticeable for instance that, even in the largest towns of the Volta and Northern and Upper Regions, towns with between 10,000 and 20,000 inhabitants, the number of persons in the median household rises to only eight and nine persons respectively. In Ashanti and Brong-Ahafo houses in towns of similar size contain on the average twice as many people. In the Accra Capital District towns other than Accra contain comparatively few persons per house, but Accra itself rivals Kumasi in that the median house contains about fourteen persons. It is probable that in Ashanti and Brong-Ahafo the strong Ashanti family system has combined with increasing revenue from cocoa to encourage the building of large town-type houses even in small towns or villages. That cocoa revenue has had this effect in the past is shown by the fact that the 1948 Census found an average of 9·3 persons and 4·8 rooms per house in Akwapim compared with 7·6 and 3·5 respectively for the *Colony* as a whole. The contrast between Accra, Brong-Ahafo and Ashanti on the one hand and the remainder of the country on the other is also clearly shown by Table 1.28. What is equally clear is the distinctive pattern of the large towns.

TABLE 1.28

AVERAGE NUMBER OF PERSONS PER HOUSE
BY REGION AND CERTAIN TOWNS, 1960

Region

Accra C.D.	13·4
Eastern	10·1
Western and Central	9·8
Ashanti	11·7
Brong-Ahafo	12·6
Volta	9·2
Northern and Upper	10·3
Ghana	10·6

Certain Towns

Accra	18·5
Kumasi	21·3
Takoradi	18·3
Bawku	9·7

Source: 1960 Census.

Two important observations should be made on the numbers of persons living in each house.

The first is that many more people live in the really large houses than might at first be indicated by the average figures. Thus in the Accra Capital District the average number of persons per house in 1960 was 13·4. Nevertheless, over half the population lived in houses containing more than twenty. Thus, as can be seen in Table 1.29, the really big house is more a feature of Accra than of Brong-Ahafo or Ashanti. This is doubtless partly attributable to the very large houses for men or for women and children found in the old Ga area of Jamestown. Throughout Ghana as a whole more than a third of the population were enumerated in houses containing more than twenty persons.

TABLE 1.29

PERCENTAGE OF PERSONS IN HOUSES BY NUMBER OF
PERSONS PER HOUSE AND REGION, 1960

Region	Number of persons per house				
	1–4	5–9	10–19	20–49	50+
Accra C.D.	5	15	26	40	14
Eastern	6	25	39	26	4
Western and Central	7	24	36	28	5
Ashanti	5	19	38	32	6
Brong-Ahafo	4	17	38	37	4
Volta	8	28	37	23	4
Northern and Upper	7	26	34	25	8
Ghana	6	23	36	29	6

Source: 1960 Census.

The second point is that a significant social change has been occurring. Overcrowding has not increased, but instead there has been a shift in the proportions of the type of house in the community. Many more Ghanaians now live in large town houses containing a considerable number of rooms. In one sense this has represented a surprisingly successful attempt to carry a village way of life to the town. Living in a town like Accra, with a population of over a third of a million, has in many cases not meant leaving the communal life of the village for residence in small lonely quarters in the town. On the contrary, often more relatives are living closely together than ever before. This is especially true of richer families with interests in cocoa or other lucrative fields rather than of poorer immigrants from further afield.

Such close residence is often mitigated by separate access to the outside or to the yard. Nevertheless, when trends towards the nucleation of the family are sought in Ghana, cognizance must be taken of the opposite tendency. Communal living certainly retards tendencies towards the concentration of expenditure on the nuclear family, even amongst the middle and upper classes. On the other hand, immediately prior to the Census and in the years that have followed, another factor has emerged. The government has been building in the larger towns many houses and flats, frequently occupied by government employees, which have apparently been planned for occupation by either nuclear families or families with comparatively few other attached relatives.

The great majority of marriages in Ghana are still of the traditional type. Such marriages usually involve one or more ceremonies, although there is great variation from one part of Ghana to another. They also usually involve the payment of money to the bride's parents. Such marriages do not in practice preclude either premarital sexual experience or couples living together without having celebrated such a marriage or without having completed all its formalities, especially the full payment of bride price. No limit is set upon the permissible number of wives. Marriage does not necessarily mean that spouses live together. Traditionally, amongst the Ashanti, husbands and wives remain with their own families, and this is still as often as not the case, while amongst the Ga many husbands still live together in one compound while wives and children live in another.[1] Such complexities have led the law in Ghana to regard any couple who are living together or who have participated in traditional marriage ceremonies as enjoying a *customary marriage*.

Other forms of marriage have penetrated Ghana from outside. Islamic marriage, registered by the local Islamic religious authorities, has long been important in the north and is of increasing significance in some of the towns of the south. In such marriages men are limited to four wives. Christian marriage in Ghana is in some ways similar to Islamic marriage. It is recorded by the local minister of religion and it is assumed that he should be consulted in case of divorce. The only form of marriage registered by the State and indissoluble except by legal divorce is *Marriage under the Ordinance*. A man cannot be married to two wives under the ordinance at the same time, but he can live with more than one woman as long as only one of the marriages has been contracted in this way. Such behaviour may constitute grounds for divorce but not for laying a charge of bigamy. This type of marriage is still comparatively rare, and hence statistics of registered marriages are not very meaningful. Nevertheless, it is gaining favour, especially amongst the middle and upper classes as a way of protecting their daughters' interests. More than one type of marriage may be performed. Some couples undergo as many as three, such as Christian, traditional and ordinance marriages successively. The Government has contemplated the creation of what might be regarded as a more modernized legal framework for marriage and divorce, but to date has met with difficulties when attempting to work out a satisfactory way of amending traditional practices. The most recent effort was the *Marriage, Divorce and Inheritance Bill* of 1963 which was subsequently withdrawn.

In a survey of conjugal condition,[2] all conjugal conditions of some permanency were defined as marriage. Only the most impermanent and casual liaisons were supposed to be excluded. In practice, field-workers were of the opinion that many respondents insisted on including only conjugal partnerships which would have been included in the legal concept of *customary marriage*. Thus, some respondents, when giving their age at first marriage, may have excluded some earlier, rather impermanent relationship. The research workers felt that very few relationships leading to the birth of children had been excluded.

In the survey the average age of females at first marriage was found to be lower in urban areas than in rural areas and lower again in the wealthier suburbs of the towns. However, this does not mean that there is necessarily a marked urban-rural differential in age at marriage in areas of homogeneous culture. The rural figure is weighted by the predominantly rural north where most female marriage occurs soon after puberty and where most females are married at 15 or 16 years of age. In most areas of the south the average age is undoubtedly higher. Thus, there probably is some urban-rural differential even here, but it is not very marked. There is some evidence of a slight socio-economic differential within the urban areas.

[1] See Meyer Fortes, 'A Demographic Field Study in Ashanti', in Frank Lorimer, *Culture and Human Fertility*, UNESCO, 1954, and Ioné Acquah, *Accra Survey*, University of London Press, 1958, p. 47, and elsewhere.

[2] See Appendix. Population Council Programme Survey, *Conjugal Biographies*.

The *Survey of Population Attitudes in Economically Superior Urban Areas*[1] produced evidence from the females of the middle and upper class suburbs of Accra, Kumasi, Takoradi-Sekondi and Cape Coast of an average age at first marriage of 22·2 years, considerably above the average for all of urban Ghana.

There may be some overstatement of the real age at marriage, for, as seen before, the most massive shift in age statement to enumerators is that by females from their adolescent years to ages over 20 years. It is possible that this is most marked amongst married women and that the same phenomenon is found when women, who married early, state their age at that marriage. On the other hand, strenuous attempts were made in the survey to reduce such errors to a minimum by making a detailed biographical record of the respondents in terms of age and by relating age to the birth of children and to their ages at the time of interviewing.

The differentials in age at first marriage can easliy be related to economic and social factors. In much of the subsistence farming area of the north there is no economic reason why a girl should not marry at 15 years. Social pressures push in the same direction. The chances are still against marriage interfering with her schooling. In 1960 only 900 of the 42,000 females aged 15–19 years in the Northern and Upper Regions were at school. Indeed there is little place in the farming compounds of northern Ghana for an unmarried woman who has reached puberty. The position is quite different in the south, especially in the towns. In Accra, where the process has proceeded somewhat further than in most areas, approximately a quarter of the females of 15–19 years of age were attending school at the time of the 1960 Census and another quarter had been equipped by previous schooling to hold office and other similar positions.

Summarizing the position, it might be said that in the far-flung rural areas of northern Ghana most females of 15–19 years of age are married. In the south this position is not reached until the 20–24 years of age range. The national position appears to be much the same as that of Burundi or the more economically developed parts of the Congo. Marriage appears to occur somewhat later than in Dahomey. But all these African comparisons are fraught with uncertainty, because they depend on the definition of *marriage* employed, and almost certainly the definition has varied very widely. At the present time the age of females at first marriage is probably no lower in southern Ghana, and more certainly in the towns of southern Ghana, than in the United States. Furthermore, whilst the average age at marriage of females in Western countries is falling generally, in Ghana it will almost inevitably rise. The extension of education alone will exert heavy pressure in this direction. In the north the winning out of the cash economy over subsistence farming will probably also act in the same way.

Preliminary analysis of the survey material on average age at first marriage of males suggests that for the country as a whole the figure may be around 25 years. The average age reported in the *Survey of Population Attitudes in Economically Superior Urban Areas* was just over 26 years. Such an age at marriage would agree with recent findings in the Congo and Guinea.

[1] See Appendix.

These findings suggest that the average age between spouses, when each is marrying for the first time, is 5 or 6 years. This is borne out for Ghana by the *Survey*. This age difference was not only approximately that usually found between spouses, but also that advocated by the majority of both wives and husbands. Experience elsewhere suggests that the social changes set in train by economic development and universal education may lead towards a reduction in the age gap between spouses. This will probably be effected by a rise in the age of marriage for females and a fall in that for males. It is likely that these changes have already been under way for a very considerable period in Ghana. In the economically better-off urban areas the age difference is now probably just under five years. This is well below that still found in rural northern Ghana, which is almost certainly similar to the pattern once found over the whole of Ghana.

Two other features of Ghanaian marriage should be mentioned. One is that of marriage instability and the other is polygyny.

Divorce is easily obtained, even from more formal marriages, with the single exception of marriage under the ordinance which can be dissolved only judicially. Other divorces require little more than agreement, or even desertion, although repayment of part or all of the bride money or consultations with religious leaders or families may also be involved. One factor which makes an unstable marriage pattern possible is the economically independent outlook of Ghanaian women. Over half of all Ghanaian adult females are employed, and most can find a living or return to their families if the need arises. In the *Survey of Population Attitudes in Economically Superior Urban Areas* nine wives out of ten claimed that they could have continued to support themselves had they not married. Although only 6 per cent stated that they were fully supporting themselves and their children while married, over half claimed to be providing some financial support. It is this possibility of economic independence which also allows later female marriage than could possibly be the case in, for instance, some of the agrarian cultures of Asia.

In Table 1.30 the effect of the 'unstable' marriage pattern is charted. In the case of males, some of the increase in the cumulative total of conjugal partners with the years is caused by polygyny. A rough measure of the extent of polygyny at some stage during the males' lives is given by the excess of conjugal partners shown for males over that shown for females in the age group 5 years younger. In the case of both sexes one of the reasons for the increase in the number of partners is widowhood and remarriage. If widows were always to remarry, and assuming past levels of mortality of the order discussed in the next chapter, this phenomenon would be sufficient to explain the entire increase of conjugal partners in the case of urban females and half the increase in the case of rural females. Such wholesale remarriage does not in fact occur, although a much closer approach to it is found in rural areas than in urban areas, for, in the former, it is much more probable that such a traditional arrangement as the polygynous marriage to the brother of the deceased husband will be adhered to. Thus, a major reason for the pattern shown in the Table remains divorce and remarriage. However, it is important that the Table should not be misread. The younger groups will not inevitably follow the pattern indicated by the Table. Some of the differences in the chart may not be merely chronological in terms of age, but may arise from cultural change, affecting the young whilst unable to affect the past behaviour record of the older.

Several points of interest arise from the Table. One is that the 'unstable' marriage pattern is much more marked in rural than urban areas. Another, using the rough check on polygyny, is that polygyny is also very much more marked in rural areas. Furthermore, an examination of the younger age groups suggests that it is proving far more resistant to social change in rural areas than in the towns. That social change, especially in the form of a diminution of polygyny has been occurring in the towns, but not to the same extent in the country, is suggested by the rise in the ratio of rural male to urban male figures when reading up the Table from the 50+ age group to the 25–29 years of age group.

TABLE 1.30

AVERAGE NUMBER OF CONJUGAL PARTNERS EVER POSSESSED BY PERSONS EVER MARRIED BY AGE AND SEX, 1963–4

Age Group	Rural		Urban		Ratio of rural to urban figures		Excess of male figure over figure for female group 5 years younger	
	male	female	male	female	male	female	rural	urban
15–19	1·1	1·0	1·0	1·0	1·1	1·0	–	–
20–4	1·2	1·2	1·0	1·0	1·2	1·2	0·2	0·0
25–9	2·3	1·3	1·2	1·1	1·9	1·2	1·1	0·2
30–4	2·4	1·4	1·3	1·2	1·8	1·2	1·1	0·3
35–9	2·4	1·5	1·5	1·3	1·6	1·2	1·0	0·3
40–4	2·7	1·7	1·7	1·2	1·6	1·4	1·2	0·4
45–9	2·7	1·9	1·7	1·4	1·6	1·4	1·0	0·5
50+	3·5	2·1	2·5	1·4	1·4	1·5	–	–

Source: *Conjugal Biographies* Survey of Ghana, 1963–4.

The 'unstable' marriage pattern may not survive. It is certainly under pressure, for it is not wholly compatible with the transition of population from a village way of life to that enforced, for instance, by working in an office job in town, while occupying a government-owned house and striving to ensure the education of one's children. The *Survey of Population Attitudes in Economically Superior Urban Areas* examined a group in which these pressures are strongest. Three-quarters of those interviewed had enjoyed a stable, monogamous marriage, in which neither partner had ever been married to another. Five-sixths favoured such marriages as the preferable way of life. The majority of those not doing so gave as their reason that such a manner of living leads to boredom.

Polygyny is by no means uncommon in Ghana. It is, however, somewhat rarer than Table 1.31 might at first seem to imply, for this Table provides a summation of the experience of those surveyed. Thus, not every man who has at some stage lived with three women simultaneously, is any longer doing so. It may be assumed that a cross-section of society taken at any given time would reveal a good deal less polygyny than is shown in the Table.

Polygyny is, as was suggested by Table 1.30, more common in the rural areas. Its frequency amongst rural males is well over twice what it is amongst urban males. However, even in the rural areas less than half of all males who have ever married have lived at any stage in a polygynous union.

It will be increasingly difficult for polygyny to survive under the pressures

TABLE 1.31

ADULTS CLASSIFIED BY THE MAXIMUM NUMBER OF CONJUGAL PARTNERS EVER POSSESSED
SIMULTANEOUSLY BY RURAL-URBAN DIVISION AND SEX, 1963-4 (PERCENTAGES)

Maximum number of conjugal partners	Rural		Urban	
	males	females	males	females
0	6·5	1·3	4·2	1·9
1	49·3	97·9	76·4	98·1
2	28·5	0·8*	13·5	—
3	10·2	—	3·9	—
4	4·2	—	1·9	—
5–9	1·2	—	0·0	—
10+	0·1	—	0·0	—
Total 2+	44·2	0·8	19·3	—

* It is not claimed that polyandry is sanctioned anywhere in Ghana. Nevertheless, in confidential interviews, a handful of females in rural Ghana maintained, in spite of being queried on the point, that at some stage in their lives they had *lived* with two men at the same time. Presumably one of the unions was loose, irregular and probably secretive.
Source: *Conjugal Biographies* Survey of Ghana, 1963–4.

of economic modernization and social Westernization. Polygynous unions are essentially a feature of certain traditional, rural societies, where a very large age gap usually exists between each husband and his wives. They can be maintained in a community where the age gap between spouses is lessening, only by failing to provide any marriage opportunity at all to a considerable proportion of the male population.[1]

If the figures given in Table 1.31 were taken to represent a cross-section of Ghanaian society at any given time, they would plainly be difficult to explain. For instance, if all age groups were of equal size, there would be 63 per cent more wives than husbands in rural areas and 23 per cent more in urban areas. However, polygynous unions do not necessarily depend for their existence on either a surplus of females or a class of males who remain unmarried throughout life. Where population growth is rapid, and where for some decades births each year have exceeded those of the year before, there will be a sufficiently pyramidal age structure for potential wives to outnumber by quite a wide margin potential husbands a few years their senior. Mortality, especially in societies exhibiting a relatively low expectation of life, reinforces this phenomenon.

Assuming an increase in the number of births per year to have been about 2 per cent in Ghana of a generation ago, and selecting life tables consonant with the discussion in the next chapter, the polygynous structure which seems to be implied by Table 1.31 could provide marriage for all males and females if the average age between spouses were about 16 and 9 years in rural and urban areas respectively. In fact, the Table does not imply such a structure. Many of the males were probably subsequently separated from one or more of their wives. If it is assumed that at any given time the real extent of polygyny were to be only half that indicated in the Table, such a pattern could provide marriage for all provided that the average age gap between spouses was about 12 and 5 years in rural and urban areas

[1] See J. C. Caldwell, 'Fertility Decline and Female Chances of Marriage in Malaya', *Population Studies*, Vol. XVII, Part I, July 1963, pp. 20–32.

respectively. Such an age gap is compatible with the previous findings on average age at first marriage. The apparently greater age difference here, especially in the case of rural marriages, can be explained by the fact that age gap is usually much greater when the male is acquiring a second or third wife. In rural areas, the greater age gap is achieved partly by relatively late male marriage. This is the explanation of why a higher percentage of single males is shown in the Table for rural areas than for urban ones.

If social and economic changes tend, as in some other countries, to reduce the age difference between husbands and wives, or if, as seems inevitable, more Ghanaians live in towns and conform to the existing urban social pattern, the practice of polygyny must be reduced or considerable numbers of males must live out their lives in a single condition. It seems likely that the former will occur. There are at present quite a number of older single males in the country, but most of them seem to be immigrants.

The 'unstable' marriage pattern means that females in their reproductive years may experience reduced fertility not merely through delay of age at first marriage but also because of one or more subsequent periods without a partner. The actual amount of time spent by the surveyed population within marriage is shown in Table 1.32. The periods which can be ascribed to each of the two causes, or in addition to widowhood, have not been separated. It is apparent that the patterns of social behaviour in modern Ghana may have reduced fertility by almost a third below what it might have been if all females married at 15 years of age and remained in a married state. This reduction is greatest in the towns where later marriages are the rule. It may provide the entire reason for lower urban fertility, for, as can be seen, urban females bear children as frequently as do rural females during the period when they are married. It is of no particular significance in the study of Ghanaian fertility that males spend less of this period in marriage, for they marry later, and their period of fertility usually extends well beyond 45 years.

TABLE 1.32

PERCENTAGE OF AGE SPANS, 15–44 AND 20–44 YEARS,* SPENT IN CONJUGAL UNION, AND AVERAGE NUMBER OF CONJUGAL YEARS PER LIVE BIRTH, BY RURAL-URBAN DIVISION AND SEX, 1963–4

| | Rural | | Urban | |
	males	females	males	females
Average percentage of time lived in conjugal union:				
15–44 years	61	71	50	63
20–44 years	77	84	64	82
Average number of years in conjugal union, 15–44 years of age, per live birth	—	3·1	—	3·1

* If younger than 45 years, restricted to period lived within this span.
Source: *Conjugal Biographies* Survey of Ghana, 1963–4.

Tropical African custom and religion have always favoured high fertility. Even today in rural Ghana the answer given to the question, 'Do you think that it is a good thing for people to have lots of children?' is in two-thirds of all cases an unqualified 'Yes'. The minority who answer 'No' or give a qualified answer, do so on the grounds of economic difficulty.[1] In

[1] See Appendix. Population Council Programme Survey, *Population Attitudes in Rural Areas.*

the economically better-off areas of the major towns answers are more cautious. There, most people claim to favour families with three or four children. However, such a fertility pattern has not in fact established itself as yet in these areas.[1]

Indeed, the Ghanaian family system could be described as a 'large family system' in contrast with the 'small family system' which has developed in most economically advanced areas. As will be seen in the next chapter, the average Ghanaian woman will, by the end of her reproductive span, have borne about seven children. This figure will vary according to where she lives in Ghana from about six to about eight. Such a level of fertility seems to be high by tropical African standards.[2] Estimates of total fertility rates in Central Africa are of the order of four to five. However, estimates for many West African countries are around six or a little higher. These differences may merely reflect weaknesses in the data collected. But the pattern is consistent enough to suggest that West Africa may have a level of fertility above the rest of tropical Africa. Its inhabitants would appear to be one of the most fertile human populations in the world. Certainly, there are very few countries, even amongst the developing ones, where the size of the completed family is as high as seven children.

Ghanaian families are big in another sense as well. Family obligations often extend well beyond any grouping formed merely by parents and their children. Many more people than the simple *nuclear* family are often found living in the same house, especially in the towns. But the more important sense in which the *extended family* exists is as a network through which economic and other assistance, as well as obligation, run. The system may not be as secure as it has been. About half the respondents in the *Survey of Population Attitudes in Economically Superior Areas*, when asked if their own households differed in any ways from those in which they had spent their childhoods, described changes which can only be interpreted in terms of some transition from *extended* to *nuclear families*. The extent of such change at the present time should not be exaggerated. Even two-thirds of university students expect to spend between 10 per cent and 30 per cent of their professional incomes on relatives other than their wives and children.[3]

5. SUMMARY AND CONCLUSIONS

By the standards of Africa and also of the world's equatorial countries, Ghana already has a dense population. By any standards its level of fertility and hence of potential population growth is very high indeed. Although high death rates have as yet prevented that potential from being fully realized, immigration from other West African countries has supplemented a substantial and increasing rate of natural growth. Thus, while the four decades up to 1960 probably witnessed a doubling of Africa's population, that of Ghana may have trebled.

A relatively higher standard of living has attracted immigrants to Ghana.

[1] See Appendix. Population Council Programme Survey, *Population Attitudes in Economically Superior Urban Areas.*

[2] Comparisons are drawn from INSEE, *Perspectives de Population dans les pays Africains et Malgashe d'Expression Française*, Paris, 1963, p. 18.

[3] See Appendix. Population Council Programme *University Survey.*

By 1960, at least a twelfth of the population was foreign born and an eighth of foreign origin. Nearly all came from West Africa, and most originated in three countries, Togo, Upper Volta and Nigeria. Thus Ghana, with 99·8 per cent of its population of African origin, had no social problems of any magnitude arising from the presence of non-Africans.

As with other countries of rapid natural increase, the most striking aspect of Ghana's population is its youth. Although census age data are somewhat defective, it can be discerned clearly that at least half the population is under 18 years of age and half the labour force under 30 years of age. Such a rapidly increasing population does give rise to many social and economic problems. However, it should also be noted that the age structure of fast-growing populations can ensure a dramatic rate of social change whenever development break-throughs can be effected. If, for instance, education could suddenly be made universal up to 15 years, it would take only another fourteen years before more than half the adult community had received some training in the new system. Alternatively, in a country with a similar level of mortality, but where population growth was negligible, the same change would take almost twice as long. Over half of all Ghanaians now alive have been born since the end of the Second World War and over a quarter since Independence. Similar fractions hold good for the attainment of voting age.

The available statistics imply a surprising degree of demographic sex equality in Ghana, and perhaps in all of tropical Africa. It seems that approximately equal numbers of the sexes are born and that the subsequent ravages of mortality show little differentiation by sex. It is, of course, possible that, with economic and social modernization, mortality will be reduced more rapidly in the case of females than in the case of males.

Demographically, economically and socially Ghana falls into two parts, the country in the south lying near the coast or within the forest, and the considerably larger area of savannah-woodland country found to the north. Living standards, levels of education and expectation of life are all higher in the south. The north presents the Government of Ghana with its greatest challenge. Solutions to its problems will not be easy to find. One palliative has been applied without planning, and that is the spontaneous short and long-term movement of northern peoples to the major employment areas of the south. Such movement arises largely because the distribution of population in Ghana does not at present coincide with economic opportunities. The major area of dense population lies in the south where such opportunities exist. But an important secondary area of dense settlement is found in the Upper Region, where the present subsistence farming economy can support the population only on a relatively low standard of living. The best immediate prospects for extending the agricultural cash economy appear not to be in the north, but in the only major forest areas remaining unused, those in the south-west of the country. Ghana has had for two-thirds of a century a genuine frontier of intensive economic development in the forest area, which has moved progressively west and north-west from the Densu Valley and Akim until it is now in south-western Brong-Ahafo. This frontier has always attracted migrants and will continue to do so. It seems inevitable that it will now move southward into the Western Region to exploit the dense rain forest of south-western Ghana.

Much of the migration from rural areas is, however, directed not towards agricultural areas but to the growing towns. The occupational balance of Ghana is changing quite dramatically. In the twelve years preceding 1960 the proportion of the labour force employed in agriculture fell from about 80 per cent to 62 per cent. By the latter year almost a quarter of the population lived in towns with more than 5,000 inhabitants. One measure of the change in conditions arising from a transfer from rural to urban life is that in 1960 seven-eighths of the labour force in the towns worked in non-agricultural employment. This change in way of life did not have an equal impact on all members of society. Most affected were the young, for, while five-sixths of the oldest labour force age groups worked in agriculture, little over half of the young adults did so. This is probably quite a good indication of the direction and rate of change in the type of employment likely to be in demand in the years ahead. It is also an indication that, if the supply of town jobs cannot keep up with the demand, the problem of unemployed younger people in the towns might become more acute.

There is probably a link between the demand for town jobs and the increased provision of education. It will be argued subsequently that the extension of schooling has encouraged the movement to the towns. At the same time, it has certainly made the migrants more fitted for those jobs. An excellent illustration of the rate at which social change can occur in a rapidly expanding population is provided by the educational statistics. In terms of the whole population, and not merely those of school age, the rather astonishing transformation should be noted from a fraction of 4 per cent who had received any schooling in 1948 to 21 per cent in 1960. By the latter year 49 per cent of 10–14-year-olds were either in school or had been there. In no single Local Administration Area had a majority of adults as yet been to school, but that position was being approached in Accra and Kpandu. Opportunity for obtaining education was becoming greater but was by 1960 by no means even. Males, people in southern Ghana, and especially people in the towns of that area, still led in terms of amount of schooling. These divisions are, however, lessening.

Coupled with other social and economic changes are various changes in the structure of the family. With urbanization, more people are living in large houses with many occupants. The emotional and economic ramifications of the Ghanaian family are under pressure with transition from a village way of life, but are far from being substantially modified. Polygyny and the unstable marriage pattern are also under pressure. The stronghold of the former is still in rural Ghana. It is less important in urban areas, and is probably less practised by the young than was the case a generation ago. Females marry later in the towns and probably somewhat later in higher socio-economic groups. Later marriage and the unstable marriage pattern mean that the possibility of child-bearing throughout the country is probably limited to only about two-thirds of the maximum time biologically available. In spite of this, Ghanaian families are very large indeed and the rate of population increase is rapid. The implications of this affect most aspects of Ghanaian society and will be the major theme of the next three chapters.

DISTRIBUTION OF POPULATION BY MAIN TRIBAL DIVISIONS ACCORDING TO REGION

	All Regions		Western Region		Accra Capital District		Eastern Region		Volta Region		Ashanti Region		Brong-Ahafo Region		Northern Region	
	Number	%	Number	%	Number	%	Number	%	Number	%	Number	%	Number	%	Number	%
Major Tribes (language groups)																
Akan	2,964,580	44·1	1,105,030	80·2	78,440	16·0	488,900	44·7	19,300	2·5	830,370	74·9	418,970	71·3	23,570	1·8
Ga-Adangbe	560,370	8·3	22,460	1·6	238,260	48·5	267,310	24·4	6,760	0·9	16,340	1·5	6,040	1·0	3,200	0·2
Ewe	876,230	13·0	45,430	3·3	71,220	14·5	130,210	11·9	571,100	73·5	35,880	3·2	13,440	2·3	8,950	0·7
Central Togo Tribes	56,740	0·8	270	0·0	430	0·1	590	0·1	54,210	7·0	530	0·0	330	0·1	380	0·0
Tem (Kotokoli)	51,020	0·8	2,500	0·2	3,670	0·7	11,650	1·1	17,730	2·3	10,990	1·0	1,890	0·3	2,590	0·2
Guan	251,810	3·7	52,650	3·8	5,450	1·1	75,540	6·7	32,680	4·2	9,810	0·9	16,850	2·9	58,830	4·6
Yoruba	109,090	1·6	24,290	1·8	9,330	1·9	27,020	2·5	7,100	0·9	22,870	2·1	8,020	1·4	10,460	0·8
Ibo	14,050	0·2	7,420	0·5	3,320	0·7	840	0·1	170	0·0	1,990	0·2	200	0·0	110	0·0
Hausa	61,730	0·9	10,610	0·8	12,350	2·5	12,220	1·1	3,690	0·5	12,090	1·1	4,250	0·7	6,520	0·5
Other Nigerian Tribes	24,350	0·4	12,870	0·9	6,000	1·2	1,960	0·2	510	0·1	2,110	0·2	530	0·1	370	0·0
Gurma	237,780	3·5	5,930	0·4	7,630	1·6	22,400	2·0	31,800	4·1	23,590	2·1	16,540	2·8	129,890	10·1
Mole-Dagbani	1,072,370	15·9	42,330	3·1	12,930	2·6	22,610	2·1	4,750	0·6	83,750	7·6	52,120	8·9	853,880	66·2
Lobi	37,550	0·6	160	0·0		0·0	30	0·0		—	900	0·1	4,140	0·7	32,250	2·5
Grusi	148,480	2·2	8,870	0·6	3,810	0·8	4,320	0·4	1,650	0·2	15,390	1·4	12,850	2·2	101,590	7·9
Mande	90,870	1·4	9,990	0·7	7,370	1·5	5,380	0·5	650	0·1	24,490	2·2	10,530	1·8	32,460	2·5
Songhai	35,930	0·5	6,200	0·4	8,450	1·7	9,960	0·9	2,130	0·3	5,920	0·3	1,910	0·3	1,360	0·1
Fulani	25,050	0·4	2,080	0·2	3,310	0·7	2,690	0·2	650	0·1	3,530	0·3	1,480	0·3	11,310	0·9
Kru	6,500	0·1	4,060	0·3	1,920	0·4	360	0·0	20	0·0	120	0·0	20	0·0	—	0·0
Other African Tribes	64,370	1·0	9,790	0·7	9,160	1·9	8,840	0·8	21,620	2·8	5,730	0·5	5,380	0·9	3,850	0·3
Other mainly Ghanaian Tribes	21,980	0·3	1,380	0·1	390	0·1	630	0·1	520	0·1	170	0·0	12,230	2·1	6,660	0·5
Not classified by Tribes	15,970	0·2	3,230	0·2	8,310	1·7	740	0·1	240	0·0	2,560	0·2	200	0·0	690	0·1
Total population	**6,726,815**	**100·0**	**1,377,547**	**100·0**	**491,817**	**100·0**	**1,094,196**	**100·0**	**777,285**	**100·0**	**1,109,133**	**100·0**	**587,920**	**100·0**	**1,288,917**	**100·0**
Largest tribe in the Region																
Name	Asante		Fante		Ga		Akyem		Ewe		Asante		Boron		Dagomba	
Number	895,360		582,690		184,230		182,990		571,100		735,330		305,850		186,970	
Percentage of population of region	13·3		42·3		37·5		16·7		73·5		66·3		52·0		14·5	

Source: 1960 Census. *Atlas of Population Characteristics.*

* This table became available shortly before publication and after the completion of the text. It is inserted here to amplify observations made in Chapter I.

CHAPTER II

POPULATION CHANGE

1. POPULATION GROWTH

There may or may not be a *population explosion* in the world today in the sense that our technology will prove incapable of supporting the generations to come at the standard of living that they desire. There is certainly such an explosion in the sense that the present rapid growth of population in almost all parts of the world is a unique phenomenon in the history of man.

This vast multiplication of the human species is a most significant event of our times. It does not merely mean that there will be two or three people in every place where one was previously to be found. Social and economic fabrics cannot be inflated in such a simple manner. New occupational positions often emerge in very different proportions from those which were to be found in the former situations. The need for new living space does not mean merely an extension of the bounds of rural settlement. It often means a substantial overflow of people into the towns. Rapid urbanization is not only a product of change of social outlook and economic change. It can be greatly accelerated by a rise in the rate of rural population increase. As we have already seen, it is often the young adults who set out to seek town jobs. If the number of young adults is increasing rapidly, then towns may grow in size much faster than does the population as a whole.

Africa is participating in this multiplication of human numbers, and Ghana is conspicuous in this regard. If the censuses can be fully trusted, the population almost trebled between 1921 and 1960. Furthermore, it would appear that the rate of growth has accelerated in recent years. The enumerated populations at the censuses of 1948 and 1960 suggest an intercensal growth rate of about 4·2 per cent per year during the intervening period. Such a growth rate would be far above that experienced by most countries, and would be likely to be the cause, as well as the result, of very considerable social and economic change.

It is of great importance for all types of governmental action that an accurate estimate should be made of Ghana's present rate of population growth. As the whole country is not covered by a birth and death registration system, such an estimate cannot be made from the results of a single census combined with the known vital rates of the time. It must depend either on two censuses or perhaps on an examination of the age structure depicted by the most recent census. Fortunately, Ghana has held two censuses since the end of the Second World War. However, the implied growth rate was so high that considerable doubt has been raised about the accuracy of the censuses, especially that of 1948. *The Seven-year Development Plan*, possibly ignoring immigration, assumed an annual rate of only 2·6 per cent. A careful examination of the two censuses is therefore warranted.

The picture painted by the two censuses is set out in Table 2.1. It can be seen that the very high rate of population growth cannot of itself be used to invalidate either census, as a considerable part of the population increment can be attributed to immigration.

TABLE 2.1

APPARENT POPULATION GROWTH, 1948–60, ACCORDING TO 1948 AND 1960
CENSUSES

	1948 Census (thousands)	1960 Census (thousands)	1948–60 Increase	
			(a) thousands	(b) percentage
Total population	4,118	6,727	2,609	63
Foreign-born	181*	560	379	209
Native-born	3,937	6,167	2,230	57

* Assuming all non-Africans to be foreign-born. The assumption is not quite correct, but the effect on other calculations is negligible.
Source: 1948 and 1960 Censuses.

During the twelve-year period the number of native-born increased by 57 per cent. It is impossible to compute a rate of natural increase for the native-born directly from this figure because that population has been augmented during the intercensal period by locally born children of foreign parentage. However, if the assumption is made that there is no difference in the fertility performance between foreign-born and native-born females, and in addition that the increase in foreign-born population between 1948 and 1960 occurred in equal arithmetical increments, the estimates shown in Table 2.2 can be obtained. It should be noted that these assumptions can be varied considerably without appreciably affecting the conclusions.

TABLE 2.2

APPARENT COMPONENTS OF POPULATION GROWTH, 1948–60

Population arising from the following subdivisions of the population of Ghana	Population growth		Percentage of total population growth	
	Natural increase (thousands)	Immigrational increase (thousands)	Natural increase	Immigrational increase
(a) Those listed as native-born in 1948	2,045	—	78·4	—
(b) Those listed as foreign-born in 1948	90	—	3·4	—
(c) Foreign-born arriving between 1948 and 1960	95	379	3·6	14·6

Source: 1948 and 1960 Censuses.

Thus, if these figures are to be believed, immigrants have been responsible, not for the seventh of population growth that is suggested by the increase in the number of foreign-born, but for over one-fifth. Immigration since 1948 has been responsible for just over 18 per cent of all growth. Therefore, if immigration had been restricted after 1948 to the point where it merely balanced emigration, Ghana's population increase in the intercensal period would have been only 2,135,000 and its 1960 population would have been 6,253,000 instead of 6,727,000.

If this picture of population growth is correct, the rate of natural increase for the intercensal period has averaged 3·5 per cent or 35 per thousand per year. This is an exceedingly high rate, but there is nothing inherently impossible in it. Equally high rates of natural increase have been known in South-east Asia and central America. Such a rate is not in too great a disagreement with the information published about Ghana in the latest United Nations *Demographic Year Book*. There, it is suggested that the birth rate might have been around 51 per thousand for the period 1950–5. This finding is based on *reverse survival* methods. It is not clear what data were available, but 1960 census material may have been used. The same publication lists death rates for the same period for the compulsory registration areas in the country varying from 19 to 22 per thousand.[1] Thus, it is suggested that the rate of natural increase for a six-year span in the heart of the intercensal period might have been between 2·9 and 3·2 per cent per year. In another Table[2] the same publication produces figures for 1960 from the compulsory registration areas suggesting a birth rate of 56 per thousand, a death rate of 26 per thousand and hence a rate of natural increase of 3·0 per cent.

However, the picture pieced together from the two censuses although plausible, cannot be correct. Although it may be possible to reconcile the total figures, it is not possible to reconcile the data for some of the subdivisions of the population. It is instructive, for instance, to examine what happened to the native-born population enumerated in 1948. Some have probably left the country for training and jobs elsewhere or because their parents came from other countries. A few, who left prior to 1948, have probably returned. It is most unlikely that the return flow has exceeded the out-flow. But the great majority will have remained in the country, where by 1960 they either formed part of the native-born population of 12 years of age and over or had already died. A comparison of the two censuses indicates that 92·6 per cent of them appear to have survived the twelve years.

This result is not possible, as it implies a level of mortality below that yet reached in any country in the world. Later in this chapter it is suggested that between 1948 and 1960 the expectation of life at birth in Ghana might have increased from about 39 years to about 45 years. If this is the case, about 82 per cent of a population with the age structure exhibited by Ghana in 1948 could have been expected to survive 12 years. The exact level of mortality is not in fact very important in the case of an age structure like that found in Ghana. For expectations of life at birth for the whole period varying as widely as 32 and 45 years, the variation in the proportion surviving is only that from 79 to 83 per cent. Table 2.3 is, in fact, only a worked out example. We are continuing to keep in mind the whole range of possibilities.

Thus, of the 3,937,000 population enumerated as native-born in 1948, only about 3,228,000 should have been enumerated as 12 years of age or over in 1960. In fact, over 400,000 more than this number were discovered. This is over an eighth more than might have been expected.

---

[1] United Nations, *1962 Demographic Year Book*, pp. 39, 469 and 517. About one-eighth of the population of the country is found in the compulsory registration areas.
[2] Ibid., p. 125.

TABLE 2.3

SURVIVAL OF NATIVE-BORN POPULATION FROM 1948 TO 1960

Native-born population enumerated in 1948 (in thousands)	3,937
Proportion expected to survive from 1948 to 1960 (per cent)	82
Expected number of native-born population 12+ years of age, in 1960 (in thousands)	3,228
Native-born population, 12+ years of age, actually enumerated in 1960 (in thousands)	3,645*
Number of persons by which 1960 enumeration exceeded expectation (in thousands)	417
Percentage by which 1960 enumeration exceeded expectation	12·9

* Approximate estimate.

There are only four ways in which this remarkable discrepancy could have arisen. There may have been underenumeration in 1948 or overenumeration in 1960; some immigrants who arrived between 1948 and 1960 may have believed that it was safer to inform the enumerators that they were born in Ghana; or there may have been massive advance in age-statement by children, who were in fact born after the 1948 census, but who claimed to be over 12 years of age in 1960.

It is quite likely that all these possibilities did occur to some extent. However, age advancement is unlikely to have been of any considerable importance. The surplus of native-born over 12 years of age could be explained only by an average advancement in age statement of $2\frac{1}{2}$ years. The examination of age structure showed that there is no evidence of such a phenomenon on anything like this scale. It can be argued that some circumstances connected with the 1960 Census could have resulted in an overcount. Such circumstances would be the enthusiasms of a newly independent country and the double-counting of people who moved from their usual residence to their native town to participate in the census night festivities. However, it is well to remember that census overcounts in developing countries are certainly not the usual experience.

The most likely explanation is that there was underenumeration in 1948 and that some immigrants did give wrong information about their places of birth. Some idea of the implications of such errors in the data can be gained from Table 2.4. Here are presented two extreme hypotheses, (A), where comparatively little of the error lies in misstatement about birthplace, and (B), where a great deal of the error lies in such misstatement. Hypothesis (C) represents an attempt to make a judicious guess at what is likely to be the real state of affairs.

What is reassuring about these hypotheses is the relatively small variation between each in the more important measures. Once the discrepancy in the claimed survival of the native-born from the 1948 Census to 1960 is recognized, corrections can be made within reasonably close limits. Estimates of growth rates are not greatly changed by allocating the error in different ways. Nor, it should be added, are these rates appreciably affected by assuming overenumeration in 1960 instead of underenumeration in 1948, or by assuming that some error lay in each census.

It is evident that the real average annual rate of population growth rate between the censuses was not 4·2 per cent, but instead probably about 3·6 per cent. This is still well above the 2·6 per cent on which the Seven Year

F

TABLE 2.4

HYPOTHETICAL CORRECTION OF DISCREPANCIES EXISTING BETWEEN THE DATA OF THE 1948 AND 1960 CENSUSES

Characteristic	Data as enumerated	Three hypotheses accounting for the extra 417,000 native-born over 12 years of age enumerated in 1960 but not predicted on the basis of the 1948 enumeration		
		(A)*	(B)*	(C)*
1948: Total population (thousands)	4,118	4,472	4,315	4,412
(a) native-born (thousands)	3,937	4,275	4,125	4,218
(b) foreign-born (thousands)	181	197	190	194
(c) percentage foreign-born	4·4	4·4	4·4	4·4
(d) percentage underenumeration in census	—	7·9	4·6	6·7
1960: Total population (thousands)	6,727	6,727	6,727	6,727
(a) native-born (thousands)	6,167	6,127	5,967	6,067
(b) foreign-born (thousands)	560	600	760	660
(c) percentage foreign-born	8·3	8·9	11·3	9·8
(d) percentage of foreign-born claiming native-birth	—	7	26	15
1948–60:				
(i) Population increase (thousands)	2,609	2,255	2,412	2,315
(a) increase in native-born (thousands)	2,230	1,852	1,842	1,849
(b) increase in foreign-born (thousands)	379	403	570	466
		percentages		
(ii) Average annual rate of population increase	4·2	3·5	3·8	3·6
(iii) Average annual rate of natural increase	3·5	2·9	2·9	2·9
(iv) Percentage of total population increase attributable to:				
(a) native-born	78	75	71	73
(b) foreign-born	22	25	29	27
1921–31:				
Average annual rate of population increase	3·2	—	—	—
1931–48:				
Average annual rate of population increase	1·6	2·1	1·8	2·0
1948–60:				
Average annual rate of population increase	4·2	3·5	3·8	3·6

* Notes on the bases of the hypotheses:

All hypotheses assume (i) the same fertility and mortality schedules for the native-born and foreign-born populations, (ii) the same degree of underenumeration in 1948 of the native-born and foreign-born populations, (iii) equal annual net immigration for each year between 1948 and 1960, (iv) that 17,000 native-born under 12 years of age stated their ages as over 12 years in the 1960 Census, (v) that the foreign-born claiming native birth in 1960 were all over 12 years of age.

The hypotheses differ in the following ways in their explanation of the enumeration of the extra 400,000 native-born in 1960 (i.e. after subtracting 17,000 for age over-statement): (A) 90 per cent of remaining error arises from underenumeration in 1948 and 10 per cent from those of foreign-birth claiming native-birth in 1960; (B) as for (A) but 50 per cent of error due to each cause; (C) as for (A) but 75 per cent and 25 per cent allocations of error respectively.

Development Plan is apparently based. Indeed, over the seven years the former rate would yield a population increase of over 28 per cent compared with under 20 per cent in the case of the latter rate. Similarly, the real rate of natural growth was probably about 2·9 per cent instead of 3·5 per cent. These adjusted 1948 Census population figures present a more plausible picture of intercensal population growth since 1921.

Any correction makes the immigrant contribution to the population growth somewhat more important. By 1960 persons of foreign-birth probably made up about one-tenth of Ghana's population. More impressively still, they had, by their arrival and by the subsequent birth of their children, probably contributed about 27 per cent of the intercensal population growth. It is not unlikely that a seventh of the foreign-born population could have achieved enumeration as native-born in 1960, for in some areas ethnic groups, such as the Ewes, live on both sides of the border. Others could probably successfully claim to be of foreign ancestry but of native birth, especially when dealing with the less zealous enumerators. This may also have been the case in 1948. No correction has been attempted for the earlier census, for the effect on the total figures would be slight. Indeed, the effect on the overall picture of growth rates of choosing Hypothesis (C) instead of Hypothesis (A), where many fewer immigrants have returned their birth-place incorrectly, is very slight.

The fact that the rate of natural increase has been slightly less than that indicated by some of the published United Nations statistics[1] suggests that mortality levels may have been underestimated by the United Nations. In point of fact the published figures do not claim to represent the country as a whole, but only the eighth of the population who live in areas covered by registration. These areas are largely identical with the bigger towns, and almost certainly exhibit better health conditions than the national average. It should also be noted that relatively few people in Northern Ghana live in such areas. Furthermore, the United Nations' attempt to estimate fertility from census age data cannot be duplicated easily for mortality. Fertility levels have a decisive influence in shaping the age structure of a population. The same cannot be said of mortality. Its influence is overshadowed by that of fertility, and can be almost entirely obscured by age misstatement. Thus, there is a strong case for beginning an examination of the level of vital rates in Ghana with an examination of fertility.

But, before beginning such an examination, certain problems should be noted.

The first relates to the Post-enumeration Survey carried out shortly after the 1960 Census. This ambitious survey will produce in due course data on fertility, mortality and migration, which will be more complete than the material gathered from the various sources used in this and the following chapters. Because of this, relatively simple methods of analysis are used here to examine the available data. The use of a complete battery of demographic analytical techniques would only be justified if new evidence were not to be expected shortly. The more exhaustive methods can be used on the Post-enumeration Survey evidence. As it is, we feel justified in erecting this temporary framework, which, in fact, interlocks sufficiently to suggest that later findings will not differ very significantly from it.

[1] i.e. 1962 Demographic Year Book, Table 18.

The second problem relates to the use of hypothetical distributions of deaths. Our knowledge of overall mortality levels in tropical Africa is deficient; our knowledge of the actual distribution patterns of deaths by age is very slight indeed. Accordingly, in the subsequent discussion mortality has been assumed to follow the patterns set out in Model Life Tables prepared by the United Nations (*Methods for Population Projections by Sex and Age*, New York, 1956). It can be argued that for African conditions, where the mortality of children of 1–4 years of age may according to some observers be disproportionately high compared with that found in other parts of the world, other life tables, such as those recently prepared in the Office of Population Research of Princeton University, are more appropriate. However, at the time of this analysis, these other tables were not available to the writer. Furthermore, it is by no means certain that Ghana is, or is any longer, subject to such relatively high child mortality. It is quite possible that the apparent very sudden rise in the number of children in recent years, which is noted later in the study, may be partly caused by the passing of this phenomenon.

Thirdly, there are problems of age distortion arising from age misstatement in the Censuses. A possible correction is suggested in a later chapter but, except in the case of young children, the corrections are not used in this chapter, although at times attention is drawn to their implications. One reason is, of course, that the exact degree of correction is by no means certain. However, the main reason is that it seems probable that such data as age at child-birth, which is related here to census data, suffer from the same age distortion. In these circumstances, the most sensible thing to do seemed to be to relate to each other the uncorrected data so as to obtain rates directly applicable to the 1960 Census population and thereby to what the population apparently believes its age structure to be. In a later chapter possible corrections to these rates are also considered. This method has dangers as well as advantages. The chief danger is that the Model Life Table mortality schedules will no longer be appropriate. But, the effects of correcting the age structure of the population have been tested in all cases where we have used the life tables. As mentioned later, the reduction of the size of the aged group and the increase in the number of infants suggested by the corrections left the population in a condition where the life tables yielded approximately the same crude death rates and the same estimates of the survival of the total population from 1948 to 1960. However, adjustments were necessary and were made when using child-woman ratios to estimate fertility.

What follows is, therefore, a demographic sketch, which, within the next few years, will probably be strengthened and corrected. We believe it to be sufficiently close to the truth to be able to support the description and analysis of other population phenomena subsequently described.

2. THE LEVEL OF FERTILITY

The 1960 Census had not at the time of writing published any data on the pattern of childbearing by age of mother. However, two enquiries have produced such data for the whole of the country and a third has yielded comparable data for certain selected areas. The first two were the 1948

Sample Survey of the Fertility of Women[1] held immediately subsequent to
the 1948 Census on a sample of one in forty of females over 15 years of age,
and the 1963–4 construction of *Conjugal Biographies*.[2] The third is the
study of *Fertility, Mortality and Family Structure in Selected Ghanaian
Communities*[3] carried out in 1961 by Friedlander and Smith. While none of
the surveys may have been successful in eliciting from respondents details
of all births, especially in those cases where the babies subsequently died,
they probably obtained a reasonably accurate picture of the age pattern of
maternity, except insofar as age misstatement occurred. In Table 2.5 the
findings of the *Conjugal Biographies* survey are shown.

TABLE 2.5

AGE-SPECIFIC BIRTH RATES, 1963–4

Age group of mothers	Live births per thousand females per year	Percentage distribution of live births by age
15–19	120	10
20–4	220	18
25–9	260	21
30–4	220	18
35–9	180	14
40–4	140	11
45–9	100	8

Source: Population Council Programme Survey, *Conjugal Biographies* (1963–4).

In Table 2.6 the findings drawn from the *Conjugal Biographies* can be
compared with the distribution of births according to the other two surveys carried out in Ghana. The agreement between the two surveys carried
out on a national scale is striking, even though different techniques were
used and over fifteen years separated the projects. The data drawn from the
other survey come only from the four rural towns surveyed. Sekondi-
Takoradi was omitted from these latter results in an attempt to balance the
omission of truly rural areas and so to improve comparability.

Comparison with other African data, as well as with some from elsewhere, draws attention to two specific features of the Ghanaian findings.
Firstly, by tropical African standards, Ghanaian females appear to give
birth to relatively few children before 20 years of age. They actually seem to
bear a smaller proportion of their children at that age than do Americans,
but do in fact bear more children because of the larger size of completed
families.

The other feature is the large number of children apparently borne by
older women nearing the end of their reproductive span. The number is so
large as to raise the suspicion that a major factor is the overstatement of

[1] The Gold Coast, *Census of Population, 1948: Report and Tables*, pp. 35–7 and pp.
395–6.

[2] See Appendix. Population Council Programme Survey, *Conjugal Biographies*
(1963–4) (unpublished).

[3] Dov Friedlander and Raymond T. Smith, *Fertility, Mortality and Family Structure
in Selected Ghanaian Communities: a preliminary report*, 1963 (unpublished), pp. 28–40.
This survey was also supported by the Population Council and carried out from its
programme at the University of Ghana.

their age by mothers. It seems most improbable that women bear a third of all their children after 35 years of age. Even amongst the population of Taiwan, an extreme example of the late bearing of children, less than a quarter of births occur to mothers of that age. Certainly the findings for Ghana do not agree with the figures presented for those tropical African countries where French is the official language,[1] but those data give the impression that they may have already been adjusted to correct age misstatement. Other evidence comes from the Ghana surveys themselves. In the two nation-wide surveys the average number of children borne by each female continued to rise slowly with the age of mothers until 60 years. In the 1948 *Census Report* the suggestion was made that the explanation for this probably lay in the greater hardihood and capacity for survival to old age of those women who had given birth to disproportionately large numbers of children. However, the real reason almost certainly is that some women who claim to be between 50 and 60 years of age are really considerably younger. It is most improbable that the explanation is biological and not social. This receives support from the fact that the Friedlander-Smith survey of towns in some of the more educated and advanced parts of Ghana exhibits this phenomenon to a smaller degree. In their towns only 29 per cent of women's children are born after they are 35 years old. Similarly, the most recent of the nation-wide surveys shows this characteristic less markedly than the previous one. This corroborates earlier findings on advancement in age statement. One of those findings was that such advancement often occurs from the 15–19 years of age group. Thus, it is probable that Table 2.6 substantially understates the proportion of births normally occurring to females before they have reached 20 years of age. The possible degree of such understatement will be discussed in a later chapter, when the adjustment of age data for the construction of population projections is considered.

TABLE 2.6

PERCENTAGE DISTRIBUTION OF BIRTHS BY AGE OF MOTHER (GHANA AND SOME OTHER COUNTRIES)

	Age of mother						
	15–19	*20–4*	*25–9*	*30–4*	*35–9*	*40–4*	*45–9*
Ghana:							
1948 Fertility Survey	10	17	17	19	17	12	8
Conjugal Biographies (1963–4)	10	18	21	18	14	11	8
Friedlander-Smith (1961)*	11	23	20	17	14	9	6
Fifteen countries of French-speaking							
Africa†	17	24	22	17	12	6	2
Taiwan‡	4	21	28	23	16	7	1
England and Wales‡	6	31	32	19	10	2	0
USA‡	13	34	27	16	8	2	0

* Survey data obtained from females in Anomabo, Tsito, Mpraeso and Larteh by enquiring about births in the preceding twelve months. This is only one of the investigations carried out.

† Source: INSEE, *Perspectives de Population dans les pays Africains et Malgashe d'Expression Française*, Paris, 1963, p. 21.

‡ Source: United Nations, *1959 Demographic Year Book*.

[1] INSEE, *Perspectives de Population dans les pays Africains et Malgashe d'Expression Française*, Paris, 1963, p. 21.

Given reasonably good information on the age structure of a population and on the distribution of births by the age of the mothers, it is possible to estimate the level of fertility. One measure of fertility, which has the advantage of summarizing a considerable amount of information in the form of a single index, is the *total fertility rate*. This rate represents the average number of children which women would bear, if age-specific fertility rates remained constant throughout their child-bearing years. In Ghana, there is no definite evidence that fertility levels have been undergoing change, and so the total fertility rate can probably be equated with the average size of completed families. The three surveys listed in Table 2.6 do provide age-specific birth rates from which the total fertility rates shown in Table 2.7 can be computed.

TABLE 2.7

TOTAL FERTILITY RATES ACCORDING TO THREE SURVEYS

1948 Fertility Survey	5·4
Conjugal Biographies (1963–4)	6·2
Friedlander-Smith (same investigation of four rural towns listed before)	7·1

Thus, the nation-wide surveys seemed to indicate that the average Ghanaian woman could expect to bear about six children during her lifetime. However, the rates suggested by these surveys cannot quite explain the number of children found in Ghana by the 1960 Census. An examination was made of the number of children enumerated as under 5 years of age and of the female age groups from which their mothers must have come. In order to determine the number of live births, an allowance had to be made for the number of children who had already died and for those mothers who had also died. These allowances, which vary somewhat with the mortality level, are made in Table 2.8. An adjustment is also shown in accordance with the previous finding that the 0–4 years of age group had probably lost slightly over 3 per cent of its number by overstatement of age.

TABLE 2.8

TOTAL FERTILITY RATE CORRECTED FROM 1960 CENSUS AGE DATA

Mortality level (expectation of life in years at birth)	Corrected total fertility rate	Total fertility rate with additional correction for age advancement from 0–4 years of age group	Apparent under-counting of births in the Conjugal Biographies (percentages)
35	7·4	7·6	16
37½	7·3	7·5	15
40	7·2	7·4	14
42½	7·1	7·3	13
45	7·0	7·2	11½

United Nations model life tables (*Methods for Population Projections by Sex and Age*, 1956) have been employed together with the age-specific birth rates from the *Conjugal Biographies*. Reverse survival methods were used with the 1960 Census data to compute the numbers of births giving rise to the 0–4 age group and the number of females from whom the mothers were drawn (i.e. 15–54 in 1960) with weighting for chance of being within the group and reverse survival methods for slightly less than 2½ years to give a true average of the dates of birth.

Thus the total fertility rate in Ghana is almost certainly higher than seven births per woman. This means that the research workers who constructed the *Conjugal Biographies* must have failed to record between one-sixth and one-eighth of all live births, in spite of painstaking efforts to avoid this error. In the 1948 *Fertility Survey* enumerators must have omitted over a quarter of all births. The explanation lies almost certainly in the reluctance of mothers to remember or to admit to interviewers the birth of many babies who subsequently died. All interviewers employed to construct *Conjugal Biographies* reported this phenomenon. Some associated the reluctance with the feeling that it was unlucky to recall the dead, especially dead infants. If the pattern of mortality follows that set out in the United Nations model life tables, the number of live births, occurring during the five years preceding the 1960 Census but failing to survive until enumeration, would have ranged between 19 and 26 per cent for expectation of life at birth varying from 35 to 45 years. Thus, if all the failure of the interviewers to list all births can be explained in this way, the *Conjugal Biographies* contain a record of only about two-fifths of those births where the child subsequently died. In the more sophisticated societies examined by Friedlander and Smith the proportion was apparently higher.

The total fertility rate reveals Ghana to be amongst the most fertile populations in the world. This agrees with what is known about the emphasis on fertility in the traditional culture of tropical Africa. Two objections may be made about the methods used to estimate the rate. The first is that the United Nations model life tables may not adequately describe the relative importance of infant and child mortality in terms of the general level of mortality. The second is that we may have underestimated the relative loss from the 0–4 years of age group arising from underenumeration and overstatement of age. If either point is valid, the total fertility rate is in reality even higher than that shown in the above calculations, for studies of mortality in Africa have shown that it may be infant and child mortality that is disproportionately high.[1]

A comparison of the level of fertility in Ghana with that found elsewhere in tropical Africa is more difficult. In Table 2.9 a comparison is made with certain data estimates for countries using French as the official language. There is some evidence that fertility is unusually high in West Africa. Indeed, on a regional basis it is probably the world's highest. That of Central Africa appears to be quite definitely lower. It is by no means certain that Ghana's rate is above that of other West African countries. The estimates given are uncertain, and past experience in the field of fertility measurement has shown that increasing accuracy of measurement is usually accompanied by a raising of the estimates. Blacker has reported total fertility rates of 7 in certain districts of Tanganyika.[2]

What is noteworthy is that Ghana's level of fertility is very considerably higher than that of Taiwan and Singapore, two Asian areas of relatively accurate statistics and of unusually high fertility. On the basis of these comparisons, it might be said that Ghanaian women tend to have twice as

---

[1] See T. E. Smith and J. G. C. Blacker, *Population Characteristics of the Commonwealth Countries of Tropical Africa*, London, 1963, pp. 39–46.
[2] Ibid., p. 66.

many children as American women, and three times as many as the Swedes do.

TABLE 2.9

TOTAL FERTILITY RATES FOR RECENT DATES
(GHANA AND CERTAIN OTHER COUNTRIES)

Ghana	7·2–7·6
Guinea	6·4
Mali	6·3
Niger	6·3
Togo	6·2
Dahomey	6·2
Ivory Coast	6·1
Upper Volta	5·6
Senegal	5·3
Chad	5·3
Madagascar	5·3
Congo	4·7
Cameroun	4·6
Mauritania	4·4
Central Africa	4·4
Gabon	3·7
Taiwan	6·1
Singapore	6·3
England and Wales	2·6
Sweden	2·3
USA	3·7

Source: All African rates except Ghana are from INSEE, *Perspectives de Population dans les pays Africains* ... , op. cit., p. 18; other rates are from United Nations, *1959 Demographic Year Book*.

Using the corrected total fertility rates for Ghana, the age-specific birth rates gathered from the *Conjugal Biographies* can now be used to determine crude birth rates. The rates vary from 52 to 54 per thousand of the population according to the exact mortality level, and would have been at much the same level in 1948 as in 1960. These figures are slightly above the finding claimed by the United Nations for its determination by *reverse survival* methods, but a little below the figure of 55·8 per thousand quoted in the United Nations 1962 *Demographic Year Book*. T. E. Smith has recently written that, 'Estimates of crude birth rates for African communities are usually between 40 and 50 births per annum per 1,000 population and sometimes higher'.[1] He pointed out that some of these higher estimates have been made for the Ivory Coast, Guinea and Dahomey amongst others. The concentration of high rates is certainly in West Africa.

TABLE 2.10

CRUDE BIRTH RATE, 1960, ACCORDING TO MORTALITY LEVEL

Expectation of life at birth (in years)	35	37½	40	42½	45
Crude birth rate	54	54	53	52	52

3. THE LEVEL OF MORTALITY

The natural growth in a community is simply the margin between the additions made to the population by births and the subtractions removed

[1] *Population Characteristics of the Commonwealth Countries of Tropical Africa*, p. 66.

by deaths. Therefore, if the rate of natural increase and the birth rate have been determined, that of mortality is at once known. In Table 2.11, our findings are set out for the period between the two most recent censuses.

TABLE 2.11

ESTIMATION OF THE AVERAGE LEVEL OF MORTALITY, 1948–60

	Possible expectations of life at birth (in years)				
	35	37½	40	42½	45
(1) Proportion of 1948 population surviving to 1960 Census (percentage)	80	81	81	82	83
(2) Annual rate of natural increase (per thousand)	28	29	29	29	30
(3) Crude birth rate (per thousand)	54	54	53	52	52
(4) Crude death rate (per thousand) calculated by subtracting (2) from (3)	26	25	24	23	22
(5) Expectation of life at birth implied by crude death rate and age structure of population	39	40	41½	42½	43½

The rounding of the figures in the first three lines has produced slight irregularities of progression in the final two lines where our interest at present lies. However, the degree of precision of any of the statistics would hardly warrant any more exact statement.

If the assumptions in Table 2.11 are correct, the average expectation of life for the period could not have been 35 years, for such a level of mortality would imply other vital rates which would in their turn imply an expectation of life at birth of 39 years. Similarly it could not have been 45 years. At only one point are the two measures of mortality identical.

Thus, the average expectation of life at birth between 1948 and 1960 may have been about 42½ years. It was not of course constant at that level for the period has witnessed a very considerable increase in living standards and health facilities in the country. If the advance against mortality has been proceeding at the same rate as that used for constructing population projections in the United Nations manual, *Methods for Population Projections by Sex and Age*,[1] the expectations of life at various dates would be those set out in Table 2.12.

TABLE 2.12

ESTIMATES OF EXPECTATION OF LIFE
AT BIRTH AT VARIOUS DATES,
1948 TO 1964

Date	Estimate of expectation of life at birth
1948	39½
1954	42½
1960	45½
1964	47½

In Table 2.13 an attempt has been made to compare Ghana's level of mortality with that of various other countries as presented in the United Nations 1962 *Demographic Year Book*. Employing the same assumptions

[1] United Nations, Department of Economic and Social Affairs, *Methods for Population Projections by Sex and Age*, New York, 1956.

TABLE 2.13

EXPECTATION OF LIFE AT BIRTH COMPARED WITH THAT ESTIMATED FOR GHANA AT THE SAME DATE (VARIOUS COUNTRIES)

Region	Country	Date	Expectation of life at birth	Estimated Ghanaian expectation of life at birth at that date	Comparison of Ghanaian expectation of life at birth with that of the other country
Tropical Africa	Ghana (my estimate)	1948–60 (average)	40	—	—
	Ghana (UN estimate)	1948	38	39½	+1½
	Central African Republic	1959–60	35	45	+10
	Congo (Leopoldville)	1950–2	38	41	+3
	Guinea	1954–5	31	42½	+11½
	Ivory Coast	1956–8	35	44	+9
	Mali	1957	26	44	+18
	Rhodesia and Nyasaland	1950	37	40½	+3½
	Southern Rhodesia (Africans)	1953–5	48	42½	−5½
	Senegal	1957	37	44	+7
	Upper Volta	1960–1	32	45½	+13½
Temperate Africa	Morocco	1960	50	45½	−4½
	United Arab Republic	1960	52	45½	−6½
	Swaziland	1946	48	38½	−9½
Asia	Ceylon	1954	60	42½	−17½
	India	1957–8	45	44	−1
	Philippines	1946–9	49	39	−10
	Thailand	1947–8	49	39	−10
South America	Brazil	1940–50	39	38	−1
	Colombia	1950–2	44	41	−3
	Chile	1952	50	41½	−8½
Europe	England and Wales	1961	68	46	−22
	France	1961	68	46	−22
	Norway	1951–5	71	42	−29
	Spain	1950	59	40½	−18½
	Yugoslavia	1958–9	62	44½	−17½
	USSR	1958–9	64	44½	−19½
North America	Panama	1952–4	60	42	−18
	USA	1961	67	46	−21
Oceania	Australia	1953–5	67	42½	−24½

Source: Except for my estimate of Ghana, 1962 Demographic Year Book. All post-World War II tropical African data have been used.

used to construct Table 2.12, expectations of life at birth have been calculated for Ghana for each of the relevant dates. Some of the figures shown
for other African countries are based on the findings of field surveys instead of complete censuses.

The most remarkable feature of the Table is that the United Nations
estimate of expectation of life at birth in Ghana in 1948, made solely from
the limited age data provided by that census, is in fairly close agreement
with that resulting from the more elaborate methods of the present analysis,
which has been able to draw on the richer material of the 1960 census as
well.

The evidence presented in the *Year Book*, of which this is only an ex-
tract, makes it clear that tropical Africa still has the highest level of
mortality of any major area in the world. However, what is equally clear is
that life expectation in Ghana is probably greater than in any other part of
the region, with the apparent exception of Southern Rhodesia. This may be
largely a product of its higher average incomes and hence of proportionately
greater surpluses for governmental action in the field of health.

Health, however, is not related solely to the standard of living. Many of
today's poor countries enjoy far lower levels of mortality than did Western
Europe when at the same state of economic development. They have been
able to reduce mortality by importing ready-made medical technology.
However, this technology has not been designed to be equally effective in
all parts of the world. To date, it has certainly raised expectations of life
in tropical Africa but not as rapidly nor to the levels that have been the
case in many other parts of the world. Thus Ghana's average income per
head is well over twice that of the UAR, but its expectation of life at birth is
considerably lower. Similarly, India, although much poorer in terms of
individual incomes, can offer its population as high an expectation of life
as can Ghana.

4. SUMMARY OF VITAL RATES

In Table 2.14, an attempt has been made to present the vital rates for the
1948–60 intercensal period and to construct a crude projection until 1975.

The rates already calculated are average rates for the period, 1948–60.
In the Table these rates are ascribed to the mid-year of that period, 1954.
Thus, at that time the crude birth rate was about 52 per thousand, the
crude death rate about 23 per thousand, and consequently the rate of
natural increase was about 2·9 per cent per year.

It has been assumed for the purposes of this simple model that the crude
birth rate has recently been fairly constant and will continue to be constant
for some years at around 52 per thousand. It has also been assumed that
the expectation of life at birth has been increasing at the rate of about one
year for each two years of time elapsed as in the United Nations model life
tables. This assumption fits in with stable population analysis of the age
structure of the 1948 and 1960 Censuses.

In fact, stable population analysis, carried out after estimates have been
made of the effect upon the age structure of immigrants and of their
children born in Ghana, suggests that the whole picture drawn in Table
2.14 of the 1948 and 1960 population characteristics is not far out. That is,
of course, if any underenumeration in 1948 was distributed proportionately

by age. This would be especially likely if whole communities were omitted from the count.

The most significant feature of the Table is the implication that the rate of natural growth is already over 3·2 per cent per year and will average about 3·3 per cent during the present Seven-Year Development Plan period.

TABLE 2.14

ESTIMATED MORTALITY, FERTILITY AND NATURAL INCREASE, 1948–75

	1948	1954	1960	1965	1970	1975
Expectation of life at birth (in years)	39½	42½	45½	48	50½	53
Crude death rate (per thousand)	24	23	21	19	18	16
Crude birth rate (per thousand)	52	52	52	52	52	52
Rate of natural increase (per cent)	2·8	2·9	3·1	3·3	3·4	3·6

The finding that the average expectation of life at birth for the 1948–60 intercensal period was about 42½ years, together with the argument summarized in Table 2.8, means that the total fertility rate is about 7.3. With a sex ratio at birth little above parity, this means that the gross reproduction rate is about 3·6. And, if the pattern of mortality approximates to that found in the United Nations Model Life Tables, the net reproduction rate during the intercensal period was about 2·2. Thus, even if the low level of mortality of the 1950s were not to be improved, the Ghanaian population would more than double by natural increase alone each generation.

These rates and also the corrected age-specific fertility rate are shown in Table 2.15. The age-specific rates have been corrected only in the sense that they apply to the population which believes its age to be as described in the census and surveys. In a subsequent chapter the correction of these rates to remove the effect of age misstatement is attempted, and only there are the rates stated in terms of real age. The greatest adjustments are at the extreme ends of the child-bearing span.

TABLE 2.15

ESTIMATED MORTALITY AND FERTILITY INDICES,
1948–60 AVERAGES

	Rate
(a) *Total fertility rate*	7·3
(b) *Gross reproduction rate*	3·6
(c) *Net reproduction rate*	2·2
(d) *Age-specific birth rates**	
(per thousand females of ages	
shown below)	
15–19	141
20–4	259
25–9	306
30–4	259
35–9	213
40–4	165
45–9	117

* See Chapter IV for modification of these figures.

5. MORTALITY TRENDS

Some indication of long-term mortality trends can be gained from the census information available. In Table 2.16, stable population analysis has been employed to examine the 1921 Census which recorded that 44 per cent of the population was under 16 years of age.

If this figure can be regarded as in any way a reliable indicator, then a birth rate in 1921 of the order of that found in the 1948–60 period would imply an expectation of life at birth of about 28 years. If the birth rate were a little higher, the expectation of life at birth at that date would have been less than 28 years. In either case the decrease of mortality between 1921 and 1954 would have been considerable, and would have been similar to that claimed by a United Nations manual[1] to have been the common experience in the world at that time.

TABLE 2.16

AN ESTIMATE OF CHANGE IN EXPECTATION OF LIFE AT BIRTH, 1921–54—STABLE
POPULATION ANALYSIS BASED ON 1921 CENSUS AGE DATA AND A CRUDE BIRTH
RATE OF 52 PER THOUSAND

Crude birth rate	52
Crude death rate, 1921	38
Rate of natural increase, 1921	1·4 per cent
Expectation of life at birth, 1921	28 years
Gain in expectation of life at birth, 1921–54	14½ years
Average gain per year in expectation of life at birth, 1921–54	0·43 years

Table 2.16 is largely conjectural, but it does give a general indication of mortality change over a third of a century. It suggests that, although the crude death rate was probably near 40 per thousand in 1921, the rate of natural increase of the population was almost 1½ per cent per year. That the population of Ghana was increasing quite rapidly 40 or 50 years ago is confirmed by the use of reverse survival methods to examine the older age groups of the native-born. There is no doubt that when these groups were born, there were many more births each year in the country than had been the case the previous year. The population was certainly not a stationary one.

The rise in life expectation this century calls for some explanation. Until recent years it was probably largely to be attributed to rising living standards and the extension of the cash economy throughout much of society, especially in southern Ghana. Great improvements in transport, first the railways and then the multiplication of roads which were used by ever more lorries, certainly helped. Strong central government with its maintenance of law and order has been very important.

However, the provision of medical services has been increasingly important and henceforth will probably be the most significant factor in the reduction of mortality. Some doctors have been available and some prophylactic methods have been used against disease all this century. Some hospitals have existed since the 1930s and some medical clinics were founded as early as the end of the Second World War. In recent years doctors and nurses have become more numerous, and since 1955 forty-seven Health Centres have been established. From about the same date a nation-wide campaign has been waged against yaws. The time may come soon when it

[1] *Methods for Population Projections by Sex and Age.*

is possible to mount a vast operation aimed at the eradication of malaria.

But there are still many problems, as is indicated by an expectation of life at birth of perhaps 48 years. Infant mortality rates, although falling, are still high. Large numbers of babies continue to die of malaria, pneumonia and diseases of the dysentery and gastro-enteritis group. In the 1960 Census, 290 doctors[1] were enumerated (one for each 23,000 of the population), but they are concentrated heavily in southern Ghana and more particularly in Accra.

Undoubtedly, a very considerable mortality differential exists between different parts of the country. In the towns of the south the expectation of life at birth is probably already well over 50 years. In the villages of the far north it may not be much over 30 years.

It is possible that Ghana is on the threshhold of a rapid advance against mortality of the type that Ceylon achieved in the early 1950s, for the establishment of many more health centres and a very considerable increase in the number of doctors in the country is assured over the next decade. In this case the reduction in mortality will be faster than that assumed in the population projections found below, where a gain in expectation of life of one year in each two calendar years is posited. For this reason the projections are, in terms of mortality change, conservative. Death rates may well fall faster, and natural increase may climb a little more quickly.

6. FERTILITY DIFFERENTIALS AND CHANGE

Fertility levels are high in Ghana. There is no certain evidence that a significant change has already taken place in the birth rate or is about to take place. However, such a change cannot be ruled out. Some fertility differentials now exist and some sections of the community desire fewer children than has been the average in the past. For these reasons, the possibility of a considerable fertility decline is taken into account in the projections.

Most Ghanaians want children in considerable numbers and their culture has long assumed this to be the 'natural' desire. In a survey of *Population Attitudes in Rural Ghana*,[2] almost two-thirds of the interviewees replied 'Yes', without qualification, to the question, 'Do you think that it is a good thing for people to have a lot of children?' Even amongst the upper and middle classes of the towns,[3] less than a tenth of all women desire completed families of less than four children. Among these women, only 7 per cent of those who were pregnant at the time of the survey were sorry that they were in this condition, while over 40 per cent of those who were not at the time pregnant, wished that it was otherwise.

An important tool in the analysis of fertility decline or in the prediction of such decline in many countries has been the study of differential fertility. If some sections of the community have begun to restrict the

---

[1] The figure of 565 for the end of 1964 is provided by the Register of Doctors kept by the Ministry of Health. Of this number 205 are Ghanaians.

[2] See Appendix. Population Council Programme Survey, *Population Attitudes in Rural Ghana* (1963) (unpublished).

[3] See Appendix. Population Council Programme Survey, *Population Attitudes in Economically Superior Areas* (1963) (unpublished).

number of children in the families, it may well mean that the practice will become more general. In the West the small family system spread from higher to lower socio-economic groups and from urban to rural areas. That there is some difference in average family size between sections of the community does not necessarily show that change in family size is under way. Such social or regional differences may exist in a perfectly static form. Even in this case, the average fertility in the country may change with a variation in the proportions of the population found in the different groups.

There is evidence of two differentials in fertility in Ghana, that between the different geographical regions of the country and that between urban and rural areas. In addition there are a few data bearing on the question of whether there is a differential between social classes.

In Table 2.17 Regional fertility differentials are examined. The methods used previously to estimate total fertility rates have again been employed, but no correction has been attempted for age advancement from the 0–4 years of age group, because the extent of such age misstatement varies from one Region to another. These rates are then compared with various other measures.

TABLE 2.17

REGIONAL VARIATIONS IN FERTILITY, 1960

	GHANA	Accra C.D.	Eastern	Western and Central	Regions Ashanti	Brong-Ahafo	Volta	Northern and Upper
Total fertility rate*	7·1	6·0	7·3	7·2	8·1	8·2	6·9	6·0
Percentage variation from Ghana	—	−15	+3	+2	+14	+16	−3	−15
Child-woman ratio†	886	789	924	903	1,006	1,017	865	756
Percentage variation from Ghana	—	−11	+4	+2	+14	+15	−2	−15
Sex ratios, 15–44 years of age‡	98	133	101	99	108	115	86	75
Percentage variation from Ghana	—	+36	+3	+1	+10	+17	−12	−13
Income per head (£)	—	105	50	50	59	56	46	23
Percentage variation from Ghana average excluding Accra C.D.	—	—	+8	+8	+30	+21	0	−50

* Estimated by the method used to obtain the national figure, but not corrected for age advance-ment.
† Children 0–4 per thousand women, 15–44.
‡ Males per hundred females.

The Table proves beyond doubt that there are very significant differentials in fertility by Region. Excluding for the present Accra, which is largely urban, fertility falls into three major divisions. In the southernmost Regions, which abut upon the Gulf of Guinea, fertility of medium range is found. In the areas of predominantly Ashanti cultural influences, Ashanti and Brong-Ahafo, fertility is extremely high. In the far north, fertility is relatively low. Women in Ashanti and Brong-Ahafo apparently bear almost a third more children than do their fellow countrywomen in the Northern and Upper Regions. These differences are real enough, although the low fertility of the north may be slightly exaggerated, for age misstatement is greatest there and the 0–4 years of age group, upon whom the calculations largely depend, may have been reduced to a relatively greater extent by premature age advancement.

It is of interest to note that an almost identical finding could have been made by relying on simple child-woman ratios. These ratios are particularly reliable in the case of a population, such as that of Ghana, with a fairly stable age structure.

Excluding once again Accra, the relation between the sex ratio in the age groups from which nearly all mothers are drawn and the level of fertility is remarkable. Except in the case of the Volta Region, nearly all the variation in fertility seems to be explicable in terms of variation in the sex ratios. It is possible that the relation is not quite as exact as it appears. For instance, we have seen, when dealing with age misstatement, that sex ratios in this age range are probably somewhat depressed in the Northern and Upper Regions by a relatively greater advance in ages from under 15 to over it in the case of females than in the case of males.

However, even when care is taken to avoid such pitfalls, it still appears that the major factor related to variation in the level of fertility in Ghana is the balance of the sexes. This in turn is controlled by migration. In the north some marriages are broken for long periods by long-term migration to the south. In many more marriages, co-habitation is reduced by seasonal and other short-term migration. It may also be that immigration into Ashanti and Brong-Ahafo ensure that the Ashanti inclination for early female marriage can easily be fulfilled. The effect is probably only marginal as interethnic marriage is not particularly common. What is important is that few Ashanti males emigrate from the Ashanti-Brong-Ahafo area. The Volta Region provides the anomaly. The explanation probably lies in the fact that migrants from the Region usually travel much shorter distances than do people from the north and hence revisit their homes more frequently. Three-fifths of the emigrant males from the Volta Region are found close by in the Accra Capital District and the Eastern Region.

Migration is also clearly related to the Regional income. Thus, when incomes are low, male emigration is high, the proportion of females living for considerable periods without husbands is great, and the level of fertility is relatively low. It is, therefore, easy and also misleading to show a direct relation between Regional income and fertility. All kinds of incorrect sociological hypotheses could be built upon this, if the migration factor were not taken into account.

Figures 2.1, 2.2. and 2.3 show that, if a more detailed analysis is made at the Local Administration Area level, the relationship between adult sex ratios, fertility levels and population increase can be observed clearly. All are high in areas of Ashanti culture and are low in the north and along much of the coast. In the more thriving coastal towns sex ratios and rates of increase are high but not child-woman ratios. In the northern parts of the Volta Region sex ratios are low, but the rate of population increase is quite high. The high rate of population growth in Ashanti and Brong-Ahafo does not arise solely out of natural increase, for, as shown above, these are also immigrant areas.

G

Figure 2:1

GHANA: SEX RATIOS OF POPULATION 15-44 YEARS, BY LOCAL ADMINISTRATION AREAS, 1960

Males per 100 Females.

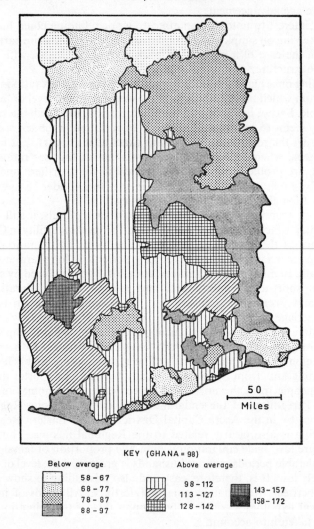

KEY (GHANA = 98)

Below average		Above average	
58 - 67		98 - 112	143 - 157
68 - 77		113 - 127	158 - 172
78 - 87		128 - 142	
88 - 97			

This type of differential fertility does not seem to presage a decline in fertility. In fact, if rising living standards and cultural change bring more jobs to the north, or make it easier to travel back home more often, or make family migration by northerners more common, the relatively depressed fertility of the emigrant areas could rise towards those levels now prevailing elsewhere.

Rural-urban fertility differentials almost certainly exist but there is some difficulty about their exact measurement. In Table 2.17 it was seen that Accra's total fertility rate was 15 per cent below that of Ghana as a whole

Figure 2:2
GHANA: CHILD-WOMAN RATIOS,
BY LOCAL ADMINISTRATION AREAS, 1960

(Population 0-4, per 1000 females, 15-44.)

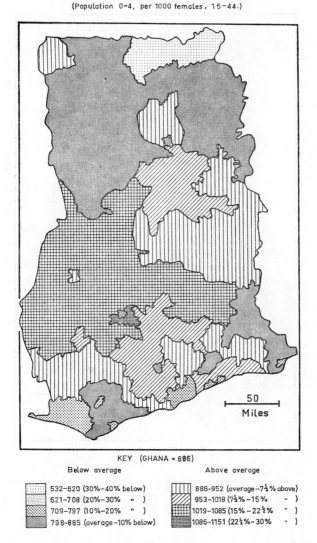

KEY   (GHANA = 886)

Below average	Above average
532–620 (30%–40% below)	886–952 (average –7½% above)
621–708 (20%–30% ")	953–1018 (7½% –15% ")
709–797 (10%–20% ")	1019–1085 (15% – 22⅔% ")
798–885 (average –10% below)	1086–1151 (22½%–30% ")

and 18 per cent below that of the rest of the Eastern Region. The position was similar but a little less marked as measured by child-woman ratios.

In Table 2.18 child-woman ratios are used to examine the comparative level of fertility in urban and rural areas. As the urban population contains great numbers of people in fairly small towns, child-woman ratios are separately compared for some of the bigger towns and the Regions in which they are found. Urban fertility appears to be 8 per cent below that of the whole of Ghana and 10 per cent below that of rural Ghana. The difference may arise mainly from the larger towns, for in southern Ghana

Figure 2:3

GHANA: PERCENTAGE POPULATION INCREASE,

BY LOCAL ADMINISTRATION AREAS, 1948-60

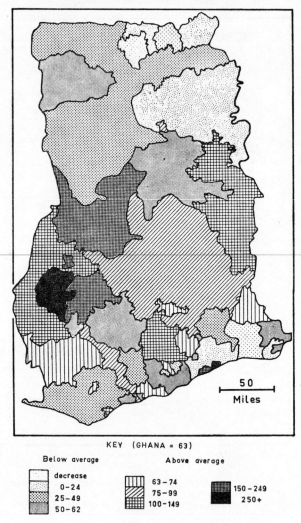

KEY (GHANA = 63)

Below average   Above average

decrease
0-24   63-74
25-49   75-99   150-249
50-62   100-149   250+

50
Miles

child-woman ratios in these towns are frequently about one-eighth below
that of the whole Region in which each town is found. The town ratios
would, of course, differ more from that of the rural population alone than
they do from the total population of which the town's inhabitants form a
part. This does not appear to be the case in northern Ghana, where large
towns are few. Urban fertility levels in the north are similar to those found
further south, but rural fertility levels are much lower in the north than in
the south.

TABLE 2.18

URBAN FERTILITY DIFFERENTIALS AS MEASURED BY CHILD-WOMAN RATIOS
(CHILDREN, 0–4, PER 1,000 FEMALES, 15–44)

Urban area	C-W ratio	Total area (or Region)	C-W ratio	Urban difference from Regional ratio (as a percentage)
All urban population*	816	All population of Ghana	886	− 8
		All rural population	908	−10
Accra†	769	Ghana	886	−13
Kumasi	827	Ashanti	1,006	−12
Takoradi	792	Western and Central	903	−12
Cape Coast	797	Western and Central	903	−12
Koforidua	797	Eastern	924	−14
Sunyani	907	Brong-Ahafo	1,017	−10
Ho	672	Volta	865	−22
Tamale	788	Northern and Upper	756	+ 4
Bawku	763	Northern and Upper	756	+ 1

* Population in centres with 5,000 or more inhabitants.
† Accra municipality ; not Accra Capital District as in Table 2.17.

Table 2.18 cannot be taken to prove beyond doubt the existence of a rural-urban fertility differential. It certainly cannot be taken to measure its extent. The reason is that the child-woman ratios, and indeed the total fertility rates calculated earlier, are based upon the number of young children and the number of women living in a particular area. It is assumed that such statistics are related to maternity. This is not necessarily so. For instance, some of the women who go from Central Ashanti to live and work in Kumasi, leave their children with their grandparents. Other town families send children back to grandparents in rural areas at times so that the children will not be brought up entirely cut off from their ancestral traditions. Such behaviour would tend to lower the apparent fertility in urban areas as calculated previously. On the other hand, the opposite process also occurs. Some rural families send children to urban relatives for schooling. However, this is unlikely to have much effect on the 0–4 year old groups. More importantly, the towns contain a bigger proportion of women in their younger and more fertile years. This difference in urban and rural age structure may mean that the real rural-urban fertility differential is greater than suggested in Table 2.18.

The *Conjugal Biographies* survey[1] and a supplementary similar study restricted to Accra[2] allow a study to be made of urban-rural fertility differentials based on the actual number of living children borne by women. These findings are presented in Table 2.19. No attempt has been made to correct the figures for failure to recall a proportion of children who subsequently died. As such failure was probably higher in rural areas, the differentials may well be even greater than suggested in the Table. Some irregularities have probably been produced by the misstatement of mothers' ages.

The Table leaves no doubt that a very considerable rural-urban fertility differential exists in Ghana. Amongst the urban population as a whole

[1] See Appendix. Population Council Programme Survey, *Conjugal Biographies*.
[2] 400 conjugal biographies made in various parts of Accra.

fertility may be a sixth less than that found amongst the rural population. It is likely that the main factor in the difference is relatively low fertility in the bigger towns. In Accra, women of completed fertility have borne about a quarter less children than have the women of the villages. On the average the former will have given birth to about six children while the latter will have borne about eight.

It is not clear whether fertility in urban areas is falling, and, if it is, whether it is falling faster than that of rural areas. At first glance the greater differentials at younger ages suggest that such changes are occurring, but the figures for completed fertility suggest that this phenomenon probably arises from a greater degree of advancement in age misstatement in rural areas.

Even if no change is occurring in such differentials, their existence implies the inevitability of some fall in Ghanaian fertility levels with increased urbanization. If a larger proportion of the country's people were to live in towns and were to adopt the levels of fertility prevailing there, then obviously the average level of fertility would fall. Such a phenomenon was quite an important factor in the fertility transition in the West. If the present proportion of urban population were to double, as it could over the next decades, and if half the urban population were to live in large towns like present-day Accra, fertility for this reason alone could fall about $6\frac{1}{2}$ per cent. This would lower the national total fertility rate from 7·3 to 6·8.

The statistical analysis does not establish why fertility is lower in urban than in rural areas.[1] Such lower fertility could be a product of the peculiar marital conditions of urban life, or it could arise from the fact that the rural-urban emigrant stream contains a large proportion of young females who have had less than the average number of children or who subsequently bear comparatively few children. It is likely that both factors are involved.

As we have already seen, females in the urban areas spend only 63 per cent of the 15–44 years of age span in conjugal union compared with 71 per cent in the case of rural females. Most of the difference is explained by later marriage in the towns. Much, but by no means all, the lower fertility

TABLE 2.19

RURAL-URBAN FERTILITY DIFFERENTIALS

	Average number of live births per female			Amount below rural survey births			
	Rural	Urban	Accra	Urban survey		Accra survey	
Age of Females	survey	survey	survey	No.	%	No.	%
15–19	0·6	0·5	0·3	0·1	16	0·3	50
20–4	1·7	1·3	1·3	0·4	24	0·4	24
25–9	3·0	2·5	2·4	0·5	20	0·6	20
30–4	4·1	3·6	3·2	0·5	12	0·9	21
35–9	5·0	4·6	4·2	0·4	8	0·8	16
40+	6·1	5·5	5·1	0·6	10	1·0	16
Completed fertility (i.e. 45+)	7·4	6·2	5·6	1·2	16	1·8	24

These figures are not corrected for age misstatement or omitted births.
Source: *Conjugal Biographies* and *Accra* surveys.

[1] A minor cause of the urban-rural fertility differential could be the greater use of contraceptives in the urban centres. See Chapter IV, p. 154.

in urban Ghana and Accra can be explained in terms of the much lower birth rates in the earliest and latest years of the reproductive span. The former is caused by delayed marriage, the latter may be largely a product of lesser age misstatement in the towns than in rural Ghana.

Preliminary findings from the rural-urban migration survey indicate that females with few children, and particularly unmarried females, are more likely to migrate to the towns than are those with more children. Thus the towns may receive a cross-section of females who are either naturally less fertile or who through accident or intention have borne fewer children.

The survey of *Population Attitudes is Economically Superior Urban Areas* collected data on births in the wealthier suburbs of Accra, Kumasi, Takoradi-Sekondi and Cape Coast. These data are not completely comparable with those for either urban Ghana or Accra. But a rough comparison suggests that amongst the upper and middle classes fertility under 30 years of age is probably slightly lower than among the entire population of these towns. This is presumably caused by a greater delay in marriage. Subsequently, the differential disappears. There is some evidence that the completed family size may be greater in urban areas amongst the economically better-off than amongst the poor. This may, however, be a statistical error arising from better reporting of the birth of infants who subsequently died.

A much more difficult question is that of long-term change in the level of fertility. It can be argued that in recent times increased urbanization may have tended to lower the level a little. But this could easily have been offset by the reduction in widowhood arising out of the decline in mortality. Even the greater stabilization of marriage may have raised fertility. On the other hand, the pattern of very early marriage, still almost universal in the north, was probably common throughout the country two generations ago. Such a pattern fits easily into a subsistence, agrarian economy.

The censuses should provide answers to the question. However, insufficient and defective age data prior to 1960 raise almost as many problems as they solve.

The 1948 Census attempted to enumerate separately children under one year of age, but enumerators appear to have erred in classifying all very young children in this way. As a result, 100,000 more infants were listed in 1948 than in 1960. In the 1948 Census, 378 children under one year of age were enumerated for every thousand females, 16–44 years old. In 1960 the number was only 220. If the 1948 figure were taken seriously, it would imply an average number of births per woman during the reproductive period of 13 to 15. This, by any international comparison, is clearly far beyond the bounds of probability. It is also at complete variance with the data published in the *Fertility Survey* of the same Census Report.

In 1948, 1,981 children, 0–15 years of age, were enumerated for every thousand females, 16–44 years of age. In 1960, the ratio was 2,134. This does not imply that fertility was 7 per cent lower in 1948, because it must be remembered that infant mortality and child mortality rates were higher. The use of reverse survival ratio methods and life tables appropriate to the estimated levels of mortality at each date, suggests that fertility in 1948 may have been slightly lower than in 1960. However, this is by no means certain.

More intriguing results arise from a comparison of the 1921 and 1960

Censuses. In 1921, the 0–5 years of age group was separately enumerated in the Colony and Ashanti. At that date there were 947 children of this age for every thousand females, 16 to 45 years of age, and probably about 814 0–4 year olds. In 1960, in the same area the ratio was 951. This does not imply equal fertility because of the decline in mortality. The implication is that fertility in 1921 was about 7 per cent lower than in 1960. This would mean that the birth rate at the earlier date was just under 50 per thousand and the total fertility rate under 7.

Some of the implications of this discussion are set out in Table 2.20. The Table is purely speculative. Age data was very rough in the earlier censuses and cannot form the basis for any definite conclusions. The division of population for enumeration purposes into four large age groups, as was done at each census, is itself evidence that social conditions preclude any great accuracy in age statement. The exact variation of the mortality level does not greatly affect the findings shown.

TABLE 2.20

GHANA: POSSIBLE FERTILITY TRENDS, 1921–61

Census	1921	1948	1960
Intercensal period*		1921–48†	1948–60
Expectation of life at birth (years)	28	39½	45½
Total fertility rate	6·8	7·1	7·3
Crude birth rate	48	50	52
Intercensal change in fertility		+4%	+3%
Average annual change in fertility		+0·1%	+0·2%

* i.e. excluding 1931 Census; 1921 is used in order to obtain a longer period.
† Comparisons were made for the Colony and Ashanti.

There is little certain evidence of fertility change between 1948 and 1960. The small apparent change quite probably arises either from a slight change in adult female age composition or from defective data. If the small increase in fertility is real, it is not much greater than might be explained by reduction in widowhood with declining mortality.

The 1921–48 rise certainly resembles the apparent 1948–60 movement. If real, it may indicate what can happen in tropical Africa with improving maternal health and a reduction in widowhood and perhaps polygamy. On the other hand, the use of suspect age enumeration, suspect to the extent that 1921 age data in Ashanti was based on 'young children' only, means that the whole comparison is of very doubtful validity.

We have no definite evidence of fertility decline. Recent evidence implies, if anything, the opposite. Indeed, it would be unwise to assume any secular trend in fertility until much more evidence is available. Nevertheless, care will be taken when constructing population projections to include the possibility of a substantial fall in fertility.

It might be noted that, when females interviewed in the survey of *Population Attitudes in Economically Superior Urban Areas* were asked to compare the numbers of children, to which they had given birth, with the numbers borne by their mothers at the same age, half said that their mothers had produced more, a third said less, and a sixth said the same number. This may show some decline in fertility. But it may only point to the lower fertility of urban populations with which we are already familiar, for all the respondents lived in large towns, while a great number of their mothers did not.

7. THE ABSORPTION OF POPULATION GROWTH

Increased population growth may now be considered in terms of the effect upon the family, the settlement pattern of the country and the rural-urban division of the population.

First, the family might be considered. There has been a very considerable decline in mortality in recent years. This must mean that living parents will on the average have more of their children surviving and needing to be reared. The extra proportion of children likely to survive could be estimated, and, in a society where all orphaned children were removed from sight into institutions, this would provide a measure of the extra pressure upon the household accommodation and family budget. This is not the case in a country like Ghana where the orphaned are adopted by their relatives. In this case the important factor is the relative numbers of children and adults who are likely to be caring for them. Between 1948 and 1960 infant and child mortality declined. So did adult mortality, but not as rapidly. Thus, as can be seen in Table 2.21, the ratio of children to adults climbed quite steeply. That is to say, in only twelve years child-dependency increased by between an eighth and a seventh. Where both parents survived, and personally cared for their own children, the average rise in dependency would have been greater still.

This is a very great rise in dependency. It is in fact considerably greater than might have been suggested by the overall gain in life expectation if mortality was distributed by age according to the pattern of the United Nations Life Tables. The gain gives some support for the belief that infant and child mortality have been atypically high in tropical Africa, and that this pattern is altering in Ghana because of disproportionately great advances against such mortality.

It is possible that child-dependency was less in 1948 than in 1921 because of fertility decline, but, as pointed out before, this phenomenon may be merely a product of defective age enumeration in 1921.

A sudden dramatic rise in child-dependency has occurred in many countries since the end of the Second World War. It is the product of the importation of a medical technology which has proved especially effective in combating the types of infectious diseases which have previously killed many children in tropical lands or in some poor lands outside the tropics. That the phenomenon is fairly general does not mean that the sudden strain thrown upon the family system or upon the national economy is any less acute. The family and the education system are already feeling this strain. On the household level the change is not going unnoticed. In the *Survey of Population Attitudes in Economically Superior Urban Areas*, three-quarters of all male respondents and three-fifths of all female respondents claimed that there are now more children in Ghana compared with the number of adults than used to be the case. The adult world has yet to face the influx of young persons growing up to adulthood. The phenomenon is similar in effect to the post-War baby boom in parts of the West. In Ghana it was a fall in mortality rather than a rise in fertility which produced this occurrence. Nevertheless, the end result is the same. In the next few years the economy will have to produce new jobs at a much faster rate. This is not always as easy in a developing economy as in a developed one. At the same time many more potential mothers will reach adulthood and will reinforce the population's tendency towards a high rate of natural growth.

TABLE 2.21

CHILD-DEPENDENCY, 1921–60

	Child dependency Ratio		
	Census 1948	Census 1960	Intercensal period 1948–60 (per cent)
Children, 0–15, per thousand **population, 16–44 years**	996	1,125	
Increase in above ratio			13
Children, 0–15, per thousand population, over 16 years	755	863	
Increase in above ratio			14
	Census 1921*	Census 1960*	Intercensal period 1921–60* (per cent)
Children, 0–15, per thousand population, 16–45 years	1,044	1,102	
Increase in above ratio			6
Children, 0–15, per thousand population, over 16 years	789	877	
Increase in above ratio			11

* Ratios for 1921 area of the Colony of the Gold Coast and Ashanti only.

Child-dependency is usually not measured by the ratios employed in the above Table, which were necessary there to allow comparability between the censuses. The usual comparison is that of the population under 15 years, the group which most countries hope eventually to remove from the labour force, and the 15–64 years of age group, in which the great majority of those employed full-time are to be found. It has already been seen in Table 1.8 that Ghana's dependency ratio is high and is at least potentially economically burdensome. In Table 2.22, it is shown that its child-dependency is high by African standards.

The difference between Ghana and some of the countries of Central and East Africa may partly arise from higher fertility in the former. This difference and that between Ghana and other West African countries may also have been increased lately by a more dramatic fall in infant mortality in Ghana. Finally, some African countries may give the appearance of lower ratios than is really the case because of the relative underenumeration of children.

Ghana's burden of child-dependency is no more than the highest levels found in Asia or Latin America. It is, however, enormously greater than that of many economically advanced countries, whose economies could better bear such a strain. For instance, in comparison with the number of adults in the main working age range, Ghana has two and a half times as many children as do the two north-western European countries listed.

TABLE 2.22

CHILD-DEPENDENCY: GHANA AND VARIOUS OTHER COUNTRIES
(CHILDREN, 0–14, PER 1,000 PERSONS, 15–64)

Ghana	852
Senegal*	764
Guinea	772
Ivory Coast*	767
Togo*	737
Upper Volta	734
Congo (Leopoldville)*	668
Tanganyika	765
Uganda	734
United Arab Republic	795
Ceylon	708
Iran	783
Taiwan	880
Mexico	853
USA	521
England and Wales	351
Sweden	333

* Some adjustment of census age data has been necessary.

Source: 1960 Census of Ghana and various United Nations *Demographic Year Books*.

The combined effect of rapid population growth and economic development upon the settlement pattern is interesting. Figure 2.4 shows that in 1960 there were two areas of above average population density. These have already been described. The large block is in southern Ghana, and contains a majority of the country's population. It is an area of ports and of extensive tree-crop cultivation in areas which were once covered by tropical forest. It is the area where the cash economy is dominant. The smaller area of dense settlement is in the Upper Region, and is largely confined to the north-east of that region. This is a region of critically densely settled subsistence farming.

Now, how is the sudden population increase being absorbed? Are the frontiers of settlement being pushed into the more sparsely inhabited areas or is the extra population pouring into those areas which are already relatively closely peopled?

The answers are provided by Table 2.23. Those areas of above average population density are just maintaining their relative position if they are examined as a single unit. However, such an examination hides the really important population shifts which are occurring. The Upper Region is absorbing less than its share of population increase, while the densely settled area of Southern Ghana is taking in considerably more than its share. In fact, this area, comprising less than a quarter of Ghana's extent, contained over three-fifths of Ghana's population by 1960. Almost $4\frac{1}{4}$ million people lived there at an average population density of above 200 persons per square mile. That population was being increasingly concentrated there was shown by the fact that, although it contained only 59 per cent of the country's population in 1948, it absorbed 68 per cent of the 1948–60 population increase.

Figure 2:4

GHANA: POPULATION DENSITY,

BY   LOCAL ADMINISTRATION AREAS, 1960

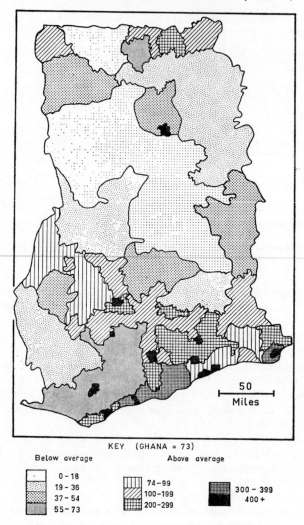

KEY   (GHANA = 73)

Below average   Above average

	0 - 18
	19 - 36
	37 - 54
	55 - 73

	74 - 99
	100 - 199
	200 - 299

| | 300 - 399 |
| | 400 + |

There are probably three reasons for this concentration. Firstly, the densely settled southern area has probably accounted for more than its share of the country's natural increase. As we have already seen, fertility levels are higher there. In addition, mortality rates are undoubtedly lower. Secondly, the developed areas of the south attract more immigrants from other countries. Thirdly, there is a net intake of migrants into the south from northern Ghana. This is partly a simple case of rural-urban migration, for most of the bigger towns are in the south. However, there is also movement to cocoa-farming and mining areas.

TABLE 2.23

POPULATION CONCENTRATION, 1948–60

	Densely settled Ghana*	Densely settled Southern Ghana*
	%	%
Proportion of total area of Ghana	27·0	23·1
Proportion of total population in 1948	70·9	58·9
Proportion of total population in 1960	70·5	62·6
Proportion of total 1948–60 population increase of Ghana absorbed	70·0	68·4

* See Figure 2.4.

There has been an even more marked disparity between the absorptive capacities of town and countryside. In 1948 only an eighth of the population lived in urban areas.[1] But two-fifths of the 1948–60 population increase went into such areas. In 1948 three-fifths of the population lived in centres with less than 1,000 inhabitants. But only half as much of the intercensal population increase was added to such areas. The towns, therefore, are absorbing a disproportionate amount of the population increase. However, they are not yet absorbing most of it, as now happens in many economically advanced countries. Even in the 1948–60 period, they took less than half of the population increase, but the fraction may never be below half again. Between the censuses, a quarter of the increase was accounted for by the Accra Capital District alone. Accra itself absorbed 20 per cent and Kumasi another 11 per cent.

Such is the general picture. The figures should be interpreted carefully. Some of the urban increase came from the natural growth of the urban population itself. Some of the rural population became town dwellers not by moving, but by remaining in their villages which meanwhile grew in population size past the minimum limit set for 'towns'. Such changes meant, of course, that they were indeed subject to a greater urban influence.

TABLE 2.24

ABSORPTION OF POPULATION INCREASE BY URBAN AND RURAL AREAS, 1948–60

	Size of Locality	
	Over 5,000 inhabitants	Over 1,000 inhabitants
Proportion of total population, 1948	13·0	40·8
Proportion of 1948–60 population increase absorbed	39·2	69·8
Proportion of total population, 1960	23·1	51·9

8. SUMMARY AND CONCLUSIONS

Population growth in recent years in Ghana has been very rapid, but it has not been as great as the 1948–60 average rate of 4·2 per cent per year indicated by a comparison of the 1948 and 1960 Censuses. The fault probably lay chiefly in underenumeration in the 1948 Census. The real figure was apparently a little over $3\frac{1}{2}$ per cent per annum. Almost three-quarters of the intercensal gain can be attributed to the natural increase of the population which was in Ghana in 1948, and a little over a quarter to immigrants who have arrived since.

[1] Urban areas were defined by the 1960 Census as localities with 5,000 or more inhabitants.

In the years immediately ahead, the rate of natural increase will probably be about 3·3 per cent per year and overall population growth will average somewhat over 3½ per cent per year depending on the net intake of immigrants. In 1965, the crude birth rate was probably 52 per thousand and nearly stationary, the crude death rate 19 per thousand and still falling, and the expectation of life at birth about 48 years and rising.

During her fertile span, the Ghanaian woman gives birth to an average of 7·3 children. This is amongst the highest levels of fertility ever recorded. There are differentials in fertility within the country. In Regional terms, Ashanti and Brong-Ahafo are about 15 per cent above the national average, while the Northern and Upper Regions are about 15 per cent below it. The main factor in reducing fertility in the north seems to be the separation of marriage partners during periods when the husbands migrate to the south. Fertility is also lower in the towns than in the rural areas by about 10 per cent. It is somewhat lower again in the biggest towns.

The drop in mortality since the end of the Second World War has led to an acceleration in population growth. So marked has been the fall in infant and child mortality, that there is a surge of population growing up. Thus between 1948 and 1960 child-dependency, which was already high, increased by about 13 per cent bringing further strains to the family and to the nation's educational programme.

Most of the extra increment which is being added so quickly to the population's size is being absorbed in the densely settled quarter of the country in the south, which took over two-thirds of the increase. Part of the explanation for this is rural-urban migration, for most of the big towns are to be found here. Two-fifths of the total population increase was absorbed by the towns, and seven-tenths of it by centres with more than a thousand inhabitants.

In the next decade Ghana will be concerned with four main demographic problems. The first is the very high birth rate, which has produced rapid natural increase, which in its turn will endanger the hard-won economic gains. The second is the high level of immigration, which aggravates the overall rate of population growth, but which, as will be seen in the next chapter, also has some compensating features. The third is the wave of youngsters, not eroded as much in number by mortality as any previous generation, who have been born during the last fifteen years, and who will soon be demanding an enlargement of employment and training facilities at a faster rate than ever before. The fourth is the fact that already probably over half of all population increase is being absorbed by the towns. There will consequently be a steep increase in the demand for town jobs, especially in the larger towns.

CHAPTER III

MIGRATION AND URBANIZATION

1. THE GENERAL PATTERN OF MIGRATION

For a predominantly agricultural population, enjoying only a low standard of living, the people of tropical Africa have always been surprisingly mobile. Their journeys have usually been based on economic necessity, but, at the same time, most of the travellers have enjoyed the movement and have often gone further than was strictly necessary. It is probable that in modern Ghana more money is spent on trips in *mammy lorries* than is necessary to maximize the financial return from these outlays. Sixty thousand Ghanaians earn their income by providing transport, and almost two-thirds of them work on the lorries. A further 11,500 people spend their working lives keeping vehicles in repair.

For much of Africa's history, movements of whole tribes caused the displacement of other weaker peoples. But the raising of frontiers controlled by central governments has stopped this, and only the folk memories linger. In the African savannah, nomadic pastoralism continues, but this is in arid country well to the north of Ghana.

The establishment of strong central government produced another type of migration. It guaranteed individual safety to an extent that men from one ethnic group could work amongst those of other ethnic groups in far away places where economic opportunities were better. Migration in modern Africa is similar to migration in present-day Europe in that it is mostly unorganized and is usually carried out for economic reasons.

Much migration in Africa has always been seasonal. In the more arid country north of the West African forest there is a dry season after the harvest when few productive activities can be carried out. This was once the time when gain could be hoped for only from intertribal warfare. It has subsequently become the time of seasonal migration, when many seek employment to the south in the cultivation of tree crops, or in the mines, or in the growing ports along the coast.

Migration from subsistence farming areas to places where cash incomes can be secured is not only a way of enlarging one's acquisitive power, but a way of opening that power to new fields. Subsistence farming products cannot usually be exchanged for manufactured goods such as bicycles or transistor radio sets or cloth or tins of sardines. There are few families left now in Ghana who do not feel the urgent need of some cash income.

There has been, at least until recently, little difference between internal and external migration. People migrate from northern Ghana to Kumasi or Accra for much the same reason as they do from Upper Volta. When they reach their destinations they have similar cultural and linguistic problems. The position is now changing. There is a greater sense of national identity and of the necessity of caring for nationals. No one will dispute the right of people from any part of Ghana to migrate to Accra. This is no longer always the case with people coming from beyond Ghana's borders. And, perhaps more importantly, foreign exchange problems and exchange controls mean that Ghanaians have undisputed rights to remit back any fraction of their earnings to their place of origin, while those from other countries have not.

It should not be thought that all migration is from savannah country or subsistence farmlands to places nearer the coast or that all migration is seasonal. Ghana is the richest land in tropical Africa in terms of average income per head. Southern Ghana is particularly well favoured and is an area where jobs have usually been fairly plentiful. It has attracted large numbers of people from other countries on the Gulf of Guinea coast, particularly from Togo and Nigeria. Most of these people come, not because there is no cash employment in their own areas, but because of the higher incomes which can be earned in Ghana. Such migrants tend to be longer-term settlers, although most hope to return home eventually. Even from northern Ghana and the savannah lands beyond, there have always been a substantial number of longer-term migrants. It is probable that in recent years their fraction of the whole movement from these areas has been increasing.

Migration has profoundly affected Ghana, and its extent is a reflection of the depth of the economic and social changes which have occurred during this century. It, in its turn, is an agent for further change.

At the time of the 1960 Census, two-fifths of the people of Ghana were living in localities other than their birth-places. Half of these had migrated either from another Region or another country. The majority of the inhabitants of the Accra Capital District had not been born there. On the whole, there was a direct relation between the attractive force that each Region exerted on people from other Regions and that which it exerted on foreign immigrants. This is clear from Table 3.1 and Figures 3.1 and 3.2. The combined figures for migrants from other Regions and other countries could almost be taken as an index of economic opportunity. The towns, cocoa-growing areas and mines are the great lures. The exceptions to the rule are the Volta Region and the Northern and Upper Regions. These

TABLE 3.1

POPULATION IN EACH LOCALITY ACCORDING TO BIRTH-PLACE, BY REGION, 1960
(All figures are in percentages)

Birthplace:	Same locality	Another locality in the same Region	Another Region	Another country
Region of enumeration				
Accra C.D.	48	6	30	16
Eastern	50	27	14	9
Western and Central	59	24	10	7
Ashanti	53	19	19	9
Brong-Ahafo	59	13	19	9
Volta	65	20	5	10
Northern	69	23	2	6
GHANA	59	21	12	8

Figure 3·1
GHANA : PERCENTAGE OF POPULATION
BORN IN ANOTHER REGION,
BY LOCAL ADMINISTRATION AREAS, 1960

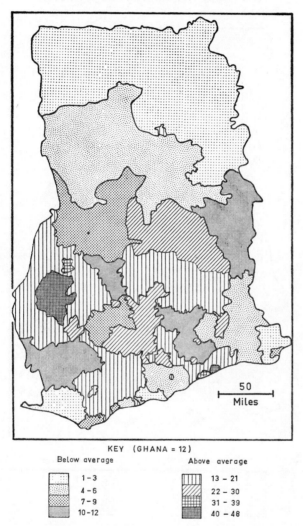

KEY (GHANA = 12)

Below average   Above average

	Below average			Above average
	1 – 3			13 – 21
	4 – 6			22 – 30
	7 – 9			31 – 39
	10 –12			40 – 48

areas attract few people from other parts of Ghana, but they do attract
substantial numbers of people from the countries immediately across the
border. Many Togolese, especially Ewes, are to be found in the Volta
Region, and many people from Upper Volta, especially Mossi, are found in
northern Ghana.

2. INTERNATIONAL MIGRATION
The flow of migrants across Ghana's borders has been much greater than
any census can indicate, for so much of it is short-term migration. It has
H

Figure 3·2
GHANA: PERCENTAGE OF POPULATION
BORN IN ANOTHER COUNTRY,
BY LOCAL ADMINISTRATION AREAS, 1960

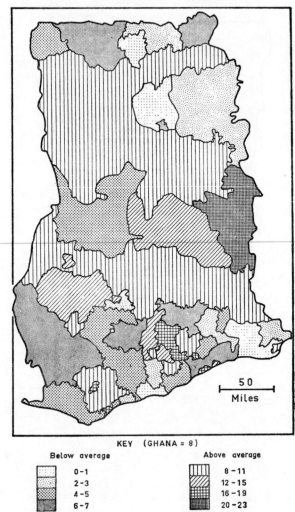

KEY   (GHANA = 8)

Below average		Above average	
	0 - 1		8 - 11
	2 - 3		12 - 15
	4 - 5		16 - 19
	6 - 7		20 - 23

been claimed that Ghana is one of the only two sub-Saharan countries where the annual flow in each direction has exceeded 300,000 persons.[1]

As already seen in Table 1.4, over four-fifths of the immigrants come from three countries, Togo, Upper Volta and Nigeria. The first two have common borders with Ghana. The explanation for the Nigerian stream is partly that Nigeria has a very big population, probably half that of West

[1] George H. T. Kimble, *Tropical Africa*, New York, 1960, Vol. I, p. 585, quoting Meredyth Hyde Clarke, 'The Labour Problem: Britain's Research into Human Relations', *The Times British Colonies Review*, London, Autumn 1954, p. 8.

Africa, and so will tend to loom large in the statistics even if its people have no greater penchant than those of other West African countries to migrate to Ghana. Part of the explanation lies also in the fact that Nigeria is the nearest ex-British colony to Ghana and from this common history stem various similarities in administration and official language which lead the potential migrant to feel that he will not be in a completely foreign environment.

Southern Ghana[1] is probably the only area on the West African coast where the main immigrant streams are no longer predominantly from the north. Immigration from countries found wholly in the savannah belt makes up little more than a quarter of Ghana's foreign immigration as shown by birthplace statistics. Immigration into southern Ghana from the savannah countries and Ghana's own north makes up only about half of the stream into southern Ghana. At the time of the 1960 Census, the population in southern Ghana which had not been born there consisted of 314,000 persons from coastal countries, 189,000 persons from the Northern and Upper Regions of Ghana, and 129,000 from countries of the interior. Thus, these three groups made up 50, 30 and 20 per cent respectively of the total of foreign and northern immigrants.

Togolese and Nigerian immigration into Ghana made up 57 per cent of all immigration recorded at the census in terms of foreign origin and 54 per cent in terms of foreign birth. Most of these migrants came not because they could not earn money in their own countries, but because they could earn more in Ghana. The migration is usually not seasonal and much of it is on a long-term basis. That it is a more settled form of migration than that from the savannah lands is shown by the fact that the sex ratio amongst foreign-born Togolese and Nigerians is only 121 and 149 males per hundred females respectively, while it is 280 amongst those born in Upper Volta. Similarly, the foreign-born Togolese and Nigerian communities have produced Ghanaian-born additions to their numbers equal to 59 per cent and 66 per cent of the size of the foreign-born community. In the case of the Upper Volta immigrants the proportion is 47 per cent. It might be noted that 93 per cent of the Togolese and 91 per cent of the Nigerian immigrants are to be found in southern Ghana.

Because it was felt that this type of migration would become relatively more common, a survey was made of migrants from southern Togo and southern Nigeria at present employed in Southern Ghana.[2] The sample sex ratio of those in employment closely approximated to the census findings. No similar test could be carried out on the age structure, as the census has not published figures on the foreign born by employment and age. In the following section, census findings will be used to analyse the position of immigrants in Ghana, and survey findings will be employed to extend this picture.

[1] For the purpose of this discussion, southern Ghana is defined as all Regions of Ghana except the Northern and Upper Regions.

[2] See Appendix. Population Council Programme, *International Migration Survey*. Eleven areas were selected in southern Ghana which the 1960 Census indicated to be especially attractive to foreign immigrants. Within these areas sampling techniques were used in May–July 1963, to carry out 634 interviews. The Togolese were restricted to Ewes from southern Togo, and the Nigerians to those born in the Western and Eastern Regions of Nigeria (this also includes what is now the new Mid-western Region).

When attempting to assess the effect of immigration on the country's economy, probably the most important characteristic of the foreign-born males is that they come to work. Thus most arrive after their rearing and training, if any, is complete. Many return home when old. Less than an eighth of those surveyed arrived in Ghana after 30 years of age.

TABLE 3.2

AGE OF MIGRANTS FROM NIGERIA AND TOGO AT FIRST ARRIVAL

Age:	Under 20	20–9	30–9	Over 40
Percentage of immigrants	43	45	10	2

Source: *International Migration Survey*, 1963 (unpublished).

This pattern of arrival and departure means that the foreign born are concentrated in the main working age groups, as is shown in Table 3.3. The foreign born, aged 15–54 years, form 77 per cent of all foreign born compared with 49 per cent which that age-group represents of the whole population and with 46 per cent among the native born. The foreign born make up a sixth of all males from 15 to 54 years of age.

TABLE 3.3

PERCENTAGE FORMED OF ALL POPULATION BY THE FOREIGN BORN IN EACH AGE GROUP BY SEX, 1960

Age group:	0–4	5–14	15–24	25–54	Over 55
Males	2	3	12	19	13
Females	2	4	8	10	6

Source: 1960 Census.

These figures are reflected in those of employment. The foreign born over 15 years of age and in employment make up 61 per cent of the foreign-born community, while the native born over 15 years and in employment make up only 36 per cent of the native-born community.

TABLE 3.4

PERCENTAGE FORMED BY THOSE OVER 15 YEARS OF AGE AND IN EMPLOYMENT OF THOSE OF ALL AGES, BY BIRTH-PLACE AND SEX, 1960

	Males	Females	Both sexes
Foreign born	78	33	61
Native born	43	30	36

Source: 1960 Census.

If this were the whole story, the economic case for unlimited immigration would be overwhelming. But it is not. For instance, Table 3.3 might seem to imply that older migrants return home in great numbers, and suggests that, if we had figures for the over 65 or over 75 years of age groups, there would be very few immigrants indeed of that age. This is not the case.[1] The decline with age merely means that massive immigration is only a recent phenomenon. This is supported by the fact that the 1948 Census enumerated only a third as many foreign born as did the 1960 Census.

[1] Indeed figures which became available after the writing of this section showed that in the population 65 years of age and over, the foreign born formed 13 per cent of males and 5 per cent of females.

Much more important is the fact that the foreign born do swell the unproductive population by giving birth to children in Ghana. These children are hidden as native born in the census statistics, but are shown together with their parents in the statistics of 'foreign origin'. This by no means wholly nullifies the implications of the above Tables for two reasons. Firstly, the disproportionate adult sex ratio, which is 189 males per hundred females in the 15–54 years of age range, together with the difficulty of achieving cross-ethnic marriages, means that a great number of immigrant males do not father children in Ghana. Secondly, between 1948 and 1960 new immigrants were arriving so rapidly that the numbers of newcomers outnumbered the older, settled, immigrant families with considerable numbers of locally born children.

Among the native born of foreign origin 73 per cent are under 15 years of age. The proportion of all persons of foreign origin between 15 and 54 years of age is 59 per cent, thus making that community about one-fifth again more economically efficient in terms of age than those of Ghanaian origin. New data also allow comparisons of the more conventional labour force age range, 15–64 years. Of those of foreign origin $62 \cdot 3$ per cent are of this age compared with $50 \cdot 9$ per cent of persons of Ghanaian origin. Thus those of foreign origin have an age structure that is about $22\frac{1}{2}$ per cent more economically efficient.

The Survey of 1963 gave support to the belief that net immigration has not recently been increasing at the rate that it did from 1948 to 1960. Only 21 per cent of those interviewed had been in Ghana less than 5 years, 25 per cent stated between 5 and 10 years, leaving just over half who claimed to have arrived before mid-1953.

The Survey yielded some interesting information on the process of migration. Only 4 per cent of the immigrants claimed to have come from large towns like Lagos, Ibadan and Lomé. The fact that another 27 per cent came from towns of some size is mainly a reflection of the large number of Yoruba migrants, who come from one of the most urbanized areas of the tropics. But even so, 69 per cent of the migrants came from rural villages, and for many their migration was in reality a form of rural-urban migration. When the time came to seek employment in the town, they decided that the move might just as well be made to a Ghanaian town as to one of their own country.

On reaching Ghana, 86 per cent went first to the towns, 4 per cent went to the mines, and 10 per cent to the cocoa-growing areas. Of those who went to the towns, almost two-thirds stopped first at Accra, which lies directly on the main coastal route from the east. Over a sixth went to Kumasi or Takoradi. In many cases the towns were the obvious stopping points *en route* to new employment. Probably no more than a third of all migrants to Ghana have remained in the towns, although almost certainly the proportion doing so has been climbing steeply in recent years.

Four-fifths of all the migrants made the original journey to Ghana on their own. Of those who did not, 58 per cent brought their wives, and half of these brought children as well. Most of the rest brought brothers or nephews. Of those who arrived alone, half have since sent for relatives. Ultimately, 42 per cent brought wives to Ghana, although others have married within their own ethnic group in the country. An eighth brought children, but over a sixth brought brothers or sisters, and others helped nephews, nieces or parents to come.

The complete marital situation of the male immigrants is that 42 per cent arranged to bring a wife from their home country, 26 per cent married in Ghana, 6 per cent have a wife only in their home country, and 26 per cent have remained unmarried. In some cases 'wives' may be read instead of 'wife'. In fact 4 per cent of those with wives in Ghana also had wives in their own country. Those who married in Ghana did not necessarily marry outside their own ethnic group. Some probably married women from their own area who had come separately and some may have married the native-born daughters of immigrants. In the case of Ewes, there is a large Ewe area in Ghana adjoining that of Togo.

The number of immigrants with children was almost the same as the number married. Of these 73 per cent had children only in Ghana, 8 per cent only in their home country, and 19 per cent in both.

It is clear that immigration has reduced the male migrants' chances of marrying. But, where marriage has taken place, most have married women from their home area, and most now have all their immediate family with them in Ghana.

This does not necessarily mean that a stable immigrant community is being formed. Most immigrants intend to return ultimately to their home country. Only one immigrant in every eighteen surveyed intended to live his life out in Ghana. However, the large number of old migrants recorded by the census suggests that perhaps a majority fail to return home. The reason may be that personal ties, especially with their own children born in the country, have multiplied, or it may be that the return journey is too expensive. Thus, although most immigrants feel that they should go back to their homelands for periodic visits, the majority of Nigerian immigrants have never managed to make a single return visit.

The Survey also provided information on the motivation of the migration and on the degree of success in achieving the desired goals. On the whole the migrants seem to have been above average in education in terms of their home districts. That it is those who have enjoyed some schooling who tend to migrate from rural areas was found in the *Rural-Urban Migration Survey of Ghana* and this situation is probably general in West Africa. In fact the immigrants from southern Nigeria and Togo do not appear to be below Ghanaian standards in education, but this certainly would not be the case with migrants from the savannah countries.[1]

Over an eighth of the foreign born studied in the Survey were brought by older relatives or husbands. Of the remainder, four-fifths arrived unequivocally in search of a job and more money. About one in twelve maintained that their chief motive was the spirit of adventure and a desire to see the world.

[1] This finding can now be supported by the new material published in Census Volume III. Of the population over six years of age, 22 per cent of Ghanaians have had some schooling. The figures for Nigerians and Togolese are 22 per cent and 16 per cent respectively. The Togolese figures, like the Nigerian ones, are for the whole country. The proportion of immigrants with some schooling would rise if the examination were confined to the southern parts of the countries because it is from there that most migrants to Ghana come. Amongst those of Nigerian origin but Ghanaian birth, 44 per cent had experienced some schooling.

Even after the passage of some years, almost half of the immigrants listed the abundance of jobs and the better wages as being the most important of Ghana's virtues. By this time about a sixth of the immigrants were homesick to the point where they could see very little to praise about life in the country.

On the other hand, over a fifth of all immigrants had no complaints at all. Of those who did have grievances, almost a third named the difficulty in remitting earnings from Ghana. This is understandable in view of the fact that 78 per cent of the immigrants claimed that they still had financial responsibilities to relatives in their home countries. Most said they had responsibilities towards several people and well over half named both parents and brothers or sisters.

To the simple query as to whether they were now happier in Ghana than they would be in their home country, about half the immigrants said 'yes', and half 'no'. The contented ones gave as their reasons the abundance of employment and the establishment of a settled family life in Ghana. The discontented ones pointed to the insecurity that a migrant African feels about both his job and his everyday life in a foreign land, or said in some way that they were homesick, or again complained of the foreign exchange controls. Almost four-fifths of immigrants agreed that immigrants never really settle down completely and feel absolutely secure in a foreign land.

About half the immigrants felt that Ghanaians liked Togolese and Nigerians. Those who thought otherwise usually quoted the type of complaint made in many parts of the world about money-seeking and somewhat insecure immigrants. They were 'greedy', 'too ambitious', 'too worldly-wise', 'too self-assured and confident' and 'too argumentative'. Some felt that they were accused of unpleasant personal habits. Others, but not as many as one might have supposed, felt that there was some bitterness over job competition.

The problem of immigration from other West African countries is a complex and important matter. The government may be led to make fundamental policy decisions in this field.

The problem is perhaps primarily an economic one. The very fact that Ghana already contains many ethnic groups speaking many languages makes the social acceptance of other African people easier. As seen above, only half of the immigrants surveyed felt that their presence was resented. This is a surprisingly small fraction in an immigrant community, whose members, like those of similar communities elsewhere in the world, are very sensitive to indications of rejection. In the *Survey of Population Attitudes in Economically Superior Urban Areas* only two-fifths of the Ghanaians interviewed preferred a smaller proportion of immigrants in the community than that now found, one-fifth favoured the present situation, and two-fifths were quite happy to see the proportion increase. These are hardly the viewpoints of a community riddled with xenophobia. Furthermore, the implications of pan-Africanism would seem to demand the freest possible movement of Africans across the continent's internal borders. It might appear to some as odd to see that flow hindered more by the new independent countries than by the old colonial powers.

But the new independent countries have problems of economic policy that the old colonial powers never had to face. The most fundamental difference is the acceleration in population growth with the revolution in mortality rates. In the years immediately ahead the population would increase by about $3\frac{1}{4}$ per cent per year even if there were no immigration. The inflow of population from outside the country could take the rate to well over $3\frac{3}{4}$ per cent.

Rapid population growth is a factor of formidable magnitude in affecting the success of economic plans to increase the standard of living. Such growth means that a large fraction of the money available for investment cannot be used for increasing production but must be employed for multiplying such social capital as houses, schools, town streets and the like to accommodate the extra population. It also means that substantially greater production of goods is needed just to maintain the average consumption per person.

In these circumstances the government might feel it should examine the possibility of reducing the immigrant flow. It is the one component of the population growth that could easily be lowered by official action. Furthermore, if any action must be taken, such action would be attractive on the grounds that it would reduce the relative size of that part of the community which is considered as yet less identified with Ghana.

However, the economic argument for action of this type is debatable. It would not yield such certain economic benefits as a substantial fall in the birth rate. The reason for this is that a disproportionately big fraction of the immigrant community works. Therefore, it may increase production by more than it removes in terms of the need for extra social capital.

In addition, much of this work is done within the modern, cash economy of southern Ghana. Immigrant labour in Africa, as in other parts of the world, is often prepared to work hard, especially in tasks not much favoured by the local population. The immigrant contribution may prove to be critical in the industrialization process and particularly in those tasks in heavy industry for which the tropical climate may prove to be rather inhospitable. In many countries of the world immigrants, driven by feelings of insecurity or a desire for greater earnings than they have previously been able to obtain, are prepared to work much harder than the native-born population. Most of the immigrants, themselves, have little doubt on this point. Over four-fifths of those interviewed claimed that immigrants in Ghana do work harder and most gave reasons similar to those we have suggested above.

Migrants, however, also create economic problems. The most difficult is that of foreign exchange. African migrants will long continue to have responsibilities to relatives left behind, and will usually have a strong desire and obligation to send some of their earnings back. This could generally be allowed by a colonial power, whose exchange problems could be dealt with in terms of a whole empire. It is an entirely different matter for a small, independent country. In tropical Africa, Ghana faces an unusually severe problem, because her relatively high standard of living has attracted an exceptionally large number of immigrants. For instance, if all the foreign born wished to remit £4 per month, the drain on foreign exchange would be about £32 million per year, which would reduce the country's ability to import by about a quarter.

Immigrants create another problem, which, paradoxically, is closely related to their possible potential for accelerating the industrialization of the country. They inevitably seek employment in the modern sector of the economy and especially in the towns. While according to the 1960 Census, only 8 per cent of the population of the whole country was foreign born, that category in Accra, Tema, Takoradi and Kumasi formed 17, 15, 16 and 12 per cent respectively of the total population. If enough urban employment can be provided, the large amount of immigrant labour being offered is economically all to the good. But, in the near future, the employment market is going to be taxed by the unusually large numbers of young people needing jobs. The position will probably be especially acute in the towns, not only because rural-urban migration is in general increasing, but also because, as has been seen, such migration is a particular characteristic of the young adult. The coming of age of all these young people will undoubtedly bring many of them into the towns.

These problems are not all insoluble, nor should they be seen in absolute terms. There is little doubt that foreign exchange controls will have to be maintained. This, in itself, will lessen the inflow of immigrants, because, unless some of the earnings can be sent back home, the whole point of the migration is, for many of the migrants, lost. Almost certainly the flow is already slackening, and almost certainly the problem of remittances is the main reason. Foreigners in Ghana do have the right to remit some of their earnings, but, for most of the poorer African immigrants, the processes involved are either not understood or are too complex to be manageable.

It is not unlikely that the flow of immigrants will be restricted without being prohibited. Probably, stricter watch will be kept over formal requirements for entry, such as entry permits or work permits or whatever may be decided upon. Undoubtedly, a considerable flow of illegal migration will exist side by side with that legally permitted, for Ghana's land borders are long and parts are difficult to police.

If the energy and willingness to work harder even in unpopular tasks is required, this will almost certainly be met for some time by migration from northern Ghana. In terms of training, the quality of these migrants will improve as the plans for providing more schooling in the north achieve success. The crowded areas of the Upper Region may eventually serve as a pool of labour for labour-hungry industries in the south, much as southern Italy today serves the factories of that country's north.

3. INTERNAL MIGRATION

At the time of the 1960 Census, about an eighth of the people enumerated in Ghana were of foreign origin and another eighth were from a Region other than the one in which they were enumerated. The census did not distinguish between seasonal and longer-term movement, but it did provide a picture of population movement at a specific point in time. Furthermore, it did so at a time when seasonal movement should have been of no great volume.

In Table 3.5 and Figure 3.3, census data on inter-Regional migration have been analysed. The Regions are large enough to ensure that most of the movement recorded is over substantial distances and that a real change in the migrants' way of life is almost inevitable. As birth-place data are employed, the flows are measured in terms of movement since birth. For this reason, it is not possible to distinguish between old flows, which are now waning, and new flows, which are still waxing.

TABLE 3.5

FLOW OF PERSONS SINCE BIRTH BETWEEN REGIONS, AS SHOWN BY 1960 CENSUS

(a) *Emigration of those born in each Region to other Regions*

Region of birth	Emigration (thousands)	Emigration as percentage of all inter-Regional migration	Emigration as percentage of all enumerated as born in the Region	Main Regions to which migrants go*
Accra C.D.	59	7	18	—
Eastern	176	21	17	*Accra, Ashanti,* Western and Central
Western and Central	138	17	11	Ashanti, Eastern, Accra
Ashanti	109	13	12	Brong-Ahafo
Brong-Ahafo	24	3	6	—
Volta	136	16	17	*Eastern,* Accra
Northern and Upper	189	23	14	*Ashanti,* Brong-Ahafo, Western and Central

(b) *Immigration into each Region of those born in other Regions*

Region of immigration	Immigration (thousands)	Immigration as percentage of all inter-Regional migration	Immigration as percentage of all native born enumerated in Region in 1960	Main Regions from which immigrants come*
Accra C.D.	149	18	36	*Eastern,* Western and Central, Volta
Eastern	158	19	16	*Volta,* Western and Central
Western and Central	137	16	11	Eastern, Northern and Upper
Ashanti	205	25	20	*Northern and Upper,* Western and Central, Eastern
Brong-Ahafo	109	13	21	Ashanti, Northern and Upper
Volta	41	5	6	—
Northern and Upper	32	4	3	—

(c) *Net inter-Regional flow of native born*

Region	Ratio of immigrational and emigrational flows†	Net migration‡ (thousands)
Accra C.D.	+2·53	+ 90
Eastern	−1·12	− 19
Western and Central	−1·01	− 1
Ashanti	+1·89	+ 97
Brong-Ahafo	+4·48	+ 85
Volta	−3·29	− 95
Northern and Upper	−5·88	−157

* Only migration flows of more than 30,000 persons shown; those of more than 50,000 in italic.
† Ratio of biggest to smallest flow; immigration shown positive, emigration negative.
‡ Immigration shown positive, emigration negative.

Figure 3·3
GHANA : INTERREGIONAL MIGRATION FLOWS
IN EXCESS OF 30,000 PERSONS
(Measured by movement since birth)

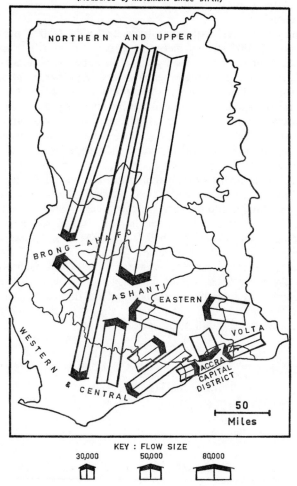

About 831,000 native-born Ghanaians are living outside their Regions of birth. Twelve flows between Regions have contained more than 30,000 persons, and, of these, ten are between adjoining Regions. That Ghanaians are mobile in all parts of the country is shown by the fact that over a tenth of those born in any Region except Brong-Ahafo were enumerated in another Region. Similarly all Regions number immigrants from other Regions as more than a tenth of their population except the Volta Region and the Northern and Upper Regions.

The net inter-Regional flows indicate clearly the Regions of high and low economic opportunity. Accra, Ashanti and Brong-Ahafo have between them attracted more of the native-born than they have lost through emigration. On the other hand, the Northern and Upper Regions and the

Volta Region have shown a net loss of over a quarter of a million persons. Brong-Ahafo's favoured position is shown by the fact that four and a half times as many people have arrived as locally born people have left. At the other end of the scale is the north where almost six times as many have left as have come.

Only three inter-Regional flows have exceeded 50,000 persons. The largest, almost 70,000 strong, has moved from the Northern and Upper Regions into Ashanti. The second greatest, numbering almost 60,000, has moved from the Eastern Region into Accra. Another, containing over 50,000 persons, and probably less strong now than a generation ago, has proceeded from the Volta Region to the Eastern Region.

A further examination of Figure 3.1, where the location of inter-Regional migrants is shown by Local Authority Areas, reveals more specifically that the main emigrant areas are the entire north, except for Tamale, the Volta Region, except for the Buem-Krachi area in the north, and the coast, except for the main towns and the area around Accra. The most important immigrant areas were Accra and Tema, Kumasi, the new cocoa areas of western Brong-Ahafo, and the thriving cocoa areas extending from east of Kumasi to Akim. Some immigration has also taken place to the food-growing areas in the transitional belt from forest to savannah woodland around Atebubu in Brong-Ahafo East.

In Table 3.6, the sex ratios of the emigrants from each Region are examined. Those of southern Ghana vary from 109 to 126 males per hundred females. The northern ratio is of quite a different order. Of those born in the Northern and Upper Regions, almost twice as many males as females are now to be found in other Regions.

TABLE 3.6

SEX RATIOS OF NATIVE-BORN FOUND OUTSIDE THEIR REGION OF BIRTH, BY REGION OF BIRTH, 1960

(Males per hundred females)

Region of birth	Sex ratio
Accra C.D.	109
Eastern	111
Western and Central	125
Ashanti	126
Brong-Ahafo	114
Volta	118
Northern and Upper	196

Most inter-Regional migrants, like migrants from foreign countries, make their first move as young adults. Table 3.7 seems to suggest that most return to their home Regions when they grow old. This may not be as clearly the case as is suggested by the Table. That more of the young are found outside their home Regions can be the result of an increase in such migration. Almost a quarter of adult males in the main labour force age range are found outside their home Region. In the case of those from the north the proportion is around 30 per cent. There is some suggestion that, relative to the number of male migrants, female migration may be on the increase. In the older age groups female migrants number only about half as many as do male migrants. However, in the 15–24 years of age group, the fraction is about three-quarters.

TABLE 3.7

PERCENTAGE OF NATIVE-BORN FOUND OUTSIDE THEIR REGION OF BIRTH, BY AGE AND SEX, 1960

Region of birth	Sex	*Age groups (in years)*				
		0–4	*5–14*	*15–24*	*25–54*	*Over 55*
All Regions	male	7	10	23	24	12
	female	7	12	17	13	7
Northern and Upper Regions	male	4	6	30	29	13

Source: 1960 Population Census.

4. URBANIZATION AND RURAL-URBAN MIGRATION

Although much of the population movement in Ghana is still directed to the cocoa farms and the gold mines, the towns have become an increasingly important destination for both internal and external migrants.

The population of the towns is quite distinctive, partly because of the nature of urban life and partly because urban areas exert a selective attraction upon rural peoples. We have seen in earlier chapters that a much bigger proportion of town people have been to school than is the case in the villages. On the average more residents are found in each house in the towns. In the towns, too, more people are unemployed, or at least more regard this as their condition.

For the rural-urban migrants the most important difference between town and village is probably that most of the employment available to those who live in the former is non-agricultural. Table 3.8 shows that in terms of change in the occupational pattern with change in the population of the settlement, there is almost a perfect continuum from the smallest villages to the largest towns. Moving from centres with fewer than 200 inhabitants to those with more than 100,000, the proportion that the agricultural work force makes up of all those in employment drops from 88 per

TABLE 3.8

PERCENTAGE OF WORK FORCE EMPLOYED IN DIFFERENT INDUSTRIES, BY SIZE OF LOCALITY, 1960

Industry

Size of locality (Number of inhabitants)	Agriculture, fishing, etc.	Mining, quarrying	Manufacturing	Construction and provision of electricity water, sewerage facilities	Commerce	Transport, etc.	Services
Under 200	88	1	4	1	4	1	1
200–499	81	1	6	2	7	1	2
500–999	76	1	7	2	9	2	3
1,000–1,999	69	2	9	3	11	2	4
2,000–4,999	56	3	11	4	17	3	6
5,000–9,999	41	2	13	6	26	4	8
10,000–19,999	22	7	15	11	28	5	12
20,000–49,999	12	5	15	9	31	11	17
Over 100,000	4	0	16	12	37	7	24
All localities	62	2	9	4	14	3	6

Source: 1960 Population Census.

cent to 4 per cent. But it is only in centres with more than 5,000 inhabitants that less than half the work force is employed in agriculture.

As agricultural employment drops, more labour is available for other industries. As yet, the towns of Ghana are chiefly commercial and service centres rather than the seats of large-scale manufacturing industry. In the largest centres, over half the work force is employed in these two categories. The great majority of those engaged in commerce are petty traders, while most of those in services are governmental administrative, clerical, educational or medical officers. In the largest towns, a sixth of the work force is employed in manufacturing, although almost half of these are engaged in small-scale textile activities. The mining industry has given rise to a considerable number of medium-sized towns but to none with over 100,000 inhabitants.

The differences in employment structure between localities of various size are largely a reflection of the total amount of non-agricultural work available. In Table 3.9, which examines employment in terms of occupation, it can be seen that non-agricultural employment in the towns is apportioned along lines surprisingly similar to those obtaining in the villages. In each, just over a third of the non-agricultural work force provides retailing services, and a slightly larger number supply skilled or unskilled labour.

TABLE 3.9

PERCENTAGE OF WORK FORCE ENGAGED IN DIFFERENT OCCUPATIONS, BY URBAN-RURAL DIVISION, 1960

Occupation	Percentage of total work force		Percentage of non-agricultural work force	
	urban	rural	urban	rural
Farmers, fishermen, etc.	18·2	74·0	—	—
Craftsmen, production process workers, labourers	29·2	11·3	36	43
Professional, technical and related workers	4·3	1·7	5	7
Administrative, executive and managerial workers	1·5	0·2	2	1
Clerical workers	5·3	0·6	6	2
Sales workers	28·2	9·0	35	35
Transport and communication workers	5·2	1·1	6	4
Miners and quarrymen	2·0	1·2	2	5
Services, sport and recreation workers	6·1	0·9	8	3

Source: 1960 Population Census.

Urban and rural Ghana also differ in sex and age structure as Figure 3.4 shows. This arises largely from the higher proportion of males and of persons within specific age ranges in migration streams. One would gather from Table 3.10 that there are two *occupational frontiers* in Ghana. One is the large towns, especially those with more than 100,000 inhabitants, which contain about one-seventh more males than females. The other seems to be the very smallest kind of village. In some cases these are undoubtedly outposts where forest is being cleared for such purposes as cocoa farming.

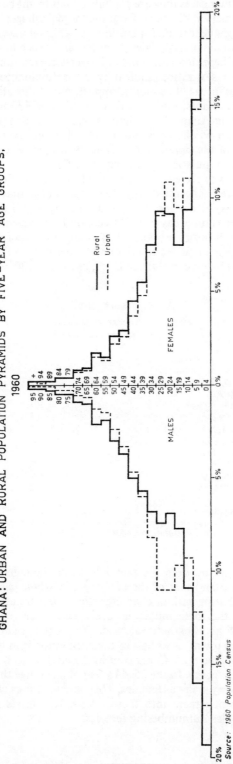

Figure 3:4

GHANA: URBAN AND RURAL POPULATION PYRAMIDS BY FIVE-YEAR AGE GROUPS, 1960

Source: 1960 Population Census

However, in other cases they are probably what might be termed subsidiary peripheral hamlets at distances from the 'home' villages. In them, villagers work for periods near to their plantings or other interests, and usually they contain a predominance of males. In other places such localities are migrant communities where either seasonal or longer-term migrants are to be found. Certainly, high sex ratios, indicating a predominance of males, are a characteristic of areas of economic opportunity. In localities with less than a hundred inhabitants, the sex ratios are 134 and 130 males per hundred females in Brong-Ahafo and Ashanti respectively, compared with 115 for the country as a whole. In Brong-Ahafo, the rural *boom* area of Ghana, 12·2 per cent of the population lives in such hamlets compared with 8·4 per cent of the population of the whole of Ghana.

The sex ratios of the employed population vary in the same fashion but in a much more exaggerated way. It would appear that economic opportunities for females do not increase as rapidly as do those for males in either urban or rural areas of rapid economic expansion.

Similarly, an unusual proportion of young adults is found in the towns. In Ghana's urban areas are to be found 23 per cent of the population. But 28 per cent of 15–24-year-olds are there, as are over 30 per cent of males of that age.

TABLE 3.10

SEX RATIOS, BY SIZE OF LOCALITY, 1960
(males per hundred females)

Size of locality (number of inhabitants)	Sex ratio total population	employed population
Under 100	115 ⎱	194
100–199	103 ⎰	
200–499	101	156
500–999	98	151
1,000–1,999	98	144
2,000–4,999	99	137
5,000–9,999	98	128
10,000–19,999	104	176
20,000–49,999	106	194
Over 100,000	114	206
All localities	102	159

Source: 1960 Population Census.

The differences between the populations of the chief focuses of rural-urban migration and that of the country as a whole can perhaps best be shown by comparing various characteristics of the population of all Ghana with those of the three municipal areas with over 100,000 inhabitants, Accra, Kumasi and Sekondi-Takoradi. This has been done in Table 3.11.

In these large towns, over half of the population is in the 15–44 years of age range compared with 43 per cent in the country as a whole. Sex ratios are well above average. In the 25–44 years of age range there are one and a half times as many males as females. These are measures of the composition of the immigrant stream into these towns. It consists mostly of young adults, with males outnumbering females.

The large towns draw people from afar and, as a result, have a rather cosmopolitan atmosphere. In the whole country one-fifth of the population comes from a Region or country other than that where it was enumerated in 1960. In each of the towns, the proportion is over twice as great, and, in fact, approaches half.

In the big towns, three-fifths of the children are at school, compared with a national figure of two-fifths. This is not merely a result of the location of these towns, for their levels of education are quite clearly above those of

TABLE 3.11

COMPARISON OF CHARACTERISTICS OF THE POPULATION OF GHANA AND THAT OF THE THREE LARGEST TOWNS, 1960
(All figures shown as percentages)

	GHANA	Accra*	Kumasi*	Sekondi-Takoradi*
Age groups (as proportion of all population):				
0–14	45	39	42	40
15–24	17	22	23	21
25–44	26	29	28	30
45–64	9	8	6	8
65+	3	2	1	1
Sex ratios:				
All population	102	114	112	117
25–44 years of age range	101	152	143	152
Birthplace (as proportion of all population):				
Same Region	80	51	58	66
Another Region	12	32	30	18
Another country	8	17	12	16
Schooling (as proportion of all in age group):				
(a) 6–14 years of age:				
never	56	31	41	38
past	4	3	4	2
present	40	66	56	60
(b) 15+ years of age:				
never	80	52	62	58
past	16	41	32	36
present	4	7	6	6
Economic activity:				
(a) (as proportion of all over 15 years of age):				
unemployed	4	10	8	9
employed	69	63	69	65
employed in agriculture	62	3	7	7
(b) (as proportion of females over 15 years of age):				
females fully occupied with home duties	37	32	32	41

* Municipal Area.
Source: 1960 Population Census.

I

the surrounding areas. Three factors are probably involved. The first is more plentiful educational facilities in the towns, the second is an above average capacity of the residents there either to meet the extra schooling costs or at least to allow the total or partial withdrawal of their children from economic activity, and the third is the greater need for education in order to obtain urban employment.

This educational differential is no new thing. Over twice the proportion of adults have been to school in these towns as in the country as a whole. Part of the reason is that the margin between schooling in urban and rural areas has been even greater in the past than it is now. However, another factor is also important. The towns attract an undue proportion of the educated from the countryside, because those who have been to school have more chance of acquiring good urban jobs than those who have not.

The occupational figures of the towns are much as the previous discussion would lead us to suspect. There is little agricultural employment and un-employment is relatively great. In Accra and Kumasi proportionately somewhat fewer adult women seem to be withdrawn from the work force on the grounds of home duties than is the case in the rest of the country. This may not in fact be so. In rural areas, where census-takers often have difficulty in deciding whether women do actively participate in agriculture or not, it would appear that there may have been an understatement of the proportion of females who actually play some active role in agriculture.

Not only is the population of Ghana growing rapidly, but the urban population is increasing at an even faster rate. According to the census enumerations, the total population rose by almost two-thirds between 1948 and 1960. At the same time it can be estimated that the urban population trebled in numbers and that of many of the larger towns was multiplied by two and a half. By 1960, Kumasi alone contained as many people as all the urban areas did forty years earlier.

In many parts of the developing world, the years of rapid population increase since the Second World War have witnessed a remarkable urban *explosion*. There is no parallel in such a short period at any time in the history of Western countries. Up to the present Ghana has experienced this change possibly to a greater degree than most tropical African countries.

As shown in Table 3.12, the proportion of the population living in towns with more than 5,000 inhabitants almost doubled in the twenty-seven years between 1921 and 1948, and almost doubled again in the twelve years from 1948 to 1960. During the thirty-nine years from 1921 to 1960, the number of people living in urban areas multiplied almost nine times.

By no means all this extra urban population poured into towns which already had more than 5,000 inhabitants at the beginning of the period under examination. Some remained in the same centres as these grew from villages to towns. Their ways of life have probably not changed as much as would have resulted from migration to a distant city. However, there has undoubtedly been change of the same type, if not the same order, in their milieu, arising directly out of the growth of their localities of residence. Those influences which we regard as urban have certainly strengthened.

The rate of growth of urban population has been far above that of rural population for almost half a century. By the 1948–60 period, the average annual rate of growth of the town population was three times that of the

TABLE 3.12

URBANIZATION, 1921–60

	1921†	1948	1960
Urban population* (thousands)	181‡	538	1,551
Total population (thousands)	2,296	4,118	6,727
Percentage of population in urban areas	7·9	13·0	23·1

* Population in centres with more than 5,000 inhabitants.
† African population only.
‡ Certain peculiarities of the presentation of the census statistics, especially in the northern Territories, affect the interpretation of the data.

rest of the population. The result of this was seen in the previous chapter. The towns, although containing only an eighth of the population in 1948, absorbed two-fifths of the intercensal population increase. The real figure may have been even higher, for underenumeration in 1948 may well have been greater in rural areas than in urban ones.

TABLE 3.13

RATE OF GROWTH OF URBAN AND RURAL POPULATION, 1921–60*

	1921–48	1948–60
	%	%
Average annual rate of growth:		
urban population	4·1	9·2
rural population	0·7	3·1
Proportion absorbed of total population growth in period:		
urban population	37	39
rural population	63	61

* Assuming all Census enumerations to be correct.

The effect of rural-urban migration and of the increase in size of many localities between 1948 and 1960 on the pattern of population distribution by locality size is interesting. The population living in small villages with between 100 and 999 inhabitants fell from 51·6 to 39·7 per cent. The proportion in towns with more than 5,000 inhabitants almost doubled, while that in towns of over 10,000 inhabitants did double. Probably, this pattern will persist. More people will live in the bigger towns, fewer will live in the smaller villages. With rapid population growth, a great number of the present small villages will probably become large villages and later small towns at a faster rate than new villages are formed.

However, there is certainly no sign as yet of the depopulation of rural Ghana. Accepting the censuses as they stand, the growth of rural population between 1948 and 1960 averaged over 3 per cent per year. The real rate was almost certainly not much less than $2\frac{1}{2}$ per cent. This is such a high rate that the expansion of cultivation must have difficulty in paralleling it and is certainly a major explanation for the flow of population from the country to the towns.

TABLE 3.14

POPULATION BY SIZE OF LOCALITY, 1948 AND 1960

Locality size	Percentage of total population		
(number of inhabitants)	1948	1960	Difference
Under 100	7·7	8·4	+0·7
100–199	10·3	7·6	−2·7
200–499	22·1	16·5	−5·6
500–999	19·1	15·6	−3·5
1,000–1,999	15·2	15·7	+0·5
2,000–4,999	12·6	13·1	+0·5
5,000–9,999	4·5	6·1	+1·6
10,000–19,999	2·5	5·4	+2·9
20,000–49,999	1·1	3·9	+2·8
50,000–99,999	1·7	—	−1·7
100,000 and over	3·2	7·7	+4·5

Source: 1960 Population Census.

The growth of urban population between 1948 and 1960 produced no major change in the Regional balance of urbanization within the country. However, two of the three least urbanized Regions, Brong-Ahafo and the Volta Region, improved their position relatively, largely at the expense of the Central and Western Region. This was not so in northern Ghana. In 1948, 7·8 per cent of the urban population was found there, while by 1960 the proportion had dropped to 6·6 per cent. The Accra Capital District alone absorbed a quarter of the entire intercensal population increase. It might be noted that Accra serves the function of the large regional town for much of the Eastern Region, and, for this reason, the Eastern Region could not in 1960 be regarded as less urbanized than the Central and Western Regions or Ashanti.

In 1960, urban Ghana could still be largely equated with the Accra Capital District, and the Eastern, Ashanti, Central and Western Regions. In 1960, 61 per cent of the people of Ghana were to be found in these Regions. But they contained 82 per cent of the urban population at that date, and in 1948 had contained 87 per cent.

TABLE 3.15

URBANIZATION BY REGION, 1948 AND 1960

Region	Urban population as percentage of Region's population		Percentage of total urban population of Ghana		1948–60 urban population increase as percentage of total urban population increase in Ghana
	1948	1960	1948	1960	
Accra C.D.	63	80	26	25	25
Eastern	10	20	12	14	15
Central and Western	20	27	33	23	19
Ashanti	14	25	16	18	19
Brong-Ahafo	2	16	1	6	8
Volta	5	13	4	7	8
Northern and Upper	4	8	8	7	6
GHANA	13	23	100	100	100

To sum up, one of the most significant and portentous developments in the contemporary history of Ghana is the swelling of the town populations. The large towns are becoming an ever more important segment of the nation's life. The most important factor in this growth has been the stream of migrants pouring from the villages into the larger towns. Whilst a few years ago it might well have been asked whether the urban population was great enough to allow the development of secondary industries, the question now is whether those industries can be created quickly enough to provide sufficient employment for the expanding populations of the towns.

The measurement of rural-urban migration from existing data for Ghana is difficult. In Table 3.16 it has been assumed that the rate of natural increase has been the same in urban and rural areas. Now, we have already seen that fertility is lower in the towns. However, this is probably entirely offset by lower mortality and by the different age structure, which concentrates in the towns those who are most likely to become parents and least likely to succumb to death. Acting to some extent in the opposite direction is the surplus of adult males in the urban areas.

In the Table, three hypotheses are examined. The first is that the 1948 and 1960 Census data are both correct. The second and third hypotheses assume that underenumeration occurred in 1948 along the lines posited in Hypothesis (C) in Table 2.4 of the previous chapter. The second hypothesis assumes that the underenumeration was experienced to an equal extent by urban and rural areas, while the third hypothesis takes it to have been an entirely rural phenomenon. Each hypothesis is subdivided into sub-hypotheses (i) and (ii), the former assuming that one-third of all foreign immigrants between 1948 and 1960 went to urban areas and the second that two-fifths did so.

The 1960 Census revealed that one-third of the foreign-born population lived at that time in towns. This is a much higher concentration in urban areas than was found among the population of Ghanaian origin, of whom only 22 per cent lived in the towns of the country. It is possible that the fraction, one-third, is a plausible estimate of the foreign contribution not only to the 1960 urban population but also to the 1948 urban population. On the other hand, as suggested in sub-hypothesis (ii), migrants before 1948 may have been attracted much more by the cocoa farms and the gold and diamond diggings. If this were the case, and the 1948 Census implies that it might have been so, perhaps less than a fifth of the urban population was foreign born in 1948, in which case 40 per cent of the 1948–60 census stream must have found its final destination in the towns. Hypothesis (2)(ii) would seem most likely to approximate to reality.

Table 3.16 allows not only a study of the components of urban population growth in Ghana, but a more precise restatement of some of the observations made in the last few pages. In no case does this restatement introduce any substantial modification to the pattern already discerned, except that it does appear that the rate of urban population growth has probably been three and a half rather than three times as great as that of the rural areas. The towns may have absorbed a little over two-fifths of all intercensal population growth instead of a little under two-fifths.

Table 3.16 reveals quite clearly the components of the rather astonishing growth of urban population between 1948 and 1960. About a quarter of the increase can probably be explained by the natural increase of the population who already lived in towns in 1948. Perhaps another quarter can be attributed to foreign immigration. Probably over half of the popula-

TABLE 3.16

RURAL-URBAN MIGRATION, 1948–60

	Hypothesis (1)*	Hypothesis (2)*	Hypothesis (3)*
1948 total population (thousands)	4,118	4,412	4,412
1948 urban population (thousands)	538	577	538
1948 rural population (thousands)	3,580	3,835	3,874
Percentage urban population in 1948	13·0	13·0	12·2
1960 total population (thousands)	6,727	6,727	6,727
1960 urban population (thousands)	1,551	1,551	1,551
1960 rural population (thousands)	5,176	5,176	5,176
Percentage urban population in 1960	23·1	23·1	23·1
1948–60 population increase (thousands)	2,609	2,315	2,315
1948–60 urban population increase (thousands)	1,013	974	1,013
1948–60 rural population increase (thousands)	1,596	1,341	1,302
1948–60 average annual percentage population increase	4·2	3·6	3·6
1948–60 average annual percentage urban population increase	9·2	8·6	9·2
1948–60 average annual percentage rural population increase	3·1	2·5	2·4
1948–60 net foreign immigration (thousands)	379	466	466
1948–60 net foreign immigration plus natural increase† (thousands)	476	616	616

	(i)	(ii)‡	(i)	(ii)‡	(i)	(ii)‡
1948–60 net foreign immigration plus natural increase absorbed by urban areas (thousands)	159	190	205	246	205	246
1948–60 natural increase of 1948 urban population (thousands)	274	274	234	234	218	218
1948–60 rural-urban immigration plus natural increase§ (thousands)	580	549	535	494	590	549
Components of 1948–60 growth of urban population						
(a) Net foreign immigration plus natural increase (percentage)	16	19	21	25	20	24
(b) Natural increase of 1948 urban population (percentage)	27	27	24	24	22	22
(c) Rural-urban immigration plus natural increase (percentage)	57	54	55	51	58	54
1948–60 rural-urban migrants (thousands)	462	437	445	411	490	456
1948–60 rural increase (thousands)	1,596	1,596	1,341	1,341	1,302	1,302
1948–60 rural increase plus rural-urban migrants and their natural increase	2,176	2,145	1,876	2,164	1,892	1,851
1948–60 rural-urban migrants and their natural increase as percentage of line above	27	26	29	23	31	30
1948–60 average per annum rate of population growth of rural population plus rural-urban migrants and their natural increase (percentage)	4·0	4·0	3·4	3·8	3·4	3·3

  * Hypotheses are based on the following assumptions: (1) All census data are correct. (2) Hypothesis (C) in Table 2.4 of previous chapter is correct and underenumeration in 1948 affects urban and rural areas to the same extent. (3) As for (2), but all underenumeration in 1948 was in rural areas.

  † Assuming equal annual increments of foreign immigrants and same level of natural increase as native-born population.

  ‡ Sub-hypotheses: (i) One-third of all 1948–60 foreign immigrants went to urban areas. (ii) Two-fifths did so.

  § Assuming same level of natural increase as the rest of the population.

tion increase has resulted from what has been described in the table as rural-urban migration. It should be noted that the last category includes persons who became residents of towns merely by remaining in their villages while these grew in size until they contained more than 5,000 inhabitants. In one sense, such an inclusion is valid, because the environment of such people undoubtedly changed considerably.

Three points are of particular importance. Firstly, in Ghana, as in the United States of three-quarters of a century ago or other countries of substantial foreign immigration, such immigration has forced the pace of urbanization very considerably. Secondly, large numbers of people have been on the move within Ghana. Much of the movement is circular, but the net movement alone from rural to urban areas, even with the omission of those who remained in the villages which grew to towns, has over the period been not far short of half a million people. Thirdly, rural-urban migration has removed a quarter or more of the rural population increase. In the modern world such large-scale rural-urban migration seems to rise inevitably from the rapid growth of rural populations. There would appear to be a limit, not in terms of potential land supplies alone, to the rate at which new farming opportunities can be made available. Without the migration to the towns, rural population in Ghana would have grown at about $3\frac{1}{2}$ per cent per year. The migration reduced the rate to about $2\frac{1}{2}$ per cent. It will be assumed, when projecting population in the next chapter, that rural Ghana can continue in the years immediately ahead to absorb population at the rate of $2\frac{1}{2}$ per cent per year.

Where the rural-urban migrants go is determined by the pattern of settlement and of economic development within the country. Three-fifths of Ghana's population was to be found in 1960 within a densely settled area (23 per cent of the country) in the south.[1] Five-sixths of the towns, 78 out of 94, are to be found in the densely settled area. There are another nine towns also in the south, and seven of them are within 10 miles of the area defined here as densely settled. Both towns with more than 100,000 inhabitants are in the south. On the other hand, northern Ghana, with a fifth of the country's population, contains less than one-thirteenth of the towns and less than one-fifteenth of the urban population.

TABLE 3.17

DISTRIBUTION OF TOWNS, 1960

Town size (number of inhabitants)	Densely settled area in south	Area in south within 10 miles of densely settled area	Remainder of south	North*
Over 100,000	2	0	0	0
20,000–100,000	7	0	0	1
10,000–20,000	19	3	1	3
5,000–10,000	50	4	1	3

* Northern and Upper Regions,
Source: 1960 Population Census.

Finally, it might be asked what proportion of the growth of urban areas has been accounted for by the largest towns. In Table 3.18 it can be seen

[1] See Figure 2.4, Chapter 2.

that the six largest towns increased in size by about 400,000 persons and that this amounted to almost two-fifths of all inter-censal population growth. Accra accounted for over half the total growth of these six towns.

TABLE 3.18

GROWTH OF THE SIX LARGEST TOWNS, 1948–60

	Population		Population increase	Population increase As a percentage of all 1948–60 urban population increase
	1948	1960	1948–60	
	(thousands)		(thousands)	
Accra	134	338	204	19·9
Kumasi	71	181	110	10·7
Takoradi	17	41	24	2·5
Cape Coast	23	41	18	1·8
Koforidua	19	35	16	1·6
Tamale	17	40	23	2·2
Total of six towns	281	676	395	38·7

Source: 1960 Population Census.

5. THE RURAL-URBAN MIGRANT

Between 1962 and 1964 a research programme was undertaken in an effort to determine the mechanics of rural-urban migration in Ghana and to discover the characteristics of the migrants. In 1963, information was obtained about more than 17,000 persons living in some 2,500 households in sixty-six localities. The survey covered the whole country and concentrated on migration to the major urban areas, and ignored movements to cocoa-growing and gold-mining areas as well as to other rural districts.[1]

The rural section of the Survey attempted a complete enumeration of both those living in village households and those members of the households absent elsewhere. The categories of the population in terms of internal migration are shown in Table 3.19. Two-thirds of the people regarded themselves as settled, but one-third of these visited a large town often. The last proportion varied of course with the locality. Furthermore, a great part of the composition of the settled population was undoubtedly made up of children, who form 45 per cent of the population of the country. Thus, although about one-ninth of the members of rural households are away in the town at any given time, a considerably larger fraction of adults belongs in this category. Most rural-urban migrants were away on something more permanent than a seasonal basis. It was, however, a period when many seasonal migrants would be likely to be back in the village. Altogether, counting those away in urban areas and those at home in rural ones at the time of the Survey, 11·6 per cent of the population were regarded as being in some way fairly permanent rural-urban migrants and a further 4·6 per cent hoped to join this category. Those now retired from this group amounted to 5·5 per cent. Those regarded as seasonal migrants totalled 3·9 per cent. Another 4·6 per cent hoped to join this category and 2·1 per cent had retired from it.

The Table is somewhat unsatisfactory in that, in order to achieve concise-

[1] See Appendix. Population Council Programme *Rural-urban Migration Survey of Ghana.*

ness, it aggregates the experience of very different parts of the country. However, it does illustrate the significance of rural-urban migration in rural Ghana and demonstrates the extent of the flow of population to the town and in many cases back again.

TABLE 3.19

RURAL GHANA: ANALYSIS OF POPULATION IN TERMS OF RURAL-URBAN MIGRATION, 1963

Primary migratory classification	Secondary classification	Percentage of rural population
(1) Has not migrated to urban areas and does not intend to do so in the foreseeable future*	(a) Visits a town often	22·0
	(b) Rarely or never visits a town	41·8
(2) Has not migrated to urban areas but intends or hopes to do so	(a) Seasonally†	4·6
	(b) More permanently	4·6
(3) Has permanently returned to rural areas after one or more periods in urban areas	(a) Seasonally	2·1
	(b) More permanently	5·5
(4) Has returned to the rural area but will go to urban areas again	(a) Seasonally	2·8
	(b) More permanently	2·7
(5) Temporarily away in urban area	(a) Visiting‡	1·3
	(b) Seasonally	1·1
(6) Now more permanently away in urban area	(a) Returns for visit at least once a year	6·4
	(b) More rarely or never returns	2·5
(7) Not included above		2·6

* Includes migrants to other rural areas whether present or absent.
† For periods of less than one year.
‡ Away for less than three months and not engaging in paid employment.
Source: *Rural-urban Migration Survey*, 1963.

An examination was also made of the immigrant population in the four largest towns. Of the Ghanaian population, originating from outside the locality surveyed, less than one-seventh had come from other urban areas, and over six-sevenths were born in rural areas. Of these people 7 per cent were on a temporary visit, 4 per cent were seasonal migrants and 89 per cent were more permanent migrants to the towns. Of the latter, five-sixths stated that they visited their home areas at least once every year. Of the foreign immigrants, 3 per cent were temporarily visiting, 3 per cent were seasonal migrants, and 94 per cent were more permanent migrants. Thus, the towns of Ghana are not large and somewhat ephemeral aggregations of seasonal migrants. The great majority of their populations either are rural-urban migrants, who have settled down as town residents, or are townsmen by birth.

A preliminary analysis of those characteristics which appear to determine whether a villager is likely to emigrate to the towns or not suggests that education is an extremely important correlate. Table 3.20 shows that over three-quarters of those with no education expect to remain permanently in the rural areas, while less than half of those with middle school education do so. The numbers with secondary and university education are comparatively small. The fact that some are found in their home areas in rural Ghana is explained by their coming back as administrators, teachers and the like to areas where they are familiar with the language and people. As might be expected, the relation between literacy and the tendency to migrate to the towns is similar to that between education and migration.

These findings were fully supported by the personal interviews. Time and time again respondents, when asked why they had stayed in the village, replied that their lack of education prevented them from getting a good town job. Others, when asked why they had migrated to urban areas, replied that they had been to school, as if this answer provided a full explanation which no sensible person would contest.

TABLE 3.20

RURAL POPULATION OF GHANA: EDUCATION AND RURAL-URBAN MIGRATION, 1963
(All figures shown as percentages)

Migration classification	No schooling	Schooling (highest level reached)			
		Primary	Middle	Secondary	University
Has not migrated to urban areas and does not intend to do so	76	69	48	34	9
Has not yet migrated but intends to do so	5	14	14	11	3
Has migrated to urban areas (whether absent or not)	19	17	38	55	88
	100	100	100	100	100

Source: *Rural-urban Migration Survey*, 1963.

TABLE 3.21

RURAL POPULATION OF GHANA: LITERACY AND RURAL-URBAN MIGRATION, 1963
(All figures shown as percentages)

Migration classification	Literacy	
	Illiterate	Literate
Has not migrated to urban areas and does not intend to do so	75	52
Has not migrated but intends to do so	6	13
Has migrated to urban areas (whether absent or not)	19	35
	100	100

Source: *Rural-urban Migration Survey*, 1963.

Almost 2,500 households were studied in detail to determine the nature of the migratory process.

Considerable attention was given to the migrants' motives. Five-sixths of all migrants or potential migrants gave as their chief reason for the move the desire for more money, or the prestige accompanying more highly-paid town jobs, or the desire to earn money to buy consumption goods, or similar economic motives. In most cases the answers suggested that the 'pull' of the towns in Ghana was still a more important factor than the 'push' of overcrowding and land hunger in rural areas. Most migrants certainly expect to raise their earning power by going to the towns.

Most of the rest of the respondents gave answers indicating their preference for town life and its sophistication, and, in some cases, its lack of the more irksome forms of rural toil. Some women go to the towns in the hope of acquiring a town husband. A few respondents argued that travel and change of environment were good things of themselves even if they did not succeed in raising living standards.

Detailed questions followed on the particular things that migrants find pleasant and unpleasant in town and village life respectively. Amongst the joys of urban life, jobs and wages were prominent. But most migrants also spoke of entertainments, holidays when no work of any kind was expected, cinemas, bars, dancing and women. Many explained that life was more exciting and faster, and a surprising number felt that Accra, Kumasi or Takoradi exhibited a visual beauty with which the forest or the woodland savannah could never compete. Over a third pointed to better shopping or marketing facilities and around a quarter referred to the water and electricity supplies. In many parts of Ghana, water carrying is still a considerable part of rural existence. A fifth approved of the better health facilities.

What are regarded as the drawbacks of town life? By far the most important failing is that the migrant must enter a fully cash economy. Rents must be paid for, and are usually thought to be high. Food must be bought, at prices which often seem to the ex-villager to be extortionate. When unemployment strikes, money runs out very quickly, and there are none of the things which seem to cost nothing and cushion hard times in the village. A third of the respondents referred to social evils which most equated with theft. The rural-urban migrants' shock at the level of theft in the towns is interesting, for most native townsmen blame this crime largely upon the newcomers. Two-thirds of both the rural and urban population feel that town life corrupts. A sixth of the migrants resent the shanty towns around the larger urban areas, which their own arrival has helped to create. Whilst the pace of the large town attracts many, it appals others. Of the rural-urban migrants, a sixth worried about the traffic accidents, an eighth complained of the noise, and a ninth just said that life was too fast. Others complained of the unfriendliness of town people.

The mirror image of the cases for and against town life are the feelings expressed about village life. Why do people stay in rural areas all their lives? Two-thirds of those who stayed explained this action by saying that they had a farm or had been occupationally successful in the village. It may be that even in some parts of Ghana, there is some degree of land hunger, and that this is a factor in rural-urban migration. A sixth had some kind of tie, such as being a chief or head of a family, which made migration difficult. Almost a third stated that they felt that they were condemning themselves to relative poverty by remaining in the village, but that they felt that the compensations of village life more than made up for this. The chief pleasures of village life were the low cost of housing and food, the mutual help of family and friends, and the quiet and security of rural life. Five-sixths of village and town population alike thought that village life was more 'manageable' than that of the towns. Those failings of rural Ghana, which were mentioned by a considerable fraction of the sample, were, in order of frequency, the inadequate water supply, the lack of suitable work for the educated, the scarcity of night clubs, bars and dances, the shortage of consumer goods, the bad roads, the dullness of life, and the inadequate medical facilities.

The high sex ratio in the rural-urban migrant streams arises not merely from the fact that there are more jobs for males in the towns. It is partly a product of social pressures. Five-sixths of the rural population think that it is a good thing for young men to go to the town for a while in order to earn money, acquire skills and achieve some sophistication. Only about half feel the same way about young women. The great majority of those who disapprove cite as their reason the danger that the female migrants will become prostitutes. On the other hand, some see the advantages of allowing females to secure town husbands who will be able to support them at a higher standard of living and allow them to live a more sophisticated, urban way of life.

Over half the rural households surveyed have lost some member to the town. On the whole, the decisions to migrate have been made without too much family friction. Only a ninth of rural-urban migrants say that any member of the family spoke strongly against their going. Only a twelfth of those remaining in the village claim to have done so reluctantly because of family responsibilities. On the other hand, a similar proportion have apparently stayed in the village in spite of encouragement from some members of the family to go to the urban areas. It is rare for a whole family to migrate, but not unknown. There are houses in some villages empty because whole families have gone at least temporarily to the town.

In a mobile and gregarious society like that found in Ghana, much learning is acquired by seeing and talking. This is especially true nowadays. Two-thirds of those intending to migrate to the towns have already been there for a visit. Most of the others have learnt what to expect through hearsay. Of the older migrants, already in the towns, only a third had visited an urban area before their migration. Very few migrants are as yet influenced in their decision to migrate by what they learn from the radio, newspapers, books or school. It should be added that most of the migrants, who had not previously visited the towns, discover that their picture of life there was surprisingly wrong. However, in about half of all cases, their misconception lay in the fact that scare stories about the strangeness of the town led them to expect greater adjustment difficulties than actually turned out to be the case. But others were surprised to find how hard it was to find jobs or earn as much money as they hoped. Many were shocked by the prices and others by the overcrowded housing conditions.

An indication of the relation between rural schooling and urban growth is the fact that a third of potential migrants hope for a clerical job or some other position that will utilize their literacy and training. One sign that rapid urban population growth may be tending to outstrip urban employment is that three-quarters of the rural-urban migrants living in the towns feel that it is now harder to get jobs than when they first arrived. This may, of course, be nothing more than the effect of rising expectations or the product of unjustifiably rosy memories.

The movement from village to town is in many ways similar to the process of international migration which has already been described. Three-quarters of intending migrants are already married and almost as many have children. However, only an eighth of those married will take their wives on the original journey and fewer still will take any children. Another three-quarters will send for their wives once they have established themselves in the town. But a twelfth of the wives and a somewhat bigger fraction of the children will remain indefinitely in the villages. Some of these wives and children belong to seasonal or shorter-term migrants. In over 96 per cent of all cases they will be looked after by relatives.

Once, large numbers of rural-urban migrants travelled on foot. But this movement is now very small. Over four-fifths now go by mammy lorry, and most of the rest use either the train or the bus. On arrival in the town, two-fifths stay at first with relatives and a quarter with friends from the same district of origin. One in twelve, having neither relatives nor friends to turn to, goes to the part of the town where migrants from their own area live. There they contact the leader or 'chief' of this group, who arranges for them to stay either with himself or with one of his people. A fifth search immediately for a room or house to rent.

When a migrant settles down in the town, he rarely cuts himself off completely from his home village. Traditional and family ties in West Africa are much too strong for such severance. Only an eighth of all migrants return home less frequently than once a year. The usual number of visits is one to three, although visits to the north of the country tend to be more infrequent. People making these visits make up a considerable proportion of the passengers who travel in mammy lorries along the roads of Ghana. The visits are short, partly because of the problem of getting time off from work, and usually average between three and seven days.

The interplay between village and town is very interesting. The returning migrant has gained in prestige. Over four-fifths of both villagers and migrants agree on this point. Some skills are brought back. About a third of migrants working in the towns intend eventually to practise their town jobs back in the village. Many use their town earnings to build either houses or extra rooms on to their families' houses in the village. Of the migrants surveyed in the towns, 30 per cent either had already built in the village or were in the process of doing so, 63 per cent hoped to do so before their final return, and only 7 per cent had no intention of building.

The movement from rural to urban Ghana is frequently a case of *chain migration* and exhibits some of the efficiency and some of the strain often associated with that process. A large proportion of rural-urban migrants seek help from relatives or fellow villagers when they reach town. Three-quarters of the migrants say that the help is willingly given. Half of them have received help in the form of temporary accommodation and feeding until they are settled. A fifth have received assistance in the search for a job. A twelfth have been helped with money, and a twelfth have been aided in finding accommodation elsewhere. The giving of assistance to poor relatives is not always absolute loss. Many relatives from rural areas, especially young ones, can be treated rather like underpaid servants. About a third of the migrants felt some resentment on this score.

Success or failure in the town can reduce or enhance the attractions of rural life. Most respondents agreed that there are people in the towns who delay visits to the village or make such visits very brief because they prefer town life and townspeople. On the other hand, considerable numbers return permanently to the village. Three times as many respondents thought that this was usually due to economic failure in the urban areas than felt that it arose from the success of the migration.

Three-fifths of the migrants had to borrow money to make their migration and subsequent installation in the town possible. In well over half of all cases such money was borrowed from relatives. In about two-fifths of all cases of borrowing, fairly formal arrangements were made for repayment by instalments. When money was borrowed from non-relatives, such arrangements often included the charging of a very substantial interest rate. In the balance of cases, there was a vague understanding in most cases that there would be some kind of repayment in the indefinite future if the migration proved to be financially successful. However, in a fifth of all borrowings no arrangements whatever were made. It was assumed that the system of giving and receiving help within the family causes over a long period flows of generosity in all directions, and, in any case, that such help should not be subject to book-keeping. There is evidence that even a substantial proportion of the more formally lent money is not repaid, and this may go some way towards explaining the high interest rates.

In rural Ghana, over a third of all households claim that they receive some money remitted from the towns. Of these, nearly half receive money at least once a month. In the majority of cases the amount sent is between £2 and £10. Much of it is sent with friends or lorry drivers or taken personally by the migrant. However, remittance through the post office is important, although bank remittances are not used on any scale.

About half of the money remitted is sent according to some regular arrangement, perhaps a third when the migrants feel they have some to spare, and the rest because of pleas of emergency from the villages. Over two-thirds of the money received in the villages is spent on the general maintenance of households. However, a smaller fraction of the urban-rural remittance stream is for specified purposes. About 9 per cent is for education, $6\frac{1}{2}$ per cent for investment in farming, 3 per cent for building and $2\frac{1}{2}$ per cent for the financing of such events as festivals or funerals. A quarter of all households receiving remittances from urban areas, and thus about a twelfth of all rural households, claim to receive more money in this way than their total rural money income. This is more often the case in northern Ghana than in the south.

The remittance of money is not a transient phase of the migrants' life. In fact, he is least likely to send any money during the first period of establishment in the town when he can least afford to. Only about half of the migrants send any money during this period, but once established, even after they have been in the town for many years, over four-fifths claim to send something. Relatives receive about 99 per cent of money sent to the villages, about two-thirds going to parents, a sixth to wives and children, and a sixth to other relatives.

The rural households surveyed claimed on the average to receive £15 17s 4d each per year in the form of remitted money. In actuality, the third of the households which received any money averaged about £1 per week. If the sample is representative of the whole of rural Ghana, the total amount received from the towns would amount to almost £8 million or about $1\frac{1}{2}$ per cent of the National Income. This figure is undoubtedly low. A check on some of the respondents showed that they were inclined to discuss the general case and to ignore special remittances received in answer to a particular plea of need. More importantly, it does not include goods sent or brought back by the traveller. The true figure might be nearer to £16 million or 3 per cent of the National Income. About a third of the respondents claimed that a rural family is likely to be very poor if none of its members works in a town.

Those sending remittances from the largest towns claimed on average, where an estimate could be made, to be remitting about £43 per year each. Most of these people were the heads of urban households and this usually represents household remittance. Household heads claimed to be remitting between one-twentieth and three-quarters of their income. This may be inflated somewhat because those unable to make estimates were probably remitting less than the average, but this is certainly compensated for by the omission of goods. It is possible that about £5 million per year, or about one-tenth of the income earned in Accra, finds its way out of the city and that most of this goes to rural Ghana.

The flow of non-monetary remittances is important. Nearly all migrants returning to their villages take some goods as gifts. Cloth or clothing is the most common type of gift, followed by foodstuffs. Less common are soap, seeds and implements for farming and various types of durable luxuries such as transistor radios. There is more chance of money or gifts brought back personally by the migrant to the village being used for village celebrations or festivals than is the case with money remitted from the town.

The fact that incomes are on the average higher in the towns does not mean that economic pressures are felt less there. Just the opposite is the case. For most Ghanaians, the town is still something of an 'unnatural' existence. Its delights can be enjoyed more easily if one is aware that welcome and security is waiting in the village as soon as things begin to go wrong in the town. Failure to help relatives in the village or to visit them occasionally could well destroy that welcome, and this is a state of affairs that comparatively few urban Ghanaians would be prepared to court. Life in town without a job can be very difficult, especially if one's family lives hundreds of miles away.

Migrants already living in the town were asked, 'Where do people worry most about not having enough money to care for themselves and their family—in the town or in the village?' Four-fifths said 'in the town' and one-tenth 'in the village'. Asked where parents could afford to have most children, one-fourteenth said the town and three-quarters the village. The answer was clearer still in the case of polygyny. Only one in sixteen said that more than one wife could most easily be supported in the town, while over four-fifths voted for the village. There are, then, economic pressures of which the urban poor are also becoming aware, and which militate against both polygyny and large families in the Ghanaian town.

How does the success of the migration measure up to the expectation? After all, most such movements must necessarily be based on uncertain knowledge. Somewhat over half those migrants still living in towns, and somewhat less than half of those who had returned to the village, thought that life in the town had generally been as satisfactory as they had hoped. The chief complaint was about prices. Migrants usually knew something about the level of wages. But many just could not visualize that everything had to be paid for. Three-quarters of the migrants still living in the town said that they had not been able to buy as many things as they had expected when they first decided to come to the urban area.

Another factor was the loneliness of town life. Accra, an 'extroverted' and 'friendly' place when compared with many cities in industrialized countries, did not appear to the immigrants in this light when compared with their villages. One of the reasons for loneliness in an African city is that one is surrounded by great numbers of people of different tribal origins. Often very few of them can speak one's own native tongue. Over half of the migrants claim that they never succeed in making as many good friends in the town as they had known in the village.

Very few of the migrants regarded their migration as something permanent. Four-fifths were quite clear that they ultimately intended to return to the village. One-third intend to return when sickness or old age affects them, and another tenth at some age between 40 and 60 years. Another sixth had some definite goal such as saving a certain amount of money or finishing their house in the village. A full third had no idea. Of those returning, nine out of every ten expect to own a house in the village by the time of their return. Of these, 22 per cent had already built it, 63 per cent intended to do so, 11 per cent hoped to purchase one, and 4 per cent expected to take over a family house.

6. SUMMARY AND CONCLUSIONS

Migration is a fundamental aspect of Ghana's society and economy. The rapid economic development which has taken place in the towns and forest of southern Ghana has been greatly assisted by plentiful supplies of Ghanaian and foreign migrant labour. The mobility of the population has had two important economic effects. The demand for transport has speeded the construction of roads and the multiplication of the motor lorry, thus helping to strengthen the economic infrastructure. The movement of much of the money earned in the more developed areas back to the largely subsistence rural regions from which many of the migrants come has helped to spread the cash economy by creating cash purchasing power to stimulate local production, especially of non-agricultural goods, even far into the hinterland.

Returning migrants are also powerful instruments for carrying social change to the furthest parts of the country. As in many other countries, the direction of change is inevitably towards the adoption by the rural, agrarian society of more and more of the values of the town. These values themselves are undergoing change, partly because the towns are the main links with the outside world and hence tend to become more cosmopolitan in values and attitudes, and partly because urban life imposes new pressures upon traditional social structures. An excellent example is to be found in the family system. The problems of urban employment, housing and way of living combine with external Westernizing influences to place unstable marriage, polygyny and pro-fertility attitudes at something of a discount. In many developing countries, there has been a tendency to regard the trend towards monogamy and greater stability in marriage as an aspect of social modernization. Such attitudes are certainly spreading at the present time amongst Ghana's urban middle class, and the great social and areal mobility within the country will facilitate the spread of these values amongst the urban workers and rural population alike.

Until recently, there was no great difference between internal and external migration. This is no longer so. Independence has meant that pressures for social and economic planning have arisen at the same time that Ghana has become administratively an autonomous unit, isolated in the sense that most sovereign nations are. Thus the question of the remittance of earnings by migrants must be seen within a framework of balance of payment problems and of decisions about investment policy. At the same time, the great and continuing reduction in mortality has meant that in Ghana, as elsewhere in the developing world, young adults are beginning to seek employment in numbers not previously experienced. Government policy may have therefore to take into account the competition for employment, and more particularly for urban employment. At the same time the demand for social services is increasing, and, whilst it is not impossible to design a welfare State which is subject to substantial immigration, such a phenomenon certainly gives rise to complex problems, especially where the flow tends to be circular and settlement is intended to be impermanent. On the other hand, migrants are economically a very efficient addition to the population in that a high proportion are of working age and many have been educated or trained elsewhere.

There is no complete solution to the problem of a migration policy. For pan-Africanist reasons alone, there could be considerable hostility to a general closing of Ghana's borders. However, it is possible that immigration may in general come to be regarded with diminishing enthusiasm. At the same time, stringent exchange control regulations will probably bring about a balancing diminution in the demand to immigrate. Further, much of Ghana's Upper Region is at present 'over-populated' in the sense that in the short-run it is unlikely to be able to offer the kind of economic opportunity found in the south. One probable result of this is continuing massive migration to the south, and a national government will almost inevitably feel inclined to give priority to the employment and housing of such migrants on arrival in the south over the needs of those from other countries. The evidence in Ghana seems to be that emigration from areas of relatively high living and educational standards is likely to be more balanced in sex composition and probably in age composition. Thus, the towns of southern Ghana will probably experience in the years ahead much more family migration from the north than has been the case in the past. It is also fairly certain that the proportion of long-term migrants will continue to rise and that of seasonal migrants will diminish.

In the last twenty years, the towns have been relatively more important as the destination of internal migration and the rural and mining industries less important than was previously the case. This trend will almost certainly continue. By now the towns are likely to be absorbing over half the total population increase, and, as will be seen in the next chapter, within a little over a generation they may well contain half the people of Ghana. This might predictably occur even sooner but for the conclusion that the rate of foreign immigration is likely to decline. For, as was seen above, such immigration has been a very significant component of urbanization in Ghana. Furthermore, such a span of time in reaching the point where half the country's population is urban, depends on the continued ability of rural Ghana to absorb population increase at a fairly high rate. This may prove to be impossible. If an extra $2\frac{1}{2}$ per cent were to be absorbed each year, it

K

would mean the settling of another 4 million farming people over the next twenty years.

The way of life of the Ghanaian people, their attitudes, culture and politics will inevitably be profoundly affected by the change in the country's balance of population from rural to urban. During the coming decades the towns themselves must change if they are not to become centres of destitution. As yet, even the major towns are chiefly commercial and service centres. And, up to now, their populations have enjoyed an average standard of living considerably above that of the country as a whole. This has been one of the major forces behind the rural-urban movement.

The future population of the towns may not be accommodated so easily. If town populations continue to increase much faster than that of the country as a whole, then it would be unreasonable to assume that commerce and the provision of services could multiply in proportion. Nevertheless, if rural Ghana is hard pressed to provide sufficient extra farm land quickly enough, the flow of people from the country could continue unabated. The only real solution is the expansion of manufacturing industry. This is realized clearly by the government. The future secondary industries will be based upon the beginnings already laid in Takoradi, Accra, Tema and Akosombo. The success of plans for industrialization will very greatly change the nature of life in Ghana's towns and, through them, in the country as a whole. But the rate at which such success is achieved may in turn depend partly upon demographic and other social factors.

CHAPTER IV

POPULATION PROSPECTS AND POLICY

1. ECONOMIC DEVELOPMENT AND POPULATION CHANGE

Ghana has experienced very great economic and social change during the present century. There is in the country a consensus that much more must occur. In his Foreword to the *Ghana Seven-Year Development Plan, 1963-64—1969-70*, President Nkrumah wrote that, 'The Plan provides the blueprint for the future progress and development of Ghana as a nation. It is a programme of social and economic development based on the use of science and technology to revolutionize our agriculture and industry.'[1] How is it planned that these aims should be achieved? The answer is that 'we must create the wealth. The only way to build up the national wealth is to maintain a maximum rate of productive investment in industry and agriculture.'[2] The planners are clear about their aims and the priorities that must be accorded their success. They state that 'the needs of economic development must precede all other considerations of policy as Ghana embarks on the new era of social reconstruction. . . . In this and subsequent plans for the development of Ghana a consistent strategy must be developed and applied to yield the most rapid rate of economic development possible within the limits of Ghana's generous endowment in human and material resources.'[3] In one sense most developing countries are finding themselves too generously endowed with human resources, for their populations have been growing in size as never before.

In the middle of the twentieth century the flow of the products and by-products of the Industrial Revolution to all parts of the world became increasingly significant. It was a flow, not only of goods, but also of techniques, ideas and ideologies. It has been a period in Africa and Asia when many countries have achieved their independence. It has also been a period which has witnessed 'a revolution of expectations' all over the world, but perhaps nowhere more markedly than in some of the newly independent countries. It is a period that has become very familiar with 'development plans', 'international assistance', 'technical aid' and vastly expanded education programmes.

One of the most remarkable features of what has been a very remarkable period has been the rapid fall in death rates in almost all parts of the developing world. Hitherto, in human history, levels of mortality had fallen, if at all, only slowly. Since the end of the Second World War advances in medical technology and public health techniques have continued. Much disease control, both preventive and curative, can now be carried out sur-

---

[1] Ghana, *Seven-Year Development Plan, 1963-64 to 1969-70*, Accra, 1964, Foreword, p. v.

[2] Ibid.

[3] Ibid., p. 1.

prisingly cheaply. Furthermore, a period of international competition without global war has produced a nearly world-wide climate of opinion strongly favouring the continued expansion of health facilities within developing countries and the provision of a considerable amount of technical assistance from outside sources.

The result has been a fall in the level of mortality at a rate far exceeding that experienced by the first industrializing countries in the nineteenth century. These countries had to create their modern medical technology parallel to the construction of their modern industrial apparatus. Contemporary industrializing countries can import much of the medical technology which they need, even if further work has to be done on the specific problems of each area.

The cutting of the death rates and the resulting ability to guarantee a greater chance of survival to old age has of itself been an immense social advance in developing countries. Similarly, the assurance that many more people will be educated and will be educated for much longer than has previously been the case has been a fundamental social advance. In social terms at least, each has very greatly raised the condition of life in developing countries.

However, each advance has raised other formidable problems, which ultimately will have to be solved if the advances themselves are to continue to be enjoyed. The falls in mortality have been so sudden, that no social adjustments could take place in time to prevent a very great rise in the rate of natural increase. Similarly, all the problems of providing suitable employment for those produced by the expanded educational systems have not yet been solved.

In many of the developing countries death rates have already fallen to the levels existing in north-western Europe early in the present century. But birth rates are higher than those which have been found in north-western Europe for centuries. The result has been a rate of natural increase much higher than that found in those countries now economically developed at the time when they were first industrializing. Between 1948 and 1960, the population of Ghana increased at an average rate of $3\frac{1}{2}$ per cent per year. In contrast, no European country exceeded the rate of $1\frac{1}{2}$ per cent per year during any decade when it was undergoing industrialization. England multiplied its population over three and a half times during the critical hundred years of economic development that formed the nineteenth century. Ghana has done as much since 1921 and by now, population is probably expanding at a rate that would mean a thirty-four-fold increase each century if sustained.

Some population growth may well assist an industrial revolution. Larger internal markets are created. The work force has a higher proportion of young workers, perhaps more ready to accept innovation, than is the case with a stationary population.

But a growth of population at the rate now found in Ghana and other parts of the developing world may well slow the rate of industrialization and the speed with which standards of living can be raised. It is not impossible that it could frustrate such a revolution altogether.

There are several reasons for this. The most important immediate reason is that each extra increment of persons added to a community means that so much more must be provided in the form of houses, schools, roads, factories and the like just in order to sustain living standards so that people may continue to enjoy the same average amount per head of these things. Furthermore, the additional population cannot quickly provide these things for itself. It must be helped at considerable cost by the rest of the community. This help is largely used up in duplicating existing facilities rather than in raising living standards by, for instance, making labour more productive through increasing the average amount of capital stock per worker. It may well be in Ghana, for instance, that the value of factories or land needed to employ an extra worker is equal to at least three years of the worker's productive output. Thus if the labour force increases in size at the rate of 3 per cent per year, the whole labour force will have to reinvest not 3 but 9 per cent of its entire output in providing the employment facilities for these extra workers. Exactly the same form of argument is valid when discussing the rise of the whole population by 3 per cent per year. It will take 9 per cent of the national income to duplicate existing facilities so that the extra population can be absorbed. In the ensuing examination of the position in Ghana the labour force approach will be used in conjunction with an examination of the problem of supporting the non-employed dependants. The problem about this extra expenditure on the additions to the population is that, in a fast growing population, it is not a single outlay made once and for all time by a heroic effort of belt tightening. If the population continues to grow at 3 per cent per year, then 9 per cent of production will always be spent in duplicating extra facilities for it.

There are other reasons why fast population growth can place a strain upon an economy. Such societies have only a low proportion of the total population in the working age groups. Furthermore, if the population continues to multiply, the time will ultimately come when land and other resources will tend to become short. This point is of less importance in an industrializing country than in a completely agrarian one. Industrial civilization has shown a remarkable ability to multiply its resources.

In the immediate future Ghana is unlikely to be concerned with the problem of natural resources. Its main worry will be the race between population and investment. The central problem will be to enlarge the amount of existing capital per worker so as to make labour more productive. Only through such an increase in productivity can higher living standards be achieved. Much the same argument can be applied to investment from outside the country. A larger population is unlikely to attract any more investment than a smaller one, and thus what it does attract will mean a lesser share per head than in the case of the smaller population.

Now, all these things were known to those who drew up the Seven-Year Development Plan. What was not available at the time was a clear picture of the level of population growth, for much of the findings of the 1960 census have only recently become available. That detailed analysis of the demographic data could not be undertaken in time to influence the planning is shown by the acceptance for the Plan period of a 2·6 per cent per annum rate of population growth.[1] Analysis in an earlier chapter has shown

[1] *Seven-Year Development Plan, 1963-64 to 1969-70*, p. 7.

this figure to be much too low, and this will be corroborated later by population projection.

The planners were keenly aware of the population problem. They drew attention to the high growth and dependency rates, remarking that, 'These facts must condition all economic policy in Ghana for years to come.'[1]

The key section of the Plan, setting out the planners' view on population growth, and explaining the absence of any recommendations to the Government for action to curb excessive growth rates is the following.

> Young people make two demands on the community and their elders. First they must be maintained and trained until they come of working age. Then the means must be found to set up the farms, factories and offices in which they can be employed. The expenditure on both their rearing and their subsequent absorption into the labour force must be financed out of the savings of their elders.
>
> A young and growing population like Ghana's means that every bread-winner has to provide for a proportionately larger number of dependants than he would in a country with a stagnant or relatively older population. The burden of savings required of the Ghanaians now working must consequently be greater than it would otherwise be. In addition, the present low levels of productivity and incomes make it harder for Ghana to save than it is for a wealthier community.
>
> This makes it necessary for the Government and people constantly to remind and rededicate themselves to the task of economic development. For it must be emphasized that the demographic situation which lays this heavy burden of savings on the population is not likely to show any significant changes in the short-run. The success that we have had in bringing down the death rate in one generation will not be matched by a similar rapid success in bringing down the birth rate. Until the birth rate is reduced the population will continue to grow and the numbers of the dependent young will remain proportionately large.[2]

We now have enough population data to be able to test this conclusion more exactly. Four surveys of population attitudes[3] throw some light on the possibility of a spontaneous decline in birth rates. Such a decline does not, of course, exhaust the possibilities of a fall in the level of fertility. Secondly, the population projections examined subsequently allow us to judge with a fair degree of accuracy whether a fertility decline or a reduction in the volume of immigration would make a significant difference to the rate of industrialization and the level of the standard of living in the years immediately ahead.

Elsewhere the Plan states, 'A growing population presents an opportunity as much as a problem. As there are more mouths to feed so also are there eventually more hands for work. A sustained stream of productive investment at an adequate rate is required to turn this opportunity into reality.'[4]

---

[1] *Seven-Year Development Plan, 1963-64 to 1969-70*, p. 7.

[2] Ibid., pp. 7–8.

[3] See Appendix, Population Council Programme surveys: (i) *Survey of Population Attitudes in Economically Superior Urban Areas*, (ii) *Survey of Population Attitudes in Rural Areas*, (iii) *Survey of Aged Population*, (iv) *University Survey*.

[4] *Seven-Year Development Plan*, op. cit., p. 8.

In fact, the only choice in Ghana during the next generation would appear to lie between a very rapidly growing population and one with a more moderate, but still high, rate of increase. Subsequent analysis in this chapter will demonstrate that the latter presents fewer problems, and indeed more opportunity, than the former. In the faster growing population there will eventually be more hands, but there will be proportionally more mouths still. One of the fundamental problems of high growth rate populations is that dependency is great and that the number of employed persons is relatively small. It is precisely this type of population that is least likely to allow the stream of productive investment to turn the opportunities for substantial gains in living standards into reality.

2. THE POSSIBILITY OF FERTILITY TRANSITION

The Industrial Revolution in the West ultimately produced no frantic race between economic growth and population increase because after about the 1880s the birth rates began to follow the death rates in decline. This was the product of the decision by many parents to limit their families to a smaller size than that normally found amongst their ancestors. For most of the nineteenth century death rates alone had been falling and consequently rates of natural increase had been rising. By the early twentieth century birth rates were declining faster than death rates, and during the 1930s both were low and the great period of population expansion appeared to be at an end. The whole transition from high birth and death rates to low rates appeared to be but a facet of economic modernization and has been called the *demographic transition*.

If the fall in fertility arose merely because of the extra population pressures upon the community and family, then one would normally expect the demographic transition, once started, to complete its course in a predictable manner. However, the mortality level in many parts of the developing world is already lower than was the case in Western Europe when birth rates first began to fall. In most of the developing world, rates of natural increase are well above those prevailing at that time in Europe. Ghana's recent rate of population increase has been two-and-a-half times that of England of the 1880s. The latter, in fact, was no higher than that probably prevailing in Ghana in 1921.

The truth appears to be that the decline of the birth rate in the West arose from a spreading desire amongst individuals in the community to limit the size of their families, and that these decisions were caused by changes in the cultural climate and in the economic and social realities of the rapidly industrializing and urbanizing societies in which they lived. Thus, in a closed society, economic and demographic transition might go hand in hand. The position in today's developing world is far more complex. Mortality transition has, in terms of economic transition, arrived in a sense 'prematurely'. It is possible that its arrival has produced population growth rates so high that economic transition will prove very difficult to achieve if demographic transition is left to follow the *laissez-faire* course taken in the West.

On the other hand, it would be incorrect to picture today's developing world as the counterpart of pre-industrial Europe. It is very different. It has been deeply affected by the changes set off by the original Industrial

Revolution. Its urban populations are growing much faster than did those of the West, its populations are recipients of ideas spread by modern means of communication, education is being attempted on a scale never imagined in the pre-industrial West, and factory-made consumer goods are flowing to those who can afford to buy them.

Thus it would be wrong to assume that, because fertility declines have not yet occurred in poor, predominantly agrarian countries, they cannot occur. One can hardly cite the experience of the last twenty years, for the time-scale is too short.

Hence, surveys have been carried out in Ghana on this and related questions. In the West, the small family system began amongst the wealthier, urban classes. It spread from the wealthy to the poor, and from urban to rural areas. Similarly, if fertility decline were to begin in Ghana, it might well commence amongst the economically better-off in the larger towns. Thus, a sample of 627 persons was drawn amongst the quarter of the population of Accra, Kumasi, Takoradi-Sekondi and Cape Coast who lived in the apparently better-off suburbs. A large proportion of the husbands worked in 'white collar' jobs. The survey examined a group who make up about 2 per cent of the population of the country and who might well be the first to be affected by any fundamental change in national attitudes towards such matters as family size.

The survey showed that amongst this group deep-seated social change is under way. Far more of them live in a house containing only husband, wife and their children than was the case amongst their parents. Most of them are in favour of monogamy and stable marriage to a degree that probably would have astonished their ancestors.

Most are still convinced that a rapidly growing population is in the national good, but most, like the West Europeans of the late nineteenth century, are beginning to find the raising of large families in a modernizing society a very considerable burden. Almost two-thirds complained about the burden of affording adequate education for their children. This is of very considerable interest because the decline in family size in Europe began at just the time when compulsory education provisions were becoming effective. The burden does not disappear when the State assumes responsibility for such costs as school fees. Education removes children at least partly from the labour market. It means that they must be clothed better both to meet the requirements of the schools and because there is more 'keeping up with the Joneses'. Four-fifths of all respondents claimed that more money was spent on school children than on others and over half said that parents actually tend to treat school children better than children who do not attend school.

There is certainly evidence that Ghanaian families of this type are undergoing some of the changes in structure that have preceded or accompanied the development of small family systems elsewhere. Two-thirds of all respondents said that they treated their children in a different way from that in which they were treated themselves as children. The differences were always in the same direction, towards more personal affection for the children, more attention paid to their points of view and more activities involving the family as a unit. In almost half the families investigated, no other relatives lived with them. In over half husbands were found to take their wives out for entertainment quite frequently and in a third the children were also often taken out. All these changes tend to increase the proportion of money spent upon the children and hence to aggravate the difficulty of rearing large families. Fourteen out of every fifteen respondents claimed that children are now absorbing a larger part of the Ghanaian family's budget than used to be the case.

Socially, the family structure amongst the better-off, urban population of Ghana has probably changed to the point where the practice of birth control could quite easily be adopted. Whether other economic and social changes tend also in this direction must be seen.

There is, in fact, no sign that these families are as yet limiting their size to below that of the rest of the urban community in which they are found. Urban fertility is, as has been seen, below that found in the rural areas. But the survey of the better-off revealed a completed family size of almost six children, the average number for each major town differing little from that found by the conjugal surveys for a complete cross-section of the population. The conclusion must be drawn that there is no clear evidence of a fertility differential by economic class as yet in Ghana. From this it follows that it is unlikely that fertility amongst the upper economic classes in urban areas is declining. It is just possible that a slight differential is hidden by a greater reluctance of the poor to remember dead children, but there is no evidence for this. The Survey did show that the parents of the interviewees had on average more children at the same age, but the margin was small and completely explicable in terms of the rural-urban fertility differential, for many of the interviewees were of rural origin.

There does not appear to be in Ghana, even amongst the group surveyed, any desire for complete or nearly complete freedom from children. One component of the decline in fertility in the West was that a significant fraction of married couples decided to have either no children at all or to limit their number to one or two. Families of this size were desired by only a negligible number of the Ghanaian respondents. On the other hand, the model number of children which male and female respondents would advise newly married friends to have was found to be three and four respectively. This indicates that the family size that has hitherto prevailed is no longer regarded as the most desirable by this type of respondent. Indeed, 28 per cent of the males and 32 per cent of the females questioned wanted no more children than they possessed at the time of the Survey. This group alone represents a substantial demand or potential demand for ways of limiting births.

Did the respondents feel that a case could be argued on either personal or national grounds for reducing fertility? Only about half the respondents felt that a wife need not give birth to so many children now in order to ensure that some grow up and are subsequently able to care for herself and her husband in their old age. Demographically, of course, this is incontestable. More significantly, nine-tenths of those who did appreciate the implications of the higher rate of survival went on to draw the conclusion that some women at least would have to discover ways to limit their number of births. Similarly, about half of those interviewed thought that the high level of natural increase might some day provide potential recruits to the labour force in greater volume than could easily be matched by the

expansion of employment. But only a quarter of the respondents concluded that the Government was likely at a future date to initiate a campaign urging parents to restrict the size of their families.

This does not mean that only a quarter of the population desire the expansion of existing family planning facilities for those who wish to make
use of them. Nor does it mean that this socio-economic group has remained so unaware of medical and social change that most of its members
do not question the age-old pro-fertility orientation of African society.
In fact a great many married couples can discuss quite freely how many
children are desirable and whether efforts should be made to limit births.
Ghanaian society is less inhibited in this regard than some social scientists
have claimed is the case, for example, in Korea or even the American Deep
South. In fact about 70 per cent of couples have had such discussions.
About 65 per cent of respondents said that they were aware that it is
possible for some people to control family size by birth control methods.

In spite of increasing interest in family size, the advent of an unexpected
pregnancy is usually not regarded as a disaster. As can be seen from Table
4.1, only one pregnant woman in fourteen regrets her condition. However,
one husband in every seven with pregnant wives regrets his wife's pregnancy. At the time of the interviews, about half of all respondents desired
pregnancy. Such a fraction is large enough to sustain the highest level of
fertility. However, it may perhaps be sustained at an unreal level by the
acceptance of pregnancy by those already in that condition. For, of those
not pregnant, 57 per cent of both wives and their husbands were pleased
about this.

TABLE 4.1

PREGNANCY CONDITION OF WIVES AMONGST ECONOMICALLY BETTER-OFF
URBAN COUPLES, 1963 (PERCENTAGES)

Pregnancy conditions of wife and attitude of husband or wife	Husbands*	Wives*
(1) Pregnant and pleased	18	15
(2) Pregnant and displeased	3	1
(3) Not pregnant but desiring pregnancy	26	28
(4) Not pregnant and not desiring pregnancy	41	44
(5) Failed to answer either question	12	11
Summary:		
Desiring pregnancy ((1)+(3))	44	44
Not desiring pregnancy ((2)+(4))	44	45

* Male and female surveys were separate and do not cover husbands and wives of
the same couples. This, and also the existence of a small amount of polygamy, explains
the inequality of pregnancies in husbands' and wives' columns.
Source: *Survey of Population Attitudes in Economically Superior Urban Areas.*

Amongst this group in Ghana, the idea of the limitation of fertility is by
no means unknown. Half of all respondents claimed to know some way of
limiting births and a third stated that they had at some time practised the
method. Indeed, a fifth said that the method had achieved its aim of postponing an unwanted pregnancy. Two-fifths stated that they would probably
use the method at some time in the future. A few had in mind continence
or *coitus interruptus*, but the great majority were referring to modern

contraceptives. In the larger towns, condoms and spermaticidal pastes and foaming tablets have long been on rather inconspicuous sale from pharmacies. Probably their most important market was originally the expatriate European population, but much of the more educated, town population of Ghana is aware of their existence. Just over a quarter of the respondents claim to use, at least on occasions, contraceptives bought from the chemist shops, and almost half say that they know people who do. However, some of these purchases are apparently imported patent pills, said to be for 'feminine hygiene' and having in fact no contraceptive properties.[1]

These figures by no means gauge the full extent of the possible future use of family planning methods. Almost two-thirds of all respondents said that they would employ means of preventing or postponing pregnancies if they were told by a doctor either a method or a better method than the one they were then employing for achieving this end. On the other hand, less than half of those making this claim said that they would be interested if the method was complicated or meant quite a lot of trouble. The majority would expect the cost of contraception not to exceed £1 10s per month, even though on the average they compute the cost of bringing up an extra child at about £3 per month when a baby and £4 or £5 when a few years older. Half of all the respondents, who were prepared to use contraceptives, said that they would do so only if the cost was not more than half that of bringing up a baby and considerably less than half that of supporting a child. This, then, is no simple question of economic substitution.

Fewer couples had discussed the possibility of actually using contraceptives than had discussed in more general terms the problems of family size and the possibility of limiting it. The number who have already done so amounted to 42 per cent of the sample, while another 37 per cent thought that such a discussion could be held. In one-ninth of all cases, one member of the couple was in favour of contraception but knew or thought that the other spouse would be against. In the majority of these cases, it was felt that the spouse's objections were in some sense religious, although in by no means all cases doctrinal.

In Ghana, where much of the economic and even social change is directed by the Government, the question must inevitably arise of the wisdom of establishing public family planning clinics. Thus, the answers, as set out in Table 4.2, to the question about willingness to use such clinics is of special interest. Seven out of every ten respondents would be in favour of such an innovation, and six out of every ten would be prepared to use the services provided. Of those who opposed the setting up of clinics, only a quarter did so on what could be regarded in any sense as religious grounds. The majority merely reacted against what they considered to be a strange, new and somewhat repellent idea.

In view of the changes in public attitudes towards abortion and sterilization which have occurred in some countries in recent years, these matters were also raised in the Survey. Abortion is illegal in Ghana, and in 1963 a Cabinet decision was announced in favour of introducing legislation to make the penalties for its practice more stringent. Therefore, no information was sought about personal abortion histories. But, in answer to the

[1] D. I. Pool, who is investigating this matter in the course of a fertility survey in the Accra-Tema area.

TABLE 4.2

ATTITUDES AMONGST ECONOMICALLY BETTER-OFF URBAN POPULATION TOWARDS
GOVERNMENT FAMILY PLANNING CLINICS, 1963

(i) *Question:* Do you think that it would be a good idea if the Government were to establish family planning clinics in Ghana?*

Answer:	Percentage of interviews		Percentage of those answering	
	males	*females*	*males*	*females*
YES	69	73	70	75
NO	29	25	30	25
Failed to answer	2	2	—	—

(ii) *Question:* If such clinics were set up, would you (your wife) ever use them?

Answer:	Percentage of interviews		Percentage of those answering	
	males	*females*	*males*	*females*
YES	65	61	69	67
NO	29	29	31	33
Failed to answer	6	10	—	—

* Preliminary explanation had already established clearly what such clinics were.
Source: *Survey of Population Attitudes in Economically Superior Urban Areas.*

general question whether abortion was commonly practised in Ghana, about half the male respondents and a third of the female thought that it was. Many discussed the case of school girls. Such girls often have more chance of escaping the watch of their families in order to have sexual relations. It is believed that contraceptives are used more in such relations than is common in the country. Nevertheless, the interviewers were informed that pregnancies among school girls are not rare. Such pregnancies raise far more serious problems than they would have in the past among the illiterate girls of rural villages. The latter would probably have been expected to marry soon anyway, and, even without marriage, the bearing of the child presented no great problem. But in the case of school girls, there has been a considerable investment of money and hope by the family and an investment of effort by the girl. Therefore, pregnant school girls quite frequently seek abortions, which are sometimes fatal and incur a certain amount of publicity.

About two-fifths of the respondents expressed themselves in favour of the right to sterilization, if desired, once a family of sufficient size had been born. However, the majority view amongst members of each sex was that the preferable form of sterilization was that which was performed upon members of the opposite sex. Of those opposed to sterilization, 26 per cent, or 13 per cent of all respondents interviewed, based their attitude on religious grounds, while 9 per cent argued that it was in the national good to prevent such interference with high fertility. But the majority, some 60 per cent of those opposed and about 30 per cent of all respondents, expressed fear of either losing fertility, potency or sexual prestige or of the operation itself.

It should be realized that we have been discussing a select group, but one that could play a key social role in any decline in the fertility level. Only one-tenth of the population lives in the four large towns surveyed, and, even in these towns, the examination was confined to less than a quarter of the population. Thus, we have interested ourselves in less than 2 per cent of the population, although, if we had investigated similar groups in other towns, the proportion might rise towards 3 per cent.

But what of the great mass of the people, over three-quarters of whom still live in the villages? To answer this question, the *Survey of Population Attitudes in Rural Ghana* was designed to give a balanced cover of rural Ghana. The interviewees did not have the sophisticated knowledge of modern contraceptives shown by the respondents previously examined, but they were aware of some of the problems of high fertility in an era when infant and child mortality has declined quite dramatically. On the whole, the economic problems of very large families were felt to be relatively more acute in the areas of southern Ghana where the cash economy predominates and less in the subsistence rural areas of the north.

In the sample as a whole, only one-third of the respondents denied that it was a good thing to have a lot of children, but almost two-thirds agreed that people with a lot of children are poorer than those with fewer. The case against having too many children was summed up in the main by the cost of supporting them and that of educating them in that order. In better-off urban areas the specific problem of education looms more seriously than the general problem of support. This is not yet the case in rural areas. The case in favour of children was more complex. In the subsistence north, more children, and even more wives, can still be a source of economic wealth. On the whole, this is no longer the case in more economically developed areas. The most important argument for large families was the extra assurance of assistance in old age or times of sickness. Personal prestige and the national good were also frequently mentioned. Only 6 per cent of those favouring large families spoke of children in some way as a 'consumption good', which could be enjoyed for its own sake. This may merely mean that Ghanaian society takes so much for granted that the possession of children is a form of pleasure it does not occur to respondents to point it out.

Perhaps the most interesting part of this survey was the enquiry into the productive work done by children either in the form of adding to the family's income directly or indirectly assisting in increasing the output of farms or other fields of occupation. In the case of children who do not go to school, one-third of respondents claim that 5–9 year olds earn their keep and this rises to almost two-thirds in the case of 10–14 year olds. The figures are highest in the north. Children are cited as doing general farm-work, house-work, water-carrying and the running of errands. However, school attendance makes a critical difference. The percentage of families claiming that school children manage to justify their existence econo-mically is for each age group only half what it was for children not attend-ing school. Nevertheless, the great majority of the rural population express themselves in favour of a further extension of schooling. In many cases this is related to long-term financial prospects, but far more often the feelings expressed are those of the general good to be obtained by reducing illiteracy, spreading enlightenment and assisting economic development. Some of those opposed to further schooling point to the cost of supporting school children. But far more are concerned about the withdrawal of

labour from their farms either because of the children's immediate attendance at school or their later tendency to go to the towns looking for
urban employment.

In spite of increasing economic pressures on some of the large families,
there is no evidence as yet that the desired family size is beginning to fall
below that which has prevailed in practice up until now. Only about one-
sixth of the rural respondents desired completed families of less than five
children. Most frequently favoured were 7 or 8 children, which has been, as
was seen previously, the approximate size of the completed family in rural
Ghana.

However, almost two-thirds of respondents agreed that attempts to prevent pregnancy or to abort unborn children are practised in the villages.
Only one-seventh of those admitting this knowledge, and less than one-
tenth of the whole sample, expressed approval of such actions. The chief
reasons ascribed to these attempts to prevent births were economic. There
were other frequently cited reasons. One was that the child was illegitimate
and that the mother or her family were opposed to a marriage with
the husband. Another was that the mothers were women of loose morals
and irregular liaisons who did not intend a pregnancy to change their way
of life.

Two aspects of the high fertility pattern are of special interest. One is the
relation between bringing up a family and having some of its members
educated, and the other is the role of the large family as a kind of insurance
policy against destitution in time of old age or sickness. These questions
were pursued further in the *Survey of Aged Population*, which was limited to
an examination of population over 65 years of age who had wholly or
partially retired from economic activity.

An investigation was made of the cost to the family of educating children
and of the subsequent returns in the form of support to the family and
help with the education of other relatives which could be afforded from the
higher income gained on the basis of the educational qualifications. This
shows that family ties are still strong enough in Ghana for the money spent
on the education of young relatives to be a sound economic investment. It
may well be the best investment open to many Ghanaians. Of all aged
respondents, 59 per cent claimed that the family had already received back
more than the original investment, and two-thirds of these said that the
return was much greater than the investment. Another 12 per cent had
received back about the same amount as had been spent, while 29 per cent
had received back less. Of the latter, about half, or one-seventh of the
whole sample, described the return as being much less. It is significant that
this group is far bigger in rural Ghana, where it makes up 18 per cent of
households, than in urban Ghana, where it forms only 5 per cent. It suggests that some of the rural households have come close to having lost
contact with their educated children who have migrated to the towns.

Since investment in education is greatest in the case of those children
who have received the longest period of education, a survey was made of
the students at the University of Ghana. Many of these students had
received a considerable part of their education before as much free education or as many scholarships were available as is now the case. On the
other hand, many had assisted their own education, often part-time, by

obtaining employment. Nevertheless, 89 per cent stated that they would not have been able to continue with their education but for private financial support. The most critical point in the educational ladder, where the withdrawal of private support would have precluded continuation at school or the obtaining of the type of employment which could subsequently support part-time education, was undoubtedly at the primary school level.

Most financial support for education came from parents, although the role of uncles and brothers was also important. Well over half the recipients regard the repayment of the assistance as a definite obligation. The two main forms of repayment will take the form of assistance with the education of brothers and sisters and the support of parents, especially when old or sick. It is noteworthy that support for education sets up a kind of chain reaction which engenders the further support of education. Most students expect to spend between 10 per cent and 30 per cent of their net income on the assistance of relatives beyond the bounds of the nuclear family consisting of themselves, wives and children, and most expect to be paying money to from four to six of such persons.

Thus, the financial obligations of the extended family remain very strong. On the whole, such obligations are not resented. Less than a tenth of all students claimed that they resented it in any way. The majority approved, and a third strongly approved. This does not mean that graduates would receive no economic benefit from limiting the number of their children. The obligation to other relatives would not show a compensatory rise. In fact one-third would expect to reap the full financial gain, and another third would expect to retain most of it.

The problem of estimating the right family size to ensure help for oneself in old age and sickness and for one's family in securing education is a difficult one. The family will be reduced by mortality. Some will not be very successful in the world and others will be somewhat grudging about sharing their success. Males are more likely to be earning income than females, and the sex balance within the family is a matter of chance. In the *Survey of Aged Population*, it was discovered that, of all children ever born to the aged parents, 63 per cent had survived and reached adulthood by the time of the survey. Only 35 per cent had become what their parents regarded as good providers, and only 24 per cent had given assistance in education to relatives. However, 26 per cent had given help to their parents in time of sickness, and 37 per cent were now assisting during old age.

Thus, it might appear that parents were likely to receive some support in old age if they had three children and some support in sickness with four children. Unfortunately, these are average figures, and many families do not fare as well. In fact, in a third of all families surveyed none of the children had been able to help with the education of relatives and in a tenth none had been able to help during sickness. In a ninth of all rural families and a sixth of urban ones no help had been forthcoming in old age. The rural-urban differential here may not be significant, because more urban retired people may receive superannuation or income from a business or houses, or something of the sort.

The reduction of infant and child mortality will allow more persons to survive from birth to adulthood. This should permit parents to reduce the average size of their families and still retain a reasonable assurance of care in old age. On the other hand, the very forces of modernization which have allowed the reduction of mortality may also help to break the bonds of family obligations, with perhaps the result that parents can trust fewer of their surviving children to give sufficient help. There are, however, other factors. Rising standards of living may well make parents less desperately in need of such support, while at the same time making it easier for others to provide it. In the long-run the Government will undoubtedly shoulder these social welfare burdens.

In the near future the State can hardly provide a comprehensive range of social welfare payments. These services are expensive even in a highly developed economy. Ghana has made a creditable start in this direction, but for the time being the needs of development investment must inevitably come first. 'It is more important that steady employment is assured to him (the worker) from the time he comes of working age till the time he retires, and that in the meantime his sons and daughters are also educated and trained so that they are able to take regular and profitable employment than that he can look forward to a small pension.'[1]

The thinking expressed in the Seven-Year Development Plan and quoted above may fall somewhat short of the hopes of most Ghanaians. This is undoubtedly because most citizens in Ghana, as elsewhere, do not fully comprehend the expenditure required to maintain a complete welfare State. Nor is the average citizen in a position to distinguish between the likely long-term returns from investment in economic development in contrast to investment in social welfare schemes.

It is of interest that, in spite of the strong Ghanaian tradition of family assistance, over 60 per cent of all aged respondents in the country answered 'Yes' and only 27 per cent said, 'No' to both the following questions. 'Do you think that it would be a good idea if the Government were to tax people more, so that any sick people could be helped by being paid money by the Government instead of by their relatives?' 'Do you think that it would be a good idea if the Government were to tax people more, so that old people could be paid a pension (i.e. money) by the Government to support them instead of their being supported by relatives?' There was no significant division in opinion in terms of either sex or urban-rural residence.

It might be noted that the enthusiasm waned somewhat when similar questions were put to university students, a group who would ultimately find jobs in the high income and high taxation brackets. Perhaps they felt that they would pay more in the form of higher taxation than in the form of private assistance, or perhaps they thought that, if they had to make the expenditure in any case, they would prefer to receive personal gratitude in return. Certainly, the private system finds somewhat more favour amongst the givers of assistance than it does amongst the recipients. The students were asked, 'Do you favour a system of private help by individuals for sick or unemployed relatives, or would you rather the Government imposed higher taxation in order to pay full sickness or unemployment pay to people not able to work?' Individual help was preferred by 46 per cent, the Government scheme by 48 per cent and neither by 6 per cent. When the same question was repeated in terms of assistance to the aged, 47 per cent

[1] *Seven-Year Development Plan*, op. cit., p. 6.

preferred private assistance, 50 per cent Government pensions, and 3 per cent neither.

The main point at issue in this discussion of the intricate system of private assistance for the needy which has developed in Ghana is whether it is the main social force sustaining high fertility. Do parents consciously endeavour to have large families so that they can minimize the danger of being left without the economic support of children in times of sickness, unemployment or old age? If this danger were to disappear, would parents immediately desire smaller families? Is there, indeed, an arguable case in terms of developmental economics for investing more in social welfare so as to accelerate the fertility decline aspect of demographic transition? There is no strong evidence that welfare payments would cause a marked fall in the birth rate. The aged were asked how many children they would advise a newly married friend to have, firstly, if the present level of social service payments were to be retained, and secondly, if a full range of pensions and disability payments were available. In the latter case, 37 per cent of respondents advocated more children, 13 per cent the same, and 49 per cent fewer. When university students were asked about the number of children they would like to have themselves in these two different sets of circumstances, 15 per cent said more under a welfare State, 66 per cent said the same, and 19 per cent stated fewer. Those preferring more children under the welfare State argued not illogically that they would then be able to afford more as their expenditures would be largely confined to their nuclear families. There is, then, considerable doubt whether on balance a substantial expansion of social welfare payments would at first have much effect upon the level of fertility. In the longer run such payments might well act in concert with other pressures towards a fall in the birth rate in that their existence would remove one of the otherwise nearly insoluble dilemmas of fertility transition.

Several conclusions can be drawn from this study of the possibility of fertility decline. One is that the economic and social change which has already occurred in Ghana is no guarantee that birth rates will necessarily fall. Nor is the decline in infant and child mortality. On the other hand, the evidence of sustained high birth rates in some of the developing agrarian countries during the last decade or two cannot be taken as certain evidence that such countries cannot expect any voluntary limitation of family size until their economic transition is far advanced. The period has been much too short to allow such generalizations to be made with certainty.

What is certain is that the urban population is growing disproportionately rapidly and that, amongst the economically better-off, in the towns at least, profound change in the structure of the family is under way. The place of women, and especially of children, in the home is improving, and children are absorbing more of the family's money and attention. These families are worried about the expenditure needed on large families and this worry centres more around the cost of the education and training of the children than on anything else. Much of the extra expenditure will remain even if all school fees are abolished. The possible relationship between the implementation of universal or near universal schooling and fertility decline should not be underestimated either in late nineteenth-century Western Europe or contemporary Ghana. The question of family size and the problems of excessively large families are already discussed widely by couples within this key urban group. So is the possible use of modern contraceptives. Indeed, a quarter of those included in the sample claimed to have used them at some stage. As a pointer to likely future developments, perhaps the most significant finding was that two-thirds of the respondents favoured the establishment by the Government of family planning clinics and that a similar number would be prepared to use such facilities.

The position is of course very different in rural Ghana, where the large family is still much admired. Nevertheless, it is in the rural areas that an important distinction can be made about the economic impact of high fertility upon the family. An understanding of this point is probably important in the assessment of the problems of many developing countries. It is this. The argument that large families can be economically advantageous in agrarian areas is apparently valid in Ghana only in the predominantly subsistence farming areas of the north. There, especially in areas where there are still ample reserves of cultivable land, a man is not impoverished by taking many wives and rearing a great number of children. His personal well-being will probably improve. But this is no longer the case in the south, where the cash economy is dominant. Here, large families do give rise to economic problems and these problems are being increasingly aggravated by the greater demands for education, although, as yet, the chief complaint of those with many children is of the general problems of support rather than of the specific difficulties of providing schooling. The pattern found now mostly in the rural south will inevitably embrace the whole country, for there can be little doubt that the north will experience increasing penetration by the cash economy, the provision of schools and the need for education to secure desirable jobs.

What of the future? Should population projections examine the possibility of a fertility decline? The answer seems to be that there are certainly forces operating towards a limitation of family size, but it can be by no means certain that they will be effective. Economic development, what might be called by some 'social modernization' associated especially with urbanization, and the related spread of the cash economy and of the pressure to educate children all work in this direction. It is less certain that in the short-term the extension of social services does.

It can be said with some assurance that fertility is unlikely to rise further. Therefore, the high fertility projection should involve the assumption of constant fertility. It is possible that the forces listed above, reinforced by a continued fall in mortality, could give rise to declining fertility. If some Government family planning clinics were established, and if contraceptives continued to come into the country without restriction for relatively cheap sale through retail outlets, a 1 per cent per year decline in fertility could be envisaged. There is much to be said for also examining the implications of a 2 per cent per year decline, for such a situation could be brought about by massive governmental intervention. In the present political and social climate of the world, and with the degree of change which occurs from one decade to another, it would be unwise for anyone constructing population projections to ignore this possibility.

3. POPULATION PROJECTIONS

Only four factors can influence the future population of Ghana, or indeed of any other country. One is the present population, by which is meant not only its total size but also its sex and age composition. Another is the pattern of fertility, which includes not merely the number of births arising from a given population at a certain time, but also the distribution of child-bearing amongst the female population in terms of age. A third is the pattern of mortality, and once again not merely the volume but also the distribution by age is important. The final one is migration, where the sex and age pattern of the migrants must also be taken into account.

Mortality and migration give us least difficulty. In accordance with previous findings, the expectation of life at birth was taken to have been 45½ years in 1960. Subsequent to that date it is assumed that it improves in accordance with the United Nations schedule of life tables so that for every year elapsed an approximate gain is achieved of half a year in the expectation of life at birth. It can be taken for granted that the country will persist with its battle to reduce death rates and that this will produce a fairly constant and predictable increase in expectation of life. Some error in the prediction of the exact rate of change will not produce very significant differences in the population projections.

Migration is subject to control by Ghana. It can be either prevented or allowed by governmental decision providing that the decision can be effectively enforced. In order to examine the economic implications of attempts to control immigration, two different sets of projections have been constructed. One assumes that migration has been halted, in that immigration has been reduced to the point where it equals emigration and so net migration is zero. The other assumes little control, but adopts the viewpoint that such measures as the control of remittances from the country will tend to reduce the rate of immigration and even the absolute number of immigrants entering per year below that obtaining in the 1948–60 period. The annual average intake in the projections has been fixed at the apparent average annual net immigration between the 1948 and 1960 censuses, if both sets of census figures are accepted without question. This is undoubtedly less than the real volume of the flow during those years. Furthermore, such immigration will represent an ever less significant element in Ghana's total population growth as the size of the population becomes bigger. The sex division of the immigrant flow is assumed to be the same as during the intercensal years and the age distribution on arrival the same as that found in the *International Migration Survey*. The same fertility schedules were applied to female immigrants and to the native born.

There is no problem in projecting average individual female fertility. The 1960 total fertility rate was taken to be 7·3 and the sex ratio at birth 101 males per 100 females. Three sets of projections were calculated, the first assuming constant fertility, the second a decline of 1 per cent per annum in fertility from 1965, and the third a decline of 2 per cent per annum from the same date. In both cases of declining fertility it was postulated that the fertility transition would come to an end when the gross reproduction rate reached 1·5, approximately the level now found in the United States or Australia. In the case of the moderate decline in fertility this would occur only shortly before the year 2060, but in the steeply declining projection this would happen about the year 2005.

The real problems of projection are those arising from census and survey age misstatement. Chronological age is a concept which has not yet become part of the everyday experience of considerable sections of the population. As was seen earlier, one effect of this in the 1960 census enumeration was to reduce the apparent population between 10 and 19 years of age and to swell that above 20 years. A disproportionate number of females was found in the 20–34 years of age range. That this age distribution was not a genuine peculiarity of the population but arose from a definite pattern of age misstatement was established by the discovery that such a pattern was found widely in tropical Africa and persisted regardless of the census date. Confirmation was received from the fact that, although the pattern is found in all regions of Ghana, it is far more pronounced in the north, where illiteracy is higher and where other indices indicate a greater degree of age misstatement.

The problem of age misstatement is not one merely of projecting forward certain distortions in the age structure. This would only be serious in so far as it affected short-term estimates of such measures as the size of the labour force. The real difficulty is that in the first few years of projection it affects the estimates of fertility very greatly. Over a decade the seemingly denuded female 10–19 years of age group is moved into the 20–29 years of age range. The apparently small group in the most fertile age range greatly depresses the estimate of births. Now, this is completely artificial. The original census data, and probably the survey fertility data as well, contained distortions. If such age-specific birth rates are to be used, the new data should be distorted again by increasing the number of 20–29 year olds by prematurely advancing females from the younger age groups. If this is not done, or if some form of correction is not carried out on the original data, highly misleading results can be obtained.

Just how misleading these results can be is shown by the projection of the uncorrected 1960 census data. The projection for the 1960–5 period produces an apparent average annual rate of population growth of 3·2 per cent per year with migration and 2·7 per cent without it. These figures are, of course, totally irreconcilable with the 1948–60 average rate of growth, which was suggested by the earlier analysis, of 3·6 per cent and 2·9 per cent respectively for that period. It is much further still from the implication of the uncorrected census data that the growth with migration averaged 4·2 per cent per year and would have amounted to 3·5 per cent without it. An acceptance of such a growth rate for the 1960–5 period would imply, with due allowance made for improvement in mortality, an average population growth rate of about 2·8 per cent per year between 1948 and 1960. This would in its turn suggest that the real 1948 population must have been about 4,960,000 and that underenumeration in the census of that year was about 17 per cent. This figure seems improbably high.

This discussion is relevant because it would seem probable that the 2·6 per cent per annum population growth figure given in the Seven-Year Development Plan is based upon such a projection from uncorrected census figures. The acceptance of such a figure seems to involve risks, although everyone may not be convinced on that point until the next census.

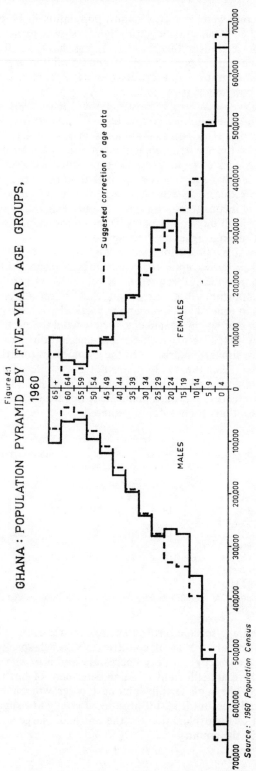

Figure 4.1

GHANA : POPULATION PYRAMID BY FIVE-YEAR AGE GROUPS, 1960

Source: 1960 Population Census

If this growth rate were correct, Ghana's population in 1970 would be no greater than 8,800,000, allowing for slightly slower growth in the early 1960s. Later projections in this chapter suggest that the real population in that year will lie somewhere between $9\frac{1}{4}$ and $9\frac{3}{4}$ million depending on the exact rate of immigration and fertility decline. A reasonable estimate for planning purposes might be $9\frac{1}{2}$ million.

An attempt was made to reconstruct the 1960 census population in accordance with the findings of this analysis on fertility, mortality and migrational trends. The results are shown in Figure 4.1. There are two major changes to the age structure which were recorded by the census. The first is that the ages of some persons enumerated as over 20 have been reduced to under that age. The second is that some of the aged have also had their ages reduced. The proportions of persons found in the older age groups were inconsistent with the mortality experience of Ghana, and confirmed that in Ghana, as in many other countries, the old are subject to the temptation to exaggerate their age.

It was not the age adjustment itself, but a by-product of it that produced the most marked effects upon the projections, and brought these in line with what had previously been learnt of the 1948–60 population growth trends. The important observation was that, if census enumeration in tropical Africa in general and in Ghana in particular is consistently marked by a certain type of age misstatement, then it would seem to be inevitable that the survey data, from which the age-specific birth rates have been constructed, are similarly marked. On the assumption that the error in the 1960 census data and the 1963 survey data was identical, age-specific birth rates were corrected to those shown in Table 4.3. The total fertility and gross reproduction rates are unaffected, but the distribution of births by the age of mothers is considerably altered.

TABLE 4.3

AGE-SPECIFIC BIRTH RATES, CORRECTED AND UNCORRECTED
(Births per thousand females)

Female age group	15–19	20–4	25–9	30–4	35–9	40–4	45–9
Uncorrected A-S B.R.	141	259	306	259	213	165	117
Corrected A-S B.R.	219	304	304	255	201	147	30
Uncorrected distribution of births (%)	10	18	21	18	14	11	8
Corrected distribution of births (%)	15	21	21	17	14	10	2
15 countries of French-speaking Africa* (%)	17	24	22	17	12	6	2

* From *Perspectives de Population dans les pays Africains et Malgashe d'Expression Franaise*, op. cit., p. 21.

The corrected age-specific birth rates are very reassuring. Their pattern is sufficiently similar to that of countries of French-speaking Africa to suggest that the correction has been necessary and is of approximately the right order. There are still signs of some deferment of birth in Ghana by later marriage. The high fertility amongst older women has been very considerably reduced but it is still prominent enough to suggest that such fertility is part of the explanation for the unusually large size of the completed family in the country.

The redistribution of age-specific birth rates reduces the average age of mothers at the time of the birth of their children. This has no effect on the eventual size of each woman's family. But, it does have a very considerable effect on the community's population growth rates. This occurs because the average length of a generation is shortened. Women have children earlier who in turn reproduce at a younger age. More generations are fitted into a century and so the same population increases are achieved in a shorter time.

It might also be noted that the redistribution of population in terms of age has no measurable effect on the mortality calculations of earlier chapters. Some population has been removed from the oldest age groups where mortality risks are high, but some have also been added to the youngest age group where the risk is also high and where the population is much greater in size. The total effect on the 1960 population is to leave crude death rates unchanged.

These, then, are the bases of the population projections. There are in all six projections. The high set assume constant fertility, the medium ones fertility declining by 1 per cent per year from 1965, and the low ones fertility declining by 2 per cent from the same date. Each is divided into a migration projection, which assumes what is likely to be the upper limit of net immigration, and a no migration projection, which assumes that Government action has reduced net migration to zero. The migration sub-sections of the projections part ways from 1960, and in truth little is yet known about migration trends since that date. The projections, taken as a whole, serve to show the relative differences between possible courses of development. These lessons remain largely valid even if some adjustments are made to the bases of the projections.

4. THE IMPLICATIONS OF THE POPULATION PROJECTIONS
The most obvious implications of the projections are those connected with total population size. These are set out in Tables 4.4 and 4.5 and Figures 4.2 and 4.3. They demonstrate the certainty of massive population increases, even if anti-migration and anti-high fertility policies were to be adopted.

In the quarter century from 1960 to 1985, Ghana will certainly double its population and may go far towards trebling it. Planners should probably aim at coping with a two-and-a-half fold increase. Their problems will be considerable no matter what course population follows, for, in so short a period, no demographic miracle can save them. Very great reductions in potential population can usually be effected only over two generations. Over a shorter period, reductions in female fertility do not achieve dramatic results, because earlier high fertility has already produced great numbers of children who will inevitably be the parents of the coming generation. Thus, in the case of Ghana, by 1985 the highest projection is less than one and a quarter times greater than the smallest.

The position is considerably different if the forty-year period from 1960 to 2000 is considered. By the latter date the highest projection is 1·6 times the size of the lowest. More significant from the planning point of view is the fact that the additions to the population in the latter part of the period are of very different magnitudes. Between 1985 and 2000, the lowest projec-

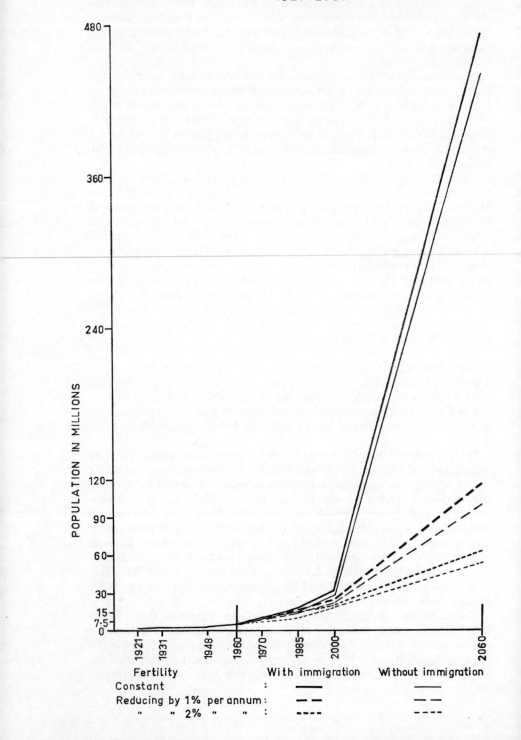

Figure 4:2
GHANA: POPULATION GROWTH and PROJECTED GROWTH,
1921 - 2060

Figure 4:3

GHANA : ALTERNATIVE POPULATION PROJECTIONS, 1960-2000

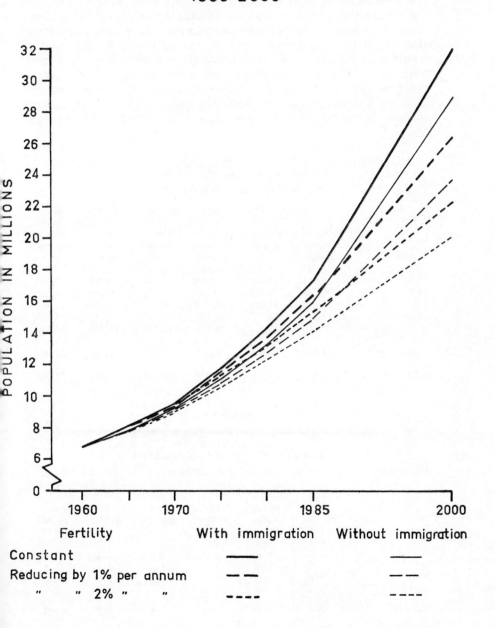

tion suggests an increase in population of just over 6 million persons. But the highest projection places the increase at more than $14\frac{1}{2}$ million, or two and a half times as many. At this stage the difference in the investment needed to absorb the extra population into the community and into employment is obviously very great indeed.

The projected populations for a century hence are not intended to be in any sense estimates. They are in fact included to show the impossibility of the continuation of certain population trends. An individual and national *laissez-faire* policy towards family size over the next century would imply that by 2060 the country's population would be greater than that of contemporary India on less than a twelfth of that country's land area. Even the lowest projection yields a population equal in size and density to that now found in the United Kingdom. All this merely demonstrates one thing. Well within the century, the higher projections must be invalidated by a rise in mortality or fertility must fall very markedly. The first could

Quote

TABLE 4.4

POPULATION PROJECTIONS, 1960–2060

(All population in thousands)

Projections	Constant fertility		Fertility reducing by 1% per annum		Fertility reducing by 2% per annum	
Date	With immi-gration	Without immi-gration	With immi-gration	Without immi-gration	With immi-gration	Without immi-gration
1960	6,727	6,727	6,727	6,727	6,727	6,727
1965	8,088	7,904	8,088	7,904	8,088	7,904
1970	9,748	9,329	9,697	9,281	9,648	9,235
1975	11,780	11,084	11,560	10,877	11,354	10,684
1980	14,279	13,267	13,730	12,752	13,233	12,287
1985	17,352	15,974	16,249	14,945	15,289	14,049
2000	31,916	28,918	26,413	23,841	22,341	20,084
2060	470,571	423,337	114,063	100,921	64,099	55,533

TABLE 4.5

MULTIPLICATION OF POPULATION, 1960–2060, ACCORDING TO VARIOUS POPULATION PROJECTIONS

(Shown as multiples of 1960 population)

Projections	Constant fertility		Fertility reducing by 1% per annum		Fertility reducing by 2% per annum	
Date	With immi-gration	Without immi-gration	With immi-gration	Without immi-gration	With immi-gration	Without immi-gration
1960	1·0	1·0	1·0	1·0	1·0	1·0
1965	1·2	1·2	1·2	1·2	1·2	1·2
1970	1·4	1·4	1·4	1·4	1·4	1·4
1975	1·8	1·6	1·7	1·6	1·7	1·6
1980	2·1	2·0	2·0	1·9	2·0	1·8
1985	2·6	2·4	2·4	2·2	2·3	2·1
2000	4·7	4·3	3·9	3·5	3·3	3·0
2060	70·0	62·9	16·9	15·0	9·5	8·3

arise from the poverty and destitution of overpopulation or possibly from a nuclear war. The alternative does mean that eventually it is inevitable that the Ghanaian population must critically examine the profertility tendencies in their culture and the social grounds on which any possible resistance to various methods of family limitation may rest.

The magnitude of the populations suggested by some of the projections can perhaps best be grasped by converting them into average population densities for the country. Ghana's population density, it might be repeated, is already high both in terms of the African scene and in comparison with all but very exceptional areas of the equatorial tropics.

Ghana still has a great deal of land which could be used for agriculture or which could be used more efficiently for that purpose. Nevertheless, it is salutary to compare Ghana's projected population densities with some of the world's most densely settled countries. Ghana's population density will reach the figure now attained by China before 1980 according to the highest projection and by 1995 according to all projections. The highest projection reaches India's present density in the year 2000. By 2000 all projections show densities greater than that of present-day France, and by 2060 all will have surpassed the contemporary United Kingdom figure and all but the lowest pair of projections Holland's present figure. At that date the high projection envisages a density six times greater than that now attained by any country.

These comparisons serve to show that in agricultural terms even the 'Fertility Reducing by 2 per cent per annum, Without Migration' projection is a radically optimistic forecast. For France, the United Kingdom and Holland have attained their present densities as a result of prolonged industrial and urban revolutions. All the countries mentioned have great areas of soils which have proved well suited to intensive crop-growing. The position in Ghana is not as optimistic in spite of striking success with forest tree crops.

TABLE 4.6

PROJECTED POPULATION DENSITIES, 1960–2060
(Average number of persons per square mile)

Projections	Constant fertility		Fertility reducing by 1% per annum		Fertility reducing by 2% per annum	
Date	With immigration	Without immigration	With immigration	Without immigration	With immigration	Without immigration
1960	73	73	73	73	73	73
1965	88	86	88	86	88	86
1970	106	101	105	101	105	100
1975	128	120	126	118	123	116
1980	155	144	149	138	144	133
1985	188	173	176	162	166	153
2000	347	314	287	259	243	218
2060	5,109	4,596	1,238	1,096	696	603

There are two ways by which Ghana's high rate of population growth could be reduced. One would be to restrict immigration and the other would be to reduce fertility. It would be possible to take one action without the other or to take both in conjunction. As, at some stage, it is possible that policy decisions will have to be taken within these fields, a close study is justified of the respective contributions of migration and natural increase to population growth and economic development.

Table 4.7 illustrates, as did Tables 4.4 and 4.5, that the prevention of immigration could slow down population growth more effectively than could declining fertility over the short run. Even the reduction of fertility by 2 per cent per year could not, if it were coupled with free entrance for immigrants, reduce total population below that which would result from constant fertility and a ban upon immigration, until 1980. And were the fertility reduction to be only 1 per cent per year, population growth would not be exceeded by the constant fertility without immigration projection until about 1990.

In the longer term the position is very different. By the year 2060, the major difference between the projections is determined largely by the level of fertility. Projections with different immigration policies but the same level of fertility display relatively similar population totals when compared with those displayed by projections with different fertility levels. Ulti-

TABLE 4.7

PERCENTAGE FORMED BY EACH PROJECTION OF THE
'CONSTANT FERTILITY WITH MIGRATION' PROJECTION AT VARIOUS DATES, 1960–2060

Projections	Constant fertility		Fertility reducing by 1% per annum		Fertility reducing by 2% per annum	
Date	With immi- gration	Without immi- gration	With immi- gration	Without immi- gration	With immi- gration	Without immi- gration
1960	100·0	100·0	100·0	100·0	100·0	100·0
1965	100·0	97·7	100·0	97·7	100·0	97·7
1970	100·0	95·6	99·4	95·1	98·9	94·7
1975	100·0	94·1	98·1	92·3	96·4	90·7
1980	100·0	92·9	96·2	89·3	92·7	86·0
1985	100·0	92·1	93·6	86·1	88·1	81·0
2000	100·0	90·6	82·8	74·7	70·0	62·9
2060	100·0	90·0	24·2	21·4	13·6	11·8

TABLE 4.8

PERCENTAGE FORMED BY THE 'WITHOUT MIGRATION' PROJECTION OF THE
'WITH MIGRATION' PROJECTION OF THE SAME FERTILITY LEVEL AT VARIOUS DATES, 1960–2060

Projections	Constant fertility	Fertility reducing by 1% per annum	Fertility reducing by 2% per annum
Date			
1960	100·0	100·0	100·0
1965	97·7	97·7	97·7
1970	95·7	95·7	95·7
1975	94·1	94·1	94·1
1980	92·9	92·9	92·9
1985	92·1	92·0	91·9
2000	90·6	90·3	89·9
2060	90·0	88·5	86·6

mately Ghana's demographic dilemma, which has arisen from economic development and the mortality decline, can be solved only by a very considerable decline in fertility. But are the chief short-term gains to be secured in this way? Table 4.8 shows that a ban on immigration could achieve a 5 per cent reduction in what would otherwise be the total population size by the early 1970s and a 10 per cent reduction by 2000. Such gains can be very tempting to the economic planner.

However, as pointed out in the earlier analysis of migration, the question of the effect of immigration upon economic development and upon the speed with which living standards can be raised must be approached cautiously. Admittedly the arrival of immigrants creates the need for more housing, roads and other facilities. But most do not demand schooling or support when young. A far higher proportion of them are found within the working age groups, for the simple reason that most make the journey in order to secure work. On the other hand, many immigrants do become the parents of children after they have arrived in Ghana, and these children are usually brought up in the country. Certainly the fertility of some male migrants is impaired by the difficulty of finding wives, for the immigrant groups exhibit sex ratios well above normal.

The immigration problem is only part of the more complex question of the short-term effect of various population growth patterns upon economic development. There is a tendency amongst economic planners to assume that fertility decline can have no significant economic effect for the first fifteen or twenty years because this period must elapse before there is any slackening in the demand for employment. This is not so, for children give rise to expenditure long before they require employment.[1] They demand extra housing, schools and an expansion of a multiplicity of other services. Their extra demands are not as great as are those of adults, especially in the case of extra children of highly fertile families who may often be crammed more tightly into houses of the same size as those that hold smaller families. In the discussion that follows, this is taken into account by assuming that persons under 15 years cost the community to which they are added only half the expenditure on the average that is demanded by the addition of persons over 15 years. This form of analysis is necessary in order to compare, for instance, two populations with labour forces of the same size but with different numbers of children. The population with the fewer children will be able to save more while maintaining the same standard of living as the other population. These are the savings which would otherwise have been spent by either the individuals or the Government on supporting the extra children. These savings, whether accumulated by individual initiative or Government taxation, can be invested to raise the capital stock per worker and ultimately the standard of living.

In Table 4.9 an analysis has been made of the economic implications of the various possible paths of population growth. The examination has been confined to the periods from 1960 until 1985 and from 1960 until 2000. Thus the findings relate solely to what might be regarded as the near future. No contemporary economic planner could hardly fail to take into account the effects of his planning during such a relatively short period.

[1] For discussion on this point, see Ansley J. Coale, 'Population and Economic Development', in Philip M. Hauser (ed.), *The Population Dilemma*, 1963.

Problems arising from the distinction between the cash and subsistence economies or between cash and labour investment have been avoided by carrying out the analysis in labour years, each of which is defined as the average amount of labour performed by a member of the labour force in one year. It has been assumed that the proportion of persons participating in gainful activity will remain in terms of sex and age at the level obtaining in 1960. It has further been assumed that the planned 15 per cent rate of domestic saving investment[1] could just be attained by the projection that stipulates constant fertility and unchecked immigration. The capital-output ratio employed was 3:1, which means that it was estimated that the average amount of productive capital per worker was valued at three times his annual output.

One can hardly omit the subsistence farming sector of the economy. Indeed it would be difficult to do so, as it is shrinking in size and it would not be easy to estimate its magnitude at any given time in the future. It should be realized that the Government intends to develop the North, and a rapid expansion of the population in the areas where subsistence farming is now practised would inevitably mean the necessity for creating more roads, schools, wells, small-scale irrigation systems and perhaps state farms. In addition the local population would have itself to undertake the building of more houses and the preparation of more farm areas. Although children in these areas now engage in farm-work at very young ages, this will be decreasingly the case as school attendance is enforced. With a reduction both in family size and in the rate of expansion of the farming communities, there would undoubtedly be available a potential pool of extra labour. This might be used in several ways. Its existence could lead to more intensive farming or farm capitalization. Alternatively it might be tapped off by the Government for organized part-time developmental schemes, or might be used for the production of some cash crops, or might allow additional migration to urban industries without jeopardizing farm production.

The analysis of investment is at this stage confined to internal savings because these can be predicted with greater certainty. The role of foreign investment will be mentioned later.

The lessons to be learnt from the Tables are clear enough. They illustrate the broad general differences between various types of population growth and the likely effect of such growth upon economic development. The exact levels of such variables as immigration or fertility are not of crucial importance. Numbers are listed with such exactitude in the Tables more to show the method of analysis than to suggest that much importance is placed upon such fine precision.

The first and perhaps most important lesson is that a *laissez-faire* population policy would be incompatible with continued economic development if such development were to be financed entirely out of Ghana's own resources and if the rate of savings were not to be raised above 15 per cent of the national income. Any substantially higher rate of savings at the present level of economic development would inflict very considerable hardship upon the community for a long period and its imposition would be

---

[1] *Seven-Year Development Plan,* op. cit., p. 18.

TABLE 4.9

INVESTMENT IN ECONOMIC DEVELOPMENT ACCORDING TO DIFFERENT POPULATION PROJECTIONS,
1960–85 AND 1960–2000

Projections	Constant fertility		Fertility reducing by 1% per annum		Fertility reducing by 2% per annum	
	With immigration	Without immigration	With immigration	Without immigration	With immigration	Without immigration
(a) *Period, 1960–85*						
(1) Total labour years* (thousands)	98,746	92,189	98,666	92,113	98,588	92,040
(2) Investment on basis of 15 per cent savings (thousands of labour years)	14,812	13,828	14,800	13,817	14,788	13,806
(3) Additional investment available because of reduction in number of dependants (thousands of labour years)	0	−920	1,579	553	2,958	1,841
(4) Total investment (thousands of labour years)	14,812	12,908	16,379	14,370	17,746	15,647
(5) Increase in labour force (thousands)	5,172	4,355	5,126	4,311	5,081	4,269
(6) Extra investment required to employ increase in labour force (thousands of labour years)	15,516	13,065	15,378	12,933	15,243	12,807
(7) Net investment available for raising productivity (thousands of labour years)	−704	−157	1,001	1,437	2,503	2,840
(8) Percentage net investment forms of total labour years	−0·7	−0·2	1·0	1·6	2·5	3·1
(b) *Period, 1960–2000*						
(1) Total labour years* (thousands)	224,160	204,690	218,360	199,268	213,275	194,526
(2) Investment on basis of 15 per cent savings (thousands of labour years)	33,624	30,704	32,754	28,890	31,991	29,179
(3) Additional investment available because of reduction in number of dependants (thousands of labour years)	0	−2,047	9,389	6,377	10,877	7,587
(4) Total investment (thousands of labour years)	33,624	28,657	42,143	35,267	42,868	36,766
(5) Increase in labour force (thousands)	11,887	10,223	10,834	9,240	9,917	8,385
(6) Extra investment required to employ increase in labour force (thousands of labour years)	35,661	30,669	32,502	27,720	29,751	25,155
(7) Net investment available for raising productivity (thousands of labour years)	−2,037	−2,012	9,641	8,547	13,117	11,611
(8) Percentage net investment forms of total labour years	−0·9	−0·9	4·4	4·3	6·2	6·0

* A labour year is the work done by one gainfully employed person during one year.

likely to transform Ghanaian society to something radically different from what we know today.

Although economic gains do come with declining fertility, such gains become greater with time. Thus, with a 1 per cent per annum decline in fertility, gains are two or three times as great in the fifteen-year period between 1985 and 2000 as they are in the twenty-five-year period up to 1985, and with a 2 per cent decline they tend to be somewhat larger in the later period than in the earlier one. Related to this is the very important point that only the projections showing steep declines in fertility reap substantial early gains. One of the projections postulating a 2 per cent per annum decline in fertility actually shows a 3 per cent investment in rising productivity in the period up to 1985.

A very important point not brought out clearly by the Tables is that the difference in investment between the various projections would be likely to be even greater than has been indicated, for there are secondary gains as well. The more money that is available for investment, the more rapidly does output per worker rise, and the more easily can higher rates of saving and investment be afforded. Such higher rates of investment will in their turn accelerate economic growth. In addition, the projections exhibiting declines in fertility are those describing populations where many more women would be potentially available for productive work in so far as fewer of them would spend the majority of their adult years caring for small children.

The actual money value to the community of fertility decline is very great indeed, even in the short run. The amounts shown here should be regarded as ceiling figures, which might be attained if the labour released by the reduction in dependency and the decline in the need for creating more employment is used in other ways just as efficiently as it would have been in circumstances of maximum population growth and pressure. In Table 4.10, the differences in investment between the most extreme projections are shown to be about £690 million for the 1960–85 period and almost £3,000 million for the 1960–2000 period. As these estimates are based on the 1960 value of a labour year, differences in investment levels and hence of productivity between the projections would make the actual contrasts considerably greater than this. Thus, in purely monetary terms, it would be a sound investment for the Ghanaian Government to spend up to £13 million per year between now and 1985 if it could ensure a 1 per cent per annum decline in fertility or £25 million to secure a 2 per cent per annum decline. Similarly, between now and 2000, an average annual investment of

TABLE 4.10

NET INVESTMENT AVAILABLE FOR RAISING PRODUCTIVITY, 1960–85 AND 1960–2000

Projections	Constant fertility		Fertility reducing by 1% per annum		Fertility reducing by 2% per annum	
	With immigration	Without immigration	With immigration	Without immigration	With immigration	Without immigration
1960–85	−137	− 30	195	280	488	553
(£G million)						
1960–2000	−397	−392	1,880	1,665	2,560	2,260

£50 million would be warranted for the lesser decline and over £60 million for the greater one. Table 4.11 shows that, in terms of annual expenditure per female in the reproductive age range, expenditures of up to £6 and £11 are warranted for 1 per cent and 2 per cent declines respectively, if the perspective is limited to 1985, and £18 and £23 respectively if the whole period to 2000 is taken as the planning period.

TABLE 4.11

AMOUNT BY WHICH AVERAGE ANNUAL INVESTMENT AVAILABLE EXCEEDS THAT AVAILABLE ACCORDING TO THE 'CONSTANT FERTILITY: WITH IMMIGRATION' PROJECTION, 1960–85 AND 1960–2000

Projections	Constant fertility		Fertility reducing by 1% per annum		Fertility reducing by 2% per annum	
	With immigration	Without immigration	With immigration	Without immigration	With immigration	Without immigration
(a) *Amount per year*						
1960–85	—	4·3	13·3	16·6	25·0	27·6
(£G million)						
1960–2000	—	0·1	56·9	51·5	73·9	66·4
(£G million)						
(b) *Amount per year per female of reproductive age**						
1960–85 (£G)	—	2	6	8	11	13
1960–2000 (£G)	—	0	18	18	24	23

* Taken here to be 15–44 years.

It is not suggested that the Ghanaian Government would wish at the present time to spend the full average annual amounts listed in Table 4.11 on an attempt to reduce the level of fertility. Quite obviously, if the full amount were to be spent, the full saving would have been dissipated. Furthermore, such average expenditure would be a relatively great strain in the early part of the period when the population and gross national income were comparatively small and a relatively light load towards the end of the period. Nor would any government wish to spend money far in excess of the likely demand for such services.

But it is suggested that the potential economic gains are so great as to warrant on economic grounds the setting up of a comprehensive network of family planning clinics throughout the towns and villages of the country. Such a network could be regarded as a direct economic investment and would cost only a fraction of the sums suggested in Table 4.11. The case against such an action would have to be a non-economic one.

Another conclusion that can be drawn from Table 4.9 is that the effect of immigration upon economic development does not have the same kind of critical significance as does that of the level of fertility. Migrants tend to pay for themselves in that such a large proportion of them are employed in the economy. However, this does not mean that there are any gains to be made because of fewer dependants. Just as immigrants are concentrated by age in the main labour force span, they are also concentrated for the same reason in the reproductive span. Thus, immigrant communities, even with an excess of males, can show unusually high crude birth rates although exhibiting no higher individual female fertility.

M

In the short-run, 1960 to 1985, there might be some immediate gains to be made by prohibiting immigration and so reducing the rate at which new employment would have to be created. This is not the case in the longer period. In the constant fertility projection the total population size becomes larger so rapidly that the volume of immigration eventually becomes almost insignificant. In the other projections, immigrants become of more value as the number of their non-economically active dependants becomes, in common with the rest of the population, smaller. With low fertility, Ghana could approach the position of modern Australia or Switzerland, where immigrants are valued on economic grounds.

The ultimate effect of immigration upon the race between population and economic growth is so slight as to suggest that questions of immigration policy must be decided upon other grounds. Many arguments can be raised both for and against the restriction of immigration. Migration policy may be affected by the general question of African unity. Immigrants do not on the whole bring to Ghana specialized skills or encourage a flow of subsequent investment as has been the case with British migration to Australia. But they may be an unusually energetic cross-section of people. They may have the disadvantage of requiring the creation of more employment, but in so far as this demand is concentrated in the more advanced parts of the economy, they may encourage economic modernization. On the other hand, this means that they will tend to concentrate in the towns with a resulting strain upon the provision of urban housing. Much may depend on the demand to remit money and on the volume of illegal remittances in the form of either money or goods.

Now, what are the implications of the figures given in Table 4.9 for 'net investment' for the future strength of the economy of Ghana and for the individual living standards of the Ghanaian people?

The projection of the economic effects of the growth of population, capital, productivity and skills is complex and is outside the range of the present study. However, it is important that the population projections should be used to indicate whether the different courses of population change would be likely to give rise to very different courses of economic change. In Tables 4.12, 4.13 and 4.14 this has been done in the simplest fashion. It has been assumed that the 'net investment' has been stored in some way and injected into the economy at the ends of the 1960-85 and 1960-2000 periods respectively. It has further been assumed that this injection of investment immediately yields the extra productive capital, which in turn results in proportional increases in productivity and national income. Such a calculation demonstrates in an accurate fashion the differences in economic efficiency between the various projected paths of population growth, but it predicts only the minimum rates of economic growth and hence the minimum rates of divergence. For, in reality, the extra investment is added gradually through the whole period under examination. Thus, where there is economic growth, productivity is rising throughout the period, and much of the extra production can be continually ploughed back to yield faster rates of economic growth. Therefore, the average annual rates of economic growth shown in Table 4.12 of 5–6 per cent for the case where the net import of foreign capital averages 5 per cent of the country's output could easily be compatible with the statement that, 'For the longer run planning in this country we should aim at rates of economic growth in excess of 7 per cent per annum under subsequent development plans.'[1]

The size of the economy as a whole, as measured by the total production of goods and services or 'gross national product', will continue to expand in two ways. Firstly, if present productivity per worker can be maintained, it will expand as rapidly as the labour force. Secondly, if productivity can be increased, there will be additional growth over and above that of the labour force. Such an increase in productivity can arise if capital growth can outstrip the increase in the labour force. One source of the additional investment required for this is the 'net investment' shown in Table 4.9. Another is capital from outside the country. The Plan concludes that, 'If a high rate of domestic savings is maintained, then it could be expected that Ghana's domestic resources for growth would be supplemented by a generous inflow of both public and private capital from abroad. The contribution of external capital to the development efforts of other countries in a position similar to Ghana's allows us to conclude that a supplement equivalent to an average of 5 per cent of the national output every year could be reasonably expected.'[2]

In Table 4.12, the expansion of the Ghanaian economy is shown for the periods 1960 to 1985 and 1960 to 2000 according to each projection. It can be seen that production would be likely to rise at an average annual rate of 3–4½ per cent without external capital and from 5–6 per cent with it. It is noteworthy that growth is more rapid in the projections which postulate declining fertility. This might have been expected during the shorter period, for at first the labour force expands hardly less rapidly in these projections. What is more remarkable is that the difference becomes more accentuated in the longer term projection in spite of the fact that in the latter years of the period both the population and the labour force of the 'declining fertility' projections are considerably smaller than those of the 'constant fertility' projections. The product increases more rapidly when immigration is allowed than when it is restricted.

But the increase in national production, taken without regard to the increase in the size of the labour force or of the population, is not a very meaningful measure. It could have some meaning if one were to take a mercantilist point of view or were interested purely in a large population as 'cannon fodder' for war. But, even war in the modern world is won less by numbers than by productive strength and by the standard of living, and hence training and skill, of the combatant. A large population may be associated with a large national product, not because the country possesses modern factories, but because an immense amount of subsistence agriculture is needed to feed it.

For our purpose, it is more to the point to ask which projection implies the most rapid rise in productivity. On the assumption that increases in productivity are proportional to increases in the amount of capital per worker, the results shown in Table 4.13 are obtained. Any relaxation in this assumption would probably increase the differences between the projections from those already shown in the Table.

[1] *Seven-Year Development Plan*, p. 240.
[2] Ibid., p. 18.

TABLE 4.12

INCREASE IN GROSS NATIONAL PRODUCT, 1960–85 AND 1960–2000

Projections	Constant fertility		Fertility reducing by 1% per annum		Fertility reducing by 2% per annum	
	With immi-gration	Without immi-gration	With immi-gration	Without immi-gration	With immi-gration	Without immi-gration
(a) *Size of product in final year of period expressed as a multiple of that of 1960*						
1960–85:						
With no external capital	2·4	2·2	2·6	2·4	2·8	2·6
With 5 per cent external capital per year*	3·6	3·3	3·8	3·5	4·0	3·7
1960–2000:						
With no external capital	4·2	3·6	5·4	4·8	5·9	5·0
With 5 per cent external capital per year	8·1	7·2	9·1	8·1	9·6	8·0
(b) *Average annual percentage growth of product during period*						
1960–85:						
With no external capital	3·5	3·2	3·9	3·6	4·2	3·9
With 5 per cent external capital per year*	5·2	4·9	5·4	5·2	5·7	5·4
1960–2000:						
With no external capital	3·6	3·3	4·3	4·0	4·6	4·1
With 5 per cent external capital per year	5·4	5·1	5·7	5·4	5·8	5·3

* i.e. a net inflow of foreign capital equal to 5 per cent of the national output.

It can be seen that productivity can be raised either by reducing fertility or by importing foreign capital. Without either, no advance in productivity can be made if the rate of saving rises no higher than 15 per cent of output. Where there are both, the greatest gains in productivity are made. A fertility decline of 2 per cent per year and an annual net import of foreign capital equal to 5 per cent of national production could produce an average annual rise in productivity of 2 per cent and could multiply productivity by two and one-third times between 1960 and 2000. Further slight gains could be achieved in the short run by prohibiting immigration. Between 1960 and 1985, much more impressive gains in productivity are secured from a rapid decline in fertility than from a more moderate one.

Gains in productivity are not identical with rises in the standard of living. Some countries may choose to reinvest increasing proportions of total production as productivity rises so as to speed up economic development. However, in international comparisons, it is rare to measure individual

TABLE 4.13

INCREASE IN PRODUCTIVITY PER EMPLOYED PERSON, 1960–85 AND 1960–2000*

Projections	Constant fertility		Fertility reducing by 1% per annum		Fertility reducing by 2% per annum	
	With immigration	Without immigration	With immigration	Without immigration	With immigration	Without immigration
(a) *Percentage growth in productivity during the whole period*						
1960–85:						
With no external capital	−3·9	−1·0	5·6	8·8	14·0	17·5
With 5 per cent external capital per year	45·7	48·6	55·0	58·4	63·6	67·1
1960–2000:						
With no external capital	−6·4	−7·1	32·3	32·2	43·7	46·7
With 5 per cent external capital per year	84·1	83·4	122·8	122·7	134·2	137·2
(b) *Average annual percentage increase in productivity during period*						
1960–85:						
With no external capital	−0·2	−0·1	0·2	0·3	0·6	0·7
With 5 per cent external capital per year	1·5	1·6	1·8	1·9	2·0	2·2
1960–2000:						
With no external capital	−0·2	−0·2	0·7	0·7	0·9	0·9
With 5 per cent external capital per year	1·5	1·5	2·1	2·1	2·1	2·2

* Assuming productivity to increase as amount of capital per worker increases.

consumption. Normally, a simple comparison is made of average national income per head, which could be taken as representing either present consumption or potential future consumption. This course will be followed here. Income per head is not identical with productivity, for some of the projected populations are burdened with a greater proportion of non-producing children than are others. It would be more appropriate in such a comparison to recognize that small children do not consume as much as adults, and so by applying weights take into account different age structures. This is hardly ever done, and we shall content ourselves here by pointing out that, were it to be done in Table 4.14, the contrasts in that Table would be slightly reduced.

As would be expected, Table 4.14 shows that the average national income per head follows the same pattern as productivity in rising most when capital is imported and when fertility decline is the fastest. Once again the gains are greatest when both conditions apply.

There are two differences. The most significant is that declining fertility raises the average national income per head, not only by increasing the capital stock and hence the productivity of the employed, but also by reducing the number of dependants. Thus, while the *'Fertility Reducing by 2 per cent per annum: With immigration'* projection, coupled with a 5 per cent per annum flow of external capital, shows an increase in productivity by the year 2000 of 134 per cent, the average national income per head by that date would have risen 188 per cent. Thus, one set of circumstances could produce a rise in living standards, as measured by the average national income per head, of almost threefold in the forty-year period from 1960 to 2000 at an average annual rate of 2·7 per cent. This would probably be sufficient to satisfy almost any community. It is a far cry from the stagnation and decline which would be produced by constant fertility coupled with negligible imports of capital.

The other difference between the productivity and national income per

TABLE 4.14

INCREASE IN NATIONAL INCOME PER HEAD, 1960–85 AND 1960–2000

Projections	Constant fertility		Fertility reducing by 1% per annum		Fertility reducing by 2% per annum	
	With immi-gration	Without immi-gration	With immi-gration	Without immi-gration	With immi-gration	Without immi-gration
(a) *Percentage increase in national income per head during whole period* 1960–85:						
With no external capital	− 8	− 8	7	9	23	24
With 5 per cent external capital per year	40	41	57	58	77	77
1960–2000:						
With no external capital	−11	−15	37	35	78	68
With 5 per cent external capital per year	70	66	131	129	188	169
(b) *Average annual percentage increase in national income per head during period* 1960–85:						
With no external capital	−0·3	−0·3	0·2	0·3	0·8	0·9
With 5 per cent external capital per year	1·4	1·4	1·8	1·8	2·3	2·3
1960–2000:						
With no external capital	−0·3	−0·4	0·8	0·8	1·5	1·3
With 5 per cent external capital per year	1·4	1·3	2·1	2·1	2·7	2·5

head tables is that the latter indicate no short-term case for restricting immigration and some long-term case for not doing so.

Several general conclusions can be drawn from the study of the implications of the population projections. One is that a *laissez-faire* population policy is not compatible with rising living standards unless the net imports of foreign capital are very considerable. If foreign capital cannot be acquired on the scale desired, or if interest rates are so high that in due course the balance of capital imports shows no very great margin over the repayment of loans and interest, an economic revolution will be able to be achieved only through declining fertility or by a drastic reduction in the level of consumption in order to increase domestic saving and investment.

Another is that, over the period 1960 to 2000, net imports of foreign capital running at about 5 per cent per year or a fertility decline of about 2 per cent per year would produce similar increases in national income per head. Both together would yield considerably greater rises than their arithmetical sum, rises of an order that would be likely to satisfy the expectations of the Ghanaian people.

5. SOME CONSEQUENCES OF POPULATION GROWTH

An examination of certain aspects of projected population growth will serve both to illuminate further the reasons for the various relationships already described between population change and economic development and to assist planning by analysing the different rates of change in some of the subdivisions of the Ghanaian society.

One of the ultimate aims of a population policy, which encourages the reduction of fertility, is not merely to lower the eventual size of the total population below what it might otherwise have been but also to reduce the rate of population increase and the increments of human beings added to the society each year. It is this marginal increase in population size which drains away investment which might otherwise have been spent on intensifying economic development.

In the very short run the most effective way of reducing population growth is through the prohibition of immigration. If, during the 1960–5 period, net immigration had continued as during earlier years, the annual growth rate could have been as high as 3·8 per cent. If it had faded away to nothing, the rate would have dropped to about 3·3 per cent. But, by the 1980–5 period, and even more the 1985–2000 period, the lowering of fertility would have a much more marked effect upon growth rates than would the disappearance of immigration.

Table 4.15 demonstrates that, while the total population exhibited by the projection with the slowest growth rate still makes up in 1985 81 per cent of that of the projection with the highest growth rate, the number of people added to the population in that year by the former projection is only 55 per cent of that added by the latter projection. The difference is much more marked in the year 2000, when the smallest population is still 63 per cent of the size of the larger but the population increment for the year is only 33 per cent of that of the other. Thus, while one projection postulates a net population growth during the year 2000 of 1,340,000 persons, the other indicates an increase of only 442,000.

It is clear that the declining fertility projections offer a slackening in the strain brought about by rapid population growth at an earlier date than the figures of total population size might have suggested.

TABLE 4.15

RATE OF POPULATION GROWTH AND SIZE OF POPULATION INCREMENTS
AT VARIOUS DATES, 1960–2000

Projections	Constant fertility		Fertility reducing by 1% per annum		Fertility reducing by 2% per annum	
	With immi-gration	Without immi-gration	With immi-gration	Without immi-gration	With immi-gration	Without immi-gration
(a) *Average annual rate of population growth* (%)						
1960–5	3·8	3·3	3·8	3·3	3·8	3·3
1980–5	4·0	3·8	3·4	3·2	2·9	2·7
1985–2000	4·2	4·2	3·2	3·1	2·4	2·2
(b) *Growth in population numbers during one calendar year* (*in thousands*)						
1985	694	607	552	478	443	379
2000	1,340	1,215	845	739	536	442
(c) *Relative size of total population and 12 months' increase in population size at certain dates* (*highest projection=100*)						
(i) 1985:						
Total population	100	92	94	86	88	81
12 month increase in size	100	88	80	69	64	55
(ii) 2000:						
Total population	100	91	83	75	70	63
12 month increase in size	100	91	63	55	40	33

One of the most remarkable features of the projections was noted above. That is that the gross output of the country was no lower in those projections which postulated very considerably reduced total populations. Much of this phenomenon is readily understood if separate examinations are made of the growth of the labour force and of the dependent population.

If the labour force is regarded as being restricted to persons over 15 years of age, then it is obvious that no fertility decline can have any effect whatsoever on its size for at least fifteen years. However, during this whole period the number of dependent children may be decreasing.

In Table 4.16 it can be seen, when the projections are grouped together according to migration policy, that the fastest decline in fertility will not lower the size of the labour force by more than 1 per cent between 1960 and 1985 and by more than 13 per cent by the year 2000. This compares with reductions in total population size by 12 per cent and 30 per cent respectively. If a *laissez-faire* policy is adopted towards immigration, the labour force will probably be two and a half times as big in 1985 and four times as big in 2000 as was the case in 1960. If immigration is prohibited, these figures would probably be reduced to about two and a quarter and three and a half times respectively.

In any case, the problem of increasing employment is going to be very great. Even in the period 1985 to 2000, only one projection shows the annual rate of increase dropping as low as 2·7 per cent. Indeed the highest projection shows it reaching 4 per cent. Between 1960 and 1985 an average of at least 120,000 new jobs a year will have to be found. Between 1985 and 2000 a wider range of prospects opens up. According to the fertility trend and immigration policy adopted, the number of positions to be created each year will be somewhere between 190,000 and 311,000. In this analysis, references made to employment always refer to all jobs, whether created by government activity or by individual action along such lines as securing extra farm land. This is apparently not so in the following statement from the *Seven-Year Plan* which presumably refers only to employment in the modern sector of the economy. 'The 1·3 million Ghanaians who were aged 0–5 years in 1960 will be aged 15–20 years by 1975. If adequate employment opportunities are to be created, then Ghana's economy by that date must be expanding fast enough to absorb more than 70,000 additional workers each year. The comparison between that figure and the 105,000 jobs created in the leading sectors of the economy during the six-year period 1955–61 provides some measure of the magnitude of the task involved in the Government's undertaking to assure full employment opportunities to all Ghanaians by the end of a twenty-year perspective plan period.'[1] If all employment were to be taken into account, the jobs to be provided each year by 1975 would be over twice as many. In 1960, 1,294,000 people were enumerated 0–4 years of age, of whom about 1,140,000 will probably still be alive in 1975. If the proportion of economically active adults remains constant, about 800,000 will wish to enter the labour market at an average rate of 160,000 a year. On the other hand, there were 180,000 50–54 year olds in 1960, of whom some 108,000 will survive to 1975. Probably about 75,000 will have been employed and they will retire at the rate of about 15,000 per year. Thus, the annual rate of enlargement of the labour force will be running at about 145,000 persons per year without counting any additions accruing from immigration.

The other aspect of the question of population growth and economic development is the examination of those sections of the community outside the labour force age range. In contemporary Ghana most of this dependent population consists of children and any reduction in the proportion of children will immediately lessen the dependency burden. According to the 1960 census, over 93 per cent of the combined population under 15 years and over 65 years belonged in the former category. Indeed, the corrected data suggested that the real figure probably exceeded 95 per cent.

The projections suggest that a *laissez-faire* population policy would result in a rise in the proportion of children as infant mortality continues to fall. By 2000 half the community would be children and a slightly higher proportion would be found amongst all dependent groups. From about 1975 the proportion of children in the projections incorporating declining fertility would begin to fall quite markedly. By 1985 the projection incorporating the 2 per cent per annum decline in fertility would have reduced

[1] *Seven-Year Development Plan*, p. 7.

TABLE 4.16

LABOUR FORCE PROJECTION, 1960–2000*

Projections	Constant fertility		Fertility reducing by 1% per annum		Fertility reducing by 2% per annum	
	With immi-gration	Without immi-gration	With immi-gration	Without immi-gration	With immi-gration	Without immi-gration
(a) Size (in thousands)						
Date: 1960	2,440	2,440	2,440	2,440	2,440	2,440
1965	2,870	2,767	2,870	2,767	2,870	2,767
1970	3,459	3,256	3,459	3,256	3,459	3,256
1975	4,170	3,866	4,170	3,866	4,170	3,866
1980	5,015	4,599	5,015	4,599	5,015	4,599
1985	6,031	5,464	5,999	5,433	5,968	5,404
2000	10,691	9,536	9,960	8,854	9,324	8,261
(b) Relative size of labour force at certain dates (highest=100)						
Date: 1965	100	100	100	100	100	100
1970	100	96	100	96	100	96
1975	100	94	100	94	100	94
1980	100	93	100	93	100	93
1985	100	91	99	90	99	90
2000	100	89	93	83	87	77
(c) Average annual rate of increase during certain periods (%)						
Period: 1960–5	3·7	3·0	3·7	3·0	3·7	3·0
1980–5	3·8	3·5	3·6	3·4	3·5	3·3
1985–2000	4·0	3·9	3·4	3·3	2·8	2·7
(d) Average annual number of jobs to be found during certain periods (in thousands)						
1960–85	144	121	142	120	141	119
1985–2000	311	271	264	228	224	190

* The labour force is confined to the 15–64 years of age range. It is assumed that the employed, economically active will continue to make up 69·4 per cent of this group as in 1960.

the proportion of children to 42 per cent and of all dependent population to 44 per cent.

Even the two lowest projections would take a considerable period to reduce the relative size of their child population to that now found in most industrial countries. By 1985 the proportion of children found in these two projections would still be amongst the world's highest, by 2000 it would be around the level now found in India, and by 2060 at about the level now found in the United States or Australia. The relative numbers of children would remain far above that now obtaining in Western Europe, because of the assumption made when designing the projections that fertility decline would cease when the gross reproduction rate was 1·5. Thus, there is no possibility that Ghana will become within the next century a society in which children play a minor role.

In the long run, dependency does not become quite as low in the declining fertility projections as might be thought from a study confined to children. It is precisely in these more slowly growing populations that the fall in mortality can eventually make itself felt by a rise in the proportion of old people. This is not very marked until after 2000, but eventually is a factor in the difficulty experienced in increasing the fraction of the population found in the 15–64 years of age range far past 60 per cent.

TABLE 4.17

DEPENDENCY, 1960–2060

(All figures are expressed as percentages of the total population)

Projections	Constant fertility		Fertility reducing by 1% per annum		Fertility reducing by 2% per annum	
	With immigration	Without immigration	With immigration	Without immigration	With immigration	Without immigration
(a) *Percentage of population 0–14 years*						
Date: 1960*	46·6	46·6	46·6	46·6	46·6	46·6
1965	47·3	47·8	47·3	47·8	47·3	47·8
1970	47·5	48·3	47·2	47·9	47·0	47·7
1975	47·5	48·1	46·4	47·1	45·6	46·3
1980	47·8	48·3	45·7	46·2	43·6	44·1
1985	48·1	48·7	44·8	45·5	41·6	42·3
2000	49·4	50·1	43·0	43·6	36·7	37·2
2060	51·9	51·9	30·3	30·3	29·4	29·5
(b) *Percentage of population 65+ years*						
Date: 1960*	2·1	2·1	2·1	2·1	2·1	2·1
1965	1·6	1·6	1·6	1·6	1·6	1·6
1970	1·3	1·4	1·3	1·4	1·3	1·4
1975	1·4	1·6	1·4	1·6	1·4	1·6
1980	1·7	1·7	1·7	1·9	1·7	2·0
1985	1·8	2·1	2·0	2·1	2·1	2·3
2000	2·3	2·4	2·7	2·8	3·2	3·4
2060	2·0	1·9	6·8	6·3	9·1	9·1
(c) *Percentage of population 0–14 years and 65+ years*						
Date: 1960*	48·7	48·7	48·7	48·7	48·7	48·7
1965	48·9	49·4	48·9	49·4	48·9	49·4
1970	48·8	49·7	48·5	49·3	48·3	49·1
1975	48·9	49·7	47·8	48·7	47·0	47·9
1980	49·5	50·0	47·4	48·1	45·3	46·1
1985	49·9	50·8	46·8	47·6	43·7	44·6
2000	51·7	52·5	45·7	46·4	39·9	40·6
2060	53·9	53·8	37·1	36·9	38·5	38·6

* All figures for 1960 are based on the corrected data used in the population projections.

TABLE 4.18

PROJECTION OF SCHOOL AGE GROUPS, 1960–2000

Projections	Constant fertility		Fertility reducing by 1% per annum		Fertility reducing by 2% per annum	
	With immi-gration	Without immi-gration	With immi-gration	Without immi-gration	With immi-gration	Without immi-gration
(a) *Average annual rate of increase of 5–14 years group* (%)						
Period: 1960–5	4·4	4·3	4·4	4·3	4·4	4·3
1965–70	4·0	3·8	4·0	3·8	4·0	3·8
1970–5	3·8	3·3	3·5	3·0	3·2	2·8
1975–80	4·0	3·6	3·2	2·8	2·4	2·0
1980–5	4·1	3·9	3·1	2·9	2·1	1·9
1985–2000	4·5	4·3	3·0	2·9	1·6	1·5
(b) *Average annual rate of increase of 15–19 years group* (%)						
Period: 1960–5	3·2	2·7	3·2	2·7	3·2	2·7
1965–70	4·4	4·4	4·4	4·4	4·4	4·4
1970–5	4·3	4·4	4·4	4·4	4·4	4·4
1975–80	3·7	3·4	3·7	3·4	3·7	3·4
1980–5	3·9	3·4	3·4	2·9	2·8	2·3
1985–2000	4·2	4·2	3·1	3·1	2·0	2·0
(c) *Numbers of children 5–14 (thousands)*						
(i) 1960*	1,800	1,800	1,800	1,800	1,800	1,800
1985	4,892	4,574	4,406	4,119	3,969	3,711
1965–85 increase	3,092	2,774	2,606	2,319	2,169	1,911
(ii) 1960*	1,800	1,800	1,800	1,800	1,800	1,800
2000	9,233	8,499	6,952	6,395	5,242	4,818
1960–2000 increase	7,433	6,699	5,152	4,595	3,442	3,018

* Figures for 1960 are based on the corrected data used in the population projections.

In the early stages of a fertility decline the most marked effect on government spending would be on the proportion of total expenditure needed to support and extend the educational system. Only five years after the onset of fertility decline, the first results would begin to manifest themselves in the schools.

By the 1980–85 quinquennium the average annual rate of increase in size of the 5–14 year old group is already far apart between the different projections, varying from a high of 4·1 per cent to a low of 1·9 per cent. In the succeeding 1985–2000 period the gap broadens to that between 4·5 per cent and 1·5 per cent, the highest rate being three times the lowest one. Even within the 15–19 years of age group, the difference between the growth rates of the different projections is very considerable by 1985.

In terms of necessary government outlays in school-building and teacher-training, the essential fact is that between 1960 and 1985, the lowest projection adds an increment of 1,911,000 children between 5–14 years of age or a little more again that those found in 1960. However, the highest projection adds more than 3 million children to the potential school population. In the forty-year period from 1960 to 2000 the lowest projection adds 3 million children to this age group, while the highest adds two and a half times as many. Part of the extra 'net investment' shown in Table 4.9 as available in the lowest projection but not in the highest is derived from the savings made through having to educate a million less children up to 1985 and $4\frac{1}{2}$ million less up to 2000.

It is difficult to project urban population growth in Ghana, partly because the degree of urbanization will depend to a considerable extent upon the success of economic development plans, which will in their turn be affected by the rate of population growth. Some pictures of possible trends can be drawn, and this has been essayed in Table 4.19. Between 1948 and 1960 the proportion of the population living in urban areas rose by just under one percentage point each year. From what is known of urbanization within Ghana during the last few years, as well as of trends in other comparable countries, it seems a reasonable guess that between 1960 and 2000 the proportion of population living in urban areas will rise by a percentage point each year, thus reaching 48 per cent in 1985 and 63 per cent in 2000. Not all this population, of course, will be city population. A very considerable fraction will live in villages which have grown first to small towns and later to larger ones. Many of the inhabitants will probably continue to practise agriculture.

According to this assumption, Ghana's urban population will multiply between 4·3 and 5·4 times between 1960 and 2000. In 1985 the urban population is likely to be between $6\frac{3}{4}$ and $8\frac{1}{3}$ million and in 2000 between 13 and 20 million. No projection suggests a decline in rural population. In fact, the various projections suggest a multiplication of the 1960 rural population of 1·4 to 1·7 times between 1960 and 1985 and 1·3 to 2·3 times between 1960 and 2000. Even the lowest projection suggests rural populations of 7,305,000 and 6,954,000 in 1985 and 2000 respectively, representing, of course, 52 per cent and 37 per cent of the total population. Thus, before 2000, there would have begun a slow decline in rural population similar to that which has occurred at some stage in the history of most economically developed countries. If this projection were to be followed, and if living standards were to rise in the way it suggests is possible, Ghana would not want a great rural population no matter what output was desired from these areas.

There is, then, going to be a problem of urban employment. As the difference between the lowest and highest projections over the years immediately ahead is more one of the number of children than of adults, all projections imply that urban employment will have to be increased five-fold by 1985 at an average rate of about 6·7 per cent per year and over ten times by 2000. Some of the employment will be city employment, for Accra should have more than $1\frac{1}{2}$ million inhabitants by 1985 and over 3 million by 2000. By the latter date Kumasi will probably have passed the $1\frac{1}{2}$ million mark.

The question may be asked whether rural Ghana can absorb the considerable population increases projected for it. It has been suggested earlier that at the outside it could probably not absorb extra population at a greater

TABLE 4.19

URBANIZATION, 1960–2000

A. Basic assumptions

Dates:	1960	1965	1970	1975	1980	1985	2000
(i) *Percentage of total population living in urban areas*	23	28	33	38	43	48	63
(ii) *Maximum population which could be absorbed by rural areas (thousands)**	5,175	5,844	6,600	7,454	8,419	9,508	13,695

B. Population projections

Projections	Constant fertility		Fertility reducing by 1% per annum		Fertility reducing by 2% per annum	
	With immigration	Without immigration	With immigration	Without immigration	With immigration	Without immigration
(i) *Urban population (thousands)*						
Date: 1960	1,551	1,551	1,551	1,551	1,551	1,551
1985	8,329	7,667	7,800	7,174	7,339	6,744
2000	20,107	18,218	16,640	15,020	14,075	13,130
(ii) *Rural population (thousands)*						
Date: 1960	5,175	5,175	5,175	5,175	5,175	5,175
1985	9,023	8,306	8,449	7,771	7,950	7,305
2000	11,809	10,700	9,773	8,821	8,266	6,954
(iii) *City population (thousands)†* Accra						
Date: 1960	338	338	338	338	338	338
1985	1,825	1,656	1,690	1,555	1,589	1,453
2000	4,390	3,984	3,618	3,312	3,208	2,872
Kumasi						
Date: 1960	181	181	181	181	181	181
1985	977	887	905	833	851	778
2000	2,352	2,138	1,938	1,773	1,719	1,538
(iv) *Multiplication of urban population since 1960*						
Date: 1985	5·4	4·9	5·0	4·6	4·7	4·3
2000	13·0	11·8	10·7	9·8	9·5	8·5
(v) *Multiplication of rural population since 1960*						
Date: 1985	1·7	1·6	1·6	1·5	1·5	1·4
2000	2·3	2·1	1·9	1·7	1·6	1·3

* Assuming a maximum growth of rural population after 1960 of 2½ per cent per annum.

† This city population is also included above in the projections of urban population. This section is neither projection nor prediction. It merely indicates what the size of these two largest urban centres would be if their populations grew at the same rate as that of urban Ghana as a whole.

rate than 2½ per cent per year. At this rate it could support up to 9½ million people by 1985 and 13⅔ million by 2000. This ceiling is somewhat above the requirements for rural absorption even of the highest projection and therefore does not invalidate the projections based on assumptions of urban growth rates.

Finally, the projections do not take specifically into account two special forces which tend to increase the rate of urbanization. One is foreign immigration and the other is economic development. It is suggested that the urban populations of the 'With immigration' projections might be somewhat higher than is suggested by the rather simple assumptions used in the construction of the Table. It is also suggested that the urban populations in the *'Fertility decline by 2 per cent per annum'* projections might be greater than indicated.

Finally, it might be asked whether the projections imply any kind of population race with food production. In the long run, there is little question that they do. No one could seriously suppose that Ghana could by 2060 feed the four to five hundred million people suggested by the constant fertility projections. Even the hundred odd million of the *'Fertility reducing by 1 per cent per annum'* projections would seem at all possible only if Ghana were to become a kind of 'workshop of the world' or at least a workshop of tropical Africa.

In the shorter run it is possible to imagine the country's agriculture and its food imports sufficing to feed a population of between 20 and 32 million in the year 2000. It is the period up to 2000 which will most concern economic planners in the immediate future.

There are, however, problems. Such a multiplication of the food supply will demand an agricultural revolution of the type that the industrial revolution has made possible in economically developed countries elsewhere. These revolutions, with their massive increases in food production through changes in the methods of cultivation, the use of fertilizers, plant breeding and the like, can presumably take place in the poor lateritic soils of the forest lands and the somewhat better, but dryer, soils of the woodland savannahs of the equatorial tropics. Little is yet known of the returns likely to be experienced from the application of scientific research and capital-intensive farming methods to these lands, except for limited knowledge in the field of plantation, and especially tree plantation, crops.

But, there is a fundamental dilemma. Such revolutions cannot easily happen in poor countries and more particularly they cannot happen amongst subsistence farmers. Much of the necessary research can be financed, at very considerable cost, by governments, but such research is meaningless unless it parallels fundamental change in the type of agriculture. The real need is not so much good farmers or clever scientists as large, rich markets. Rapid urbanization in Ghana will go some way towards providing these markets, but very much higher living standards are also needed. Ultimately, neither private farmer nor government can successfully practise capital-intensive agriculture without such markets. Agricultural development is an aspect of overall economic development. It is not absolutely necessary that all the agricultural market should be within the country. Denmark has thrived on the nearby industrial markets of her bigger neighbours and New Zealand has used her cultural links with

Britain to find markets across the world. However, both countries have long had internal markets with demands similar to those of their external markets. In Ghana's case, with the non-tree crop section of her agriculture fashioned to produce tropical foodstuffs for a population accustomed to such a diet, and with poorer neighbours on all sides, much of the success of an agricultural revolution will depend on rising living standards within the country. Ultimately it is the purchasers of food who pay for an agricultural revolution in the food-growing section of the economy.

This brings us to the paradox of the projections. It is the '*Fertility reducing by 2 per cent per annum*' projections, with their rapidly increasing levels of national income per head, which can be imagined as supporting an agriculture capable of feeding by the year 2000 not only the 20 or 22 million people posited for them, but perhaps even the 29 or 32 million suggested by the highest pair of projections. Such increases in national income would not only provide the larger agricultural markets needed, but would make possible the provision of better schooling and agricultural extension services which would educationally equip farmers to adapt themselves to an agricultural revolution.

On the other hand, it is very difficult to imagine population growth of the type posited in the '*Constant fertility*' projections producing an agriculture capable of feeding adequately 30 million people by the year 2000 and vastly more in the succeeding years.

6. POPULATION POLICY

The discussion in this chapter might best be summed up by attempting to state what the implications of these matters might be for the formation of government policy.

Everything mentioned above should be seen as a discussion of possible trends and the likely results of such trends. There is no attempt at prediction. If there were, only one population would have been projected for each future date instead of half a dozen. Similarly, the exact level of each projection is not of critical significance. It is of no special importance whether a *laissez-faire* population policy would result in 30 or 32 million people in the year 2000.

What is of importance is that very different paths of economic growth have been shown for the various patterns of population growth. It has been shown that declining fertility can speed and, in certain circumstances, perhaps even allow economic development. It has been further shown that the speeding up of economic growth accelerates with the rate of fertility decline.

These demonstrations have usually been confined to the period up to the year 2000. It is suggested that economic planners, even if employed specifically on a seven-year plan, must think in periods of at least this length. After all, at the present level of mortality and at that projected for the next few decades, the majority of Ghanaians now living will still be alive in 2000. In many planning projects, whether they involve the building of harbours like that at Tema or the establishment of an institute to study the selective breeding of tree crops, investment is being made in the belief that really substantial returns will be earned only over decades.

The pattern of population growth is determined by three factors in addition to the initial structure of the population. They are the courses of mortality, fertility and migration. Each could conceivably be the subject of a governmental policy.

It has been assumed in this study that there exists in the Government of Ghana, as well as in the country as a whole, a consensus on the subject of mortality. It is agreed that the battle to minimize sickness and death should continue indefinitely and that the expansion of medical services and the increase in the number of doctors should go on. The assumption that this will be so has underlain the whole of the projections. No exaggerated claims have been made for the likely falls in the death rate. On the contrary, the projections may have been unduly cautious, for at no stage do they consider the possibility of mortality improvement at a faster rate than a gain in expectation of life of half a year for each elapsed calendar year. Yet in many developing countries in Asia and other parts of the world, gains during the last twenty years have been considerably greater than this. However, we have taken into account the substantial medical and economic problems of tropical Africa.

There is, of course, the possibility that *laissez-faire* population growth will slow down economic growth to the point where no increase could be afforded in the amount of medical attention per head of population. If this were to occur at the same time as the swollen population began to put increased strains upon the country's food supplies, mortality could cease to decline and could even increase. In this case the *Constant fertility* projections at least would be invalidated. This possibility has not been analysed in detail, because it must presumably be the policy of any government to avoid it if possible. Its threat might well lead to changes of governmental attitudes towards intervention in the field of fertility.

It has already been shown that governmental action with regard to immigration is likely in the long run to have only marginal significance in terms of either population size or economic development. There is some possibility that the latter assertion is wrong. If it is true that economic breakthroughs have sometimes been critically affected by such economic attitudes as developed amongst the Protestants of north-west Europe or the immigrants in the United States, it is possible that the energy of immigrants into Ghana, an energy which is as elsewhere in the world sometimes frantic and based on feelings of insecurity, could be important in key stages in the process of industrialization.

It may well be that the Government will not be forced to decide on any hard and fast immigration policy. It seems probable that for many years to come Ghana will have to maintain a tight control over foreign exchange and hence over immigrants' remittances to their home countries. Unless very great change occurs within the West African family structure, such control, if efficiently enforced, could dramatically reduce the volume of net immigration. This occurrence may already be under way.

The real matter which will require some serious thought is whether the Government should at some stage take any action which could encourage a reduction in the level of fertility and hence of the rate of population growth.

Perhaps one of the most profound ways in which the Industrial Revolution has affected mankind is by upsetting the near equilibrium between births and deaths. The first major area of the world to experience this

N

phenomenon was nineteenth-century Europe. However, nineteenth-century Europe provides no more exact guide to social change in the developing world of the second half of the twentieth century than it does to economic change. Mortality rates fell only slowly throughout the century and were still quite high at its end. Fertility at the beginning of the period was much below what it is in contemporary Ghana. As a result, Europe's industrializing countries were not called upon to cope with population growth rates above $1\frac{1}{2}$ per cent per year. Indeed, the annual growth rate was often nearer $\frac{1}{2}$ per cent, compared with $3\frac{1}{2}$ per cent in Ghana of today. There was a second way in which the European situation differed. A considerable fraction of the surplus population could either emigrate to settlement lands overseas or could pour from the rural areas into industrial cities which were already well established. Neither possibility exists in modern Ghana. Certainly, the industrial cities may some day exist. But the vast factory agglomerations which have so profoundly affected Ghanaian consumption patterns, mortality levels and other aspects of living are found, on the whole, not a few miles from the farms, but thousands of miles away in Western Europe or even further afield. Modern migration restrictions and the cost of fares almost rule out these areas as an ultimate destination for the population beginning to move out of rural Ghana. The fact must be faced that Ghana's population problem is largely an internal one and that the ultimate receptacles for most of its population increase are going to be its own larger towns.

There are many who claim that fertility control is merely the corollary of mortality control. If a nation wishes to enjoy the luxury of low death rates, it will eventually be forced to accommodate itself to facts by reducing the size of its families. In the long run, this will certainly be the case in Ghana. It is not really conceivable that modern science will advance so rapidly that over 400 million people will be able to live in tolerable comfort in the country a century hence. However, such a fall in fertility will not necessarily begin in the immediate future.

It is necessary to be quite clear about the issues involved in any current 'population debate' about the position in Ghana or presumably elsewhere in tropical Africa. In terms of the possible carrying capacity of the country or of the likelihood of famine, Ghana could probably sustain a *laissez-faire* population policy until at least the year 2000. In terms of economic development and raising the standard of living, continued high fertility could leave the Ghanaian people still relatively poor a generation hence unless massive outside aid could be relied upon. On the other hand, declining fertility could bring very substantial economic gains even over two or three 'Plan' periods and these gains would be much greater with steeper declines in fertility.

This does not necessarily mean that the Ghanaian Government should decide to encourage family limitation. But it does mean that policy makers should be absolutely clear about the issues involved. Even in the short run, money spent on reducing fertility would be a sound investment, and there is no economic case against such investment. If fertility remains high, it is because certain non-economic considerations were held to out-weigh the economic ones. It might be felt that large families provided a greater source of joy than the accumulation of possessions. Or it might be considered that certain means employed to reduce fertility were fundamentally immoral. But, if a decision not to encourage reduced fertility is made on these grounds, the fact should be realized and appreciated. No attempt should be made to bolster the decision by creating economic arguments of dubious worth to support it.

If the Government does decide to encourage or at least to allow fertility decline, the earlier the decision is made the better economically. For, no matter when the decision is made, the country will still have to wait the same length of time before the largest gains are made. A later start would mean commencing with a much bigger base population than might have been the case and hence a much bigger investment in duplicating services before growth could be slowed down.

It is the delay in the maturation of the population to working age which means that some of the benefits claimed from sustained high birth rates do in fact eventuate even with a dramatic fall in the fertility level. Thus, even the lowest projection pictures Ghana with 20 million people in 2000 and 55 million in 2060. Presumably, this meets the wishes of all who desire to see the country's resources fully utilized. Similarly, even the lowest projection shows that fertility decline will not greatly affect the size of the labour force this century. Planners could hardly desire a labour force in excess of $5\frac{1}{2}$ million people by 1985 or $8\frac{1}{4}$ million by 2000.

Modernization, and especially the financial strain of keeping children at school, together with other pressures arising from rapidly declining mortality, will probably create some tendency towards reduced fertility regardless of government policy. Probably, then, population growth would not tend to be quite as great as is pictured by the *Constant fertility* projections, unless the Government prohibits the import of contraceptives and the establishment of family planning clinics, while at the same time vigorously proscribing illegal abortion.

Consideration must also be given to the possibility that the Government will decide to pursue a more positive population policy. That such a decision is possible is shown by the fact that developing countries elsewhere have moved in this direction. For instance, at the time of the 1955 United Nations Asian population seminar in Bandung,[1] most Asian countries found themselves in agreement on economic planning, but few favoured intervention in the population field. At the 1963 United Nations Asian Population Conference,[2] it was reported that most governments were now prepared to incorporate population planning as an aspect of overall development planning. It should also be noted that Ghana was one of the sponsors of the resolution on 'Population Growth and Economic Development' in the 1962–3 Session of the United Nations General Assembly, which drew that body's attention to problems of rapid population growth in developing countries and which, at least in its original form, advised that the United Nations might assist in seeking solutions.

The surveys have shown that indirect investment in such things as social welfare services or even the education of females is not likely to pay off in terms of fertility decline except over a very long period. If short-run econo-

[1] United Nations Seminar on Population in Asia and the Far East, held at Bandung, November–December 1955.

[2] United Nations Asian Population Conference, held at Delhi, December 1963.

mic returns were required, the investment would inevitably have to take the form of an improvement in family planning facilities. It is legitimate, when weighing possible future trends, to ask whether such an event is at all probable in Ghana, and whether it would be likely to produce any significant change in the pattern of population growth. It is quite possible that, if a planning body were to be asked at some stage to suggest possible steps for achieving a 1 per cent reduction in fertility, it would make recommendations along lines now being increasingly investigated in other developing countries. It might well recommend that family planning clinics should be established first in the big towns and then progressively throughout the country, that these should be run by nurses and other trained persons, and that contraceptive materials and services should possibly be provided free. It would probably recommend that clinics be set up in conjunction with hospitals and medical centres and especially the envisaged rural health services. Nurses might be told to follow up the cases of all mothers after the birth of a child to ask whether they desired assistance in postponing the next birth for a reasonable period. The claim might be made that the use of such contraceptives as the intra-uterine contraceptive devices, along the lines now being tried in Ceylon by the joint Swedish and Ceylonese team, could be effective in rural Ghana. Such a committee would probably take the attitude that the provision of these services for those who desired them, with government publicity about the existence of the clinics without the advocacy of their use, would merely be a case of providing services for those desiring to use them, and that it could hardly be construed as putting pressures on those whose viewpoints were not in accord with using them. At first such a programme, if adopted, would merely mean utilizing features of the demographic scene already in existence, rather than creating new features.

The possibility cannot be ignored that over the next thirty or forty years viewpoints about governmental intervention to reduce fertility will change radically in the developing world, because steep fertility declines are desired to assist economic development or because the kind of measures outlined above prove insufficient to bring about a satisfactory decline in fertility and in the rate of population growth. Technically, solutions can usually be found to such dilemmas. The real problem is often a moral one. Often, however, change is eventually facilitated because of alterations in moral outlooks. Such has certainly been the case in the West over the last century.

It is by no means impossible that birth rates will eventually be slashed in developing countries by the legalizing of abortion and the establishment of free or cheap government abortion services along the lines practised in Japan or more recently in Eastern Europe. None of the arguments often raised against the complexity of contraceptives and the difficulty of encouraging their mass use except in the most sophisticated and educated societies applies in these circumstances. It is also possible that the creation of a small family system by such vigorous methods could produce the rising standard of living which would finally give rise to the required levels of education and sophistication. Whether this could happen in Ghana is by no means clear. In 1963 a Cabinet decision was announced to provide harsher penalties for the practice of abortion, but to date no such legislation has been enacted. Survey experience showed that abortion is by no means unknown in the country.

However, for the present such matters must remain speculation, although a speculation that must necessarily be undertaken by anyone commenting on the probable interrelation of population growth and economic development. It is perhaps a pity that in the intellectual climate of the contemporary world such discussion must be carried out largely in economic terms. In fact, the creation of a small sized nuclear family has been an important part of social modernization in many countries and has a significance quite distinct from its economic one.

APPENDIX

I. THE 1962-4 POPULATION COUNCIL SURVEY PROGRAMME

The 1962-4 Population Council Survey Programme was carried out as part of the research programme of the Population Council Demography Post at the University of Ghana. The research programme included eight surveys designed to illuminate some of the findings of the 1960 Population Census of Ghana and to extend knowledge of the population of Ghana and of some of its social and economic characteristics. The analyses of all surveys are being carried out in conjunction with analyses of the material available in the Census Reports. These Reports and the accompanying maps served, where possible, as a basis for sampling frames.

Research work was carried out by students of the University of Ghana, and the key personnel had all received training in the two-year Demography Course given in the Sociology Department. These students and others had also received specific training for the survey and processing work within the Demography unit. Interviewing formed only a part of the investigation of and preparation of localities for study.

The research was wholly financially supported by the Population Council. Facilities of the University of Ghana were used, and the assistance of many members of the staff was sought. For the final processing and preparation for publication of the material, the facilities of the Australian National University have been employed.

Detailed technical presentations of the findings of these studies will be published as soon as possible.

LIST OF SURVEYS

1. *Rural-urban Migration Survey*
The survey concentrated on migrants to urban areas with populations in excess of 50,000, from rural areas (i) within 100 miles radius of Accra, (ii) in the area stretching southward from the northern border of Ghana to Kumasi. Migration to rural areas, including migration to cocoa-growing and gold- and diamond-mining districts, was specifically omitted.

Information was obtained about 17,399 persons living in 2,378 households in 63 localities. Surveying was carried out both in rural emigrant and urban immigrant areas. The survey schedule contained an elaborate grill for identifying the migrant by type of migration and for linking this and other personal characteristics, as well as 94 questions or sections of questions.

The chief aspects of the rural-urban migration process examined were (i) the analysis of households according to the migratory characteristics of the members of each and the distribution of various migratory patterns within Ghana, (ii) the relation between the migratory and other characteristics of individuals, (iii) reasons for migrating, (iv) mechanism of migration, (v) social and economic effects on rural areas of emigration, (vi) various economic aspects of the phenomenon.

2. *International Migration Survey*
Eleven areas in southern Ghana, known to receive a substantial number of international immigrants, were surveyed. Information was obtained from 634 persons of Nigerian or Togolese origin. The question schedule sought personal information on 13 points and contained an additional 25 questions or sections of questions.

The chief aspects of the international migration process examined were (i) the relation between the migratory and other characteristics of individuals, (ii) reasons for migration, (iii) social and economic aspects of the migrants' lives in Ghana, (iv) return movement, (v) support of relatives in and outside Ghana.

3. *Population Attitudes in Economically Superior Urban Areas*

The purpose of this survey was to examine those sections of the population, who, from experience elsewhere, would seem to be the most likely to be the first to develop a small family system, to see if they were doing so or if their attitudes were becoming more favourable to such a development. Because it is felt that these groups are likely to be influential in determining public attitudes, questions were also asked about attitudes to foreign migration into Ghana and about views on the relation between population growth, economic growth and resources.

Economically superior residential areas were surveyed in the four centres in Ghana considered fully urban in terms of size and length of urban tradition (Accra-Tema, Kumasi, Takoradi-Sekondi and Cape Coast). 627 persons were interviewed in 23 different localities. The question schedule for males differed slightly from that for females. Information was sought on 19 personal characteristics and a further 102 questions or sections of questions.

4. *Population Attitudes in Rural Areas*

In 28 different localities throughout Ghana 709 persons were interviewed. The interviewing schedule was short (20 questions and sections of questions) and was aimed mainly at identifying economic and other pressures on family size, and at finding out whether these pressures are at all effective. The economic productivity of children was especially examined.

5. *Conjugal Biographies*

In 68 localities throughout Ghana 1,933 conjugal case histories were constructed. Information was sought on the history of conjugal condition, change in that condition, parenthood and child-survival. Some investigation was also made of forms of adoption.

6. *Registration Survey*

The subsequent history of 1,000 children, whose births were registered in ten of the thirty-nine Compulsory Registration Areas was discovered by quite laborious field investigation. The samples drawn from the Registers were carefully graded by sex and age. Attention was paid to the comparison between real age and that stated to enumerators, infant and child mortality, infant and child migration, registration of infant deaths, and real residence of parents at time of registration.

In parallel investigations, representative areas or tracts of registration areas were studied to identify all births and deaths within given periods, and checks were then made to ascertain whether the events had been registered. Checks were made on 908 births and 435 deaths in ten Registration Areas.

7. *Survey of Aged Population*

Throughout Ghana 800 persons, who had wholly or partially retired from active employment because of advanced age, were surveyed in thirty-two localities. The attention of the survey was sharply focused on the relationship between the number of children born and surviving and the degree of economic protection ensured to parents in sickness and old age. Some attention was given to assessing what changes might be caused by Welfare State types of expenditure. Some investigation was also attempted into the question of the economic return on the education of children (or other relatives) regarded as a form of investment. A limited amount of personal data was collected and eighteen questions were asked.

8. *University Survey*

A sample of three students in eleven (systematic sample by residence within Halls) of the University of Ghana was selected. Three hundred students were questioned, and anonymity of replies was ensured.

The Survey was focused on questions of family and extended family financial assistance at various stages of education. Questions were then asked about expected future assistance to be given by students, when in professional employment, to relatives beyond their own nuclear families, and this was related to a study of pressures upon the professional classes acting towards the limitation of family size. A limited amount of personal data was sought and fifteen questions were asked.

II. LOCATION OF PUBLICATIONS ON POPULATION SURVEY PROGRAMME

Location of Survey Material published or available in Conference Proceedings to date (relevant investigation is bracketed).

J. C. Caldwell, 'Africa', in Part I, 'National Programs: Achievements and Problems', in Bernard Berelson and others (ed.), *Family Planning and Population Programs: A Review of World Developments*, University of Chicago Press, 1966.

— — —   'Family Formation and Limitation in Ghana: A Study of the Residents of Economically Superior Urban Areas', in Part IV, 'Research and Evaluation', in Bernard Berelson and others (ed.), *Family Planning and Population Programs: A Review of World Developments*, University of Chicago Press, 1966. (Population Attitudes in Economically Superior Areas.)

— — —   'Demographic Training and Research in Tropical African Universities which employ English as the Medium of Instruction', *Proceedings of the United Nations World Population Conference*, Belgrade, August–September 1965, at present being published by the United Nations.

— — —   'Extended Family Obligations and Education: A Study of an Aspect of Demographic Transition amongst Ghanaian University Students', *Population Studies*, Vol. XIX, No. 2, November 1965. (University Survey.)

— — —   'Population Policy: A Survey of Tropical Africa', *Proceedings of the First African Population Conference*, Ibadan, January 1966, at present being prepared for publication.

— — —   'Demographic Training and Research in Tropical African Universities', *Proceedings of the First African Population Conference*, Ibadan, January 1966, at present being prepared for publication.

— — —   'The Erosion of the Family: A Study of the Fate of the Family in Ghana', *Population Studies*, Vol. XX, No. 1, July 1966. (Survey of Aged Population.)

— — —   'A Study of Age Misstatement amongst Young Children in Ghana', *Demography*, Vol. 3, October 1966. (Registration Survey.)

— — —   'Fertility Attitudes in Three Economically Contrasting Regions of Ghana', *Economic Development and Cultural Change*, at present being prepared for publication. (Population Attitudes in Rural Areas.)

CHAPTER V

MARRIAGE, FAMILY AND HOUSEHOLD[1]

1. INTRODUCTION

Murdock defines the family as 'a social group characterized by common residence, economic co-operation, and reproduction'.[2] This definition of the family to include common residence is not necessarily true for many societies including the majority of Ghanaian societies.

In Ghana, when the word 'family' is used it does not usually refer to the nuclear or elementary family based on the husband-wife relationship but to the extended family based on descent. However, it is possible to distinguish both forms although neither is characterized by co-residence. Because of the lack of uniformity in the use of the concept it is necessary to be clear as to which type of family one is referring to. In this discussion both the extended family and the nuclear family will be treated as non-residential social units, while the concept 'household' will be used for the residential domestic unit.

2. MARITAL STATUS OF THE POPULATION

Marriage is the normal state among adults in all ranks of Ghanaian society. Almost everyone unless handicapped by physical or mental illness is expected to get married at least once upon the attainment of adult status. The results of the Post Enumeration Survey (P.E.S.)[3] of the 1960 Population Census showed that 91 per cent of all females and 65 per cent of all males aged 15 or over were married, divorced or widowed. Thus nine out of ten adult women and seven out of ten adult men had married at least once during their lives. The women appear to enter the married state much earlier than the men and this accounts for the statistical difference between these two groups. Within the 15–24 age group, 70 per cent of the females were currently married while 14 per cent were either widowed or divorced, making 84 per cent who had been married at one time or another. Only 16 per cent of the males in the same age group had ever been married. Much of the gap is narrowed for the males in the 25–34 age group by which age 72 per cent of them had been married while the women increase their lead to 98 per cent. Thus for a woman in the 25–34 age group there is almost 100

[1] The author is indebted to Mr A. F. Rutter for reading the draft of the manuscript and making many suggestions for its improvement.

[2] George Murdock, 'The Universality of the Nuclear Family' in Bell, Norman W., and Vogel, Ezra F., *The Family*, London: Routledge and Kegan Paul Ltd, 1960, p. 37.

[3] This survey was based on a 5 per cent sample of the population. The author is indebted to Mr E. N. Omaboe, Government Statistician, Dr B. Gil, United Nations Population Expert, and Mr K. T. de Graft-Johnson, Head of the Demographic and Social Statistics Division of the Central Bureau of Statistics, for permission to use the figures from the survey ahead of publication.

per cent probability that she has been married while a 90 per cent probability is reached for males in the 35–44 age group.

Although this broad picture of marital status does not vary much from region to region the Accra Capital District and the Northern Region[1] appear to be at opposite ends of the range. In almost every age group the Accra Capital District has the highest percentage of unmarried males and females while the Northern Region registers the lowest percentages. Since the Accra Capital District is an urban Region and the Northern Region is the least urbanized Region of Ghana one may take the differences in the figures recorded for both Regions as probably reflecting urban-rural differences.[2]

TABLE 5.1

PERCENTAGE OF ADULTS WHO HAVE NEVER MARRIED IN SELECTED AGE-GROUPS
IN ACCRA CAPITAL DISTRICT AND NORTHERN REGION

	Accra C.D.		Northern Region	
Age-group	males	females	males	females
15 and over	43·4	14·0	24·1	2·6
15–24	86·8	34·2	72·2	8·0
25–34	35·4	3·6	21·7	0·9
35–44	10·0	0·9	6·9	0·3
45 and over	5·8	1·1	2·1	0·4

Source: Unpublished Data from the Files of the Central Bureau of Statistics, Demographic and Social Statistics Division.

It will be observed from Table 5.1 that even though, in general, the proportion of unmarried males in Accra Capital District is higher than the corresponding proportion for the north, this proportion becomes rather small as one approaches the higher age-groups. Thus the difference is greatest in the lower age-groups, reflecting the trend towards later marriage in urban areas.

The Post Enumeration Survey did not enquire directly into the ages at which people marry. A survey of Yeji, a rural-farm community, and the adjacent Salt Town, a rural non-farm community, both near the banks of the River Volta, gives some indication of the relatively low ages at which people marry in the rural areas.[3] In Salt Town 25 per cent of the girls were first married *before* the age of 15 and 74 per cent of them were first married before the age of 19. In Yeji the proportion of girls first married before the age of 15 was comparatively very low at 3 per cent but 63 per cent of them were first married before they were 19 years old. The age at which men first married was somewhat higher than for females, but in both settlements about 60 per cent were married before the age of 24. Although one cannot quote comparable figures for the urban areas one can infer from the data on marital status in the Post Enumeration Survey that the age at first marriage in the urban areas is much higher. One of the reasons for this is the length of time taken for formal education in urban areas. The 1960

[1] This is constituted by the present Northern and Upper Regions.
[2] Urban-rural breakdowns were not available for the Post-Enumeration Survey information at the time of writing.
[3] The information is derived from a sample survey carried out by the author in the two settlements in August 1962.

Population Census showed a positive correlation between the size of a settlement and the education of its inhabitants as measured by the number of years spent in school. Not only do more children go to school in the urban settlements but the urban children also spend longer at school in order to acquire higher qualifications. Even when they have finished school, they like to work for some years to acquire some property before getting married.

A second reason which might delay marriage is that educated young persons in the city may have the responsibility of financing the education of their younger brothers and sisters. This burden prevents them from marrying early as they cannot afford to look after a wife at the same time as they are looking after their brothers and sisters. In the case of women who have such responsibilities the prospective husbands may be frightened away by the possibilty of taking over the responsibilities. Sometimes the women themselves do not wish to marry while they have these responsibilities for fear that they may not have the opportunity, within marriage, to discharge their responsibilities adequately. A third reason, which applies mainly to the class of persons educated to school certificate level and above, is the high cost of marriage and the inadequacy of suitable housing in which to set up a home. The high cost of marriage under the Ordinance reported by Busia for Sekondi-Takoradi[1] has not been appreciably reduced, and since there are social pressures on the persons in this class to perform their marriages under the Ordinance they usually wait until they have accumulated the large sums necessary for the ceremonies. The shortage of suitable housing also militates against early marriage because the ideal of persons in this class is to live with their wives in the same house, so that they wait until such time that they can get a suitable house at a reasonable rent.

A fourth reason is that many migrants who may wish to marry partners from their home villages take a long time to save the money necessary to pay for the long holiday at home and for the ceremonies which marriage involves. All these factors contribute to later marriages in urban centres.

3. PRE-MARITAL SEXUAL RELATIONSHIPS

The factors which lead to late marriages in the towns do not also lead to a postponement of the start of active sexual life. In the past girls were not expected to have sexual relations before their puberty rites were performed. These took place shortly after they had had their first menstruation. Contravention of this requirement was regarded as a public offence and was punished with penal sanctions in many of the societies of Ghana. Since girls were usually married shortly after this ceremony many entered their first conjugal unions as virgins. This was particularly so among the ethnic groups of the south where pre-nuptial chastity was valued. Among some of the ethnic groups of the north, however, pre-marital chastity was not and is not valued. Among the Konkombas, for example, many women are pregnant when they enter their first conjugal unions and the 'husbands show

[1] K. A. Busia, *Social Survey of Sekondi-Takoradi*, London, Crown Agents for the Colonies, 1950, p. 4. The Ordinance in this context is the *Marriage Ordinance* Cap. 127 of the Laws of Ghana.

not the slightest sign of displeasure at the pregnancy of a bride'.[1] The Tallensi also attach no value to pre-marital chastity and justify their attitude by the sociologically correct observation that 'Copulation and marriage are not the same thing'.[2] While premarital sexual relations have always been permitted in many parts of the north, the south has arrived at a situation whereby the practice has become very common although it is frowned upon.

This increase in sexual freedom is not always confined to the urban areas but is also sometimes found in the rural areas. In Ashanti, for example, puberty rites are now performed in very few cases even in the rural areas. As soon as a girl menstruates for the first time her mother informs the Queen-mother of her community about the event, and from that time the girl is free to have sexual affairs with members of the opposite sex. Since, in a matrilineal society, the offspring of the girl will belong to *her* family, the girls' mother does not always discourage her daughter in her sexual adventures. The older women are anxious to have many grandchildren to increase the size of their matrilineage, and the early pregnancy of their daughters helps to achieve this. Thus the later marriage of girls in the towns does not necessarily mean that they also start having their babies later. These urban girls usually develop friendships involving sexual intimacy with boys and older men while they are at school. At school they manage to avoid pregnancy through the use of contraceptives but when they leave school many of them have one or two babies whom they subsequently leave in their home villages before coming to town to look for work and a husband. The girls talk freely and proudly about their babies and do not regard this as an impediment to subsequent marriage.

In the higher socio-economic status groups also, premarital pregnancy is now becoming the accepted thing. Two reasons are responsible for this trend: firstly, the emphasis on children as the *raison d'être* of marriage in Ghanaian society, and secondly, the difficulty in dissolving marriages contracted under the Ordinance. The bearing of children is the cornerstone of marriage and where a couple are childless there is tremendous pressure from the extended families of the partners to dissolve the marriage. The men are encouraged to marry another wife while the women are pressed to find other husbands. In customary marriage, where divorce is easy and polygyny is permitted there is no difficulty in changing one's spouse or, in the case of a man, getting an additional spouse. For people who contemplate marriage under the Ordinance it is not so easy to change spouses or take on additional ones in the event of a childless marriage. For this reason, the men insist on pregnancy as a prior condition of marriage, and until pregnancy occurs the pair remain intimate friends or dissolve the relationship when it becomes clear that they cannot have children.

Another reason for the prevalence of pre-marital sex in the towns is due to the values which girls come to adopt in the urban areas. They adopt high standards of dress, and they come to enjoy the good things of urban living. Since their incomes are generally too small to enable them to buy all the

---

[1] David Tait, *The Konkomba of Northern Ghana*, London, Oxford University Press, 1961, p. 99.

[2] M. Fortes, *The Web of Kinship among the Tallensi*, London, Oxford University Press, 1949, p. 101.

dresses they want or to own cars, refrigerators and expensive furniture, they acquire boy friends who are in the position to provide them with these things. The fact that some of these boy friends may already be married is immaterial. They are quite happy with the situation.[1]

The comparative freedom with which young persons now enter sexual unions means that parents are no longer able to exercise much control in the selection of mates. The practice of betrothing small girls is still found in rural areas but in many cases the girls refuse to marry the men to whom they have been betrothed and marry men of their own choice. The role of the parents and the extended families in the choice of mates is limited to advising the young persons to avoid certain categories of mates. When two young persons intend to marry they inform their respective parents and/or heads of their extended families. Each family then tries to find out all it can about the other family. If a family finds out that the other family has a bad reputation, for example, as quarrelsome people or criminals or if there is a history of hereditary disease or mental illness, than it advises the son or daughter of the family not to contract the marriage. In many cases the advice is taken if offered on these grounds. Again if there is a dispute between the two families the marriage is unlikely to be contracted until the dispute has been settled. Sometimes men who work in the urban areas get wives selected for them by their parents in their home villages. In some cases these marriages are calculated to strengthen certain ties at home, and the men are not always able to reject the girls given to them. In such cases they usually marry other wives of their own choice in addition to the one selected for them by the parents. Thus, in the main, the choice of the spouse is left to the individuals themselves.

4. FORMS OF MARRIAGE

There are three basic methods of contracting a valid marriage in Ghana. These methods are:

(a) customary marriage.

(b) marriage under the Ordinance.

(c) Christian church or Muslim marriage.

(a) Much has been written about customary marriage in Ghana. The principal feature of such marriage is a series of presentations by the man to the family of the girl he proposes to marry. These presentations may be made all at once or, as in the case of the Konkomba, over a period of several years. The presentations are generally made in three stages. There is a first presentation of drinks to a girl's parents when making preliminary enquiries about one's acceptability to them. This is known as 'knocking the door'. When permission is granted to 'enter', it becomes clear that the girl's parents have no objection to the young man who seeks to marry their daughter. The man then makes a second set of presentations. This is sometimes referred to as the engagement. But, in fact, it is this second set of presentations which validates the marriage. It is known among the Akans as *tsir nsa* or *tiri nsa*. Consisting of money and drink, the payments re-

---

[1] These factors have militated against girls being married as virgins. This does not mean that virginity is no longer valued. The men do not expect to find their brides *virgines intactae* because it is no longer realistic to do so but when a man finds that his bride is a virgin he is very glad about it.

ferred to above vary in value according to the status of the girl. In Accra, for example, the usual amount is twelve guineas plus twelve bottles of beer, one bottle of whisky, one bottle of gin, one bottle of aperitif wine, two bottles of soda water and seven bottles of assorted drinks. When girls of high socio-economic status are involved, the monetary part of the presentation can be increased. The gifts are normally taken to the bride's parents by the groom's female relatives, usually sisters, aunts and cousins. The bride's parents invite members of their own extended families to be present when the gifts are brought. These gifts are distributed among the relatives as an indication that they are witnesses to the marriage of a daughter of the family. The third set of presentations is made when the marriage takes place. These final presentations are for the bride.[1] At the present time, a cash payment is normally made to the girl.

The higher the socio-economic status of a girl the more elaborate are the procedures for entering the marital union and the greater the expenditures which have to be made. For most people of low socio-economic status it is only the *tiri nsa* which is necessary as that validates the marriage and gives the husband exclusive sexual rights over the woman. This *tiri nsa* may be as low as two guineas in some communities.

(b) The designation 'marriage under the Ordinance' refers to a marriage contracted according to the provisions of the *Marriage Ordinance* (Cap. 127 of the Law of Ghana). The most important features of this form of marriage are that it is monogamous and cannot be dissolved except by a valid judgment of divorce. When persons married under the Ordinance or issues of such marriages die intestate, the rules governing the distribution of their property are different from those applying to persons married under native custom. In such cases the personal property of such intestate persons is distributed in such a way that two-thirds of the property is disposed of in accordance with the provisions of the laws of England 'relating to the distribution of personal estates of the intestates in force, on the 19th day of November, 1844'. The remaining one-third is distributed in accordance with the provisions of customary law. However, real property, the succession to which cannot be the subject of testamentary disposition under customary law, is distributed in accordance with customary law. The effect of the provisions of the Ordinance is to make it possible for widows to take a share of the estate of their deceased husbands which they would not normally have had under the provisions of customary law.

Thus, if a man married under the Ordinance dies intestate and he is survived by the widow of such a marriage and by children of whatever marriage, the widow is entitled to two-ninths (i.e. one-third of two-thirds) of the whole estate and his children will share the remaining four-ninths equally. If such a man is survived by a wife but no child, the widow takes one-third of the whole estate.[2] The women therefore have definite advantages in entering unions of this kind and are always urging their husbands to marry them in this manner.

[1] Some of the items which a man buys for his bride as part of these final payments are listed in K. A. Busia, op. cit., pp. 144–5.

[2] N. A. Ollennu, *The Law of Succession in Ghana*, Accra, Presbyterian Printing Press, 1960, p. 46.

(c) A church marriage is a ceremony performed in a Christian church to bless the union of a couple, one or both of whom are members of the church.

Muslim marriage is contracted under the Marriage of Mohammedans Ordinance (Cap. 129 of the Law of Ghana). This requires that the marriage performed by Mohammedan priests in accordance with Muslim rules should be registered in the office of a District Commissioner before it can be recognized as valid under the laws of the country. When a person married under this Ordinance dies intestate, succession to his estate is in accordance with Mohammedan Law.

Customary marriage is still the basic and normal method of entering marital unions in Ghana and persons who marry in church or in a registrar's office under the Ordinance do so only after they have performed the necessary customary rites. In the 1960 Post Enumeration Survey sample, 86 per cent of persons who had ever been married had been married under customary law only. In Northern Ghana 92 per cent of the adults had been so married.

The next popular form of marriage appears to be Muslim marriage which was contracted by about 5 per cent of the sample population. This form of marriage seems to be more prevalent in Ashanti and Brong-Ahafo than in any other Region of the country. In Ashanti about 7 per cent, and in Brong-Ahafo about 10 per cent of the sample had been married in the Muslim manner. In the Kumasi City Council area the proportion was 15 per cent. In the Northern Region Muslim marriages accounted for only 5 per cent.

Customary marriage followed by a combined church and Ordinance marriage was contracted by 2·3 per cent of males and 1·2 per cent of the females in the sample. This type of marriage is associated with urban areas and a high socio-economic status. Accordingly, the proportions are highest in the large urban centres. In Accra and Sekondi-Takoradi about 7 per cent of the marriages were contracted in this way. The lowest proportions were in the predominantly rural regions of Volta, Northern and Brong-Ahafo Regions, where less than 2 per cent of the married adults had been married in this manner.

Sometimes people enter upon a marital union through customary marriage followed by a blessing in the church. This sort of marriage does not have any legal effect different from that of customary marriage. Some of the churches have regulations governing the disposition of the property of those entering such marriages in the event of their dying intestate. Such regulations do not, however, have any effect in law.[1] This sort of marriage is common in areas where the Presbyterian Church is very strong. The high.st proportions of marriages in this category are found in the Volta and Eastern Regions where the Presbyterian Church has large flocks. In Akwamu-Anum-Boso local council area where the highest proportions were found, about 9 per cent of the males and 3 per cent of the females had contracted marriages of this sort.

Where the two persons to be married belong to different churches and neither is willing to marry in the church of the other, or, where the couple

[1] N. A. Ollennu, op. cit., p. 13.

are married under customary law followed by marriage under the Ordinance, their marriage is contracted in the office of a Registrar of Marriages.
This mode of marriage is contracted mainly in large towns and involves
only about 1 per cent of all marriages.

No discussion of the forms of marriage in Ghana can be complete without
mentioning a form of union which, although not constituting legally valid
marriage, nevertheless appears to be an important form of marital union.
This is co-habitation of persons of opposite sex without the formality of
marriage.[1] In the Post Enumeration Survey sample 4 per cent of the males
and 5·6 per cent of the females were living in this sort of union. An interesting feature of these unions is that they are not more important in the
larger urban centres than in the rural areas. They are most prevalent in the
Brong-Ahafo, Ashanti, Eastern and Volta Regions. In the Ashanti Region
8 per cent of the males and 12 per cent of the females were living in such
unions. In the other three Regions the corresponding proportions were as
follows: Brong-Ahafo, 9 per cent for males, 12 per cent females; Volta,
6 per cent males and 9 per cent females; Eastern, 6 per cent males and 8
per cent females. The local authority area with the highest proportion of
such marriages in Brong-Ahafo Region was the Brong-Ahafo Central
Local Council with 12·7 per cent males and 13·5 per cent females living in
such unions. Sunyani Urban Council had the lowest proportions in the
Region being 0·6 per cent for males and 2·4 per cent for females. In
Ashanti, Kumasi West had the highest rates—12·5 per cent males, 18·1
per cent females; while the lowest rates were in Kumasi City Council area
and the Obuasi Urban Council area. In the Volta and the Eastern Regions
also the highest rates were recorded in rural districts and not in urban
districts. The proportions for the Accra City Council area were at 2·1 per
cent males and 4·4 per cent females, that is, below the national average.
One may conclude that these unions are not necessarily the result of urbanization. The explanation is to be sought in the indigenous social arrangements of the various ethnic groups. In many of these groups a period of
cohabitation may precede the marriage proper. Among the Ashantis, for
example, Fortes has pointed out that 'a marriage may begin with a period
of cohabitation approved by the parents of the couple and accepted as
proper marriage for all practical purposes'.[2] In such cases the husband does
not have exclusive sexual rights in the wife. This means that he cannot
claim damages if his wife commits adultery with another man and he
cannot claim paternity of a child conceived by his wife with another man.

Apart from this recognized custom of co-habitation there are other
circumstances which favour such unions. Among the Krobos, a patrilineal
people, the first child born by a girl belongs to the girl's family. The rights
in *genetricem* which a husband has over his wife are therefore transferred
only after the girl has had one child.[3] This being the case, the girls are not
so anxious to contract valid marriages before the birth of their first child.
In such circumstances many first babies are likely to be born in common

[1] Otherwise known as Common Law Marriage.
[2] M. Fortes, 'Kinship and Marriage Among the Ashanti' in Radcliffe-Brown and
Daryll Forde (eds.), *African Systems of Kinship and Marriage*, London, Oxford Univer-
ity Press, 1962, pp. 279–80.
[3] Verbal Communication from Mr E. Ampene, University of Ghana.

law unions and many young girls are likely to be living in such unions. This probably accounts, at least in part, for the high proportion of adults (males 16 per cent, females 19 per cent) in the Manya-Yilo-Osudoku local council areas who were living in such unions.

Apart from such social arrangements which favour the contracting of common law unions, the high rate of conjugal separation may be a factor in some of these unions. When a woman has contracted more than one marriage a subsequent husband does not usually feel obliged to perform the necessary customary rites to validate the marriage. The women do not insist on these payments for fear of losing the husbands on whom they depend for sexual satisfaction and economic support. The greater the number of marriages a woman has contracted the less likely is she to contract a legally valid marriage. As a woman gets on in years her bargaining position is weaker and she finds it harder to get a man. Therefore she is not in a position to insist on the formalities.

Although the proportions for the urban areas are low there is no doubt that such unions are becoming increasingly common in the large centres. The fact that there are many single women in the towns who are living away from the control of their families makes it relatively easy for such unions to take place. In Ghana, unlike British Guiana, these unions are not confined to the lower socio-economic groups.[1] They are found among members of the higher socio-economic groups as well as the lower ones. A man in a high socio-economic status group will contract a number of such unions concurrently. Sometimes he will have a wife or wives married under customary law in addition to keeping women in these non-legal unions. He would establish each of these wives in a house in the city and visit her regularly. These common law marriages cannot be considered as a deviation from the norm but as an integral part of the system of marriage.

5. THE STRUCTURE OF MARITAL RELATIONSHIPS

Although polygyny is permitted in many of the societies of Ghana monogamy is the statistical norm. In the Post Enumeration Survey Sample (1960), about 74 per cent of the married males were monogamously married. Twenty per cent had two wives and 5 per cent had three wives. It is only in the Northern Region and in the Volta Region that the proportion of males with more than one wife exceeds the national average. In general, the proportion of monogamously married males is higher in the urban areas than in the rural areas. This reflects the difficulty of maintaining more than one wife under the conditions of urban life. A wage earner in the town does not normally earn enough to support more than one wife at a time.

Even in the rural areas few men have the means to enable them to become polygynous. Even though the proportion of the males who are polygynously married is low the number of wives, in the 1960 sample, per 100 males was, at 135·1, higher than in many other countries.

The Post Enumeration Survey did not enquire into the frequency of marriages but there are many indications that this would tend to be high. In the sample 5 per cent of males and 7 per cent of females aged 15 and over

[1] See Raymond T. Smith, 'Community Status and Family Structure in British Guiana'. in Bell, N. W., and Vogel, E. F., *The Family*, London, Routledge and Kegan Paul, 1960, p. 260.

were reported to be divorced, the highest rates being recorded in Ashanti and Eastern Regions where the proportion of divorced was about 10 per cent for females and 6 per cent for males. In the 45 and over age group these proportions rise to 20 per cent and 11 per cent, respectively. As the proportions are much higher for older persons above the age of 45 one may infer that some of the instances of divorce recorded are cases of terminal separation of marriage without necessarily entailing the formalities of divorce. As Goody has shown for the Gonja, many women return to their kin in old age to spend the remainder of their lives among their kinsmen.[1]

This sort of situation is not uncommon among people with virilocal marriage and such cases may be treated as the equivalent of divorce by enumerators since the couple are no longer living together. It is therefore difficult to get a useful idea of the frequency of divorce by looking at the proportions of divorced persons in the population. Few women have long periods of waiting between two marriages. They are usually in the process of contracting another marriage before the previous one has been terminated. The data from Yeji and Salt Town seem to indicate that marriages are more frequent in communities based on a trading economy than in communities with a predominantly agricultural economy. In Yeji, a predominantly agricultural community, 25 per cent of the males had been married twice and 10 per cent three or more times. Only 7·4 per cent of the females had been married twice or more. In Salt Town, whose inhabitants exist primarily on trading, 40 per cent of the males had been married twice, 14 per cent three times and 7 per cent four times. Of the females, 27 per cent had been married twice and 7 per cent had been married three times. Of the two communities, Yeji is ethnically homogeneous, while Salt Town is ethnically heterogeneous. In a trading economy a man does not have to support his wives wholly from his own resources since the wives can also engage in trade and support themselves to a great extent. The men are therefore more able to afford a plurality of wives.

Many men are unable to afford more than one wife at a time, but extramarital sexual affairs have been very common traditionally and today are still practised by married adults of both sexes and by members of all socioeconomic groups. In the towns men have regular girl friends who bear them children. In many cases the men acknowledge paternity of such children and regularly contribute to their support. Apart from the desire of the marriage partners to obtain some variety in their sexual life, certain circumstances are especially conducive to this phenomenon. Where a man submits to the requests of his parents to marry a wife provided by them, the man does not always have that emotional attachment to his wife which would lead him to be faithful. He wants to make his own choices and expresses this desire in his extra-marital adventures. Where, as in many cases, his wife is of a much lower educational status, he will often indulge in love affairs with girls of higher educational status. He enjoys a full social life with these girls outside the home, and in such cases his wife is reduced to the status of a housekeeper and procreator of children. Girls who marry men against their will also indulge in such affairs for the same reasons.

[1] Esther Goody, 'Conjugal Separation and Divorce among the Gonja of Northern Ghana' in M. Fortes (ed.) *Marriage in Tribal Societies*, Cambridge University Press, 1962, pp. 14–54.

Another factor which contributes to extra-marital sex relations is the emphasis on children as a *sine qua non* of marriage. Women who do not have children by their husbands have sexual relations with other men, usually youths or men reputed to be very fertile, in the hope that they will become pregnant. In some cases they do become pregnant and give their husbands the paternity of the child. One can say, however, that women indulge in extra-marital sex less than the men.

Some men indulge in extra-marital sex in order to produce a large number of children and thus demonstrate their sexual and reproductive powers. Others do so because they are expected by their friends to do so, and not because they themselves feel the urge or the necessity to behave in that way.

Although the general attitude towards extra-marital sex is permissive the marriage partners affected do not always take kindly to such adventures. This is especially so in cases where the marriage has been contracted under the Ordinance. The women involved are usually educated and have acquired the Euro-Christian values associated with such marriages. Here lies a potential source of conflict between the spouses and frequent quarrels and separations often result. The Euro-Christian ideal of chastity outside marriage does not fit in very well with a traditional situation in which the male is free to have many concurrent marriages. Thus a man who is compelled to have one wife only because he has married under the Ordinance or in a church, finds himself in a cultural situation where men are permitted to have many wives. He solves this dilemma by refusing to adopt the value of chastity.

The educated wife faces other problems in the home today which were not faced by wives in the past or by illiterate wives in the rural areas. Many wives of educated men have had enough education to enable them to take up jobs other than trading. It is now the idea of the educated wife to go out to work and earn an independent income. This creates problems of child care and home maintenance. Since both wife and husband go out to work the household jobs and the care of children have to be left in the hands of paid servants. In the past it was possible for young couples to have young maid servants chosen from among their illiterate relatives. In fact, every educated bride had, at least, one such girl given to her by her parent's family to act as maid-servant. Nowadays, the greater awareness among all classes of the population of the advantages to be derived from education has made it more difficult to recruit such maid-servants. The 'Country relatives' want their children to go to school and are reluctant to send them to the towns as maid-servants. Thus the modern educated housewife has to do the housework without the assistance of maid-servants. Where the couple can afford it, paid servants are hired but these are not as good as the former relations since, in general, they have no real interest in such work. The sort of situation in which both spouses go out to work may lead to conflict when the husband is dissatisfied with the food prepared by maids and feels that his children are neglected by them. Some women avoid this conflict by not resuming their career until they have sent all their children to boarding school.

Among the higher socio-economic groups and in the towns, there is increasing emphasis on the conjugal family consisting of a man, his wife and their children as an autonomous social unit. This is especially so in marriages involving more than one ethnic group. In such cases the married couple are thrown more and more on their own resources and do not lean so much on their respective families of orientation. Busia found about 31 per cent of his sample in Sekondi-Takoradi were inter-tribally married.[1] He concluded from this that such marriages were on the increase in urban areas. It is possible that this is indeed so, but, nevertheless, there are still tremendous social pressures against this. On the individual level, many persons wish to contract such marriages but they are apt to be discouraged by their friends and relations. The opposition of the relatives, especially the elder ones, is mainly caused by their ignorance of the customs and way of life of the members of the ethnic group their child wishes to marry into. Since their ignorance makes them uncertain of the kind of life their child would be living they are unwilling to let their child loose on such 'uncharted seas'. Sometimes this ignorance is reinforced by unfavourable stereotypes of the other tribe. When this happens the opposition is more severe. Other persons discourage their friends from entering such unions because of the differences in language. They do not want to visit their friends and be forced to converse in English because their friend's spouse does not understand their language. In many cases, however, such objections are overcome and the couple become married. With the extensive improvements in transport over the past fifteen years making it possible for people to travel more widely than before, and the growth of residential educational institutions in which persons of different ethnic groups live and study together, the expected trend is towards more and more marriages involving persons of different ethnic groups.

6. PATTERNS OF RESIDENCE

The 1960 Post Enumeration Survey data show that the statistically normal form of residence of marriage partners is one in which both partners live in the same house. Of the married females interviewed in the sample, 66·7 per cent had their husbands living in the same house with them. A similar percentage, 63·7 per cent of all wives reported by married males were also living in the same house with their husbands. In spite of this high association between marriage and common residence of the conjugal pair, co-residence, as Goody has pointed out, 'is not an essential corollary of marriage'.[2] In many societies the ideal is for husbands to set up their own households when they marry but various circumstances make it difficult to realize this ideal. Sometimes a husband is not able to set up an independent household where his wife can join him. At the same time he does not want his wife to come and live in his parents' home because of possibilities of conflict between her and his mother and sisters. The result is that the wife tends to live in her parents' home instead of living together with her husband. In Ashanti and Brong-Ahafo these factors are reinforced by the strong ties that exist between children of the same mother which make them continue to live in their mother's domestic group even when they

---

[1] K. A. Busia, op. cit., p. 29.
[2] J. Goody, 'Fission of Domestic Groups among the Lodagaba', in *The Developmental Cycle in Domestic Groups*, Cambridge University Press, 1958, p. 56.

become married. In Agogo, Fortes found that 80 per cent of married women were living in their matrilineal family groups.[1]

In the Post Enumeration Survey sample about 20 per cent of the married females were living in the same town with their husbands but in houses other than those in which the husband was staying. Another 20 per cent were living in towns other than those in which the husbands were living. There was no appreciable difference between urban and rural districts, but in Brong-Ahafo, the Sunyani Urban Council Area has a greater proportion of wives staying in other houses in the same settlement than in the rural districts. Forty per cent of the married females of that district were living in houses other than those in which their husbands were staying.

Among the Gas, the expected pattern is separate residences for the spouses. The women cook and send food to their husbands' houses during the day and go there to sleep during the night. Children stay with their mothers, but male children leave for their fathers' homes at about the age of six or seven. This custom probably accounts for the high rate (30 per cent) of married women who stated that their husbands were living in houses in the town different from those in which they themselves were staying.

The larger towns of Ghana usually have a large core (40–50 per cent) of the population who are members of the indigenous ethnic group in whose territory the town is founded. These ethnic groups have ways of behaviour which do not necessarily reflect the current trend among the other members of the population. Because of this situation it is difficult to discern current trends in social behaviour from a statistical enumeration of occurrences in these towns. The pattern of residence is one such case in which statistical procedures do not throw light on current trends. In the large urban places the current trend, especially among the educated groups, is towards co-residence of the marriage partners. As has been pointed out above, the practical difficulties of realizing this ideal can sometimes lead to a postponement of marriage. Modern, educated couples want that constant companionship of their spouses which can only be realized in a common residence, this residence to be separate from that of either family of orientation.

Another factor leading to common residence in the urban areas is that when people migrate from rural areas to live in towns, they prefer their wives to live with them, since, in what to them is a 'foreign' settlement, the informal social controls to ensure their wives' fidelity might be lacking. Furthermore, in the urban situation, it is rather expensive to set up separate houses for wives unless one happens to be a wealthy man. The husband is also answerable to the wife's family for her health and safety. It is only when he lives in the same house as his wife that he can effectively protect her from the numerous hazards of the strange urban environment.

7. HOUSEHOLD SIZE AND STRUCTURE

The observation that household size decreases as one moves from the rural to the urban areas sometimes creates the impression that rural households are generally very large groups consisting of many persons. This impres-

[1] M. Fortes, 'A Demographic Field Study in Ashanti', in F. Lorimer, *Culture and Human Fertility*, Paris, UNESCO, 1954, p. 270.

sion is created because most of the time the concept 'family' is used instead
of the concept 'household'. When we think of the family in the rural
situation we think of a large extended family all the members of which may
not necessarily be staying together, whereas when we think of the family in
the urban situation we usually think of the household which is necessarily a
co-residential unit. Thus we imagine a considerable shrinkage from the
large rural group to the small household unit in the town. If we define the
household as a social group consisting of persons who live together and
share the same housekeeping arrangements we find that this picture is somewhat exaggerated. In the Post Enumeration Survey Sample the average size
of the household for the country is 4·3 while the smallest average size for
an urban or city council area recorded was 3·2 in the Accra City Council
area. The difference between town and country is, therefore, not very great
especially if we consider the fact that, apart from the Northern Regions,
the average for almost every other local authority area is below the national
average.

Many surveys of rural households confirm the fact that these households are not very large. The Government Statistician's survey of cocoa
producing families in the Oda area, for example, found that the average
size of a household was 4·41. During a survey of Nungua village in 1954
the author found that 50 per cent of the households consisted of four
persons or less. It is possible that the definition of household adopted in the
various surveys has resulted in the artificial splitting of significant social
units in the house. If this happened, then it did not occur in the majority of
cases since in many rural studies the proportion of houses with single
households exceeds 60 per cent.

Although the *average* size of households in the rural areas is not very
large there is no doubt that, in general, very large households are found
more often in rural than in urban areas. For example, in the Post Enumeration Survey Sample 7·3 per cent of all households were composed of ten
persons or more for the country as a whole, while for the urban areas this
proportion was only 3 per cent. The occurrence of these large households is
not high enough, however, to affect significantly the average size of household. In the northern region the occurrence of large households is sufficiently frequent to influence the averages for the various local council
areas. In that region the average household size was 6·7. The highest
average size of household (11·4) was in Tumu Local Council area. The
large households in the north may be accounted for by the fact that in that
part of the country the members of the extended family tend to live together in one compound. Since, in many cases, they have common housekeeping arrangements under the overall direction of the head of the compound, all the inhabitants of a compound were in such cases treated as
one household.

The important feature of the urban household is not so much its size as
its composition. The rural household is usually composed of persons who
are held together by bonds of consanguinity. The relationship between the
members is based on descent. In the urban situation there is a greater emphasis on the husband-wife relationship. The husband, his wife and their
children form the central core of the household. Either of the spouses may
have a relative or relatives staying with him or her but these relations have

little say in running the affairs of the household. Thus the trend in the urban areas and among the educated classes especially is for the conjugal family to be the household unit. The conjugal family emerges, in the urban situation, as a distinct autonomous unit. This means that the influence of the extended family on the lives of the marriage partners is not as great as it is under rural conditions. This influence tends to be in inverse proportion to the distance between the home towns of the marriage partners and their town of residence. Where the couple reside in the home town of one of the partners this influence may be great.

As one example of this, some non-Ashanti girls married to Ashanti men find that when they are living in towns outside Ashanti their relations with their husbands are much stronger than when they live in Ashanti. In neutral territory, the conjugal family is a more cohesive social unit. In Ashanti, especially in the hometown of the husband, the strength of the sibling bond militates against the cohesion of the conjugal family. The husband tends to spend a lot of time with his mother's family. The members of this family also make financial demands on him and he is obliged to support them. He begins to lean more and more on his mother and sisters for advice, and the centre of his domestic life shifts from that of his own conjugal family to that of his extended family. It is possible that such extreme cases are rare but they illustrate the degree to which the extended family can affect the life of the individual even under urban conditions. Even when the extended family does not influence the life of the urbanite to any great extent, the urbanite still has strong loyalties to his extended family and keeps contact with its members. The existence of a family in the home town is one factor which keeps the widely scattered members together. When they visit their home town they are always assured of a home in the family house. Most extended families also have shrines of their ancestors, and even highly educated and high status persons come to these shrines to ask for the blessing of the ancestors in any important projects they want to undertake. If a man is going abroad he pours libation to his ancestors to ask them to protect him in foreign lands. If a man is not getting on well in his job he comes home to the family shrine to ask the help of his ancestors in improving his circumstances in his job. Since the head of the family is usually the custodian of the family shrine he is in a position to influence, to some extent, the actions of the members, and he also acts as a focal point of unity for the family.

Funerals and memorial services for the dead also contribute to the continued integration of the extended family. At these functions members of the extended family from widely scattered parts of the country come together to pay homage to the memory of a departed member. Many members meet each other for the first time and children are introduced to their aunts and uncles. The members of the extended family act as one unit and make a common contribution to the expenses of the funeral and any debts incurred in connection with the funeral are shared by the members.[1]

To sum up, the most salient features of the emergent patterns of family life and household structure are the following:

[1] Such joint activities help to reinforce social ties among members of the extended family, ties that might otherwise weaken in the face of increasing regional and social mobility.

(i) Prevalence of pre-marital sex relations which is explained, in part, by the tendency for people in urban areas to marry at relatively later ages; in part, by the permissive attitude towards such matters in certain areas and by the breakdown of traditional controls in yet other areas.

(ii) Greater freedom of choice in the selection of mates.

(iii) Prevalence of extra-marital sex relations, especially on the part of males, due, in part, to the conflict between the Christian ideals of monogamy and the traditional practice of polygyny.

(iv) Possibility of greater incidence of inter-tribal marriage thanks to improved communications, greater freedom of mate selection, and the impact of residential educational institutions which cater for all the ethnic groups of the nation.

(v) Greater emphasis on the conjugal family in the urban areas but with the ties of the marriage partners with their extended families continuing to remain fairly strong.

CHAPTER VI

EDUCATION

1. THE DEVELOPMENT OF THE EDUCATIONAL SYSTEM[1]

In the traditional societies of Ghana education was informal and was carried out by the community as a whole, with the child's own family playing the most important role. It was, in fact, identical with the process of socialization by which the culture of the society was passed on to the young generation. In such relatively homogeneous, slowly changing societies such a system was adequate to meet the needs of the society. Consequently, when the first European type schools were introduced to West Africa there was no popular demand for their services. The chequered history of the early schools clearly demonstrates this, and the only schools to achieve any degree of success were those which catered largely for the inhabitants of the coastal castle-towns. The slow growth of the early schools and the closing of many of them soon after their foundation are usually explained in terms of the financial and health problems which were encountered. The main factor in their failure, however, was that the African population was not interested in them. Once this lack of interest was overcome the other factors melted into relative insignificance. Moreover, the interest of the local population in formal schools was not gained until social and economic changes had occurred which made the old type of education inadequate. As Philip Foster states in his pioneering study of education in Ghana, 'in the initial stages there is no demand for education unless significant changes have already taken place in the traditional structures'.[2] In the case of Ghana the significant changes in the social structure which led to a situation conducive to the growth of specialized educational institutions were brought about in the first place by the presence in the coastal towns of increasing numbers of European traders. During the eighteenth and early nineteenth centuries, the coastal peoples gradually became more and more involved in trade with the Europeans. With the increase in trade, urban areas began to grow and a comparatively rich group arose, a group which owed its wealth and position, not to the tradi-

[1] A short analysis such as this is not the place for a chronological history of education in Ghana. Those who are unfamiliar with this history would do well to consult the detailed material which it is not possible to discuss here. I have drawn on the historical material in order to attempt some explanatory generalizations about the development of the educational system. The best known historical sources are: F. M. Bourret, *Ghana: the Road to Independence*, London, Oxford University Press, 1960, Chapters 8 and 11; F. H. Hilliard, *A Short History of Education in British West Africa*, London, Nelson, 1957; D. Kimble, *A Political History of Ghana 1850–1928*, Oxford, Clarendon Press, 1963; H. O. A. McWilliam, *The Development of Education in Ghana*, London, Longmans, 1959; W. E. F. Ward, *A History of Ghana*, London, Allen and Unwin, 1958; C. Wise, *A History of Education in British West Africa*, London, Longmans, 1956.

[2] P. J. Foster, *Education and Social Change in Ghana*, London, Routledge and Kegan Paul, 1965, p. 43 ff.

tional society, but to trade. It was these merchants who were the first to see the advantages of the Western type of education. Some of them sent their children to Europe to obtain such an education, but increasingly they sought educational opportunities locally.

Thus the missionaries who responded to invitations to visit the coast in the 1830s, 1840s and 1850s found a situation which was already in a process of change. Because far reaching changes in the traditional society were already under way, their attempts to plant education were more enduring than previous attempts had been. The schools which were set up were modelled on the English charity schools. As in the English case there was at first no government direction nor supervision, and the curriculum was limited almost entirely to basic literacy and simple arithmetic. The great difference was that in West Africa this was the *only* type of formal education available, and the pupils could therefore look forward to relatively well paid and highly prestigious jobs as clerks and assistants to traders, missionaries, teachers, and in the second half of the century, in government service. But this development was confined to the coastal area, and even here the extent of the influence of education should not be exaggerated. By 1844 the Wesleyans had only eighteen schools, while the Basel mission had a similar number and opened their seminary at Akropong four years later.

After this time a further factor in the spread of education in the south was the extension of effective British political control, culminating in the annexation of the colony. The influence of the Government was indirect since the amount of money available for grants to education was small, and the policy was to give aid to the missionary societies rather than to participate directly in education. Later, however, there was an attempt to regularize education in the Education Ordinance of 1882, and by the appointment of an inspector the Government tried to exert some influence on the schools and especially on the standards of instruction.

There was still no government influence on the siting of schools, however, and the missionaries, finding their reception in Ashanti anything but friendly, were forced to concentrate their activities in the south. By the turn of the century there was considerable African demand for their services in this area. Nor was this demand restricted to schools of an elementary level. The Fanti Public Schools Fund, for example, was an (unsuccessful) attempt by a group of well-educated Africans to form a chain of secondary schools throughout the colony. More successful ventures were to lay the foundations for the later extension of secondary schools, and all of these attempts were the outcome of African educational demand. By 1910 there were four institutions giving secondary instruction. But at this time only a small minority of those who attended school managed to complete even their primary schooling. Primary schools in those days comprised an infant year followed by seven years of 'standards'. In the year 1911, there were 10,874 pupils enrolled in the infant classes. In Standard 1 the number had fallen to 2,057, and there were only 387 pupils in Standard 7—the final year of primary school.[1]

In contrast with the demand for education in the south, Ashanti views about education are well illustrated by the statement of the Asantahene in 1876 that 'Ashantee children have better work to do than to sit down all

[1] Education Department records.

day idly to learn hoy. They have to fan their parents, and do other work which is better.'[1] It was not until the annexation of Ashanti in 1901 and the proclamation of a Protectorate in the Northern Territories that the area of educational activity was extended. There had, however, been little contact with the Europeans and little modification of the traditional Ashanti society, and the demand for formal education in Ashanti remained low for many years. Even by 1919 the total number of schools in Ashanti was only twenty-three. Thus, although the political barriers to expansion in Ashanti had been removed, it was still in the Colony that most of the educational expansion took place. In the same year of 1919, for example, there were 186 schools in the Colony.

There was even less demand for education in the Northern Territories, which had been correspondingly less exposed to outside influences. Moreover, government policy was opposed to giving the missionaries a free hand in the north, partly because it was feared that they might be a disturbing influence making the nothern tribes more difficult to rule, and partly because the Government, particularly later under Guggisberg, wanted to avoid the haphazard spread of education which had characterized the southern development. Even so, the White Fathers were allowed to open a school at Navrongo, and in 1909, a government school was opened in Tamale. As late as 1928, however, we read of some of the few schools closing down because of lack of support, and education had made little progress.

These regional inequalities in the provision of education which were so marked in the early years of the twentieth century have continued up to the present time. They are to be traced basically to the differential contact with Europeans, their trade and their ideas, but they have also been strengthened by the Government's unwillingness, in the first half of the century, to direct educational development. Hence, the areas where the demand for education was highest, that is to say the southern areas and especially the towns, were provided with most of the new schools. This in turn created even more demand, thus intensifying the differences.

The period of the First World War therefore saw a further increase of educational demand in the south, a demand to which the government was sympathetic but which, in spite of a period of unprecedented prosperity in the 1920s it could not meet. One of the limiting factors in the numerical growth of the system was the Government's policy of restriction at the primary level until such a time as there were enough trained teachers to staff new schools. Indeed, during Guggisberg's term of office 150 schools were closed down because they did not meet the required standards of efficiency. At the secondary level, too, there was a policy of restricting the growth of the existing secondary schools, which were described as secondary in name only, in favour of the new *élite* institution at Achimota. Hence, contrary to popular opinion, the expansion of education under Guggisberg was not faster than it had been previously. Likewise, expenditure on the education system, although showing higher absolute figures, showed a rate of growth similar to that of previous decades.

However, the rate of growth of the system did not slow down much

[1] D. Kimble, op. cit., p. 75.

during the 1930s despite the shortage of money, while the demand for education grew even stronger, linked as it was with competition for the now fewer jobs in the modern sector of the economy. As well as a wider demand for primary (infant) schooling there was increased pressure for education in senior primary schools up to Standard 7 and for secondary schooling. The Government's policy of restricting expansion at all levels was never in fact fully carried out, because the pressure for more education was met by the proliferation of privately operated schools. For example, in 1930, there were six secondary schools in the country—two government, two government-assisted, and two private (non-assisted). By 1940 one of the non-assisted schools had been absorbed into the assisted category, but eleven new private secondary schools had opened and were to be found in the non-assisted category. After 1940 this growth of the private sector continued. Similarly, in spite of government policy, the number of children in primary schools rose from 53,000 in 1930 to 88,000 in 1940.

The late 1920s and the 1930s also saw the quickening of educational expansion in Ashanti. It has already been suggested that educational expansion is likely to take place on a large scale only if the traditional social structure has already been modified by other forces. Both political and economic forces entered into the changing situation in Ashanti. In the first place, the extension of British rule at the beginning of the century had brought the area directly into contact with personnel of the colonial government. This had the dual consequences of disrupting important elements in the traditional political structure, and of creating a situation in which the missionaries could work. Nevertheless, we have seen that these factors did not result in an immediate expansion of education, and that it took some time for a local demand for education to grow. A further, and crucial, factor bringing about social change was the spread, in the late '20s and '30s, of cocoa farming into Ashanti from the Akwapim area. The significant factor about cocoa farming is that although it is still carried out on the basis of peasant farms, it essentially represents a change to a cash crop economy from the earlier forms of subsistence agriculture. The rapid spread of cocoa farming meant that the whole of south Ashanti became involved in a cash crop economy with all the changes in the traditional structure that this implies. It was only after this change had taken place that the rate of educational expansion quickened, so that cocoa farming may be said to have performed the same function for education in southern Ashanti as the expansion of trade had earlier performed for the colony.

Since the Second World War, and in particular since an elected majority took charge of domestic affairs in 1951, expansion of the educational system has accelerated on every level. In so far as this expansion has been due to the ever increasing demand for education at ever higher levels, a large part of it would probably have taken place irrespective of government policy, much as the system had earlier expanded against the policy of the Government. But the fact that the Government was a popularly elected one made it politically impossible to ignore the demand, with the result that the expansion has come under some government control and has been given government encouragement and direction. Moreover, now that the demand for education is high, it is possible for government policy to have an influence on growth that it could never have had when the demand was lower. Hence the political pressures of the 1950s and the 1960s have hastened the expansion of the system. One should perhaps also mention the facilitating factor of relative prosperity based on the high price of cocoa for fifteen years after the war. This prosperity has enabled an enormous growth in numbers of pupils to take place, especially at the primary level, and has also financed major educational projects such as the building of universities.

The frequently heard argument that the growth of the educational system has also been brought about by the needs of an industrializing country for technically skilled manpower is easy to overstate. Certainly an industrializing country has occupational needs which may act as a stimulus to certain sections of the educational system. For example, the rapid expansion of the university institutions and of the secondary schools can be related to the perceived need for high level personnel to staff both the growing administration and the growing industrial sector. But the spectacular growth of the primary school system after 1951, culminating in the establishment of free and compulsory primary and middle school education in 1961, cannot be understood in these terms. There is not at present a high demand for the services of those leaving middle school, although less than 40,000 reach this level annually. Indeed, it is difficult for these young people to find any employment at all. When the annual output of the middle schools rises to a quarter of a million, as is planned by 1970, it is difficult to imagine the economy expanding fast enough to be able to absorb the young people entering the labour market.[1]

Throughout the post-war period, as was to be expected, the regional inequalities in the provision of education have persisted. Indeed an unanticipated consequence of the declaration in the Accelerated Development Plan in 1951 of free but not compulsory education was to make these differences even more pronounced. The Government has made strenuous efforts to redress the balance, efforts which include the provision of free secondary education in the north.[2] But, as has been indicated above, the development of a local demand for education is a slow process, and there is still much less interest in and appreciation of education in the north than in the south. Nevertheless, the introduction of compulsory primary education should mean that within a generation there will be something approximating to regional equality in the provision of primary education at least.

To sum up. The first formal schools were ignored even by that small minority of Africans who had the chance to attend them. It was only when strategic changes had already taken place in the traditional social structure, largely through the growth of foreign trade, that social conditions suitable for the growth of education emerged in the coastal areas. The spread of British rule and the desire of the missionaries to spread Christianity were further factors influencing this growth. The differential provision of education reflects the different degrees to which these economic, political and religious forces were present. All three have obtained in the south for a

[1] See below, pp. 231–5.
[2] For a period of some four months after October 1965, tuition in secondary schools has been free throughout the country.

longer period than in the north, and thus educational demand, which, because of the Government's reluctance to direct the provision of education, has been the key factor in development, has remained lower in the north than in the south. Moreover, once the schools were established, they in turn operated to hasten the process of social change, thus creating a still higher demand for education.

One final word on the development of the educational system should be devoted to the question of the curricula of the schools. It will be noticed that no reference has been made to technical education. This is because, in spite of the frequent references to technical education in government policy statements, and in spite of the space devoted to it by historians, technical education has, *in fact*, been unimportant in the development of Ghanaian education.

It has been common ever since 1850 for politicians and administrators to to criticize the curriculum in Ghanaian schools as being too academic.[1] This criticism perhaps reached a peak in the 1920s with the castigations first of Governor Guggisberg, then of the 1920 committee of educationalists, and finally of the Phelps-Stokes commission. The critics further accused the schools of alienating the pupils from the community through their bookish curriculum, and advocated more agricultural and technical elements in the curriculum. In the event, *despite* government policy, no such reforms took place, largely because of the resistance of the educated Africans who were most emphatic in their demand that education should be of an academic nature. The academic element in the curricula has from the earliest times been governed by the occupational opportunities available to the school leavers.[2] Academic education has, in the event, proved to be the most useful vocational education the schools could have given, for it has been in the clerical occupations that the most numerous and best paid jobs for educated Africans were to be found. Even the few who were trained in the Trade Schools of the 1920s could not find employment, hence the expansion of technical education could hardly be expected to be popular. At every level of the educational system an academic type of education developed although the policies of the Government and of the educationalists were in every case opposed to such a development. We may conclude that it was the dictates of the occupational structure rather than any slavish imitation of British education that conditioned this development.

2. THE STRUCTURE OF THE EDUCATIONAL SYSTEM

The education system of Ghana is now made up of a public sector, consisting of schools which are either run by or assisted financially by the Government, and a small private sector. Contrary to the situation in most countries, the private schools have less prestige and lower standards than the public schools, and they invariably transfer to the public sector when they reach the required standards. Since the Accelerated Development Plan of 1951, the great majority of schools in Ghana have been supported by the Government, and recent legislation has made it impossible to open a private school without special permission from the Ministry of Education.

[1] P. J. Foster, op. cit., contains a detailed and illuminating discussion of this problem, pp. 52–8.
[2] Ibid., pp. 64–7.

The primary schools provide a basic six-year course which has been designed for children aged from about six to twelve years, during which basic literacy and arithmetic are taught. At the time of writing (1965), middle schools offer a four-year course for primary school leavers.[1] Both primary and middle schools are fee free and text books are also provided free of charge. At the end of the four-year middle school course pupils may sit for the Middle School Leaving Examination. This examination 'does not represent a high standard of educational achievement but is nevertheless a useful guide to employers and others and indicates, at the least, that its holder has enjoyed ten years formal education and therein acquired the basic accomplishments of an educated citizen'.[2] Middle school pupils, however, may be selected for transfer to secondary school from forms II, III, and IV of the middle school, although there has for some time been a tendency to give preference to the younger children from forms II and III. The eventual aim is that all selection for the secondary schools should take place at the end of primary education so that those selected would by-pass the middle school altogether.

Selection for secondary school is by competitive common entrance examination, conducted by the West African Examinations Council. At the time of their examination, candidates indicate the schools of their choice, and allocation of pupils to the various schools is made, not by locality, but by reference to the examination marks. The reason for this method of selection is that it is recognized that the secondary schools are of different quality and that most of the best are situated in Cape Coast, Accra and Kumasi. It is therefore felt that to allocate pupils to schools on a local basis would unfairly favour the children living in these areas. One of the consequences of the present system of allocation, however, is the perpetuation and exaggeration of the present differences between the schools, since, on the whole, the good schools get the best pupils (in so far as this is measured in the common entrance examination). The best known and most popular schools receive a large proportion of the first choices and so it is possible for them to be highly selective, even within the group of successful candidates. The normal age for entry to secondary school is between twelve and seventeen but many of the schools only admit the younger candidates.

The main secondary school course lasts for four years, and at the end of this time pupils are prepared for the School Certificate examination of the West African Examinations Council. This certificate is awarded in three divisions and those who pass in divisions I or II are eligible for entry to the VIth form. Only about a quarter of the schools have VIth forms, and at this stage pupils may again make known the school they wish to attend, thus providing the popular and prestigious schools with another opportunity of attracting the pupils with the best results. Many pupils therefore change schools between the Vth form and the VIth form. The normal VIth

[1] Senior Primary Schools were renamed Middle Schools in 1951. It is planned to reduce the middle school period from four years to two years, and to run these schools as 'continuing schools' of a vocational nature. See *Seven-Year Development Plan*, Accra, Government Printer, 1964, p. 151.

[2] Ministry of Education, *Education Report 1960–2*, Accra, Government Printer, 1963, p. 13.

form course is of two years' duration and leads to examinations for the General Certificate of Education (Advanced level). Those who pass at 'A' level in two or more subjects qualify for entry to a degree course at one of the three university institutions. So far there have been university places available for all those who have qualified so that there are no problems of university selection, and it is unlikely that this situation will change for many years.

The Teachers' Training Colleges of Ghana recruit mainly from middle school leavers. Since September 1962 the course has been a four-year one leading to the award of a teaching certificate. In the first two years of the course 'the educational standards of the students are to be raised to a level roughly equivalent to that of a third year secondary school pupil and special stress will be laid on science subjects. In the third year of the course there will be a small amount of professional training but the emphasis will still be on the student's own education. The fourth year will be devoted to professional training'.[1] A small minority of training college students are recruited from the secondary schools and for these a two-year course leading to a teaching certificate is available. There are also two-year courses available to enable those practising teachers who possess the old two-year 'Certificate B' to improve their qualifications and salaries.

Technical education is available to middle school leavers in Technical Institutes, which select their students by reference to the Middle School Leaving Examination. Now that occupational prospects for technicians are brightening, these Institutes are becoming a popular alternative for those who fail to get secondary school places. The Government Secondary School at Takoradi is a part of the secondary system but it provides an education with a technical bias up to 'A' level. There is also a Technical Teachers' Training College at Kumasi, and Kwame Nkrumah University of Science and Technology runs scientific and technical courses of a pre-university or VIth form level in addition to its degree and diploma courses.

A remarkable growth has been effected in the fields of primary, middle and secondary education since 1950. In that year there were just over 1,000 public primary schools, just over 500 public middle schools, and twelve public secondary schools. By the 1963–4 school year the numbers were 7,490 primary schools, 2,224 middle schools, and 85 secondary schools. Table 6.1 shows the increasing number of these three types of school for each year since 1950. The unusually large increase in the number of public primary schools between 1951 and 1952 was chiefly due to the absorption into the public sector of 1,400 schools which had previously been run privately. On the other hand, the equally large increase in the 1961–2 school year almost entirely represents new growth consequent upon the introduction of compulsory primary education. Compulsory education caused less immediate pressure upon the middle schools but nevertheless over 300 new middle schools were added to the public sector in September 1961. The number of secondary schools has also been growing over the period, and ten schools were added to the public sector at the beginning of the 1963–4 school year. Moreover, at that time, the number of secondary schools with VIth forms increased from twenty to twenty-six.

---

[1] Ministry of Education, *Education Report, 1960-2*, p. 21.

TABLE 6.1

NUMBER OF PUBLIC PRIMARY, MIDDLE AND SECONDARY SCHOOLS, 1950–64

Year	Primary	Middle	Secondary
1950	1,081	511	12
1951	1,083	539	13
1952	3,069	667	26
1953	3,131	704	30
1954	3,136	717	31
1955	3,210	786	31
1956	3,312	862	35
1957	3,372	931	38
1958	3,402	1,030	39
1959	3,428	1,118	39
1960*	3,452	1,177	39
1960–1	3,552	1,252	59
1961–2	5,451	1,575	68
1962–3	6,873	1,809	75
1963–4	7,490	2,224	85

* January 1960–September 1960: Before 1960 the school year started in January; after 1960 it started in September.
Source: Education Statistics (Accra, Government Printer), Ministry of Education reports (Accra, Government Printer), and unpublished data supplied by the Ministry of Education.

TABLE 6.2

ENROLMENTS IN PUBLIC PRIMARY, MIDDLE AND SECONDARY SCHOOLS, 1950–64

Year	Primary	Middle	Secondary
1950	144,300	60,000	2,800
1951	154,400	66,200	2,900
1952	335,100	80,000	5,000
1953	372,400	88,600	5,100
1954	396,900	97,400	6,900
1955	419,400	105,000	7,700
1956	436,900	108,500	8,900
1957	455,700	115,800	9,900
1958	455,100	125,300	10,400
1959	465,300	140,000	11,100
1960*	478,100	147,500	†
1960–1	520,000	157,700	†
1961–2	701,000	176,000	†
1962–3	801,100	204,900	22,800‡
1963–4	927,500	222,800	28,100

* January–September
† Figures not available.
‡ Estimated from 1963–4 figures.
Source: Education Statistics (Accra, Government Printer), Education Reports (Accra, Government Printer), and unpublished data supplied by the Ministry of Education.

Similarly the overall enrolment at the schools has shown a dramatic increase. Table 6.2 shows that, between 1950 and 1964, primary school enrolments increased nearly seven times, middle school enrolments nearly four times, and secondary school enrolments ten times. Almost all of these increases represent new enrolments rather than transfers from the private sector of the education system. Thus, even in 1952, the year in which 1,400 primary schools were transferred from the private to the public sector, the

P

transfer only accounts for 80,000 of the new enrolments in the public primary schools in that year. Similarly in the secondary schools, apart from 1952 when rather more than half of the 2,000 new enrolments in the public sector were transfers from the private sector, almost the whole of the very large increase in enrolment represents new secondary school enrolment.

The increased enrolment in all three types of school has been evident throughout the country, but regional differences in enrolment continue to exist in spite of free primary and middle school education, and in spite of government measures to eradicate such differences. For example, the figures of the 1960 Census show that Brong-Ahafo and Northern Regions provided only 14 per cent of the primary school pupils in the country, although rather more than one-quarter of the population, aged 5–14, lived in these Regions. Moreover, these two Regions provided only 11 per cent of the middle school pupils and 6 per cent of the secondary school pupils. Thus in 1960 these disadvantaged Regions were under-represented in all three types of school, but especially so in secondary schools. Table 6.3 shows that the situation for the school year 1963–4 was substantially unchanged. Brong-Ahafo, Northern and Upper[1] Regions in 1963–4 provided 17 per cent of the primary school pupils in Ghana, less than 11 per cent of the middle school pupils, and less than 8 per cent of the secondary school pupils. Table 6.4 shows further that the proportion of the population of school age that was attending primary and middle school in 1963–4 ranges from over 80 per cent in some regions to less than a quarter in others.[2]

At all levels of education in Ghana there are more boys enrolled than girls. This is especially so at the secondary level where, in 1959, 82 per cent of the pupils were boys. In the same year 73 per cent of the middle school pupils and 65 per cent of the primary school pupils were boys (see Table 6.5). A comparison of the enrolments in 1959 and 1962–3 which is also made in Table 6.5, shows that there has been an increase in equality between the sexes at the primary and middle school levels. There are no figures available for secondary schools but it is unlikely that there has as yet been as great a change in the proportion of girls at this level since 1959. It is also interesting to note that, because of the overall increase in numbers, the absolute difference between the sexes has grown larger at all levels during the period 1959–63.

A further problem is evident if we attempt to trace any given cohort of children through their educational life. In the past by no means all of those who started primary courses completed them. This is clearly illustrated in Table 6.6, which shows the 'drop out' of those pupils who entered the primary schools in 1955. Little more than one half of these pupils completed the six-year primary course and of all those who failed to complete the course more than two-thirds left during or at the end of their first year and consequently received virtually no education. The advent of compulsory

[1] Two new regions have been created since 1960. Northern Region has been divided into the present Northern and Upper Regions, and Western Region has been divided into the present Western and Central Regions.

[2] The Ministry of Education report for 1960–2 defines the school age population as those aged 6–14, although there are still many pupils older than this in the middle schools. It should perhaps be pointed out that Table 6.4 overestimates the percentage of the population attending schools, as the total school age population in 1963–4 will have been larger than that for 1960.

TABLE 6.3

REGIONAL DISTRIBUTION OF THE SCHOOL AGE POPULATION AND OF THE
PUPILS ENROLLED IN PRIMARY, MIDDLE, AND SECONDARY SCHOOLS IN 1963–4

Region	Population aged 5–14 (1960) (a) Per cent	Primary (b) Per cent	Middle (b) Per cent	Secondary (b) Per cent
Eastern	16·9	19·0	20·8	19·4
Ashanti	16·8	20·5	21·2	13·0
Volta	12·4	14·1	16·0	11·2
Central	11·5	11·7	12·3	19·0
Upper	10·5	5·1	3·2	1·4
Western	9·0	10·6	9·1	10·7
Brong-Ahafo	8·8	9·0	6·3	3·3
Northern	7·6	3·0	2·0	3·0
Accra C.D.	6·5	7·1	9·1	19·0

(a) Source: 1960 Census (Accra, Government Printer).
(b) Source: Unpublished material supplied by the Ministry of Education and the Census Office.

TABLE 6.4

PROPORTION OF SCHOOL AGE POPULATION ATTENDING SCHOOL IN EACH REGION

Region	Population aged 5–14 (1960) (a)	Enrolments in primary and middle schools (1963–4) (b)	Percentage of school age population attending school
Eastern	288,482	222,295	77·1
Ashanti	285,973	236,832	82·9
Volta	209,977	166,723	79·5
Central	195,065	136,095	69·7
Upper	178,606	54,559	30·7
Western	152,769	118,471	77·6
Brong-Ahafo	150,317	97,229	64·7
Northern	128,792	32,194	24·8
Accra C.D.	109,900	85,897	78·0
GHANA	1,699,881	1,150,295	67·6

(a) Source: 1960 Census (Accra, Government Printer).
(b) Source: Unpublished data supplied by the Ministry of Education and the Census Office.

TABLE 6.5

SEX PROPORTIONS IN PRIMARY, MIDDLE AND SECONDARY SCHOOLS, 1959 AND 1962–3

		1959 Per cent	1962–3 Per cent
Primary schools:	Boys	65·5	60·0
	Girls	34·5	40·0
	Total	100·0 (483,400)	100·0 (801,100)
Middle schools:	Boys	73·3	69·0
	Girls	26·7	31·0
	Total	100·0 (154,700)	100·0 (204,900)
Secondary schools:	Boys	82·4	*
	Girls	17·6	*
	Total	100·0 (15,300)	100·0 (22,800)

Source: Education Statistics 1959 (Accra, Government Printer), and unpublished data supplied by the Ministry of Education.
* Figures not available.

education should do much to ameliorate this situation, particularly as the Government is also making attempts to overcome some of the economic barriers to staying at school. We must expect, however, that school attendance will be irregular in some parts of Ghana for many years to come.

The rate of 'drop out' from middle schools is insignificant and the vast majority of those who enrol in middle schools either complete the course or transfer to secondary schools. Moreover, of those who completed primary school in 1963 an estimated 90 per cent enrolled in middle school Form I the following September. The problem of 'drop out' for voluntary reasons or from economic necessity is thus concentrated in the primary school.

TABLE 6.6

'DROP OUT' OF PUPILS ENTERING PRIMARY SCHOOLS IN 1955

Primary form	Year	Number enrolled	Drop out
1	1955	109,000	34,500
2	1956	74,500	3,700
3	1957	70,800	4,900
4	1958	65,900	5,500
5	1959	60,400	2,600
6	1960	57,800	—

Source: Ministry of Education, Education Report 1960–2, Accra, Government Printer, 1963.

After entry to the middle school, early leaving because of the factors mentioned above becomes insignificant until entry to secondary school is contemplated when there are many who cannot afford to pay the fees of the secondary schools. Because of the manner of transfer from middle school to secondary school, it is difficult to estimate the proportion of middle school leavers who go on to secondary school, but an estimate may be obtained by relating the numbers in middle school Forms II and III (the forms from which most secondary school students come) to the numbers in secondary school Forms I and II (the forms into which they are placed). In the school year 1963–4 there were 13,800 pupils in secondary school Forms I and II, whereas in the previous year there had been 101,800 pupils in middle school Forms II and III. Therefore as a rough approximation we may say that 13 or 14 per cent of those who were passing through the middle schools at this time went on to secondary school.

Once entry to secondary school has been obtained, the next hurdle in Ghanaian education is the entry to the VIth Form. Very few secondary school pupils leave school before the Vth Form stage, but in 1963–4 there were 3,200 Vth Formers in the schools and only 800 in the first year of the VIth Form. This suggests that irrespective of their performance at the West African School Certificate examinations, places can only be found in the VIth Forms for a relatively small proportion of those who leave the Vth Form. With the vast expansion of enrolment which has recently taken place at the lower levels of the secondary schools it is unlikely that this proportion will be raised in the near future, even with the rapid expansion in size and number of VIth Forms which is currently taking place.

The final step on the ladder of academic education in Ghana leads to the three university institutions. The combined enrolment of these three in 1963-4 was just over 2,400, rather more than half being at the University of Ghana. The normal channel of entry has been through the VIth Form, but many people have managed to obtain the entrance requirements by other means, notably through working privately to prepare themselves for their 'A' level examinations. This accounts for the fact that the annual intake of the universities is higher than the annual output of the VIth Forms. At the University of Ghana, for example, about one-third of the total enrolment had never been through a conventional VIth Form course, and the proportion is much higher at the University College of Science Education, which has close links with the teaching profession and draws many of its students from the ranks of practising teachers.

3. THE MAJOR FUNCTIONS OF EDUCATION

Educationalists in Ghana, as in the rest of Africa and indeed throughout the world, have in the past been unduly influenced by the stress which most anthropologists place upon the function of education as a transmitter of the cultural heritage. This emphasis is entirely valid in a very simple society which is changing very slowly and which has no formal educational institutions, but it is totally inadequate for an understanding of education in a rapidly changing society which has had specialized educational institutions for many years. An analysis of the past statements of educationalists and policy makers (for example, the Phelps-Stokes Committee in the 1920s) reveals that this is the only function of education that they have understood. But it is an element which has hardly entered into the educational scene of modern Ghana. Rather a whole series of unintended consequences have resulted from the development of education.

To begin with, far from passing on and strengthening the traditional culture, the introduction of specialized institutions for education has in itself helped to alienate pupils from the traditional society, thus furthering a process already set in motion by economic factors. A second function of education has been in the political field, in the fostering of nationalism and the hastening of independence. Thirdly, in the economic field, the spread of education has been accompanied by varying degrees of unemployment. And finally, in the social sphere, the educational system operates as a mechanism of social selection, and as a means of determining which individuals become socially mobile. Many of these processes are themselves inter-connected but for the sake of brevity and clarity they must be treated separately here.

(i) *Alienation from the Traditional Society*

The traditional societies of the various parts of Ghana had no formal educational institutions.[1] It was only when substantial changes had taken place in some parts of the traditional social structure that formal schools became established. I have already indicated that education was not in itself able to *instigate* changes in the traditional society, a factor which explains the length of time which it took for education to become popular

[1] See, for example, M. Fortes, 'Psychological Aspects of Education in Taleland', *Africa*, Vol. XI, No. 4, 1938, Supplement.

even in the south. But once changes were in progress, the provision of education of a Western type did much to hasten these changes and to spread them to other parts of the country. The gradual breakdown of traditional concepts of prestige and authority; the trend from rural to urban patterns of living; the transfer from a subsistence economy to an exchange economy; all these processes were encouraged by the establishment of formal education. Furthermore, the individuals who underwent this process of education were oriented towards the modern sector of the society rather than the traditional. Entrance into the modern sector of the economy through education, however rudimentary that education may have been, provided access to situations where prestige and power were accorded on grounds other than traditional. Thus education provided a channel for rebellion against traditionalism for those who were able to take advantage of it.

The products of the schools took jobs in trade, commerce, teaching, government service and, recently, in industry. In every case these occupations had not existed in former days and they were invariably located in the towns. The towns became the centre of anti-traditional feeling and activity, and the early days of indigenous Gold Coast politics consisted largely of a struggle between the educated *élite* of the towns and the chiefs.[1] For example, in the controversy over the London deputation of 1920, Nana Ofori Atta denounced the leaders of the delegation: 'If this [visit to London] is the sort of benefit to be derived by the country from our sons and relatives who are educated then the position of the Gold Coast is in great danger.'[2] He further rejected the claims of the educated to any voice in the Legislative Assembly, speaking of 'this bosh that an ordinary native, simply because he is educated, becomes the natural leader of the State to which he belongs. It is a wrong doctrine.' The chiefs looked to the rural areas for their allegiance, while the educated *élite* drew their support from the urbanized and partially de-tribalized society of the coastal area, thus exercising some political power on the municipal councils. In the first instance both groups owed something of their position to the support of the British, who failed to see the contradictions involved in supporting both groups. Both the educated intellectuals and the tribal chiefs thought of themselves as the successors to British power. But the increasing numbers who had been to school looked more and more to standards and criteria other than the traditional. In short, they found themselves giving support to the modern rather than the traditional aspects of the society both socially and politically. Thus education was the basis of the early opposition to the chiefs.

(ii) *Nationalism*
Closely connected with the challenge to the traditional leaders was the rise of modern nationalism. Even the first of the nationalist movements in Ghana—the Fanti Confederation of 1872—had drawn some of its leaders from the products of the castle schools, and by the time of the First World

---

[1] See Legislative Assembly Debates, April 25, 1921. Also D. Kimble, op. cit., pp. 389–96, and D. Austin, *Politics in Ghana 1946–60*, London, Oxford University Press, 1964, Chapters 1–3.

[2] Legislative Assembly Debates: December 30, 1920.

War an educated *élite*, drawn mainly from the wealthy families, was firmly established in the coastal towns and was demanding control of local government. In the period after the Second World War the moderate nationalist party—the United Gold Coast Convention—grew out of this highly educated group. But education at the primary level was also reaching the rank and file members of the society and continued to do so to an increasing extent throughout the inter-war years. Many of these young men became clerks or teachers, but their aspirations were often higher than this. In the immediate post-war years they accepted the *élite* leadership provided by the intelligentsia of the UGCC, but in the split between Nkrumah and the UGCC they supported Nkrumah.

In its early years the Convention People's Party was always strongest in the towns where the mass of those with education lived. Indeed, Professor Apter contends that a good deal of the CPP's early support came from the largely unemployed 'Standard VII' boys. 'Its membership', he writes, 'was primarily the partially educated, the Standard VII boys, those whose urban affiliations made possible quick and effective organization.'[1] Others have reiterated Apter's belief, but unfortunately such statements have been supported with little or no evidence. Dennis Austin has, however, undertaken an analysis of the educational background of the national leadership of the CPP in 1951, and of local branch leadership in a rural constituency (Amansie East) and a south Kumasi constituency in 1954.[2] The results of his analysis have been brought together in Table 6.7 and they suggest that men with elementary education played a leading role in party affairs both at the local and at the national levels. But this is not to say that the majority of the party's support came from this source. Although this may have been so in the very early days of the party, it is clear that by the election of 1951 party support was widespread among all sections of the population.

TABLE 6.7

EDUCATIONAL EXPERIENCE OF SOME CPP LEADERS

Educational level reached	CPP *assembly* members, 1951	CPP *constituency* executive in Kumasi South, 1954	CPP *constituency* executive, Amansie East, 1954
University	8	—	—
Secondary School or Teachers' Training College	13	—	2
Standard VII	18	4	13
Standard III	—	1	3
No formal schooling	—	2	6
Total	39	7	24

Source: D. Austin, *Politics in Ghana, 1946–60*, London, Oxford University Press, 1964, pp. 195–9.

(iii) *Employment*

The relationship between education and the economy is always a complicated one, but it has been suggested in the earlier discussion on the

[1] D. Apter, *Ghana in Transition*, New York, Atheneum, 1963, p. 167.
[2] D. Austin, op. cit., pp. 195–9.

development of education that the education system has never, as yet, been a primary factor in bringing about economic change. In spite of this many commentators speak of education as bringing about unemployment in Ghana. This usually goes with criticism of the type and content of the education provided, and there is still a widespread belief that unemployment only exists because school leavers refuse to accept manual employment on account of their 'academic' education.[1] These beliefs must be rejected as inadequate and we must enquire more closely into the relationship between education and unemployment.

The implication behind this whole discussion (an implication which usually goes unstated) is that the education of an individual implies that he will enter the modern sector of the economy. Those who have received formal education, whatever its content, are not prepared to return to traditional occupations. Such a return is seen as failure to achieve the object of education which is conceived in occupational terms. On the other hand, there is no evidence to suggest that school leavers are averse to manual work as such. The unwillingness to enter farming, which is so often commented upon, must be explained as reluctance to enter a traditional type of employment rather than as reluctance to enter a manual type. Unwillingness to enter farming, with all the implications this has for unemployment, will not be overcome as long as school leavers see farming as an occupation where traditional methods of work and traditional patterns of authority prevail.

As early as 1870 some of the literate products of the schools were finding it difficult to find work in the modern sector of the economy.[2] Much of this unemployment was ascribed to the academic nature of the curricula of the schools, but those with the more technical education provided by the Basel Mission schools were in an even worse situation.[3] From that time until the present some unemployment in the coastal towns has been a permanent feature. It is impossible to judge the extent of changes in unemployment in Ghana since there have never been any comprehensive records of unemployment. A small, but unknown proportion of the unemployed now register at the labour exchanges but no trends can be inferred from these registrations since they include those registered in newly-opened exchanges. The number of unemployed registered at labour exchanges throughout Ghana in 1961 was 14,743, but in the same year the Ministry of Labour disclosed that there were more than 31,000 unemployed in Accra alone.

A further idea of the extent of this problem can be derived from a consideration of the numbers of middle school leavers in the past ten years. About 20,000 young people left middle school to take up employment in 1954, whereas in 1964 twice that number of middle school leavers were looking for jobs.[4] In contrast, the modern sector of the economy has been expanding more slowly, from a total employment of 224,329 in 1953 to 350,000 in 1962. This increase is less than the number of school leavers for

[1] See, for example, T. Solarin, 'The Secondary Schools Africa Needs', *West African Journal of Education*, Vol. 7, No. 2, June 1963, pp. 77–9.

[2] P. J. Foster, op. cit., p. 132.

[3] Ibid., p. 133 ff.

[4] Figures from unpublished data supplied by the Ministry of Education.

the years 1961–4 alone. Bearing in mind our contention that school leavers are unwilling to return to traditional occupations we may suggest that the unemployment situation among school leavers has worsened in the last ten years.

The relationship between the schools and unemployment is often expressed in terms of education having brought about an increase in unemployment. But the only way in which the educational system could have *created* unemployment in Ghana would have been by luring people from a situation of full employment in the rural areas to a new situation of unemployment in the towns. It seems far more likely that there has existed in the rural areas in the past a considerable degree of *under*employment. By entering the schools, boys and girls who would otherwise have been under-employed in the villages enter upon a process which turns their attention and aspirations towards the towns and the modern sector of the economy. But because of the relatively slow rate of growth of the economy there have, in the past, been too few jobs in the modern sector of the economy to absorb these school leavers. Thus, rather than creating unemployment, it is more likely that the expansion of the educational system has merely changed rural underemployment into the more easily visible urban unemployment.

The problem of unemployment has been and still is an economic problem rather than an educational one. The only educational solution would have been to stop the expansion of education, and in Ghana this has never been a practical possibility for political reasons. Nor would many people con-sider it in the long term interest of the country. The only solution to the problem of unemployment lies in the expansion of the modern sector of the economy at such a rate that employment is created for those who at present have none, as well as for the increasingly large number of school leavers who enter the employment market each year.

The Seven-Year Development Plan recognizes this, and envisages an expansion which will take up the vastly increased output of the schools. At the lower levels this is no mean task, for the annual output of the middle and continuing schools will, by 1970, be nearly a quarter of a million.[1] Between 1965 and 1970, 752,000 middle school leavers are expected to enter the labour force, and a further 110,000 will enter from other educa-tional institutions. But if the plan's target of over a million new jobs by 1970 can be reached the present rate of unemployment will be reduced in spite of these large numbers.[2]

The details of the expected manpower situation in Ghana for the next seven years are shown in Tables 6.8 and 6.9. Table 6.8 shows the manpower needs of Ghana in 1970 as they are presented in the Seven-Year Develop-ment Plan, and Table 6.9 shows the expected employable output of the various educational institutions by that date.

A comparison of the two tables will show that if the higher level occupa-tions are to expand at the planned rate they will take up the whole output of the educational system other than that of middle and continuing schools. The middle and lower level occupations will therefore recruit from the middle and continuing schools. It will also be noticed that the agricultural

[1] *Seven-Year Development Plan*, Accra, Government Printer, 1964, p. 153.
[2] Ibid., p. 146.

TABLE 6.8

THE OCCUPATIONAL NEEDS OF GHANA BY 1970

Type of occupation	New places required by 1970	Replacement for wastage by 1970	Total intake needed by 1970
High level:			
Professional, Administrative, Technical, Teachers, Skilled crafts	77,000	32,000	109,000
Middle level:			
Clerical, Transport, Trade, Semi-skilled	203,500	155,500	359,000
Unskilled:			
Labourers	64,500	44,000	108,500
Petty traders, Tailors, Bakers	60,500	156,000	216,500
Agriculture:	87,500	212,500	300,000
All occupations	493,000	600,000	1,093,000

Source: Ghana Manpower Projections: 1963–70, *Seven-Year Development Plan*, Accra, 1964, p. 145.

TABLE 6.9

PRODUCTS OF THE EDUCATIONAL SYSTEM ENTERING THE EMPLOYMENT MARKET BY 1970

Type of Institution	Number entering employment market
Universities	9,050
Secondary Schools	46,600
Teacher Training Colleges	31,000
Clerical and Commercial Schools	12,000
Apprenticeship and Technical Training	14,550
Middle and Continuing Schools	752,500
All Institutions	865,700

Source: *Seven-Year Development Plan*, Accra, 1964, p. 146.

sector is expected to employ 300,000 persons new to agriculture and that other occupations in the traditional sector of the economy are expected to employ 216,000 of the school leavers. In view of the prevalent conception of the educated person as one who works only in the modern sector of the economy, it may well be that these will prove to be the most difficult places to fill. Nor is it possible to make the unskilled level of 'petty traders, tailors and bakers' more attractive by modernization, although the fact that these are largely women's occupations may lessen the seriousness of the con-sequences. In the agricultural sector it may well be possible to make employment prospects more attractive by developing more modern tech-niques. Such modernization will be expensive, but if it is carried out there should be less difficulty in recruiting school leavers to agricultural work. On the other hand, mechanization in agriculture often involves a reduction in labour so that the employment situation may not be helped by such modernization.

In any case, one of the major problems in the relationship of education to employment during the next few years will be to get people to accept the fact that universal education implies that all jobs in the community must eventually be done by people who have had some education. As I have suggested, this is only likely to come about when the distinction between the modern and the traditional sectors of the economy has been attenuated and has ceased to have a strong hold on the minds of the people of the country.

(iv) *Social Selection*
It is a well-established fact that in industrial countries the system of formal education acts as an agent of social selection. For example, in England the children of professional and managerial occupational groups are over-represented in grammar schools, while the children of unskilled workers are under-represented.[1] Similarly, in America one finds that lower class children are under-represented in the college preparatory streams of High Schools. An enquiry into parental occupation of students in Ghana shows that a similar process of social selection is taking place in the Ghanaian education system.

The first attempt to document this at the school level was made in 1960 by P. J. Foster in the course of an investigation conducted among secondary school Vth Formers.[2] He found that 40 per cent of the Vth Formers' parents were in the Professional, Technical, Administrative and Clerical occupational categories, although less than 7 per cent of the total working population were in these categories at the 1960 Census. Conversely, nearly 63 per cent of the working population were farmers, but only 32·5 per cent of the parents of Vth Formers were farmers. These findings are presented in column two of Table 6.10. Columns three and four of that table are drawn from a study of VIth Formers and university students in Ghana made by the present writer and T. J. Johnson.[3] It will be seen that broadly the same picture of social origins emerges in the VIth Form as was found in the Vth Forms except that the position is exaggerated in that rather fewer children of farmers and rather more of professional families are to be found in the VIth Form. The University of Ghana, on the other hand, has a rather larger representation of farmers than either the Vth or VIth Forms. This is due to the existence of widely used channels of entry to the university which by-pass the normal route through the VIth Form. In fact one-third of the students at the University of Ghana had not attended secondary school VIth Forms.

Among this group there was a considerably higher proportion of farmers' children (51·5 per cent) than among the group that had passed through the VIth Forms (30·1 per cent). Conversely, fewer of them were the children of persons in occupational group I (30 per cent as compared with 60 per cent). A comparison of the figures in the various columns of Table 6:10 suggests that even if the child of a farmer manages to gain entry to a secondary school, his chances of entering the VIth Forms are still less than those of his fellow-pupils whose fathers are in higher

[1] See, for example, J. E. Floud, A. H. Halsey, and F. M. Martin, *Social Class and Educational Opportunity*, London, Heinemann, 1956.
[2] P. J. Foster, Secondary Schooling and Social Mobility in a West African Nation, *Sociology of Education*, Vol. 37, No. 2, Winter 1963, pp. 150–71.
[3] The information on the students from the University of Ghana has been derived from questionnaires made available to us by the courtesy of Mr C. Scott and the Institute for the Training of Statisticians at Achimota. Our investigation is still in progress and these are some of the preliminary findings.

TABLE 6.10

REPRESENTATION OF OCCUPATIONAL GROUPS IN VTH FORMS, VITH FORMS
AND AT THE UNIVERSITY OF GHANA

Occupational group	Working population 1960 (a)	Fathers of Vth Formers 1960 (b)	Fathers of VIth Formers 1964 (c)	Fathers of University students 1964 (c)
	per cent	per cent	per cent	per cent
I Professional, Administrative, Higher technical, Clerical	6·9	40·3	55·0	45·6
II Private traders	3·8	10·3	7·8	3·5
III Skilled workers and Artisans	11·8	12·1	6·3	5·8
IV Semi-skilled and unskilled workers	13·4	1·5	0·2	0·3
V Farmers and Fishermen	62·8	32·5	23·3	37·7
VI Others (including armed services and police)	1·3	0·7	2·6	2·0
VII No answer, don't know, retired, dead	—	2·6	4·8	5·1
Total	100·0	100·0	100·0	100·0

(a) Source: 1960 Population Census, Advance Report of Vol. III and IV (Accra, Government Printer).

(b) Source: P. J. Foster, Secondary Schooling and Social Mobility in a West African Nation, *Sociology of Education*, Vol. 37, Winter 1963.

(c) Source: Study of VI formers and university students by G. E. Hurd and T. J. Johnson. See note 3, p. 235.

occupational categories. Having crossed the threshold into the VIth Form, however, they stand an equal, or even slightly better, chance of proceeding to the university.[1]

Table 6.10, however, conceals many differences within these broad occupational categories. There is considerable internal differentiation within the professional category and within the farming category. Occupational group I is broken down into smaller and more homogeneous groups in Table 6.11. Figures for the Vth Formers of 1960 are not available in this form, but the situation for the VIth Formers and students at the University of Ghana in 1964 can be seen. In the VIth Form the Administrative, Executive and Managerial sub-group is clearly the most over-represented with about fifty times as many representatives as a random distribution would give.

This sub-group is followed by the Higher Professional group,[2] with about twenty times the representation it would have under a random distribution. At the other end of the scale, the Clerical group and the Lower Professional

[1] Thus of the university students who had passed through the VIth Form, 30 per cent were the children of farmers, i.e. a *higher* percentage than in the current VIth Form survey.

[2] The occupational category 'Higher Professional' included occupations such as doctor, lawyer, lecturer, engineer, Member of Parliament, secondary school teacher, i.e. occupations for which a degree or equivalent qualification is usually required. The category 'Lower Professional' included primary and middle school teachers, nurses, and other occupations which are usually classified as professional but which in Ghana are held in low esteem, command low salaries, and have low educational standards of entry.

TABLE 6.11

REPRESENTATION OF SUBGROUPS WITHIN OCCUPATIONAL GROUP I IN VITH FORMS
AND AT THE UNIVERSITY OF GHANA

Occupational subgroup	Working population 1960 (a)	Fathers of VIth Formers 1964 (b)	Fathers of students at University of Ghana (b)
	per cent	per cent	per cent
Higher professional	0·5	11·1	10·7
Administrative, Executive, Managerial	0·3	15·8	3·8
Lower professional	2·3	9·6	10·0
Supervisory	0·6	4·8	4·2
Clerical	2·7	10·4	11·7
White collar non-clerical	0·5	3·3	5·2
Total in occupational group I	6·9	55·0	45·6
Other occupational groups	93·1	45·0	54·6
Total	100·0	100·0	100·0

(a) Source: 1960 Census, Advance Report of Vol. III and IV (Accra, Government Printer).

(b) Source: Study of VI formers and university students by G. E. Hurd and T. J. Johnson.

group have only four times as many VIth Formers as they would have under random distribution. At the University of Ghana the picture is somewhat different in that the proportion of children from the Administrative group falls sharply. The reasons for this are not yet altogether clear, but it is possible that a large number of young people in this group go abroad for higher education. The proportions of the children in the other groups remain about the same as for the VIth Formers.

The category of farmer—group V in Table 6.10—is also a heterogeneous grouping. Some farmers are very wealthy and command high prestige; others scrape a bare subsistence. On the whole, cocoa farmers are more wealthy than farmers who grow food crops, and they are certainly more involved in the cash crop economy of modern Ghana and consequently are less likely to be traditionally oriented. Table 6.12 shows that most of the VIth Formers from farming backgrounds come in fact from the wealthier and more modern cocoa farmers, although such farmers constitute rather less than one-third of the farming community in Ghana. Only a quarter of the VIth Formers from farming families come from the subsistence farms, although this type of farming accounts for more than two-thirds of the farmers of Ghana. Furthermore, in our VIth Form survey, one-half of the 98 fathers who were farmers owned three or more farms. Thus, in terms of the amount of land which they own as well as the crops they grow, they are likely to represent the better-off section among the farmers. This internal differentiation between farmers is a factor which has invariably been over-looked in the interpretation of data on social selection. Thus Foster suggests that the remarkable fact about the composition of the secondary schools is that as many as 32 per cent of the pupils should be from the under-privileged farming community, a fact which he puts down to the egalitarian nature of African society.[1] But as we have seen, this conclusion

[1] P. J. Foster, Education and Social Mobility in a West African Nation, *Sociology of Education*, Vol. 37, No. 2, Winter 1963, pp. 168 ff.

is affected by the large-scale presence of the children of cocoa farmers—a group whose under-representation is statistically only marginal. When we turn to the under-privileged farming group—the bulk of the farming population—we find that they are heavily under-represented.

TABLE 6.12

REPRESENTATION OF SUBGROUP OF FARMERS IN VITH FORMS

Occupational subgroup	Working population 1960 (a) per cent	Fathers of VIth Formers 1964 per cent
Cocoa farmers	20·1	15·9
Food farmers	42·7	7·4
Total farmers	62·8	23·3
Other occupational groups	37·2	76·7
Total	100·0	100·0

(a) Source: 1960 Census, Advance Report of Vol. III and IV (Accra, Government Printer).

This, combined with the virtual absence of the children of semi-skilled and unskilled workers from these schools and from universities, leads us to conclude that the open nature of Ghanaian secondary education has yet to be demonstrated. All the evidence points towards the conclusion that secondary education in Ghana has similar functions of social selection to those observed in the West, although in its present stage of development the situation in Ghana is, of course, considerably more extreme. Nevertheless, as in the West, the system also operates as a channel of social mobility for the few under-privileged children who gain entry to it. Indeed, with the increasingly bureaucratic nature of Ghanaian society, education has become the principal channel of social mobility. A combination of two factors, however, minimizes the mobility functions of the educational system and maximizes the functions of social selection. The first is the relatively small number of secondary schools, and the even smaller number of VIth Forms, which ensure that secondary schooling will, in the foreseeable future, be available only for a minority; and the second is the striking difference in patterns of living between the *élite* group and the under-privileged groups which ensures that the educational chances of the former will remain far higher than those of the latter even after secondary education is free. One might even suggest that the presence in secondary schools of children of the under-privileged groups is due largely to the fact that there are more secondary school places than there are children of the *élite* to fill them. More evidence is needed before such a statement passes beyond the realm of conjecture, particularly evidence on the determinants of educability in the Ghanaian situation, but if it is so, only a large scale expansion of the secondary school system will broaden the social composition of these schools.

SELECTED BIBLIOGRAPHY

I. Books and Articles
APTER, D. E., *Ghana in Transition*, New York, Atheneum, 1963.
AUSTIN, D., *Politics in Ghana 1946–60*, London, Oxford University Press, 1964.

BOURRET, F. M., *Ghana: the Road to Independence*, London, Oxford University Press, 1960.

CLIGNET, R. P., and FOSTER, P. J., Potential Elites in Ghana and the Ivory Coast :A Preliminary Comparison, *American Journal of Sociology*, Vol. 70, No. 3, November 1964, pp. 349–62.

FOSTER, P. J., *Education and Social Change in Ghana*, London, Routledge and Kegan Paul, 1965.

FOSTER, P. J., Ethnicity and the Schools in Ghana, *Comparative Education Review*, Vol. 6, No. 2, October 1962, pp. 127–35.

FOSTER, P. J., Secondary Schooling and Social Mobility in a West African Nation, *Sociology of Education*, Vol. 37, No. 2, Winter 1963, pp. 150–71.

FOSTER, P. J., Secondary School Leavers in Ghana: Expectation and Reality, *Harvard Educational Review*, Vol. 34, No. 4, Fall 1964, pp. 537–58.

HILLIARD, F. H., *A Short History of Education in British West Africa*, London, Nelson, 1957.

JAHODA, G., The Social Background of a West African Student Population, *British Journal of Sociology*, Vol. 5, No. 4, 1954, pp. 355–65 and Vol. 6, No. 1, 1955, pp. 71–9.

KIMBLE, D., *A Political History of Ghana* 1850–1928, Oxford, Clarendon Press, 1963.

KITCHEN, H. (ed.), *The Educated African*, London, Heinemann, 1962.

MCWILLIAM, H. O. A., *The Development of Education in Ghana*, London, Longmans, 1959.

WARD, W. E. F., *A History of Ghana*, London, Allen and Unwin, 1958.

WISE, C., *A History of Education in British West Africa*, London, Longmans, 1956.

WYLLIE, R. W., The Ghanaian Teacher and His Profession, *West African Journal of Education*, Vol. 8, No. 3, October 1964, pp. 171–6.

II. Government Publications and Reports

Accelerated Development Plan for Education, 1951.
Census Reports. Various years.
Department of Education Reports. Various years.
Education Act, 1961.
Education Statistics. Various years.
Ministry of Education Reports. Various years.
Seven-Year Development Plan, 1964.
Survey of Standard VII Boys, 1951.

CHAPTER VII

ASPECTS OF RELIGION

1. INTRODUCTION

It has been said that in respect of religion Ghana is a very hospitable country. The followers of the different prevailing religions naturally exert, with varying zeal, whatever pressure is in their power in order to win converts to their own ranks, but there has been little or no evidence of religious intolerance and fanaticism as these are known elsewhere. With the breaking of the political power of the indigenous States there broke down also whatever force had been employed by them to resist the encroachments of the impinging faiths. In addition, the *Pax Britannica* put an end to thoughts of any undertaking even remotely resembling a *jihad*. The sectarian groups recently arrived from the USA, who justify their coming by fiercely exalting their own distinctive tenets, and proceed in this effort by means of a vitriolic disparagement of all other forms of religion, have not succeeded as yet in introducing any widespread habits of religious strife or acrimony in the discussion of religious issues. In the smaller mixed communities some strain, capable of erupting occasionally into violence (though still only on a very minor scale), is often present, but on the whole the various religious communities live peacefully together and their relationships are generally neighbourly, courteous, and even friendly. The fetish priest and the chief malam of a locality would often support a Church Harvest Thanksgiving festival or contribute to the cost of building a Christian school or even a church. Relatives and friends of deceased persons would attend memorial worship services for them with religious groups different from their own; Christian festivals such as Christmas and Easter are occasions of celebration and rejoicing for many beyond the folds of the Churches, while some Christians would pour libation to the ancestral spirits or be present at strictly animist ceremonies and customary rituals, especially on tribal or family occasions.

This fraternization often goes well beyond the limits permitted by the authorities of the organized religions, and indeed runs counter to the tenets professed as when, for example, Christians accept traditional charms or Muslim talismans, or Christians and Muslims participate in traditional religious festivals with all their animist ceremonial, or have recourse to the traditional sorcerer's magical help. The representatives of traditional religions see no objection to this state of affairs, but the leaders of the impinging faiths have to keep reminding their faithful that all religions are not the same.

It is interesting to note that the points at which the religions introduced from outside come into sharpest conflict with African religion—i.e. spirit worship, ancestor veneration, and, in the case of Christianity only, the concept of family—remain the principal stumbling-blocks in the practice by Ghanaians of the adopted faiths.

Three major complexes of religion are current in Ghana: the indigenous beliefs and traditional religious practices and the two impinging faiths, Christianity and Islam. It is difficult to establish precise and agreed criteria for deciding in any given case what faith a person belongs to. A Muslim has been described as 'a man who says that he is one, wears Muslim dress whenever he can and has at least one Muslim name'. For the purpose of this analysis the first only of these requirements will be adopted, and therefore anyone will simply be regarded as being what he himself says that he is. This was the basis of the recent census count and is the only one appropriate to our survey.

2. INDIGENOUS RELIGION

Indigenous Ghanaian religion, since it is not laid down in literary documents, does not present itself as a systematic body of doctrines, but rather consists of a number of traditional beliefs and certain patterns of religious practice and general behaviour which give them expression. Although only vaguely conceptualized, these traditional religious beliefs, which are abundantly evidenced in the proverbs, common sayings, myths, poetry and folklore of the people, have a unity and comprehensiveness all their own, and afford a quite coherent and adequate world-view from which the general directions of common thinking, feeling, action and life attitudes may be derived.

In broad structure this Ghanaian 'world', with its varying emphases, is not only the common heritage of all the various communal groups within the country, but it is also of a piece with the understanding of reality that obtains amongst the other peoples of Western Africa and largely of Negro Africa in general. On the whole, it remains effective even after Ghanaians have adopted other philosophies of the universe and of life.

The central concern and motivation of religious aspiration is the attainment, maintenance, protection and maximum increase and enjoyment of life and vitality in all its forms and functions, with a particular accent on fertility. Individual and corporate life that is full-blooded, pulsating, abundant and prolific in its self-expression is felt to be the greatest value within human experience, the best that existence affords. That is perhaps not to be wondered at in view of the many threats to life and physical vigour that prevail in tropical countries. This basic apprehension of things, yielding an intensely life-affirming and life-relishing general approach, constitutes the common ground and ultimate explanation of the almost endless variety of religious preoccupations and activities. A typical Ashanti libation prayer well sums up the essence of indigenous African religiosity:

> Give me help and strength, and give health to
> the king of B . . ., the people of B . . ., and
> to the women of B . . ., and to the strangers
> in the town. May the women bear children, the
> house animals and fowls increase, and the men
> gain riches. Any one who wishes evil to the
> town may that evil fall upon himself.

So vivid is the sense of the supernatural or spiritual world that its distinction from the natural world is not always clearly present to the

Q

common awareness. The whole universe is held to be peopled by countless personal spirits of all kinds. The first and greatest of them all, in a class quite apart, is the Supreme Being, original Creator and still constantly creating, the Source of all might and power, the Unexcellable, Alone the Great and Wise One, the Dependable One, Helper of the helpless, Vindicator of the wronged, by Whose grace men are alive. The twin ideas of His self-sufficiency and His being all-in-all for men, are reflected in the concept that He is both Father and Mother. Assumed to be incapable of causing harm to men, He has not received direct worship and sacrifices except in Ashanti and perhaps in parts of Eweland. But His name is constantly on peoples' lips and He is spontaneously invoked in all situations of painful shock or distress.

In the regions of less highly developed cultures, the image of the Supreme Deity, though present, is rather dim and occupies the background only, making the 'earth gods' loom more largely in the consciousness of the people.

Next in the hierarchy come the tribal deities connected with outstanding natural phenomena such as rivers, lakes, hills, rocks, trees and other objects, particularly those of striking shape. These are regarded as the sons of the Supreme Deity, who is their Creator and the source of their power. Below them are the lesser spirits who are in much closer contact with men at the individual and family levels. A good deal of religious practice relates to dealings with them in order to avoid evil or to obtain some good. Contact with them is made through their priests at the shrines, the most notable of these being the Bruku, Lakpa, Sarkamo, Kwaku Firi, Kratchi Dente and Kofi Onisumanka. A shrine has been defined as 'any place where the machinery for establishing contact with the spiritual world exists, or where spiritual beings make their existence felt by mortals through possessed mediums'. Apart from these major shrines there are countless minor ones all over the country.

Judging from common religious activity, perhaps the most important class of supernatural beings is that of a person's own (or his immediate community's) ancestors, who are believed to continue to take an interest in the affairs of their descendants, and who reward or punish them according to their deserts. They are remembered on certain fixed dates, but may be invoked at any other time to hear the prayers of their descendants. The practice of making food and drink offerings to the ancestors, the latter commonly known in Ghana as libation, is a universal and very persistent one.

In the sphere of indigenous religion, perhaps the most recent development of note is the formation of a Ghana Psychic and Traditional Healing Association which, with government help, purports to research into African mysticism as employed in traditional healing. The pharmaceutical values of known medicinal herbs are being investigated as well as the therapeutic claims of shrine personnel and the efficacy for this purpose of their paraphernalia. As in the 'spiritual church' sects, the most striking successes so far obtained appear to have been with the mentally depressed, but it is too soon to tell whether these efforts will succeed in achieving a symbiosis of scientific and spiritist medical practice, or in offering a viable basis for either religion or healing.

3. ISLAM

Islam had a start of several centuries over Christianity in coming to Ghana. This should cause no surprise since the great empires of the Western Sudan one after the other adopted this religion. The spread of Islam into what is now Ghana is linked particularly with influences emanating from Mali. While, by the close of the fourteenth century, this Empire was itself in decline, its principal trading classes, namely, the Muslim Dyula and Soninke, commonly known as the Wangara, were establishing trading posts far beyond Mali's territorial limits. By 1400 there was such a post at Begho near Nsokaw in what is now the Brong-Ahafo region, and Wangara merchants were already trading at Elmina when the Portuguese first arrived there in 1471. While the motivation of this activity was mercantile rather than missionary, the Muslim religious ethos made it quite inevitable that some spread of the faith should have accompanied it.

A chronicle in Arabic, compiled by the Muslim authorities in Gonja around the middle of the eighteenth century, gives an account of efforts at Islamization centred on Begho and of the resulting conversion of Gonja rulers about 1585. Having in one of his wars received the very effective assistance of the Faqih Muhammad in putting his enemies to flight 'by the power of Allah', the King of Gonja came to know 'that the religion of Islam surpasses all others . . . so he was pleased to join Islam and he is the one who built the mosque at Ghofe (i.e. Buipe)'.

Islam was consolidated in Gonjaland during the seventeenth and eighteenth centuries by the growth and organization of the lineages of the *malams* and by the maintenance of their constitutional relationship with the rulers. One of the latter stated the effect of this bond as follows: 'Actually if you want to wage war and you do not find a malam, then it is impossible for you to do so.' It was also believed that by the power of Islam, bullet-proof garments could be made by the malams, and some of these were procured for Ashanti generals.

As trade in Northern Ghana increased in importance, other Muslim elements from the neighbouring territories and from Nigeria were attracted there and took up permanent residence. By the middle of the eighteenth century, the expanding Ashanti empire had embraced several Muslim communities, and in particular Mampong, as its most northern sector, had lively contacts with them. When Osei Kwame, whose father hailed from Mampong, went to Kumasi as King of Ashanti, he took with him a personal retinue of Muslims who became the nucleus of the now well-known Asante *Nkramo* (Muslims). This king was believed to have turned Muslim though he dared not declare himself openly. He was eventually destooled because his sub-chiefs feared that he was intending to introduce Koranic Law with its egalitarian principles. It is significant that revolts ensued in the Muslim parts of the empire upon his destoolment, but they were firmly repressed and faded out completely when he died.

From this time onward Muslim influence steadily increased in Ashanti. In the north the spread continued, covering Dagomba and Mamprusi as well as Gonja. Indeed, in the early nineteenth century, with the added impact resulting from successful Fulani *jihads* under Uthman dan Fodio in most of the Western Sudan, it looked as if Ashanti would become a Muslim State. Even pagan States such as Grunshi now contained substantial Muslim elements, and the faith soon had followers as far south as Fantiland. However, this advance was broken probably because Muslims, in having to fight on the side of pagan rulers against their co-religionists, had such severe conflicts of conscience that they weakened in giving this support to their patrons, and lost initiative accordingly.

So far no exhaustive survey of the incidence of Islam in Ghana has been attempted, but the 1960 Census figures confirm the estimates previously made to the effect that Muslims form between 10 and 15 per cent of the total population. Apart from Northern Ghana, the biggest concentrations are to be found in the larger towns of the south, particularly in Accra and Kumasi. In practically every other town or sizeable village of the south, there is a Zongo where northern Muslims and others speaking their languages, as well as similar peoples from neighbouring territories, live together as distinct communities. Each tribal or language group selects its own chief, and the chiefs in turn elect a 'Zerikin Zongo', who represents the entire community before the traditional or central government authorities.

Most Ghana Muslims are *Sunnis* following Maliki law and both the Qadari and Tijani orders are well established. Since 1920, Ahmadi missionaries coming from Pakistan via Nigeria, have worked in the country with their headquarters at Saltpond and major establishments in Kumasi and Wa. In accordance with their general principles they have established schools conducted on Western lines in contrast with the traditional Koranic schools. A Muslim Association founded in 1932, which endeavoured to obtain government recognition of Koranic law for separate application to Muslims within the country's judicial and administrative structure, was disbanded in 1957. At present the political self-expression of Ghana Muslims is represented by the Muslim Council which is a wing of the ruling Convention People's Party.

4. CHRISTIANITY

Azurara, the chronicler of Prince Henry the Navigator, lists the last of Prince Henry's reasons for undertaking his sea-faring ventures to Africa as follows: 'The fifth reason was his great desire to make increase in the faith of Our Lord Jesus Christ and to bring to him all the souls that should be saved.'

The record states that when the Portuguese paid their second visit to the Gold Coast in 1482, with the express purpose of starting there the first European settlement on the Guinea Coast,[1] 'on the following morning they suspended the banner of Portugal from the bough of a lofty tree, at the foot of which they erected an altar, and prayed for the conversion of the natives from idolatry, and the perpetual prosperity of the Church which they intended to erect upon the spot'.

The Portuguese and the other European traders coming after them, as a rule, maintained chaplaincies in their settlements, but the responsibility for these was usually restricted to the European garrisons and their families, in some cases including their children by African mothers. Portuguese Augustinian and French Capuchin missionary-priests, during the course of

[1] They landed on January 19th at Edina which, because of the gold they found there, they subsequently named Elmina, meaning 'the mine'.

the fifteenth to the seventeenth centuries, made a few sporadic attempts at evangelizing the indigenous population, and some baptisms are on record, notably that of the Chief of Efutu, together with 1,300 of his subjects, in the year 1503. However, this event appears to have been related more to trading than to religious interests. In any case, these efforts were superficial and unco-ordinated, so that, like the much larger similar undertaking in the Congo, they soon came to grief and petered out, leaving hardly a trace.

But informal Christian contacts at the individual level continued to be made, the most effective of these being the adoption by Europeans of African youths whom they sent, or took back with them, to Europe for education. Thus, already before the middle of the eighteenth century, two Gold Coast lads had studied at famous European universities. Anthony William Amo of Axim won the Ph.D. degree in 1734, after having studied at Halle and Wittenberg Universities in Germany. Jacobus Elisa Johannes Capitein in 1737, at about 20 years of age, entered the University of Leyden in Holland and after five years' study there became the first African ever to receive Protestant Ordination. He was sent back to Elmina by the Dutch Reformed Church as a chaplain and a missionary to his own people, and promptly started work in vernacular Christian literature, publishing, in 1744, a translation into Fanti of the Twelve Articles of the Apostles' Creed.

Organized and systematic Protestant missionary work also began about this time. The first mission was that of the Moravian Brethren of Germany, which started in Ghana in 1737, but after many ups and downs was abandoned in 1776 because of the staggering mortality of 100 per cent in a staff of nine missionaries within the preceding two years.

In 1752, the Anglican Society for the Propagation of the Gospel sent the Rev. Thomas Thompson, who had volunteered 'to make a trial with the Natives, and see what Hopes there would be of introducing the Christian Religion'. In 1754, he sent three Cape Coast lads to England for education. One of them died of tuberculosis, another lost his reason and died in hospital. The sole survivor, Philip Quaque, completed his training, took Anglican orders (the first non-European to do so), and was appointed by the SPG 'Missionary, School Master and Catechist to the Negroes at the Gold Coast'. Returning home in 1766 he gave fifty years of service in these capacities as well as being Chaplain to the Company of Merchants, and died in 1816. Only in 1904 did the SPG resume work in the Gold Coast.

Really effective and lasting missionary work began with the arrival of the Basel Mission in the east in 1828, and of the Methodist Mission in the west in 1835. While the rate of expansion was rather slow during the nineteenth century, it quickened greatly in the early years of the twentieth, reaching its fastest pace in the 1920s.

Andreas Riis, the Basel pioneer, penetrated inland into Akwapim, Akim, and even Ashanti, and made a happy choice in selecting Akropong with its healthy hill climate for his headquarters. Taking to heart a remark once made by the chief of Akropong to the effect that his people would become Christians only if they could see some other Africans who followed this religion, Riis soon arranged for a contingent of Christian West Indian Negro families to be brought to Ghana in order to demonstrate that coloured people could also be Christians. Even though the experiment was only partially successful, it was effective in bridging, to a certain extent, the racial and cultural gap between the European missionaries and the people. This mission very early introduced a whole range of useful tropical plants from the West Indies and, apart from formal school education, undertook a lively programme of apprenticeship training in handicrafts and trades of all kinds. This practical and useful orientation, combined with the fact that a relatively large number of missionaries (some of them, by any standards, quite remarkable personalities) were able to give long and continuous service, accounts for the outstanding quality and success of their work. So sound was the foundation laid that when, at the out-break of the First World War, all the German missionaries were removed and the Church of Scotland Mission was called in to help, the latter were able to proceed almost immediately (in August 1918) to the constitution of an African Church, the Presbyterian Church of the Gold Coast (now Ghana) under African leadership, with the Scottish missionaries only assisting in the posts requiring advanced education.

Owing to the many formal and informal Christian influences that had been operating in and around Cape Coast for centuries, some voluntary Bible reading groups came to be formed there and at Elmina. One Captain Potter, a commander of an English vessel, visiting Cape Coast in 1831, was given money by some members of these groups with the request that he would bring them Bibles from England on his return. When he told the Methodist Missionary Society in England about this, the Society decided to send not only Bibles, but a missionary as well, and so in 1835, Joseph Dunwell arrived at Cape Coast. In this mission, too, the climate took a heavy toll of lives. Thomas Birch Freeman, a mulatto, became the most outstanding missionary of this Society. With a short break, he worked from 1838 to 1890 and made a quite remarkable contribution all round, particularly in respect of public relations with both indigenous and governmental authorities. Until 1962, the Methodist Church was administered by a District Synod under the authority of the British Conference, but in that year, it was established as an autonomous body with an independent Conference and a Ghanaian President. This is at present the largest Protestant Church in Ghana.

Next followed the Bremen Mission from North Germany, which started work with Lorenz Wolf at Peki in 1847 and, after a break, again at Keta in 1853 through the missionaries Daeuble, Plessing and Brutschin. At one with the Basel society in doctrinal matters, form of organization and working policies, this mission's development closely paralleled that of its bigger counterpart. Much of its work was carried out in what was formerly the German colony of Togoland. In 1922 an African Church was constituted with two synods, one on each side of the territorial border: the Synod of the Ghana side was called the Ewe (now Evangelical) Presbyterian Church, and that on the other side adopted the name of Eglise Evangélique du Togo.

Roman Catholic Missions resumed in the Gold Coast in 1880, under the Society for African Missions of Lyons. Disposing of large resources in well-trained personnel and finances, their work soon covered the whole country, growing by leaps and bounds. In the north, the White Fathers made a particularly notable impact. In 1950, the Gold Coast became an

Ecclesiastical Province with an Arch-episcopal See at Cape Coast, and Episcopal Sees at Accra, Keta, Kumasi, Tamale and Navrongo. In 1960, the Ghanaian Bishop John Kojo Amissah, who had been Auxiliary to Archbishop Porter since 1957, became himself Archbishop of Cape Coast and Head of the Ghana Catholic Church. In the same year, a Dagarti, Peter Dery, was raised to the episcopal status, and appointed to the newly-created See of Wa. In 1962, Joseph Amihere Erzuah was appointed Bishop of Kumasi.

Several smaller missionary societies followed these four major ones during the course of the years. The Seventh Day Adventist Mission came in 1894. The American (now African) Methodist Episcopal Mission, an American Negro enterprise, started work at Keta in 1896, and at Cape Coast in 1903, and at first attracted much interest as a Christian mission manned, led and financed entirely by Americans of African descent.

The Salvation Army appeared on the scene in the early 1920s, as did such other faith-healing sects from the USA as the First Century Gospel and Faith Tabernacle. These were joined in 1957 by the Apostolics who, however, split from them eventually because they would admit no use of medicine whatsoever, and became the Ghana Apostolic Church, now the Church of Pentecost. The emphasis of the last-named is upon an intensely emotional appeal which has found quite widespread response. There are also Jehovah's Witnesses and still other small groups. However, as is evident from the 1960 Census figures these are small groups with relatively minor influence in the country as a whole.

Since the First World War several religious groups arising from indigenous African initiative, generally known as 'spiritual churches', have come into being. This development was touched off by the visit to Ghana in 1914 of the Liberian evangelist, Prophet Harris. Following on his success in the Ivory Coast, he effectively urged whole villages to abandon their idols, with the result that several thousand people were baptized. The Church of the Twelve Apostles in the Western Province is a continuing memorial of this activity. Some 'spiritual churches', as, for example, the largest of them, the Musama Disco Christo Church, originated as break-aways from the older missionary related Churches, whereas others are independent new creations.

To a greater or lesser extent, these groups attempt to offer African solutions to unsolved conflicts within the older Churches: polygyny, the use of livelier forms of worship involving drumming and dancing as well as clapping, stamping, shouting and other signs of intensely emotional religious experience. Owing to these practices, and much-reported claims of healing successfully ailments of all sorts, they have attracted considerable notice. For the most part, however, their congregations are floating ones, people coming and going again as they feel inclined. Being preoccupied with the practice of faith-healing almost to the exclusion of any other interests, all the groups of this kind endeavour to address themselves to, or employ, such features of the traditional religious background as prophesying, witchcraft, spirit possession, exorcism or taming of evil spirits, divination, and essentially magical practices (though this is not admitted). While they treasure the Christian name and hold themselves to be 'purely Christian' groups, they are regarded by others as only marginal to the main stream of this religion and as illustrating rather the confluence of Christian and indigenous African religious influences.

The whole Christian movement has come in for abundant and often very severe criticism, particularly on the grounds of disrupting and disintegrating African societies, destroying their culture, and thereby 'softening them up' for undue foreign influence and domination. Whatever measure of justification such charges might contain, if indeed in view of the extremely complicated situation at the advent and during the early history of Christianity in Ghana any such blame could be so clearly apportioned, it can hardly be the case that the general effect of the Christian impact has merely or even predominantly been a negative one. The truly remarkable achievement of the various Christian bodies in public education and, to a lesser extent, in the provision of medical and other useful facilities, must be duly acknowledged. Besides, it must be kept in mind that in Ghana, the joining of a Church or submission to its guidance has always been an entirely voluntary affair.

Knowledgeable leaders within the Churches are nowadays very much alive to the necessity of putting their house in order wherever in the light of the criticisms referred to, it would appear necessary and feasible to do so. They are also concerned to meet adequately the challenge of revolutionary and very rapid social change. A good deal of thinking and discussion is being given, for example, to the problem of finding for Ghanaian Christianity a genuine individuality in self-expression, a selfhood and personality which would at the same time reflect the true character of and fully represent the Universal Church. In this context, the need for better and more relevant training for ministry and laity alike is recognized and several training centres (e.g. the Women's Training Centres at Kwadaso and Begoro and the Retreat and Conference Centre at Abetifi) have sprung up in recent years.[1] Scholarships for further study both at the University of Ghana and abroad, have been more numerous of late than ever before.

Also of general interest are the conversations that have been in progress during the past seven years or so between the four largest Protestant Churches (the Anglican, Methodist and the two Presbyterian Churches), with a view to organic union. These discussions have now reached an advanced stage and an agreed proposed basis of union, which has already been published, has received welcome from all sides. The intention, as stated, is not to level out the differences in theological emphasis and Church practice which at present prevail, so as to obtain a unified type of religious self-expression, but rather to unite into a single organization, with a single, unified ministry, the various traditions represented in these four separate denominations. If and when this union is achieved, the new United Church will alone embrace practically 23 per cent of the entire population of Ghana.

Since the reign of Pope John XXIII, relations between the Roman Catholic Church and the Protestant Churches represented on the Christian Council have become progressively more cordial and steps are likely to be

---

[1] Perhaps the most notable move in this direction is the transfer, now taking place, of Trinity, the joint Methodist and Presbyterian Theological College which has so far been situated at Kumasi, to the precincts of the University of Ghana, in order to ensure broader horizons and contacts for the future ministers during their course of training.

taken to find a basis for regular mutual consultations with a view to practical co-operation on public issues falling within the sphere of religion and morality.

5. RELIGIOUS AFFILIATION

Although membership figures are available from the larger Churches, they are not provided here since they are not really comparable. While, for example, communicant status is regarded by all as the standard requirement for full membership, the age of admission to communion is fixed so variously that those who in one Church would be recorded as full members would in another be classed as minors. Besides, many of the figures given are stated to be mere estimates. The basis used for the 1960 Census computation is the population 'aged 15 and over', and each person's own declaration of his affiliation. As already noted, this is the most useful one to follow in the present context. None of the Churches uses this basis for reckoning its membership; as a rule they take account only of those persons who somehow participate in their activities.

TABLE 7.1

POPULATION AGED 15 YEARS AND OVER BY SEX AND RELIGION
(Percentage distribution)

Religion	Total	Male	Female
All religions	100·0	100·0	100·0
Christians: Roman Catholic	13·4	14·9	12·0
Methodist	10·3	9·9	10·7
Presbyterian*	9·9	10·2	9·5
Anglican	2·6	2·8	2·4
African Methodist Episcopal Zion	0·4	0·4	0·4
Seventh Day Adventist	0·7	0·7	0·7
Apostolic	2·4	2·0	2·8
African Christian	1·5	1·2	1·8
Other	1·6	1·7	1·6
Moslem	12·0	14·2	9·8
Traditional	38·2	34·9	41·5
No religion	7·0	7·1	6·8
Others (e.g. Buddhist, Hindu, Jewish)	0·0	0·0	0·0

* Includes also Evangelical Presbyterian.
Source: 1960 Census (information supplied by courtesy in advance of publication).

TABLE 7.2

POPULATION BY MAIN RELIGIONS ACCORDING TO REGION (PERSONS AGED 15 AND OVER)
(Percentage distribution)

	All Regions	Western Region	Accra Capital District	Eastern Region	Volta Region	Ashanti Region	Brong-Ahafo Region	Northern Region
All religions	100·0	100·0	100·0	100·0	100·0	100·0	100·0	100·0
Christian	42·8	62·1	60·5	50·2	43·1	47·5	38·6	7·5
Moslem	12·0	11·0	13·4	9·4	7·0	15·3	13·5	14·4
Traditional	38·2	18·1	18·6	29·5	47·5	27·7	43·3	75·0
No religion	7·0	8·8	7·4	10·9	2·4	9·5	4·6	3·1

Source: 1960 Census, *Atlas of Population Characteristics*.

Doubtless many will be surprised to discover that, if all the many sorts of Christians are taken together, they represent the majority religion of Ghana, taking up, as they do, 42·8 per cent of the entire population as compared with 38·2 per cent followers of the indigenous traditional religions, 12 per cent Muslims and 7 per cent of people recorded under 'no religion'. As to the last-named category, probably the intention of those who so declared themselves was merely to indicate that they did not belong to any organized religious group. There is little common evidence that such a considerable proportion of the population has in fact abandoned the basically theistic Ghanaian world-view or achieved the degree of sophistication necessary to support the strict meaning of the statement.

SELECTED BIBLIOGRAPHY

ACQUAH, I., *Accra Survey*, London, University Press, 1958.

BAËTA, C. G., *Prophetism in Ghana*, London, SCM, 1962.

DEBRUNNER, H. W., *Witchcraft in Ghana*, Kumasi, Presbyterian Book Depot, 1959.

FIELD, M. J., *Search for Security: an ethno-psychiatric study of rural Ghana*, London, Faber and Faber, 1960.

FORDE, D., *African Worlds*, London, Oxford University Press, 1963.

GROVES, C. P., *The Planting of Christianity in Africa*, Vols. I–IV, London, Lutterworth, 1948–58.

MANOUKIAN, M., Akan and Ga-Adangme Peoples of the Gold Coast (*Ethnographic Survey*, 1950).

MANOUKIAN, M., The Ewe-speaking People (*Ethnographic Survey*, 1952).

PARRINDER, G., *West African Religion*, London, Epworth Press, 1961.

PARSONS, R. T., *The Churches and Ghana Society*, 1918–55, Brill, Leiden, 1963.

RATTRAY, R. S., *Ashanti*, London, Oxford University Press, 1923.

RATTRAY, R. S., *Religion and Art in Ashanti*, London, Oxford University Press, 1927.

RATTRAY, R. S., *The Tribes of the Ashanti Hinterland*, London, Oxford University Press, 1932.

WILKS, I., Article on Ghana in the *Encyclopedia of Islam*, ed. J. H. Kramers, H. A. R. Gibbs and E. Lévi-Provençal, Leiden, Brill, 1954–61.

WILKS, I., Islam in Ghana History: An Outline (article in the *Ghana Bulletin of Theology*, December 1962).

WILKS, I., The Position of Muslims in Metropolitan Ashanti in the Early Nineteenth Century (Paper presented at the *International African Institute Seminar*, Zaria, 1963).

WILTGEN, R. M., *Gold Coast Mission History* 1471–1880, Divine Word Publications, Techny, Illinois, USA, 1956.

CHAPTER VIII

ASPECTS OF LAND TENURE

1. INTRODUCTION

From the earliest times land in Ghana has been closely associated with 'life'. 'Life', that is existence of any form, was believed to emanate from the supernatural. Thus entrance upon life, like the birth of a child or even that of an animal or the sprouting of seeds, has always been hailed with religious ceremonies. For the same reason the termination of life—harvesting of crops, for example—was observed with solemn rites. Therefore land, through which all life other than human is believed to be transmitted, and by means of which all life (including human and animal) is sustained, is treated as a sacred gift from God and it used to be, and in some places still is, an object of worship. But it is not worshipped as God the Almighty Himself, upon whom men lean and do not fall, but is worshipped as one of the most effective agencies through which God who creates life maintains it. This is because it is the final element into which the material body of all things, animal, vegetable or mineral, must return at the appropriate time when life is terminated by Him who gave it.

This is why land used to have, and in some parts of Ghana still has, shrines and fetish groves set aside for its worship, and the priests of the land generally used to be, and still are in some places, among holders of high traditional offices.

In the predominantly agricultural areas, the priest of the land is the chief of all the priests; while on the coastal areas where fishing is the principal occupational pursuit of the people, the priest of the sea takes precedence over all other priests. The waters on the land in rivers, streams, lakes and lagoons are believed to be indispensable to the regenerative forces of the land and are therefore held to be sacred in varying degrees of importance. Each river, lake or lagoon once had a priest.

2. OWNERSHIP OF LAND

As a sacred object which sustains all life, land is fundamentally not regarded as capable of being owned. It can only be used by any person or group of people who happen to settle upon any portion of it. Eventually the area over which members of one community, with its various sections exercised acts of user, say, for cultivation, fishing, or hunting, or over which they maintained successful patrols to keep off migrating invaders or hostile neighbours, came to be identified with the particular community. In case of an invasion from, or conflict with, occupiers of adjacent land, the leader of the community had a responsibility to marshal the able-bodied men of all sections of the community to fight in order to maintain their hold upon, and if possible extend the area over which they exercised their rights.

In the past the priest of the land had charge of the land and performed annual ceremonial rites to ensure the fertility of the soil and the fertility of vegetable and animal life on it. Such ceremonies were supposed to secure the fertility and prosperity of the people as well.

The priest performed ceremonies for sowing and ceremonies for harvesting. These rites are still performed in some parts of the country though they are disappearing fast. In Accra, the rite is preserved in the symbolic ceremonies known as *Nmaa Dumo* (sowing of guinea corn) and *Nmaa Kuu* (harvesting of guinea corn) which form part of the Ga national feast of *Homowo*. Similar symbolic ceremonies exist in other tribes in some places, and new yams are not eaten until the harvesting rites have been performed by the Stool or Skin at a ceremony known as the yam festival. There are also special rites for opening and closing fishing seasons.

These annual ceremonies are performed on behalf of the whole community. There are also *ad hoc* rites for individuals who start the cultivation of virgin land or reap the first crops of the land.

By reason of his office the priest came to be regarded as the 'owner' or caretaker of the land and the officer of State in whom is vested the right to make grants of land. In some parts of the Northern and Upper Regions the priest—*Tenyona* or *Ten'dana*—is still regarded as 'owner' of the land, or the holder of the absolute title in the land, although he holds it as a trustee for the people.

Although land in ancient days was used mainly for subsistence—crop farming, breeding of livestock, and for fishing—threat of invasion and domination from outside made it imperative that for the preservation of the land and life and liberty, the community should have a political or war leader who would lead the people to battle to preserve or win more land. Since the duty of the priest in time of war was to be near the shrine continuously and to invoke intercession for victory, he was not the type of functionary to be the war and political leader. The captains of the companies, the heads of the sections of the communities with a supreme commander, qualified for that most important office and eventually assumed administrative control of the land, the priest being confined to his proper role—the performance of religious rites and ceremonies pertaining to the fertility of the land, for the general good health and well-being of man and beast, increase in population, comfort in family life and prosperity for the community as a whole.

The supreme war commander and political leader became the chief of the area, the head of the clan or tribe, and his captains became the subchiefs and the heads of the sections. But whether it is the priest or the chief who holds the land, he holds it not strictly as owner thereof, but as a trustee holding it for the whole community, the heads of the sections being responsible jointly with him to direct and ensure the peaceful and beneficial use of the land without molestation from outside.

The word 'Skin' in Northern and Upper Ghana, and the word 'Stool' in all other parts of Ghana, have come to symbolize the community as a whole; its head is installed in office by his people, and as part of the installation ceremony, he is placed on a stool or skin dedicated and set aside by the community as the physical embodiment of the soul of the community, the clan, the tribe or family on whose behalf the land is held.

Land so held is therefore called Stool land or Skin land and is defined as follows:

'By Stool land we mean, land owned by a community, the head of which occupies a Stool, such that in the olden days of tribal wars the said head of the community carried the ultimate responsibility of mobilizing the community to fight to save it, and in modern days to raise money from the subjects to litigate the community's title to the land. We may put it in another form, any land in respect of which an occupant of a Stool is the proper person to conduct its extra-territorial affairs is a Stool land. The occupant of the Stool may not be the appropriate internal administrative authority, e.g. the Stool may not be the appropriate authority to make direct grants of portions of the land to subjects, that right may be vested in a subordinate authority, e.g., a sub-stool, a quarter, a village council or in a family; but so long as the extra-territorial relations, e.g. settlement of the boundaries of any particular land with land occupied by adjoining States or communities vests in the occupant of the Stool, i.e. in the community generally and not in a section of it, that land is a Stool land.' [Ameoda v. Pordier and Ameoda v. Forzi & Anor. Consolidated, High Court, March 30, 1962, unreported.]

A recent Act has defined it as follows:

' "Stool land" includes land controlled by any person for the benefit of the subjects or members of a Stool, clan, company or community, as the case may be and all land in the Upper and Northern Regions other than land vested in the President and accordingly "Stool" means the person exercising such control.' [Administration of Lands Act, 1962 (Act 123), section 31.]

We may say then that absolute ownership of land is vested in the community represented by the Stool or Skin.

3. LAND TENURE

A study of land tenure in Ghana opens up a wide question concerning the attitudes of man to his use of the soil and to the waters upon it. In all this the individual is very important. But until very recently, this importance of the individual in the matter of land cultivation and the exploitation of its natural resources has been overshadowed by his role with regard to the acquisition of land for the family and ultimately for the community.

However, as will appear presently, developments in society have now enhanced the individual's economic role, and have lessened some of his more onerous obligations to smaller groups such as the family and the quarter. Now his obligations are recognized in certain respects to be more concerned with wider units such as the town, the 'State' under the new designation of 'Traditional Area', and ultimately with the nation.

Since land belongs to the community, every individual member of it is entitled to the use of the natural products of the soil which have not previously been appropriated for use by any other member of the same community. He is therefore entitled to collect such things as snails, crabs, wild fruits, wild mushrooms, to hunt game, fish in the public lagoon or streams, cut grass, take fire-wood or fetch water from a river, stream or well.

All forms of use of the land for his subsistence is an inherent right of the individual member of the community, and carries a responsibility to give some portion of what he collects for the performance of the periodic rites and ceremonies for the land, the sea, river, or the lagoon. Such a general form of use of land does not vest the individual with ownership or right of exclusive possession in any particular portion of the land.

In the past the general right of the members of the society was exercised by small settlements of the community over areas which had not become vested in another community. Consistent unchallenged use of land in this way made the area over which it was exercised one for which the community as a whole became responsible for religious performances, and protection from invasion; this was one of the ways in which community or Stool land was acquired. Other methods by which communal or Stool land was acquired were: conquest, settlement on unoccupied land, gift by a community which had occupied it previously, and purchase.

The basic unit of Ghanaian society is the family, not the individual. Almost everything affecting the individual is dealt with by his family. When the individual offends any one, his conduct is reported to the head of his family who, with his elders, will go into the matter and, if they should find the offence proved, take appropriate steps to make amends; if he achieves something good, his family get the praise. It is the responsibility of the family to set the individual up in life. His family marries him off, they perform the naming ceremony of his child; they bury him when he dies. Within a farming community the young man works on his father's farm, but that does not make him joint owner of the farm with the father; he does not share the proceeds of the farm with him either. His right is to be maintained by the father. When he reaches marriagable age, the family, upon the request of the father, provides him with land which, with the guidance of the father, and the assistance of relations, he cultivates. The land given to him may be a portion of a large area of the communal land which in ancient times was occupied in one form or another by ancestors of the family and therefore belongs to the family. At the same time that family land may be part of the general communal land under a sectional head. Thus, while the absolute or allodial ownership of land is vested in the community or the Stool, the general administration of its several parts may be vested in sectional or family heads, while the usufruct—the actual possessory title— is generally vested in the individual members of the family. So that the effective use of the land, the grant of any rights or interests in it, or the transfer of right to the user, is bound up with the family organization.

Where population was sparse, and land plentiful, the land was used for subsistence economy only, and shifting cultivation was the general form of agriculture. In places like the Frafra area, where population is dense and the land of the community small, settlement and continuous farming on a particular area is inevitable. With primitive methods of farming the fertility of such land soon becomes exhausted, but with modern methods of cultivation there is no danger of this happening. We shall revert to this subject later.

In addition to his right to take from the natural product of the land, the member of the family or community is entitled to occupy and possess as much agricultural land as he can reduce into his possession by his own or employed labour. He needs no formal permission of the head of the family or of the occupant of the Stool to do so. In practice, however, he usually informs the head of the family. He gets possession of building-land through a formal grant; for this grant he provides drink; he also gives drink to the head of the family when he informs him that he is farming on part of the land. With the drink he provides, the head of the family pours a libation to call the ancestors to witness the grant and invokes the blessing of God and the ancestors of the family to protect the member in any project he undertakes on the land and to make him prosper. This possessory or usufructuary title which a member of the family or community gets is the highest form of tenure an individual may acquire in land.

The oil-palm industry, which flourished from about the middle of the last century, introduced the cash economy into agriculture. The oil-palm was grown alongside food crops and not in palm plantations. That industry served as an impetus for the growing of food crops for cash, and also paved the way for the establishment of the cocoa industry which has subsequently become the dominant sector of agriculture.

Under subsistence farming, the villagers joined together every year to make new food crop farms for each other and to harvest the ripe crop. Even the manufacture of palm-oil and kernel-oil from the fruits of the oil-palm was carried on under similar arrangements whereby families and villagers assisted one another in turn to enable each family or household to produce marketable quantities. The introduction of the cocoa industry during the closing decades of the last century brought about a significant change in the economic value of land, and threw into more prominent relief ownership and other forms of tenure of land which had not previously attracted much attention.

The cocoa industry began on the Akwapim range. As the cocoa tree is a forest tree and cannot thrive on the coastal plains and the grass lands, farmers of the plains who wished to go in for the cocoa industry had to leave their homes, the shrub and grass lands, for the forest areas first in Akwapim, then Akim, Kwahu, Ashanti, Brong-Ahafo, and parts of the Central, Western and Volta Regions in order to cultivate cocoa. Not being members of the communities which owned the lands the emigrants needed for growing cocoa, they were obliged either to acquire rights by purchase, and, if they had enough money, to pay a large sum once and for all for the use of the land without further payments, or to occupy the land on terms, e.g. in consideration of sharing the proceeds. At the same time commercial developments taking place in the towns brought about a situation which necessitated sale and purchase or lease of building-land.

The sale of agricultural land was accompanied by a ceremony signifying change of hand, or transfer of possessory titles from the family or member of the community to the stranger. These ceremonies of transfer are known by various names—*Guaha, Twa Gwan, Yibaa Pom, Yibaa foo, Akatutu, Anyigba Dzi, Tsogbedita*. So important is the function of this ceremony that cases have occurred when, although purchasers have paid a major part of the purchase-price, the sale has been avoided because of the non-observance of this custom. On the other hand, once the custom has been observed, ownership in the land is transferred, however small a portion of the price might have been paid on account. The vendor is then left with only his right as a creditor to pursue any action for the non-payment of the sum at which the land was sold and conveyed.

The tribes which are predominant in the purchase of land for farming are the Akwapims, the Krobos, the Gas, the Shais and some Ewe tribes, e.g. Anlos.

A group of people, being either members of one family, or simply friends, may join together under a leader to purchase land, and apportion it among themselves according to each person's contribution to the purchase price. An example of this is the *Huza* system of the Krobos. The principal members of a family may also buy an area of land, in which case portions of it are allotted to members of the family who may wish to cultivate it. The company or syndicate of purchases build villages on their areas and this constitutes a new community; they organize their social life and their village administration. The man who led the purchase conducts the transaction of the purchase in his name and he is looked upon as the head, father or chief of the new community. When he dies the successor to his estate may be recognized by the company as the head. Usually he is accepted as such by all, but there is nothing to prevent members of the company from electing any other person to that office, the office not being hereditary.

Group purchase does not create corporate ownership of the land purchased. Each member of the company becomes the individual owner of the portion allotted to him, either in his own right, or as head or representative of his family.

The success of the cocoa and the oil-palm industries led many of the forest land owners to prefer a system of land tenure based on crop sharing and called the *Abusa* system, to an absolute sale of the land. Strangers who have not much money for the capital outlay usually accept the *Abusa* tenancy. The *Abusa* tenancy is a system under which a stranger with his own capital or labour, including the labour of members of his family, develops land belonging to another person either for a permanent crop like cocoa, oil-palm, coffee, or rubber, or even a food crop, and gives one-third of the proceeds thereof to the owner of the land. In all other respects his position with respect to the land is as permanent as that of the purchaser of the possessory title. Where, for example, he is a cocoa *Abusa* tenant, he can grow any amount of foodstuff on the land without having to give the land owner a share of it.

Formerly a man worked on his land together with his family and friends and at harvest time obtained the co-operation of his neighbours. On such occasions he made a feast for them. The custom still goes on in some areas, but not on the same scale as before. The fact that nearly all children go to school and the youth who have had the benefit of a formal education often leave the villages to seek employment in the towns, not being content to pursue peasant farming, raises the problem of employed labour on the farms. At the same time, mines and other industrial and commercial firms can offer monthly wages to the potential farm labourer which the farmer cannot. The problem has been solved by a device which is as attractive to the labourer as the wage system, the system known as *Abusa* farm labourer. Such a labourer has no tenure whatsoever in the land. He is provided with shelter on the farm and he may take from the farm food he requires for his personal use; he helps to carry the produce to the market, and is given one-third of the proceeds of the sale.

English forms of conveyance have been used many times to convey land; but except in the case of lease and mortgage the tenures transferred by this form of conveyance are not higher than the tenures governed by custom.

The usufructuary title which a person gets by occupying a portion of the Stool land is alienable and inheritable as is the right of occupation and use of land which the *Abusa* tenant acquires; but in the case of the *Abusa* tenant he can only alienate with the consent of his landlord, and he must give the landlord the first refusal. Again a successor to an *Abusa* tenant must introduce himself to the landlord in a formal way with drink. A libation is poured with this drink calling upon the spirit of the ancestors to accept him as the new tenant and he is then introduced to all the people in the various cottages of the area and formally accepted into their community.

But although the emigrant farmers form a new community they retain their affinity with their home-towns, regarding their villages merely as a temporary residence. In the village they group themselves according to their tribes, each with its own head, and observe the customs of their tribes in marriage, child-birth, puberty rites, funerals etc., and many of them go home once a year at least for their annual national festivals like *Odwira*, *Homowo*, *Nmaayem*.

Along the coast line are settlements of emigrant communities engaged in fishing, mostly Anlos and Adas. These obtain their right of occupation of the land and the use of the sea, river or lagoon, on terms similar to the *Abusa* system of land tenancy. These fishing communities maintain a government and social organization similar to those obtaining in the farming settlements.

An owner of land in need of money may pledge his farm to raise money; the pledgee in such a case is given possession of the land and uses it as his own; his right as user is the same as that of the pledger, that is, if the pledger had possessory title the pledgee will also have possessory title; if he was an *Abusa* tenant, the pledgee will be an *Abusa* tenant. No time need be fixed for redemption of the pledge, it may be redeemed at any time the pledgee is ready. The pledgee, too, need not account for profits he derives out of the land.

The acquisition of the right of title or interest in the land may be for a person's individual use or for the use of his family. Where the purchase is made with family money, or by contribution made by members of a family the title or interest acquired will vest in the family.

Again when a member of a family acquires land for himself with his own money as his individual property and other members of the family develop that land with their own money or labour by building on it or farming it, the property immediately acquires the character of family property, and neither the purchaser nor the person who developed it can dispose of it; the two or three of them may together alienate it, but upon the death of any one of them the property becomes full family property.

Property owned by an individual becomes family property upon the death intestate of the original owner, and property which has descended

R

from an earlier ancestor becomes the property of a group all of whose members trace descent from that original owner.

Family property is under the administration of the head of the family, or of any one to whom the head and elders of the family may delegate that right. Such property is used for the benefit of all the principal members of the family; the proceeds therefrom are used to maintain and improve the property, to acquire more property, to maintain the head, the aged and disabled members of the family, to assist in the education of children of the family, to meet all the social responsibilities of the family, e.g. funeral expenses, the celebration of family or national feasts, and many miscellaneous responsibilities of the family. Where there is no property from which the family derives funds, contributions are made by principal members of the family to meet family responsibilities.

Each member of the family is entitled to occupy his fair share of vacant agricultural land, and is entitled to be allotted a portion of vacant building land owned by the family. The allotment has to be made by the head and the principal members of the family.

4. SUCCESSION

The mode of life of Ghanaians is communal, therefore no Ghanaian stands alone. He is linked in an unbroken chain with many who are dead—his ancestors—and many who are living—lineal and collateral kin, that is, his family, and he is their property. While he is of age and possessed of his mental faculties, he is left in entire control of himself and of his self-acquired property. The moment he becomes incapable due to death or mental debility of exercising proper control of himself and his property the family will immediately assume absolute control of his body and his substance and deal with them in their absolute discretion within the family set-up. Thus when a person dies intestate, he is succeeded by his family and his self-acquired property becomes family property. The family are responsible for giving him a decent burial, performing for him the customary funeral rites obtaining in the tribe or community, for the education and maintenance and proper upbringing of his infant children and for maintaining his wife so long as she remains his widow or marries in the same family.

As pointed out earlier then, property which today is individual property, may tomorrow be family property. Consequently a study of property in Ghana cannot be divorced from a study of the structure of the family.

Each person is born into two families; the family of the mother, known as the family of the blood, and the family of the father, known as the family of the spirit or personality.

For the purpose of ownership of and succession to property, a Ghanaian belongs to either the maternal family or to the paternal family. There are instances where he may succeed with the maternal family, and at the same time succeed with the paternal family; this occurs in the case of a person whose father belongs to a paternal family system for the purpose of succession, and the mother belongs to a maternal family system for the purpose of succession.

When they inherit from a deceased member, the family appoint one of themselves successor to the deceased; this is done whether or not the deceased left any property.

The last census shows that the population of the country has risen sharply, and that it continues to maintain a steady increase. The basis of the economy of the country is also changing very rapidly; from being mainly agricultural it is becoming industrial and commercial. Dense populations are growing in the industrial and commercial centres, and large communities are being moved from certain areas to be resettled and rehabilitated in other areas. Elementary education is now both free and compulsory so that within the next ten years or so, all young people should be literate. Commercial and industrial development calls an increasingly large number of people into industrial occupations, leaving smaller numbers to be employed in agriculture. At the same time it calls for an increase in the production both of cash crops, to earn foreign currency, and of food crops to feed the increased population and to supply industry. The system of shifting cultivation of food crops used hitherto cannot, in these circumstances, meet the requirements of the country. This form of agriculture will not attract the literate youth; and certainly conditions of labour on the permanent crop farms will have to change if the rising generation of educated youth is to be convinced that stability can be found in working on the family's cocoa, coffee, coconut, oil-palm or rubber farm. Consequently existing methods of farming will have to give way to modern scientific methods; such changes are likely to effect and necessitate some changes and adjustments in the land tenure system. For example, it may mean that peasant farming will have to give way to co-operative agriculture, and that corporate holding will take the place of individual holding in certain fields of agriculture.

5. LEGISLATIVE DEVELOPMENTS
Some consideration will now be given to changes which have taken place in recent years and, in conclusion, to some of the changes which in turn suggest themselves.

Schemes for the commercial and industrial development of land in Ghana began during the latter half of the last century, when foreigners, both individuals and companies, began to acquire land for mining, exploitation of timber and other purposes. Grants to these foreigners were made in the language of English conveyancing and purported to convey the 'fee simple' or grant conditions of leases which conflicted with the inherent rights of subjects of a Stool or members of a family.

Since the British Government, which then administered the country, considered that it had a duty to protect the people, it sought power to control all public or Stool lands. In pursuance of that intention, the *Land Bill* of 1894, entitled '*An Ordinance to vest waste-land, forest-land and minerals in the Queen*' was introduced in the Legislative Council in 1897. Section 3 of the Bill provided that all waste-land, i.e. public land and all forest-land in the Colony should be vested in the Queen for the use of the Government of the Colony. The Bill met with vehement opposition from Chiefs and people of the country. The late John Mensah Sarbah played an important role in that opposition. The Bill was passed into law in spite of all protests, but Queen Victoria refused to give it her assent, and it therefore never became law. In its place the *Colony Concessions Ordinance* No. 14 of 1900 and the *Ashanti Concessions Ordinance* No. 3 of 1903 were passed. These two Ordinances were repealed and re-enacted by the *Concessions Ordinance* (1939) Cap. 136 [1951 edition of the *Laws of the Gold Coast*]. The object of these Ordinances is summed up as follows:

> 'the protection of land owners from being fraudulently dealt with, to prevent the tying up of large areas of land in the hands of speculative or impecunious concessionaires who, from want of capital or other causes, are unable to work the land comprised in a concession granted of mining rights, rights of cutting timber. etc., and for regulating the rights of competing concessionaires by establishing priority among them *inter se*' [*Wassaw Exploring Syndicate* v. *African Rubber Co. Ltd.* (1914) A.C. 626].

Because of the failure of the 1897 Land Bill, the Government was not able to gain administrative control over Colony land, that is land now included in the Eastern, Central and Western Regions. However, it did succeed in obtaining control over lands in the then Northern Territories. This was done by an Ordinance enacted by the Governor who, prior to 1951, was the sole legislative authority for those territories. The enactment is *The Land and Native Rights (Northern Territories) Ordinance* [No. 1 of 1904 and No. 1 of 1927 repealed and re-enacted by 1931 (Cap. 147)]. The purpose of the Ordinance was in the main exactly the same as that of the Land Bills of 1894 and 1897. Section 4 of the Ordinance provided as follows:

> 'All native lands and all rights over the same shall as from the commencement of this Ordinance be under the control and subject to the disposition of the Governor, and shall be held and administered for the use and common benefit, direct and indirect, of the natives; and, subject to the particular reservations set forth in section 3, no title to the occupation and use of any such lands shall be valid without the consent of the Governor.'

The concern of the Governor to prevent the exploitation of lands in the Northern Territories in such a way as would affect the customary land tenure, related not only to prospectors from overseas, but also to all persons who were not members of any of the tribes of the Northern Territories. Section 17 of the Ordinance, therefore, provided that:

> '17 (1) It shall not be lawful, without the consent of the Governor:
> (a) for any native to purport to alienate any estate, right, or interest in, or with respect to any land lying within the Northern Region to a non-native;
> (b) for any occupier to purport to alienate his right of occupancy granted under this Ordinance, or any part thereof, or interest therein, either (i) to a non-native; or (ii) otherwise than in accordance with regulations made under section 24,
> and any conveyance, grant, mortgage, transfer of possession, lease,

bequest, or other instrument or transaction (whether in writing or not) which purports to effect an alienation in contravention of this section shall be void of effect.'

With that aim in view the term 'Native' was defined in section 2 as follows:

' "Native" means a person whose parents are or were members of some tribe or tribes indigenous to the Northern Region and any descendant of such a person, and includes:

(a) Any person one of whose parents was a member of such tribe, and

(b) Any person who shall have obtained a certificate from the Governor in the form set out in the First Schedule, which certificate the Governor is hereby authorized to grant, as his discretion, to any native of Africa who shall declare his intention of making the Northern Region his permanent domicile and who shall have satisfied the Governor that he has obtained the consent of the native communities concerned.'

When the former Togoland, under United Kingdom Trusteeship, came under the administration of the Government of the Gold Coast, it was divided into 'Northern Section' and 'Southern Section'. By section 3 (1) of the Administration (Togoland) Ordinance, No. 1 of 1924 (Cap. 112) it was provided that the laws for the time being in force in the Protectorate of the Northern Territories should be construed, subject to such verbal alterations and codifications as might be necessary, or applicable to the Northern Section of Togoland, and section 3(2) made the laws for the time being in force in the Colony, applicable to the Southern Section of Togoland; but provision was made in section 4 of the Ordinance limiting the definition of the term 'Native' exclusively to 'a person who belongs to a tribe indigenous to the Northern Section or the Southern Section as the case may be', and provision was also made prohibiting alienation of land in either section to a person who did not belong to a tribe indigenous to the particular section. Thus after a time, a number of strangers—Akwapims, Krobos, Gas, Shais and Anlos—who at one time or the other, had acquired land in the former Southern Section of Togoland for agricultural development, came to realize that they had no tenure in the lands they had developed, and at best were mere licensees holding the land at the pleasure of their Southern Togoland vendors. Thus in *Viesa & ors.* v. *Asinor*, [14 W.A.C.A., 419] it was held that purchasers of land in Southern Section of Togoland acquired no title to land purported to have been sold and conveyed to them.

Section 4 of the *Administration (Togoland) Ordinance* [Cap. 112] was repealed by *The Togoland (Assimilation of Law) Act*, 1958, [No. 54 of 1958]. The repeal came into force on October 31, 1958; from that date on, transactions in tenure of land in that part of the country have been made on the same principles as obtain in any other part of Southern Ghana, and are regulated by the customs and usages of the tribes and clans concerned.

6. THE TEMA RESETTLEMENT

There have been some economic and other schemes in Ghana which have involved the use of large areas of land for industrial and commercial

enterprises. Prominent among these are the mining and the timber industries. These, however, have not involved movements of people from
their homes and their resettlement in other areas. The reason for this is
that most of the acquisitions of land for these schemes have been made by
private persons, individuals, or corporate bodies and not by the Government. Such acquisitions have been made under the Concessions Ordinance,
section 13(8) which provides that 'No concession shall be certified as valid
if it grants or purports to grant rights to remove natives from their habita-
tion within the area of such concession.' Therefore a concession which is
validated by the Court cannot result in the eviction of persons in occupation of the land prior to the grant of the concession and the beginning of
operations. However, housing schemes have been developed on some of the
concession lands, either for housing employees or for general purposes. In
the case of housing estates for the concessionaires' employees, the tenancy
is either tenancy subsisting for the duration of the occupant's employment
or as part of the conditions of service. In either case the tenure is personal
to the occupier, and not inheritable. It is an incident of the employment.
A dwelling may carry with it a licence to cultivate some arable land on
certain areas within the concession, but the licence does not extend to the
cultivation of tree crops. The successors of any such licensee may harvest
crops growing on the land at the date of his death, but they may not continue to farm the area, except in their own right as employees. In the case
of private housing estates on concessions, persons may acquire building
plots within the estate to erect their own buildings. The tenure such a person acquires is leasehold under the common law, a sub-demise, the duration of which at its highest may be one day short of the term of years
granted under the concession.

Unlike concessions which cannot remove people from their homes, the
acquisition of land by Government for public services, e.g. for the Air
Port Extension, has sometimes resulted in the removal of people from their
villages and from areas farmed by them, and their resettlement in new
areas. The problems which these resettlements have involved as far as land
tenure is concerned, have been very simply and easily solved.

The simplicity of the problem has been due to two main reasons: the
communities involved have been small and the villages have been few,
consequently resettlement has been relatively easy; members of the communities have all, or in the main, been subjects of one and the same Stool,
and the land to which they have been removed has been land belonging to
their Stool. Being subjects of the Stool, they are by custom entitled to be
allocated building plots in the new areas as in the old area; and as to farming, they have the same rights in the new area as in the old, namely, to
occupy and become owners of any area of unoccupied land of the Stool
which they are able to reduce into their possession through their own
labour. If there is sufficient land in the new area, as has always been the
case so far, there is no need to limit the extent of agricultural land which
each evacuee may occupy in the resettlement area.

Furthermore, no improved or scientific scheme of agriculture has had
to be devised for the resettlement area, and so the old system of peasant
farming and shifting cultivation has continued.

In the case of rehousing necessitated by natural disasters such as earthquake and floods, or for general rehousing schemes, the Government has acquired land under special enactments, and built houses which have been handed over to people under hire-purchase schemes, or on ordinary tenancy. The tenures granted over such plots of land and buildings are tenures under the common law.

Prior to the Volta River Project, the scheme which raised new problems was the Tema Harbour and Township Development Scheme. This scheme involved the removal of a fairly large fishing and agricultural community from a sizeable ancient township. Resettlement involved the provision of housing, areas for farming and new landing places for their fishing industry.

The community involved in that scheme was larger than any which hitherto has had to be removed in an acquisition. The only feature which is the same as in previous ones is that the people in that community are all subjects of one and the same Stool. One feature, however, is peculiar to their case. Because the whole of the land owned by the Stool upon which they could settle and carry on their fishing industry was acquired, as well as similar lands of adjoining Stools, there was no land nearby to which they could move and in which they would have inherent rights either for purposes of dwelling or for their work of farming and fishing. At the same time the displacement would have caused very great hardship if they had been removed to an area far remote from their ancient environment, and in which alternative land would have been vested in their Stool over which they could exercise customary rights, and acquire customary tenure in portions of it, as was the case of New Juabeng.

They have had to be settled on a portion of the land acquired from their Stool. In compensation for their houses which were destroyed, improved houses were given to them with room for expansion. A modern fishing harbour suitable for their type of fishing crafts and industry has been provided for their use, and arable land left for them to farm, but no specific portions of such lands have been allotted to any of them. In effect, therefore, most of them continue to farm on lands which they previously farmed, where such lands have not yet been affected by the large-scale development which is taking place. Again since the lands were acquired for industrial and commercial development, no improved scheme for agricultural development can be planned to take place within the area, so that the old system of farming is pursued.

It does appear in the circumstances of the Tema community that the people have no tenure of any sort in the lands they occupy, and that they are mere licensees. This is satisfactory as far as agriculture goes. But in the case of their dwelling houses, their continuance as licensees or as free owners will conflict with the policy upon which the acquisition of the land was made. Therefore, the most likely thing to happen to ensure the security of their tenure will be to give them leases for the plots they occupy at pepper-corn rents and free use of the harbour which can descend to their successors. The free use of the fishing harbour in perpetuity would constitute an inducement to them to improve their fishing methods including, of course, their crafts.

7. THE VOLTA RIVER RESETTLEMENT

The Volta River Project has raised problems of resettlement and land tenure which are bigger and more difficult than any which have hitherto been tackled in Ghana. The project is intended to provide for 'generating electricity by means of the water power of the river Volta, and by other means, and of supplying electricity through a transmission system; for the construction of a dam and power station and for the creation of a lake by the damming of the river'; for giving (to a Statutory Authority) 'power to administer certain lands liable to be inundated and lands adjacent thereto, and for dealing with the resettlement of people living in the lands to be inundated'. [Cf. title to the Volta River Development Act, 1961 (Act 46).] The area to be inundated or otherwise affected is approximately 3,775 square miles. This involves the destruction of a large number of cottages, villages and towns comprising about 14,000 dwelling-houses accommodating approximately 80,000 inhabitants. The principal employment of the people in the basin is farming and fishing. The plan provides for the resettlement of these people in about fifty-two townships, each with sufficient land on which the evacuees can carry out their occupation of farming, and with facilities for those whose trade is fishing to carry on their business of fishing.

Some of the communities to be displaced are subjects of the Stools owning the land which they have hitherto occupied and where they have carried on their work. They had therefore acquired the land they occupy in the river basin in the customary way as subjects of the owner Stool. Others are mixed communities, some of whom got their land by purchase from Stools or from individual families or persons. Others, too, hold their land by other forms of tenure like *Abusa* tenancy or as food crop tenants, pledges and so on. All these would have to be given land in replacement of what they would lose in the river basin.

It would appear from the spirit of the Act creating the Volta River Authority (Act 46) that the displaced persons should, as far as possible, be placed in a similar position to that existing prior to their evacuation. This applies to the land for their dwelling, as well as to the land for farming. It will be expecting too much to hope that the evacuees will have as much land as they had in the river basin.

In conjunction with the resettlement there is a scheme for improved farming, using mechanization and other modern methods like crop rotation, all of which will produce larger yields per acre of land than could be produced under the peasant shifting cultivation method. This means that for the economic production of food crops under the mechanization scheme, peasant farming may have to give way to co-operative farming, but may be retained in the case of tree or permanent crop farming like cocoa, coffee, coconuts, and also in purely subsistence farming in food crops.

There is no evidence that any Paramount Stool and all its subjects would be evacuated and deprived of all lands owned by the Stool. If such displacement of a Paramount Stool should happen, an easy way of solving the problem would be for the Government to acquire an alternative area of land and vest it in the Stool, settle the subjects in new towns and villages on the new land, and leave the subjects to acquire arable land according to the customary methods by which subjects acquire the title to portions of Stool land. In such a case the tenure of the land would include the free use of the land or other interests in it with the right to alienate it *inter vivos* or by testamentary disposition to any person outside the family. In this connection it must be observed that the policy to be inferred from the Administration of Lands Act, 1962 (Act 123) will not favour continued administration of lands by Stools.

The Stool's absolute title attaches to land which the subject holds for his free use on a tenure which is alienable by the subject and inheritable from him. Therefore, upon the acquisition of land within the river basin for the project, the Stool is entitled to some compensation for the determination of its absolute title, while the subject in occupation is entitled to compensation for disturbance of his possession in addition to compensation for structures and for farms he has on the land. Accordingly if the Stool has other lands to which the displaced subject could move and settle upon, the Stool is under a responsibility to offer it without further compensation. It is otherwise in the case of a stranger evacuated to land owned by a Stool different from the Stool which owned the land of which he was dispossessed. In that case the obligation is upon the Government or the dispossessing authority to provide land for the resettlement. The land for the replacement may be land acquired by Government under section 1 of the State Lands Act, 1962 (Act 125) in the case of non-Stool land, and in the case of Stool land vested in the President as trustee under section 7(1) of the Administration of Lands Act, 1962 (Act 123). The most likely thing to happen is the dissociation of the Stools from replacement grants made to individuals, since the State, i.e. the President, can, under the Administration of Lands Act, make direct grants to individuals, and since the policy revealed in the Act is to relieve Stools of the administration of land.

Whether the displaced person is settled on the land of a Stool to which he owes allegiance or not, it appears that the building land which will be given to him for resettlement should be on a tenure which is alienable, and without encumbrance, while the right to free use and alienation should be evidenced by a document. This must be so because, unlike the case of Tema, the land upon which evacuees are to be settled would be acquired specifically for the purpose of resettlement, and not for any other purpose. The tenure for farming land could also be upon the same tenure, save that in cases where the individual or family may not be able to raise the capital necessary to carry on the improved farming (and it is most likely that none of the evacuees can provide such capital), co-operative farming will take the place of individual farming, in which case the tenure may involve a right to a share in the produce or proceeds of an area of land. Such a tenure would be analogous to *Abusa* tenancy—an inheritable interest in land; but in this case, not in an identified area of land, but to a proportionate portion of the area on which the co-operative farming is operated. This tenure should, of course, be distinguished from *Abusa* labour, since unlike *Abusa* labour, it is an interest in land and is transferrable. On the principles of *Abusa* tenancy one may conjecture that an *inter vivos* alienation of the co-operative interest could be made with the consent of the other members of the co-operative, and may require that the continuing members in the co-operative movement be given the first refusal to buy his interest.

There is one other point which deserves consideration, namely, that each individual may hold an allotment in free use and contribute to a fund from which the cost of mechanized and other improved schemes of farming in the area is communally provided for.

Again non-economic rents provided under the Rents Stabilization Act, 1962 (Act 109) as amended by Act 168 may appeal to some persons who may wish to hold the land as tenants.

In the case of peasant or tree crop farming, individual holding would not be incompatible with co-operation, and can co-exist with it. In these cases co-operation may be more in the field of marketing produce than in cultivation and production. Consequently the tenure which is most likely to give satisfaction on resettlement in such cases is the free inheritable possessory title, particularly if that was the title held by the evacuee in the land of which he has been dispossessed.

These problems raised by the Volta River Project are being actively tackled both by the Government and the Volta River Authority; and it is hoped that satisfactory solutions will be arrived at before the completion of the scheme.

SELECTED BIBLIOGRAPHY

Urbanization in African Social Change: Proceedings of the Inaugural Seminar held in the Centre of African Studies, University of Edinburgh, 5th–7th January, 1963.

DANQUAH, J. B., *Akan Laws and Customs*, London, Routledge, 1928.

ELIAS, T. O., *The Nature of African Customary Law*, Manchester, University Press, 1956.

FIELD, M. J., The Agricultural System of the Manya-Krobo of the Gold Coast, *Africa*, April 1943.

FIELD, M. J., *Social Organization of the Ga People*, London, Crown Agents, 1940.

FORTES, M., *The Dynamics of Clanship among the Talensi*, Oxford University Press, 1945.

HAILEY, LORD, *Native Administration in the British African Territories*, Part III, West Africa; Nigeria, Gold Coast, Sierra Leone, Gambia, London, HM Stationery Office, 1954.

HILL, POLLY, The Migrant Cocoa Farmers of Southern Ghana, *Africa*, July 1961.

MANOUKIAN, M., *The Ewe-Speaking People of Togoland and The Gold Coast* (Ethnographic Survey of Africa, Part VI), London, International African Institute, 1952.

MANOUKIAN, M., *Tribes of the Northern Territories* (Ethnological Survey of Africa, Part V), London, International African Institute, 1951.

MEEK, C. K., *Land Law and Custom in the Colonies*, Oxford University Press, 1946.

OLLENNU, N. A., *The Law of Succession in Ghana*, Accra, Presbyterian Printing Press, 1960.

OLLENNU, N. A., *The Law of Testate and Intestate Succession in Ghana*, London, Sweet and Maxwell, 1966.

OLLENNU, N. A., *Principles of Customary Land Law in Ghana*, London, Sweet and Maxwell, 1962.

POGUCKI, R. J. H., *Report on Land Tenure in Native Customary Law of the Protectorate of the Northern Territories*, Accra, Lands Department, 1950.

POGUCKI, R. J. H., *Report on Land Tenure in Customary Law of the non-Akan areas of the Gold Coast Colony*, Part I, Adangme, Accra, Lands Department, 1952.

POGUCKI, R. J. H., *Report on Land Tenure in Customary Law of the non-Akan areas of the Gold Coast Colony*, Part II, Ga, 1954.

POGUCKI, R. J. H., *A Handbook of main principles of rural land tenure in the Gold Coast*, Accra, Lands Department, 1956.

POGUCKI, R. J. H., *General Principles of Land Tenure in Ghana*, Accra, Lands Department, 1957.

RATTRAY, R. S., *Ashanti*, London, Oxford University Press, 1923.

RATTRAY, R. S., *Ashanti Law and Constitution*, London, Oxford University Press, 1929.

RICHARDS, A. I., *Land, Labour and Diet in Northern Rhodesia*, an economic study of the Bemba tribe, published for the International African Institute, London, Oxford University Press, 1939.

WHITE, C. M. N., *A Preliminary Survey of Local Rural Economy*, published on behalf of the Rhodes-Livingstone Institute, Manchester University Press, 1959.

INDEX

GEORGE ALLEN & UNWIN LTD

London: 40 Museum Street, W.C.1

Auckland: P.O. Box 36013, Northcote Central, N.4
Bombay: 15 Graham Road, Ballard Estate, Bombay 1
Barbados: P.O. Box 222, Bridgetown
Buenos Aires: Escritorio 454-459, Florida 165
Calcutta: 17 Chittaranjan Avenue, Calcutta 13
Cape Town: 68 Shortmarket Street
Hong Kong: 105 Wing On Mansion, 26 Hancow Road, Kowloon
Ibadan: P.O. Box 62
Karachi: Karachi Chambers, McLeod Road
Madras: Mohan Mansions, 38c Mount Road, Madras 6
Mexico: Villalongin 32-10, Piso, Mexico 5, D.F.
Nairobi: P.O. Box 4536
New Delhi: 13-14 Asaf Ali Road, New Delhi 1
Ontario: 81 Curlew Drive, Don Mills
Rio de Janeiro: Caixa Postal 2537-Zc-00
São Paulo: Caixa Postal 8675
Singapore: 36c Prinsep Street, Singapore 7
Sydney, N.S.W.: Bradbury House, 55 York Street
Tokyo: P.O. Box 26, Kamata